SAINT AUGUSTINE was one of those towering figures who so dominated his age that the age itself bears his name. The Age of Augustine was a time of transition, and Augustine was a genius of such stature that, according to Christopher Dawson, "he was, to a far greater degree than any emperor or general or barbarian war-lord, a maker of history and a builder of the bridge which was to lead him from the old world to the new."

Augustine was born in the Roman province of Numidia, North Africa, in 354. His father was a pagan and his mother, Monica, a Christian who was later to be proclaimed a saint. He received the classical education of the young pagan gentleman and became a teacher of rhetoric, first in North Africa and later in Milan. During those years he acquired a mistress, a son, and an interest in the religious teachings of the Persian prophet Mani, who was all the rage at the time. But after nine years Manicheanism proved sterile and he became a Catholic. His exceptional talents were recognized and he was consecrated Bishop of Hippo, North Africa, in 395.

His remaining thirty-five years were a torrent of activity. He was the ablest religious thinker and controversialist at a period when theological controversy reached a level of intellectual refinement never achieved before or since. He was a tireless preacher. And he wrote 118 treatises, including the most famous spiritual autobiography of all time, *The Confessions*. Of all these works, the one most prized by Augustine was his *City of God*—a veritable encyclopedia of information on the lives, thoughts and aspirations of ancient and early Christian man.

SAINT AUGUSTINE
The City of God

An abridged Version from
the Translation by

GERALD G. WALSH, S.J.
DEMETRIUS B. ZEMA, S.J.
GRACE MONAHAN, O.S.U.
and
DANIEL J. HONAN

With a Condensation of the Original
Foreword by ETIENNE GILSON

Edited, with an Introduction, by
VERNON J. BOURKE

AN IMAGE BOOK
Doubleday
NEW YORK   LONDON   TORONTO   SYDNEY   AUCKLAND

An Image Book

Published by Doubleday, a division of
Bantam Doubleday Dell Publishing Group, Inc.,
666 Fifth Avenue, New York, New York 10103

Image, Doubleday and the portrayal of a cross
intersecting a circle are trademarks of Doubleday, a
division of Bantam Doubleday Dell Publishing Group, Inc.

Image Books edition 1958
by special arrangement with Fathers of the Church, Inc.

PRINTING HISTORY

Image Books edition published February, 1958

Imprimi Potest: John J. McMahon, S.J., *Provincial*
New York, August 3, 1949; August 17, 1951; August 15, 1953

Nihil Obstat: John M. A. Fearns, S.T.D.
Censor Librorum

Imprimatur: ✠ Francis Cardinal Spellman
Archbishop of New York
December 19, 1949; January 7, 1952; November 15, 1953

Cover by Paul Galdone
Typography by Joseph P. Ascherl

ISBN: 0-385-02910-1

Printed in the United States of America

28 30 32 33 31 29 27

Contents

Introduction

IN THE HISTORY of world literature we find many authors who have achieved fame and lasting influence through the writing of one great work. Augustine of Hippo produced several masterpieces. His *Confessions* is doubtless the outstanding spiritual autobiography by a Christian writer; his *Literal Commentary on Genesis* sets the standard for later Biblical interpretation; and the *Enarrations on the Psalms,* his longest writing, was most prized by the humanistic scholars of the Renaissance. In the sphere of formal theological writing, his fifteen books *On the Trinity* are unequaled in the early Church. Even the little dialogue called the *Soliloquies* has been put in a class by itself, as an example of spiritual introspection.

However, the work which Augustine considered his masterpiece is the *City of God.* He devoted a good part of fourteen years to its composition, starting the first book at the age of fifty-nine (when many a lesser man would be thinking of retiring) and completing the twenty-second book in A.D. 426, when he was seventy-two years old. His life had been rich in personal experiences. The son of a Christian mother and a pagan father, Augustine grew up in the Roman province of Numidia, North Africa. In spite of the saintly life of his mother, Augustine was not baptized as a child. His education was that of a young pagan. His studies in rhetoric, at Carthage, prepared him to teach that subject, first in Roman Africa and later at Milan in the heart of the Empire. It was while engaged as a teacher of rhetoric in the city schools of Milan, where the Roman emperors then lived, that Augustine decided to join the Church of his mother. He was in his early thirties when he took this momentous step. During his twenties he had sought religious guidance in the strange teaching of the Persian prophet Mani. The nine years spent as a Manichee were ones of frustrating search for understanding of the fabulous stories of two great gods, one who causes all that is good, the other who is the source of all evils. Influenced by the reading of some treatises in Neoplatonic philosophy, by discussions with a group of Milanese students of philosophy,[1] and by the preaching of the great Catholic Bishop of Milan, St. Ambrose, Augustine underwent a famous conversion, of which the *Confessions* and the early *Dialogues* are a moving record.

Abandoning his profession as a teacher of rhetoric, Augustine eventually returned to his African home at Tagast, in the present Tunisia. One of the best educated Christians of his day, Augustine was soon prevailed upon to become a priest. He was consecrated bishop at the nearby town of Hippo in 395. The last thirty-five years of his life were spent there, including those in which he wrote the *City of God*. Never one to shirk work or hide his light under a bushel, Augustine soon came to be recognized as the outstanding churchman of his day. Like St. Paul, he was untiring in his travels, in his preaching, in his controversies with non-believers, and in his writing.

In the midst of this active ecclesiastical career, a shocking political and military event occurred. The supposedly impregnable City of Rome was attacked and ravished by the Goths in the year 410. Suddenly the Empire which had ruled most of the civilized world for centuries was dying. Throughout the Roman world, astonishment was followed by recrimination: one persistent rumor was that Christianity had sapped the strength of Rome. The officials and citizenry of Rome were still divided into Christian and pagan groups. It takes no powers of imagination to picture the situation.

A Roman official in North Africa, the Christian Marcellinus, wrote to Augustine, telling him about this charge against Christianity and asking him to refute it. This was the setting, then, which occasioned the writing of the *City of God*. The reader will find a much fuller account in Gilson's Foreword, which follows this, and in the opening books of the treatise itself.

The first ten books of the *City of God* constitute the answer to this charge. Augustine is there concerned to show that the greatness that was Rome's was not due to the "old" religion of pagan polytheism. He studies at great length the powers and functions of the many gods and goddesses, in order to convince his readers that these mythological beings have bene-

[1] Recently studied by P. Courcelle in his *Recherches sur les Confessions de saint Augustin*, Paris 1950.

fited the Roman people neither physically nor morally. These books are a mine of information on ancient polytheism, on the social and political institutions of the pagan world, on the early history of mankind. Many of Augustine's sources of information are now lost, notably most of the encyclopedic works of the pagan historian of religion, Varro. It must also be recalled that Augustine's whole early education was in pagan literature. The *City of God* is a primary source for the study of paganism as well as Christian thought.

It is in the tenth book that Augustine begins to expound the world view of Christianity and to contrast it with paganism. In a sense he rises above the theme set by Marcellinus and argues that the breakdown of the Empire is but a small event in world history, viewed from the perspectives of eternity. Books XI to XXII offer a positive interpretation of human society, in which the protagonists are not Rome and its enemies but two radically different cities. The seeds of this interpretation are Biblical, as is the terminology, for the "City of God" is a commonplace in the Psalms. A Donatist writer named Ticonius had previously contrasted two cities, of God and of the Devil. But, if the terminology and root ideas are not original with Augustine, the development of the theme of two opposed societies bears the mark of his own genius.

The distinction between the two cities is grounded in the religious psychology of Augustine. For him, men (and angels) are created, finite spirits existing on a plane of reality below the immutable and unique being of God, but above the essentially mutable and transitory natures of bodies. Created spirits are capable of turning upward to God with their wills (*conversion*) or downward toward bodies (*aversion*). Thus there are two distinct commitments of will—or two loves.[2] Good men and even good angels cherish God and so constitute a special society, or city, of spirits devoted to divine truth and goodness. On the other hand, evil men and angels spurn God with their wills and love the bodily things of this world; they make up another society, the earthly city, which has its own lesser values. All human history and culture may be

[2] See the description of these two "loves" in the *Literal Commentary on Genesis*, XI, 15, 20; the text is translated in my *Augustine's Quest of Wisdom*, pp. 249–250.

viewed as the interplay of the competing values of these two loves and of these two cities.

The citizens of God's society are not merely all good men: the good angels belong in the City of God. Nor is Augustine so provincial as to claim that only Christians are members of the divine city: there are bad Christians and they belong to the other city; there were good men before Christ and they belong in the City of God. The members of the two cities are intermingled in actual human societies on earth, throughout the course of time.

One of the finest attributes of the City of God is peace. At the end of a justly famed discussion of peace,[3] Augustine defines it as "the perfectly ordered and harmonious communion of those who find their joy in God, and in one another in God." Whether such peace is possible on earth is a question faced by Professor Gilson in his Foreword. Augustine's message is not without optimism; he obviously felt that some measure of earthly peace had been achieved in the better days of the Empire. Yet it is a mistake to take the *City of God* as a charter for an earthly kingdom. This was a mistake made by Charlemagne and his associates, who thought to realize the Heavenly City in the Holy Roman Empire. Still, out of the impetus of the civilization and political states which they established to fill the void left by the destruction of Rome have developed the social and political institutions of modern Europe and America. In part, at least, the *City of God* has given us our ideals of national and international morality. To read this work is one way of coming to realize and to appreciate the potentialities and the limitations of all plans for peace on earth.

Many, perhaps most, readers never finish reading the *City of God* in its original form. It is a very long work. Augustine was forced to put aside his task of composition, time and again. Each new start was the occasion for summarizing what had gone before and for repetition of earlier themes. Moreover, it was a rhetorical convention of the period (in which Augustine was only too well trained) to indulge in the *excursus*. This is but a technical name for getting off the subject—a practice not unknown to modern writers and preachers. The digres-

[3] See Book XIX, 13.

sions in the *City of God* are often of great length.[4] Finally, there are in this work very detailed accounts of ancient history, of Biblical events, of the teachings of Greek and Roman mythology, and of contemporary incidents of no great importance today. Most of this digressive material is omitted in the present edition. The consequent drawing together of the parts of the *City of God* which bear directly on the major theme —the origin, development, and destiny of the two cities—may serve to heighten the impact of Augustine's thought. In any event, it brings the work within the compass of one volume and within the reading time of the average modern book.

Where chapters have been omitted, this fact is indicated in the present printing by transitional summaries of the deleted passages. A few examples of Augustine's digressions are retained, so as to give some inkling of the color and vast range of Augustine's knowledge and speculative interests. It appears that he did much extra reading, even in Greek sources, in the course of his writing.

By arrangement with the original publishers, the present edition of the *City of God* is reprinted from the three-volume translation published by the Fathers of the Church, Inc. (New York, 1950, 1952, and 1954). The chapters which have been retained are printed here in their entirety, without any change in the translation of Augustine's own words and with the original numbering of book and chapter. This means that the reader may quote or cite the present version, by internal reference to book and chapter, with full confidence that his reference will correspond with the words and numbering of the original Latin. The best Latin edition is that by Dombart and Kalb, in the Teubner series.[5] The division of five parts, introduced in the present edition, is taken from Augustine's own recommendations for dividing the text. Both the *Retractations* (II, 43) and the recently discovered *Letter to Firmus*[6] suggest these five parts and their titles.

---

[4] Augustine frequently accused himself of prolixity; see Book XV, 4; XVIII, 54; XX, 19; XXII, 30; *Retractations*, II, 43.

[5] S. Aurelii Augustini, *De civitate Dei Libri XXII*, 2 vols., ed. B. Dombart et A. Kalb, Leipzig (Teubner) 1928–1929.

[6] Edited by C. Lambot in *Revue Bénédictine*, LI (1939), pp. 109–121.

The Fathers of the Church translation is prefaced by a Foreword written by the noted historian of mediaeval philosophy, Etienne Gilson. His original essay runs to almost ninety pages and is a profound study of the meaning of the *City of God* for the modern reader. It has been possible to print a good part of this Foreword in the present volume. The elided portions are indicated by asterisks.

For those who may wish to read further about the *City of God* and its background, the following English studies are suggested: J. N. Figgis, *The Political Aspects of St. Augustine's City of God*, London, 1921; J. Rickaby, *St. Augustine's City of God, A View of Its Contents*, New York, 1925; C. Dawson, "St. Augustine and His Age," in *Monument to St. Augustine*, London, 1930; J. H. S. Burleigh, *The City of God, A Study of St. Augustine's Philosophy*, London, 1944; V. J. Bourke, *Augustine's Quest of Wisdom* (Chapter XIII: "God and Society"), Milwaukee, 1945; C. N. Cochrane, *Christianity and Classical Culture*, London, 1944; W. G. Most, *St. Augustine's De civitate Dei, Selections with Notes and Glossary*, Washington, 1949. The main studies in other languages are cited in the footnotes to Professor Gilson's Foreword.

VERNON J. BOURKE

Foreword

ETIENNE GILSON

THE CITY OF GOD (*De civitate Dei*) is not only one of St. Augustine's masterpieces, but ranks, along with the *Confessions*, among the classics of all literature. It is hardly possible to analyze the contents of this vast work, which, in spite of its overall plan, is marked by so many digressions. The purpose of this Foreword is to focus the reader's attention on Augustine's main theme, and to emphasize its historical importance. In his notion of a universal religious society is to be sought the origin of that ideal of a world society which is haunting the minds of so many today.

Augustine, it is true, did not pose exactly the same problem; that is why we should not read the *City of God* in the hope of finding therein the solution. Nevertheless, the problem posed and resolved by Augustine is certainly the origin of ours, and, if we are failing to resolve our problem, it is probably because we are forgetting that its solution presupposes a solution of the problem resolved by Augustine.

Our contemporaries aspire after a complete unity of all peoples: one world. They are quite right. The universal society which they are endeavoring to organize aims at being a political and temporal society. In this regard they are again right. Perhaps their most serious mistake is in imagining that a universal and purely natural society of men is possible without a universal religious society, which would unite men in the acceptance of the same supernatural truth and in the love of the same supernatural good.

1. *The Problem of a Universal Society*

Christianity was born in the Roman Empire, which itself was merely a vast extension of the City of Rome, or, if the formula seems imprudent, which owed to Rome its laws, its order and whatever unity it possessed. But, first of all, what

was Rome? Many and divers explanations of its origin have
been proposed; and, since the specialists themselves have not
as yet found a solution of the problem acceptable to everyone,
it would be imprudent to make a choice for them, and still
more imprudent to build upon any one of their hypotheses.[1]
No one, however, doubts that Rome, as Athens, was one of
the ancient cities, each of which was either a state or the
center of a state. We are safe in admitting that these cities
were, first of all, peopled by men united by the bond of common blood.[2] At the time of Pericles, 451 B.C., it was still the
law that only the children of a legitimately married Athenian
father and mother could be citizens of Athens. The division
of the Greek cities into phratries and associations, a division
found again in the *familia* and Roman *gens,* soundly confirms
this hypothesis.

However, it in no way rules out the penetrating views formerly developed by Fustel de Coulanges in his classic work,
The Ancient City. Therein, the family was described as already
bound to religious beliefs and sacred rites, from which it was
inseparable. In direct opposition to historical materialism, de
Coulanges professed what might not too incorrectly be called
an 'historical spiritualism.' By this is meant simply that, if man
is no longer governed in our day as he was twenty-five centuries ago, it is because he no longer thinks as he thought
then.[3] Thence comes the basic thesis that 'history does not
study material facts and institutions alone; its true object of
study is the human mind; it should aspire to know what this

[1] A. Piganiol, *Essai sur les origines de Rome.* (Paris 1917).

[2] Wilamowitz-Moellendorf, 'Staat und Gesellschaft der Grie-
chen,' in *Die Kultur der Gegenwart,* II, 42–51, IV, 97, 100. Cf.,
also, Ernest Barker, *Greek Political Theory. Plato and his Predecessors* (London 1917), a complete revision of the same author's
Political Thought of Plato and Aristotle, published in 1906. Note
the interesting remark in the Preface (p. viii) to the effect that the
Laws are the most modern (or mediaeval) of all the writings of
Plato.

[3] Fustel de Coulanges, *La Cité Antique* (Paris 1924) 2–3. All
quotations to this work are taken from the translation by Willard
Small (Boston 1894). Haunted by the harm done to France in the
attempt to imitate the ancient democracies during the revolution
of 1789, Fustel de Coulanges wanted to prove above all else that
they are inimitable.

mind has believed, thought and felt in the different ages of the life of the human race.'[4]

From such a viewpoint, it is religion which dominates from on high the family and the ancient city. Founded on the religious worship of the hearth, that is, of the household fire, which was not simply metaphorical but real, each family constituted first and foremost a closed society, which its own worship separated from all other families. 'Religion did not say to a man, showing him another man: That is your brother. It said to him: That is a stranger; he cannot participate in the religious acts of your hearth; he cannot approach your family's tomb; he has other gods than yours, and cannot unite with you in a common prayer; your gods reject his adoration, and regard him as their enemy; he is your foe, also.'[5] In order to constitute larger social groups it was necessary, first of all, to overcome the separation of families.

Let us suppose that families were grouped into *gentes* or associations, *gentes* into tribes, and tribes into cities. There, also we shall meet with worship: that of another group of divinities, such as Zeus or Heracles, whose origin is uncertain, but whom we know to have been placed above the worship of the household gods, without, however, eliminating this latter worship. The recognition of gods common to several families alone made possible the birth of the city. 'Society developed only so fast as religion enlarged its sphere. We cannot, indeed, say that religious progress brought social progress; but, what

[4] *Ibid.* II, 9, 103–104; Small, p. 123.

[5] That is doubtless why love played a secondary role in the ancient family. 'The members of the ancient family were united by something more powerful than birth, affection or physical strength; this was the religion of the sacred fire, and of dead ancestors,' (*ibid.* II, 1.40; Small, p. 51). To guarantee a continuous worship of the dead, marriage was necessary, since children were necessary to perpetuate it. Whence, the sacramental formula pronounced in the marriage contract: *ducere uxorem liberum quaerendorum causa* (*ibid.* II, 3.52; Small, p. 65). 'Everything in the family was divine' (*ibid.* II, 9, 109; Small, p. 129). 'Then a man loved his house as he now loves his Church' (*ibid.*). Even the slave was made a part of the household of the family by a religious ceremony analogous to that of marriage, and took part in the worship of the hearth. He was buried in the burial ground of the family whose Lares had been his gods (*ibid.* II, 10, 127; Small, p. 150).

is certain is that they were both produced at the same time and in remarkable accord.'[6]

* * * *

On August 24, 410, Alaric entered Rome, and, although a Christian, pillaged the city for a period of three days. On the fourth day, his troops left the city, carrying off vast booty and leaving behind a mass of corpses and ruins. Thus, for the first time, an empire fell at the very moment the Church was hoping to find a support in it. This was not, however, to be the last time. Nevertheless, out of many similar experiences, this one remains, in a sense, the most striking; for, it seemed at first glance that the fall of Rome would bring about that of the Church. However, it was the body of the faithful united only by the faith of Christ, rather than the political Colossus united by arms, which survived.

Such a lesson is not easily forgotten. The capture of Rome by the barbarians made a deep impression upon the entire Empire. The endless polemics between Christians and pagans increased in violence and bitterness.[7] To analyze all the arguments of both sides would be a task both long and detailed, and, like the polemics themselves, would not bring us to any goal. On the pagan side, there were two principal and simple arguments from which all the others directly or indirectly stemmed. First of all, Christian doctrine taught renouncement of the world; consequently, it turned the citizen away from the service of the state, a fact which brought about the fall of Rome. Secondly, the destiny of Rome was always bound up with the worship of her gods. When the Christian religion first began to spread, the pagans proclaimed that their betrayed gods would visit terrible punishments upon the Empire. No one would listen, but the turn of events finally had justified their prophecy, and to such an extent that it was no longer possible to refuse them a hearing. The Empire had become Christian and it was during the reign of a Christian emperor that Rome, for the first time in her long history, was conquered and sacked. How could anyone fail to understand a lesson so tragically clear?

[6] *Ibid.* III, 3, 147; Small, pp. 172–173.
[7] Cf. G. Boissier, *La fin du paganisme* (Paris 1909), especially the chapter entitled 'L'Affaire de l'autel de la Victoire' II, 231–291.

These objections were set down, as clearly as one could want, in a letter from Marcellinus to the Bishop of Hippo. In 412, the pagan Volusianus had addressed these objections to Marcellinus, who in turn immediately begged Augustine to write a reply. According to Marcellinus, Volusianus raised the objection that the preaching and teaching of Christ was in no way compatible with the duties and rights of citizens; for, to quote an instance frequently alleged, among its precepts there is found: 'Do not repay injury with injury,'[8] and, 'if a man strikes thee on thy right cheek, turn the other cheek also towards him; if he is ready to go to law with thee over thy coat, let him have it and thy cloak with it; if he compels thee to attend him on a mile's journey, go two miles with him.'[9] Now, it seems clear that such moral norms could not be put into practice without bringing ruin to a country. Who would suffer without retaliation the seizure of his goods by an enemy? Would anyone, thenceforth, refuse to punish according to the laws of war the devastation of a Roman province? These are arguments with which we are familiar, and which are constantly being revived by 'conscientious objectors.' They are based upon the deepest convictions of a Christian conscience, whose strength it would be wrong to ignore. It is worth noting that the Christian Marcellinus, and not the pagan Volusianus, raised the last and most formidable argument, namely, that 'it is manifest that very great calamities have befallen the country under the government of emperors practising, for the most part, the Christian religion.'[10]

The objection was urgent, and St. Augustine was not slow to reply. He had been asked how it was possible to live in the State as a Christian, and how it was possible for a State composed of Christians to endure, since the practice of the Christian virtues would infallibly bring about the ruin of the State. To this St. Augustine makes an unexpected reply, namely, that the pagans themselves have already preached the same virtues for which the Christians are being blamed. It was scarcely necessary to recall this fact to such a cultured

[8] Rom. 12.17.
[9] Matt. 6.39–42.
[10] St. Augustine, *Letter 136* 2, trans. by J. G. Cunningh edition by Marcus Dods (Edinburgh 1875) II, 175.

man as Volusianus. Did not Sallust praise the Romans for having chosen to forget injuries rather than punish the offender? Did not Cicero praise Caesar because he was wont to forget nothing but the wrongs done to him?[11] If we are to judge from the history of Rome, the observance of these laws has not worked out too badly. Again, it is necessary to understand what the Gospel teaches. There are no commandments compelling Christian soldiers to lay down their arms or to refuse service. In fact, no one is forbidden to give himself generously to the service of the State. On the contrary, rather, let them give us such husbands and wives, parents and children, such masters and slaves, such kings and judges, such taxpayers and tax collectors, as the Christian religion has taught that men should be, and then let them dare say that it is adverse to the State's well-being; rather, let them no longer hesitate to confess that this doctrine, if it were obeyed, would be the salvation of the Empire.[12]

But, how explain the fact that these calamities have befallen Rome at the hands of certain Christian emperors? Simply by denying the fact. It was not the Christianity of the emperors which brought ruin upon the Empire; rather, it was the vices within the Empire itself. For, whither might not men have been carried away by the flood of appalling wickedness, had God not finally planted the Cross of Christ there? Read Sallust and Juvenal, and the lengths to which immorality had gone will readily be seen.[13] Nascent Christianity is being blamed; the blame, however, should fall upon dying paganism. Christian revelation had two distinct ends: first, to save human society; second, to build up a society which could be divine. It is difficult to see what the State could fear from this twofold endeavor; but, what the State could gain thereby is readily apparent, for Christianity will achieve the first in striving after the second.

First, to save the political, human and natural society from the inevitable ruin whither its corruption was ineluctably leading it. It is not ignorance of the virtues required to secure

---

[11] Sallust, *The War with Catiline* 9.5 (Loeb, p. 17). Cicero, *Pro Ligario* 12.35. Cf. St. Augustine, *The City of God* 2.18.2.
[12] St. Augustine, *Letter 138* 2.15 (Dods ed. 206).
[13] *The City of God* 2.19.

happiness and prosperity which is endangering Roman society. Its members are very well aware of the obligations imposed by a merely natural love of the Empire, whose greatness was due to its past virtues, but which its citizens have not the courage to put into practice. But, what they did not have the strength to do out of love of country, the Christian God demands of them out of love of Himself. Thus, in the general breakdown of morality and of civic virtues, divine Authority intervened to impose frugal living, continence, friendship, justice and concord among citizens. Henceforth, everyone professing Christian teaching and observing its precepts will, out of love of God, perform whatever the welfare of the country demands out of self-interest and on its own behalf.[14] Augustine was already enunciating the great principle which is to justify, always and everywhere, the penetration of the Church into every human city: Take to yourselves good Christians and you will be given good citizens. Of course, the exigencies of the Gospel will never be fully satisfied in this way. But, neither will those of the world be satisfied in any other way, once the most ardently genuine followers of the Gospel are resigned finally to live in it; and whose goods, in spite of everything, it is difficult to enjoy without ever making any return. On the supposition that Christ did not expressly reserve for Himself the things that are Caesar's there still remains the problem of moral equity, concerning whose correct solution there could be no hesitation.

Let us admit that the Christian virtues are useful to the good order and prosperity of the commonwealth; still, it is no less true that this order and prosperity cannot be their proper end. This fact makes it quite clear that, to the extent the State can be sure of the practice of the natural moral virtues, of itself it can secure its own prosperity. Such was eminently the case in the early days of Rome, whose virtues St. Augustine, following the best traditions of the Latin historians, did not hesitate to praise. Did not ancient Rome owe its great success to the frugality, strength and purity of its way of life? Again, do not the origins of its decline date from the decadence of its way of life, described so often by its historians and poets?

[14] St. Augustine, *Letter* 138 3.17 (Dods ed. 208).

Far from being embarrassed by the memory of a prosperous, although pagan, Rome, St. Augustine sees in this prosperity the sign of a providential plan. If God allowed this temporal greatness, which was obtained through mere civic virtues, it was precisely in order that no one might be deceived about the proper end of the Christian virtues. Since the world can enjoy prosperity without the Christian virtues, then, certainly, they do not exist in the view of the world. 'For in the most opulent and illustrious Empire of Rome, God has shown how great is the influence of even civil virtues without true religion, in order that it might be understood that, when this is added to such virtues, men are made citizens of another Commonwealth, of which the king is Truth, the law is Love and the duration is Eternity.'[15] The sufficiency of the political virtues in their own order testifies to the supernatural specification of the Christian virtues both in their essence and their end.

Thenceforth, two cities would always be present to the thought of St. Augustine. To free the Church from all responsibility for the evils which had befallen Rome was, for him, something else than to plead a losing cause after the fashion of a shrewd lawyer. Since, as the Roman writers admit, the decadence of the Empire and the causes of the decadence antedate the advent of Christianity, responsibility for the decadence cannot be laid upon Christianity. Nevertheless, the disaster of 410 faced them. Moreover, the pagans never wearied of using this argument to the full, an argument which, it must be agreed, was clothed in the garb of apparent truth. That is why, in 413, St. Augustine took upon himself the task of writing a reply. In his *Retractations*, St. Augustine writes: 'When Rome was devastated as a result of the invasion of the Goths under the leadership of Alaric, the worshippers of the many false gods, whom we are accustomed to call pagan, began, in their attempt to blame this devastation on the Christian religion, to blaspheme the true God with more bitterness and sharpness than usual. Wherefore, fired with a zeal for God's house, I determined to write my book, *The City of God*, against their blasphemies and errors.'[16]

Of the twenty-two books which make up this work, the last

15 *Ibid.*
16 St. Augustine, *Retractations* 2.43.2.

twelve are principally dedicated to a retracing of the history of the 'two cities,' the City of God and the city of this world, from their beginnings until their end which is yet to come. If the work is entitled *The City of God*, it is only because he has chosen the title from the more noble of the two; nevertheless, it contains the history of both cities. Augustine was not deceived about the real object of his work, an enterprise dictated by the pressure of circumstances and perhaps suggested by a question of Marcellinus, to whom the work was dedicated.[17]

The work actually contains a great deal more than a vindication of the Church from the accusation of a given moment. The drama, whose vicissitudes the work aims at relating and interpreting, is literally of cosmic significance, because it identifies itself with the history of the world. The message which the Bishop of Hippo addresses to men is to the effect that the whole world, from its beginning until its final term, has as its unique end the constitution of a holy Society, in view of which everything has been made, even the universe itself. Perhaps never in the history of human speculation has the notion of society undergone a change comparable in depth, or provoked such an enlarged perspective in view of the change. Here, the City extends more than to the very limits of the earth or world; it includes the world and explains even the very existence of the world. Everything that is, except God Himself whose work the City is, is for the City and has no meaning apart from the City; if it is possible to have faith in the ultimate intelligibility of the smallest event and the humblest of creatures, it is the City of God which possesses the secret.

II. *The City of God and Universal Society*

What is a city, considered not in the material, but in the social, sense of the term? In vain would we search *The City of God*, vast as its scope is, for an abstract and general dis-

---

[17] St. Augustine, *The City of God* I (Preface). A recently discovered letter of St. Augustine, (C. Lambot, 'Lettre inédite de s. Augustin relative au De civitate Dei,' *Revue Bénédictine* 51 [1939] 109–121), bears upon the author's purpose in composing the work and gives his summation of the contents of the several parts. [Eds.]

cussion of the problem as the philosophers envisaged it in
their attempt to define the nature of the social bond. St. Augustine pursued his proper objective through innumberable
digressions, which can be called, not improperly, apolo-
getic.[18] In more than one discussion, however, he does come
to grips with the problem, where philosophy as such is judged
from a Christian point of view. This is precisely the case with
the notion of the term 'city.' He does not discuss the nature
of the city as a philosopher indifferent to Christianity, nor as a
Christian indifferent to philosophy, but as a Christian who
judges and, if necessary, reshapes its elements in the light of
faith.

When St. Augustine speaks of a human city, he is first of
all thinking of Rome and its history, such as the Latin writers
had described it to him.[19] If he was able to refute the charge
that the Church had caused the ruin of Rome, it was, as we
have seen, because Sallust himself had considered Rome to
be in ruins as a result of its own vices, and that even before
the advent of Christ. When St. Augustine asked himself at
what moment of its history Rome merited the name of city,
it was to a pagan definition of a city that he appealed. Thus,
in passing judgment on pagan society according to the laws
set down by that society, he drew his inspiration from rules
which pagan society itself had to admit.

As St. Augustine saw it, the dominant feature in the pagan
concept of the city, which is both a political and a social body,
was the notion of justice. As Cicero, for example, conceived it,
every society should resemble a symphonic concert, in which
the different notes of the instruments and voices blend into a
final harmony. What the musician calls harmony, the politi-

---

[18] H. Scholz, *Glaube und Unglaube*, iv. The author contradicts
those who see in *The City of God* a philosophy of history. In this
he is quite correct; however, it does not exclude the possibility of
a philosophy of history being derived several centuries later from
The City of God. According to Scholz, the central theme of the
work is the struggle between faith and infidelity (p. 2). This is a
quite reasonable conclusion; however, the simplest view, it would
seem, is to admit that the central theme of *The City of God* is,
precisely, the City of God.

[19] City signifies society: '*civitas quae nihil aliud est quam
hominum multitudo aliquo societatis vinculo colligata*' (*The City
of God* 15.8).

cian calls concord. Without concord, there is no city; but, without justice, there is no concord. Consequently, justice is the first condition required for the existence of the city. That is why St. Augustine felt justified in concluding that, in spite of appearances to the contrary, Rome had ceased to exist at the moment when, according to one historian, Rome had lost all justice. It was not enough to declare, along with Sallust, that Roman society was then corrupt; it was necessary to affirm even as Augustine did, in the words of Cicero, that, as a society, Rome had totally ceased to exist.[20]

But, was that going far enough? If we recall the thesis already maintained by Augustine,[21] namely, that the republic of Rome had prospered because of its virtues, it would seem quite possible to grant that it was a society worthy of the name. The reason was, as St. Augustine had written to Marcellinus in 412, that God wished to make manifest the supernatural ideal of the Christian virtues, by permitting ancient Rome to prosper without them. He thereby granted a certain temporal efficacy to the civic virtues of the pagans, and to Rome itself the character of an authentic society. Certainly, Augustine would never completely deny it. For certain reasons, whether divine or human, ancient Rome was, in its own way, a true society. The republic was certainly much better administered by the more ancient Romans than by their successors; but, in the final analysis, and in its own way, it was a society. However, in the very context where Augustine made this admission,[22] he added that it was not a society; this fact

[20] *The City of God* 2.21. St. Augustine somewhat forces the text of Cicero which he quotes.

[21] Cf. pp. 19–21 above.

[22] *The City of God* 2.21: Rome 'never was a republic, because true justice never had a place in it. . . . But, accepting the more probable definition of a republic, I admit there was a republic of a kind, and certainly much better administered by the more ancient Romans than their successors. But true justice exists only in that republic whose founder and ruler is Christ; if anyone sees fit to call this a republic, since we cannot deny that it is a commonweal. If, however, this name which has become a commonplace in other contexts is considered foreign to our way of speaking, we can certainly assert that there is true justice in the City about which Sacred Scripture says: *Glorious things are said of Thee, O City of God*' (*Ps.* 86.3). This eloquent text settles several points. First, the

he proves later, using as his authority the definitions of the social body already proposed by Cicero. There had never been a true Roman society, because true justice had never reigned in Rome. There, we are clearly facing a problem which cannot be resolved simply. In a sense, there was a Roman Republic, especially when, at its origin, there did reign a kind of justice which in turn gave birth to a kind of society. However, since that justice was not a true justice, the society it engendered was not a true society. Here, for the moment, let us yield to the exigencies of logic and admit that there never has been a Roman society, because there has never been a true society; for, not to be a true society is to be no society at all.

Taken in its strict meaning, this thesis implies that there exists and can exist but a single city worthy of the name, one which is truly a city, because it observes the laws of true justice; in short, the City whose head is Christ. Doubtless, there ought to be a second at least, namely, one which is constituted by all men, whose head is not Christ. But this latter is scarcely more than the castoffs of the former, and exists because of that former. There could be no city of injustice if there were no City of true justice. Every society worthy of the name is, therefore, either the City of God or defined in relation to the City of God.

* * * *

From among the innumerable cities throughout the world, only two are of interest to St. Augustine: two cities, that is, two societies of men.[23] Since the individual is to the city as the letters of the alphabet to the word, we must seek the origin of the two societies, into which men are divided, by examining the component parts of the societies themselves. There was a moment in history when the unity of mankind was perfectly realized, that is, when it was composed of a

---

body of men in submission to Christ forms a people; it could be called a republic of Christians. The term "republic" had already been appropriated to Rome; hence, it could be called a city. The term City of God was borrowed from Scripture. However, we can still agree with H. Scholz, *op. cit.* 78, that the notion of two opposed cities was suggested to St. Augustine by Ticonius: '*Ecce duas civitates, unam Dei et unam diaboli.*'

[23] *The City of God* 15.1; cf. above, n. 2.

single man. In fact, it was precisely to secure this unity that God first created a single man, from whom all others are sprung. In itself, this was not necessary; the earth could be peopled today with the descendants of several men, simultaneously created at the beginning of time, to whose stock each and every one would belong. Even so, the unification of mankind would still be both desirable and possible; but, through the one ancestor, from whom all men are sprung, this unity is not only a realizable ideal, it is a fact. It is a physical fact, since all men are related. Likewise, it is a moral fact, for, instead of considering themselves bound together by a mere likeness of nature, men are conscious of a real family bond. None of the faithful could doubt that all men, regardless of race, color or appearance, have their origin in the first man created by God, and that this first man was alone of his kind.[24] There was no doubt in St. Augustine's mind that God Himself had created the human race in this way so that men might understand how pleasing unity, even in diversity, was to God;[25] nor could they doubt that their unity was a family unity.[26] Thus, men are naturally brothers in Adam even before being supernaturally brothers in Christ; of this we are assured by faith.[27]

[24] The anti-racism of St. Augustine embraces all men whatsoever their state, even the pygmies, if there are such creatures; St. Augustine was not sure if there were. He even included the Sciopodes, who shelter themselves from the sun in the shade of one foot, and the Cynocephali, who had dogs' heads and barked. Whoever is rational and mortal, regardless of color or shape or sound of voice, is certainly of the stock of Adam. None of the faithful (*nullus fidelium*) is to doubt that all the above originated from the first creation. God knew how to beautify the universe through the diversity of its parts. Cf. *The City of God* 16.8.

[25] *The City of God* 12.22.

[26] 'God, therefore, created one single man, not, of course, that he was to be deprived of all human society, but rather that in this way the unity of society and the bond of concord might be more strongly commended to him if they were joined together, not only through a likeness of nature, but also by a family affection.' (*The City of God* 12.22.)

[27] The fact that there is a natural unity in the human race is known only by faith; Christians believe that God created a single man and took from him the first woman, and that from this first couple all humanity is sprung. The Creator could have done other-

Nevertheless, two kinds of men appear at the very dawn of human history: Cain and Abel. They were reasonable beings, born of the same father, from whom their own mother also came forth. They were both equally men, but of two radically different wills, in which there is portrayed the possibility, at least, of two radically distinct societies. Accordingly, as men follow the example of Cain or Abel, they place themselves within the ranks of one or the other of two peoples: of which one loves the good; the other, evil. The first has as its founder Abel; the second, Cain.[28] From this beginning the history of the two peoples is identified with universal history; rather, it is universal history. St. Augustine has reviewed the highlights of this history; others after him have repeated and enlarged it. It is not our purpose to follow in the same path, but to examine how Augustine himself envisaged the two societies of which he speaks, and which we have to define.

We said that societies are divided according to the division of loves. When St. Augustine speaks of a 'City,' it is in a figurative sense, or, as he himself states, a mystical sense, that he does so; and it is in this sense that the term must be understood. There is, on the one hand, the society or city of all men, who, loving God in Christ, are predestined to reign eternally with God. On the other hand, there is the city of all those men who do not love God, and who are to suffer eternal punishment along with the demons. St. Augustine has, therefore, never conceived the idea of a single universal society, but of two, both of which are universal—at least in the sense that every man whatsoever is necessarily a citizen of one or the

---

wise. If He acted thus, it was precisely that the elect might be fully aware of their unity. The unity of the human race is a model and figure of the unity of the holy people called to adoption through Jesus Christ. This whole outlook is based upon the faith. Cf. *The City of God* 12.22.

[28] *Enarrationes in psalmos* 142.3: '*Antiqua ergo ista civitas Dei, semper tolerans terram, sperans coelum, quae etiam Jerusalem vocatur et Sion.*' Cain was the first-born of the parents of the human race; he belonged to the city of men. Then came Abel, who belonged to the City of God. Cf. *The City of God* 15.1. To be noted here is the fact that the term "city of men" does not signify the state or nation, but the people of men whose end is not God. This is evident, since, as men, Cain and Abel were in no way different.

other.[29] In this sense, it is true to say that two loves have produced two cities: one, in which the love of God unites all men; a second, wherein all citizens, regardless of time and place, are united by their love of the world. Augustine has differentiated the two societies in several ways: love of God or love of the world; love of God to the point of self-contempt or love of self carried to a contempt of God; love of the flesh or love of the spirit. In every case, however, they are distinguished by love, which is their very root. Yet, by whatever name they are designated, it is still true to say that two loves have produced two cities.[30] While *The City of God* was still a project, and long before he wrote its history, it was thus that St. Augustine conceived it. After he had distinguished between a distorted love of self and holy charity, he immediately added: 'These are two loves, the one of which is holy, the other, unholy; one social, the other individualist; one takes heed of the common utility because of the heavenly society, the other reduces even the commonweal to its own ends because of a proud lust of domination; the one is subject to God, the other sets itself up as a rival to God; the one is serene, the other tempestuous; the one peaceful, the other quarrelsome; the one prefers truthfulness to deceitful praises, the other is utterly avid of praise; the one is friendly, the other jealous; the one desires for its neighbor what it would for itself, the other is desirous of lording it over its neighbor; the one directs its effort to the neighbor's good, the other to its own.

'These two loves were manifested in the angels before they were manifested in men: one, in the good angels; the other, in the bad. These two loves have created the distinction between the two cities, the one the City of the just, the other the city of the wicked. Established among men in accordance with the wonderful and ineffable providence of God which governs and orders all His creatures, and mingled together, they live out their life upon this earth, until separated at the last judgment: the one, in union with the good angels, to enjoy eternal life in its King; the other, in company with the

[29] There is but one human race divided into two peoples. Cf. *De vera religione* 50; *The City of God* 15.1; also, below, n. 35.

[30] *Enarr. in ps.* 64.2. *The City of God* 14.1 and 27; 15.1. *Duas civitates faciunt duo amores; fecerunt civitates duas amores duo.*

bad angels, to be cast along with its king into everlasting fire.[31] In this historical sketch of the two loves, there is contained universal history itself, as well as the basis of its intelligibility. Tell me what a people loves and I shall tell you what it is.'[32]

What, exactly, are these two cities? They are, as we have said, two peoples whose nature is determined by the object of their love. The term 'city' is already a symbolic mode of designation, but there are terms still more symbolical: Jerusalem, that is, vision of peace; and Babylon, that is, Babel or confusion.[33] No matter the name, it is always the same thing referred to, namely, two human societies.[34]

To examine the notion still more closely, the surest method is to describe the members of which these two societies are composed. This St. Augustine has done in so many ways that the reader's hesitations on the point are quite excusable, as are some of his interpreters who have become lost in their task. However, there is a guiding thread which leads us securely through the labyrinth of texts. It is the principle, several times enunciated by St. Augustine, that the two cities of which he speaks recruit their citizens in accordance with the law of the divine 'predestination' alone. All men are partisans of one or the other society because they are predestined to beatitude

[31] *De genesi ad litteram* 11.15.

[32] *The City of God* 19.24.

[33] Every kind of society, however numerous and diversified, is reducible to two. St. Augustine has derived the term 'city' from Sacred Scripture. He does not quote the texts, but he has already given an indication; cf. above, n. 5; also, *Ps.* 47.2,3,9; 45.5–6. H. Scholz, *op. cit.* 71, n. 1, gives other references to the New Testament (the last reference he gives should read *Apoc.* 21.2). Cf. Scholz (pp. 71–81) for a fruitful discussion of the notion anterior to St. Augustine. The texts borrowed from Ticonius are particularly important (pp. 78–81). Ticonius had already spoken of Babylon as the City of the Impious, and Jerusalem as the Church of the living God. Jerusalem means 'vision of peace'; Babylon, as Babel, means confusion. Cf. *The City of God* 16.4; 18.2; 19.9.

[34] St. Augustine remains faithful to the Greco-Roman tradition regarding city and people. He distinguishes three organic forms of social life (*vita socialis*), the family, the city, the globe. Cf. *The City of God* 19.7. Scholz is correct in pointing out (pp. 85–86) that it is generally quite wrong to translate *civitas* as 'state,' even though in a few rare cases it would be correct.

with God, or to eternal despair with the Devil.[35] Since there
is no conceivable alternative, it is possible to assert without
fear of error that the quality of the citizen of one or the other
society depends, in the final analysis, on the divine predestination, whose object every man is.

It is in this sense that we must interpret the terms used by
St. Augustine to designate the two cities. Some of the terms
offer no difficulty, as, for example, the City of God, or of Christ
and the city of the Devil;[36] or, the family of men who live by
faith and the family of men who do not live by faith; the body
of the faithful and the body of the unfaithful; the society of
religious men and the society of the irreligious, that is, of
those whom love of God unites and those united through love
of self.[37] On the other hand, doubts arise when St. Augustine
contrasts the earthly city and heavenly City, the temporal city
and the eternal City, or even the mortal city and immortal
society.[38] Both cities are in fact immortal; the predestined
who live in time are, nevertheless, members of one of two
eternal cities, and even on this earth it is possible to be a member of the heavenly City by the very fact of being predestined
to it.[39] Sometimes, St. Augustine uses formulae which are
precise; sometimes, not. In case of doubt, the first should serve
as a rule of interpretation of the second. Every city, regardless
of how it is called, is reducible to that whose King is God,
or to that wherein the Devil reigns. The different terms of
designation never signify other than that.

[35] *Quas etiam mystice appellamus civitates duas* (*The City of
God* 15.1).

[36] St. Augustine speaks several times of a City of God and a city
of the Devil. Christ is King in the first; the Devil, in the second.
He also calls the City of God the *libera civitas*. Cf. *The City of
God* 17.20; 21.1.

[37] *The City of God* 19.17.

[38] *The City of God* 11.1. Also to be noted is the statement that
'There is a City of God whose citizens we long to be with a love
breathed into us by its Creator.' Cf. also, *The City of God* 5.18;
21.11.

[39] St. Augustine often and in exact terms presents the two cities
as intermingled in this life. There is a part of the City of God
which lives on earth by faith during its heavenly pilgrimage. Cf.
The City of God 19.17; 22.6.

* * * *

The two cities are alike contained in a single universe whose head is its Creator, God. Contrary to the Stoics, however, St. Augustine did not conceive of the universe as a city. Never did he speak of the *cosmos* as the City of God in the same sense as a Stoic could speak of it as the City of Zeus. For Augustine, a society can exist only among beings endowed with reason. That is why we have seen him posit the universe as the stage on which the history of societies unfolds; and if on more than one point the universe is affected by this history, it is not precisely its own proper history. In this sense, Augustine profoundly differs from the Stoics. When he speaks of a city, he has in mind not an order of things but a veritable society.

If we take into consideration the sum total of rational beings, including the angels, all appear to be subject to the same history, which was prepared from all eternity in the depths of the divine Providence and which began with the creation of the world and of time, and will finish only with the end of the first and the consummation of the second. Augustine, in fact, took up the task of writing a universal history; if he was not the last to do so, he certainly seems to have been the first. In what particularly concerns the nature of man, this project implied the preliminary recognition of the unity of mankind and consequently the unity of its history. That is what he meant when he proposed to treat all men as a single man whose history would be unfolded without interruption from the beginning till the end of time. Although the expression itself is lacking, the notion of a universal history is clearly implied in the work of St. Augustine.

* * * *

When it is a question of philosophy of history, the problem becomes more complex, for then we must ask whether, from the point of view of St. Augustine himself, history was open to an overall and purely rational, yet true, interpretation, without the light of Revelation. It is certain, however, that St. Augustine never attempted to formulate such a philosophy. His explanation of universal history is essentially religious in the sense that it derives its light from Revelation. He was,

therefore, actually a theologian of history. The interpretation
which he proposed gets its inspiration less from what we today
call philosophy than from what he himself called Wisdom;
by that he means the Wisdom which is not only from Christ,
but is Christ. Had he been questioned on this point, which no
one ever thought of doing, he would have been considerably
surprised. But, would he have admitted that reason alone
could take from universal history a sense which, within its
proper limits, would be both intelligible and true? Since the
case did not arise, the question has no historical meaning. And,
if there are strong reasons for thinking that he considered that
such an attempt would have been ruinous, there is no possibility of proving it.

Must we conclude, therefore, that St. Augustine has no
place in the formation of a philosophy of history? This is still
another question, quite distinct from the previous two; for,
if he did not think about it because the question never occurred to his mind, there is no ground for saying that his
work is not at the origin of the problem. On the contrary,
everything invites us to believe that the diverse philosophies
of history which developed after St. Augustine have been so
many attempts to resolve, with the light of natural reason
alone, a problem which was first posed by faith alone and
which cannot be resolved without the faith. In this sense, the
first theologian of history[40] would be the father of all the
philosophies of history, even if he had no such intention, and
even if they were not recognized for what they are: the ruins
of a vaster edifice in which alone they could find a full justification of their own truth, taken in an authentic sense, of which
they themselves were quite unaware.

[40] It is a question here of theology in the sense of a speculative
doctrine. The entire Old Testament, together with the interpretation which the New Testament gave to it, was already actually a
universal history of the known societies treated from the point of
view of Revelation. The history of the people of God was a history
of the divine plan for all peoples. A sketch of this history can be
found in Wisd. 10-19, which narrates how wisdom has directed
the people from the creation of Adam. It is already a discourse on
universal history.

Thus, at the time, when it posed the faith as the frontier of
any universal society, St. Augustine's teaching suggested an
ever-increasing effort to push back this frontier to the very
limits of the earth. In spite of mishaps, Rome already had
Christian emperors and remained Rome. If, perchance, St.
Augustine did not clearly conceive of a world united and at
peace under a Christian emperor, who would find in the Christian faith itself the foundation of a kind of temporal peace in
this world while awaiting the perfect peace of the next, he
was not slow in pointing out to sovereigns that such a policy
would be a mark of wisdom as well as their duty. With such
a beginning, the changing circumstances of history could suggest still more. St. Augustine did not bequeath to his successors
an ideal of a universal human city united in view of purely
temporal ends proper to it; but it was enough that the City of
God exist in order to inspire men with the desire to organize
the earth into a single society made to the image and likeness
of the heavenly City.

If we examine St. Augustine's own teaching more closely,
we shall see why the notion of a temporal human society,
endowed with its own unity and including the whole human
race, could not present itself to his mind. The two cities which
he describes are, as we have seen, mystical, that is, supernatural, in their very essence. The one is the City of truth,
of the good, of order, of peace; it is, indeed, a true society.
The other, since it is defined as the denial of the former, is
the city of error, of evil, of disorder and confusion; it is, in
fact, a mockery of a society worthy of the name. Midway between these two cities, of which one is the negation of the
other, there is situated a neutral zone where the men of our
day hope to construct a third city, which would be temporal
like the earthly city, yet just in a temporal way, that is striving
toward a temporal justice obtainable by appropriate means.
Such an idea seems never to have occurred to St. Augustine;
at least, he never spoke of it.

It was not through any failure to foresee the beneficent influence that the City of God, by the very fact of its existence,
can and ought to exercise on temporal societies, that the possibility of a unified temporal order, valid and justifiable in it-

self from the point of view of its proper end, did not suggest itself to St. Augustine; rather, it was due to the close association between the two notions of *world* and of *evil*, so spontaneously linked together in his mind. He neither excluded nor thought about such a possibility. He no more thought of that than of a philosophy which, through the purely rational methods at its disposal, would free itself from the confusion of thought of the ancients and correctly resolve the problems which belonged to its domain. He was prevented from doing so less from principles than from his personal experience, for the reading of Plotinus had sufficiently drawn his attention to the incapacity of unaided natural reason fully to discover truth. Granting Christianity, everything seemed to take place for Augustine as if such a problem no longer existed, and ought nevermore to arise; or, perhaps, as if the transcendent importance of the building of the City of God relegated the temporal order to a place so clearly secondary that it was no longer worth the trouble to consider it for itself or to organize it in view of its own ends.

In pressing this point still further, we finally come to realize both the innermost meaning of *The City of God* and its historical significance.

III. *Christian Wisdom and a World Society*

The historical significance of *The City of God* can hardly be exaggerated. From the point of view of St. Augustine himself, it was a companion to the *Confessions*, whose final books deal with the history of Creation as told in Holy Writ. With Creation the history of man began; that is, the centuries-old tale of two cities, a tale which will end with the final triumph of the City of God, the ultimate end and true final cause of the divine work of Creation. Seen in the light of Christian wisdom, the evolution of world history is a no less striking 'confession' of the love and power of God than the sight of His creation, and the awareness of the wonders wrought by grace in the soul of His servant Augustine. Here all is of a piece, and no great effort is needed to discover in the *Confessions* the same general purpose as in St. Augustine's monumental *City of God*. The great Bishop of Hippo probably would never have written it except for the fall of Rome and the ensuing controversies to which that event gave rise; nevertheless, when the challenge came he was prepared to meet it.

To his successors, St. Augustine bequeathed the ideal of a society whose bond of union is the Divine Wisdom. Often forgotten, sometimes even for centuries, this ideal has always found men to bring it forth once more into the light of day to be their inspiration. Frequently, the price of revival has been the distortion of the ideal.

* * * *

The desire of the world-wide unity which fills the heart of man will, in all likelihood, never die. Since the time it was proffered them, even though in a mystical sense and on a supernatural level, it has never been forgotten. Generation after generation has honestly attempted to gather all men within the walls of an earthly city modeled upon the heavenly Jerusalem. They have studied everything except the Christian faith in order to find a common bond, but they have met with failure. Perhaps the time is ripe to recall the age-old metaphysical principle that the only force capable of preserving a thing is the force which created it. It is completely useless to pursue a Christian end except by Christian means. If we really want one world, we must first have one Church, and the only Church that is one is the Catholic Church.

Had we religious unity, we could peacefully enjoy all the other unities. Basically, there is nothing wrong in attempting to achieve philosophical unity by philosophical means, nor in trying to establish world unity through philosophical unity. Philosophy really is a unifying force, as are science, art, industry and economic forces. There is no single factor in human unity that we can afford to despise. But, just as every metaphysical undertaking is doomed to failure if secondary principles replace those which are primary, so also all efforts to unify mankind are bound to fail if the sole principle of unification is overlooked, especially when that principle is the unifying force of all the others. Philosophy, science, art and economics all can help in achieving the great work of uniting mankind, but neither individually nor collectively is it in their power to accomplish it. The besetting sin of all such undertakings is in the fact that they attempt, without Christ, to fulfill the promise made by Christ to men.

Such an achievement is quite impossible. It is conceivable that a number of men, more or less large, be unified under the domination of other men or even of one individual; however, if we are striving toward the unity of all men, we must look beyond mankind for the unifying principle. The only possible source of future unity lies not in multiplicity, but above it. *One World* is impossible without *One God* and *One Church*. In this truth lies the ever timely message conveyed to man by St. Augustine's *City of God*.

SAINT AUGUSTINE
THE CITY OF GOD

PART ONE

THE PAGAN GODS AND EARTHLY HAPPINESS

BOOK I

Christianity Did Not Cause the Fall of Rome

Preface

MY DEAR MARCELLINUS:[1] This work which I have begun makes good my promise to you. In it I am undertaking nothing less than the task of defending the glorious City of God against those who prefer their own gods to its Founder. I shall consider it both in its temporal stage here below (where it journeys as a pilgrim among sinners and lives by faith) and as solidly established in its eternal abode—that blessed goal for which we patiently hope 'until justice be turned into judgment,'[2] but which, one day, is to be the reward of excellence in a final victory and a perfect peace. The task, I realize, is a high and hard one, but God will help me.[3]

[1] Marcellinus, fervent Christian and, until his death in September, 413, close friend of St. Augustine, was appointed by the Emperor Honorius (395–423) as a Commissioner to deal with the dispute between Catholics and Donatists in North Africa. Eager for the conversion of the pagan but well-disposed imperial proconsul, Volusianus, he sought the help of Augustine and was thus the occasion for the correspondence between the proconsul and the saint which still survives and throws much light on the beginnings of the *City of God*. St. Augustine began in 412 (and finished in 415) the first five Books which, as he tells us in his *Retractations* (chap. 69), were meant as a refutation of the pagan position that polytheism is necessary for social prosperity and that the prohibition of pagan worship 'is the source of many calamities.'

[2] Ps. 93.15.

[3] Ps. 61.9.

I know, of course, what ingenuity and [...]
are needed to convince proud men of the [...]
Its loftiness is above the pinnacles of earth[...]
are shaken by the shifting winds of time—n[...]
man arrogance, but only by the grace of [...]
Scripture, the King and Founder of the Cit[...]
undertaken to speak revealed to His people[...]
divine law: 'God resisteth the proud and gi[...]
humble.'[4] Unfortunately the swollen spirit [...]
claims for itself this high prerogative, which [...]
alone, and longs and loves to hear repeated [...]
the line: 'To be merciful to the conquere[...]
haughty down.'[5]

Hence, in so far as the general plan of the [...]
and my ability permits, I must speak also of [...]
—of that city which lusts to dominate the w[...]
though nations bend to its yoke, is itself domi[...]
sion for dominion.

Chapter 1

From this earthly city issue the enemies against whom the
City of God must be defended. Some of them, it is true, abjure
their worldly error and become worthy members in God's
City. But many others, alas, break out in blazing hatred
against it and are utterly ungrateful, notwithstanding its Redeemer's signal gifts. For, they would no longer have a voice
to raise against it, had not its sanctuaries given them asylum
as they fled before the invaders' swords, and made it possible
for them to save that life of which they are so proud.

Have not even those very Romans whom the barbarians
spared for the sake of Christ assailed His Name? To this both
the shrines of the martyrs and the basilicas of the Apostles
bear witness: amid the city's devastation, these buildings gave
refuge not only to the faithful but even to infidels. Up to the
sacred threshold raged the murderous enemy, but the slayers'
fury went no farther. The merciful among the enemy conducted to the churches those whom they had spared even out-

[4] James 4.6; 1 Peter 5.5.
[5] Virgil, *Aeneid* 6.853.

side the holy precincts, to save them from others who lacked such mercy. Even these ruthless men, who in other places customarily indulged their ferocity against enemies, put a rein to their murderous fury and curbed their mania for taking captives, the moment they reached the holy places. Here, the law of sanctuary forbade what the law of war elsewhere permitted. Thus were saved many of those who now cry down Christian culture and who blame Christ for the calamities that befell the city. Indeed, that very mercy to which they owe their lives and which was exercised in Christ's Name they ascribe not to our Christ but to their Fate. Yet, if they only had sense, they would see that the hardships and cruelties they suffered from the enemy came from that Divine Providence who makes use of war to reform the corrupt lives of men. They ought to see that it is the way of Providence to test by such afflictions men of virtuous and exemplary life, and to call them, once tried, to a better world, or to keep them for a while on earth for the accomplishment of other purposes. As for the fact that the fierce barbarians, contrary to the usage of war, generally spared their lives for Christ's sake and, in particular, in places dedicated to Christ's Name—which by a merciful Providence were spacious enough to afford refuge to large numbers—this they should have credited to Christian culture. They should thank God and, if they would escape the pains of eternal fire, should turn to His Name with all sincerity—as many have, without sincerity, in order to escape the results of the present ruin.

For, many of those whom you see heaping impudent abuse on the servants of Christ would not have escaped the ruin and massacre had they not falsely paraded as servants of Christ. Now, with ungrateful pride, impious madness, and perversity of heart, they work against that Name. They who turned to that Name with a lying tongue, in order to enjoy this temporal light, deserve the penalty of eternal darkness.

Chapter 2

The chronicles are filled with wars waged before Rome was founded, and since it rose and grew to be an empire. Let the pagans read these chronicles, and then adduce one single instance of a city falling into the hands of a foe disposed to spare men seeking refuge in the temples of their gods. Or let them even point to a single barbarian chieftain who captured a town and then ordered his soldiers not to kill those caught in any of the temples. Did not Aeneas see Priam cut down before the altar, 'polluting with his blood the altar fires of his own consecration'?[1] And did not Diomedes and Ulysses 'cut down the sentries in the towered height; since they grasped the holy image and dared with bloody hands to touch the maiden chaplets of the goddess'?[2] Nor did that which follows come true: 'Since then the hope of Greece ebbed and slid away.'[3] For, after this, they conquered; after this, they wiped out Troy with fire and sword; after this, they cut off Priam's head before the altar to which he fled. Nor did Troy perish because it lost its Palladium—Minerva. And what had Minerva herself first lost that she should perish? The guardians of her statue? To be sure, once they were slain, Minerva could be taken away. It was not the effigy that guarded the men, but the men who guarded the effigy. For what earthly reason was Minerva worshiped as the protector of the land and people, when she could not even protect the guards of her temple?

Chapter 3

Just think of the kind of gods to whose protection the Romans were content to entrust their city! No more pathetic illusion could be imagined. Yet, the pagans are angry with us because we speak so frankly of their divinities. However, they feel no anger against their own writers. They even pay them a fee to teach such nonsense, and think such teachers worthy of public salary and honors. Take Virgil. Children must read this greatest and best of all poets in order to impress their tender minds so deeply that he may never be easily forgotten, much as the well-known words of Horace suggest:

> The liquors that new vessel first contains
> Behind them leave a taste that long remains.[1]

---

[1] *Aeneid* 2.501.   [2] *Ibid.* 2.166ff.   [3] *Ibid.*

[1] Horace, *Epistles* 1.2.69.

Now, in Virgil, Juno is pictured as the foe of the Trojans and as saying, while she goads Aeolus, King of the Winds, against them:

> The nation that I hate in peace sails by,
> With Troy and Troy's fallen gods to Italy.[2]

Did they act wisely in placing Rome's immunity from defeat in the hands of such vanquished deities? Even assuming that Juno spoke these words in a fit of feminine anger, not knowing what she said, does not Aeneas himself, so often styled 'the pious,' relate how

> Panthus, a priest of Phoebus and the Tower,
> Rushed with his nephew and the conquered gods
> And, frantic, sought for shelter at my door.[3]

Does he not admit that the very gods, whom he declares 'conquered' are entrusted to his protection rather than he to theirs, when he is given the charge, 'To thee doth Troy commend her gods, her all'?[4] If, then, Virgil describes such gods as vanquished, and, because vanquished, needing a man's help even to escape, surely it is folly to believe that it was wise to entrust Rome to the safe-keeping of such divinities, and to believe that Rome could never be destroyed unless it lost its gods. In fact, to worship fallen gods as patrons and defenders is more like having poor odds[5] than good gods. It is much more sensible to believe, not so much that Rome would have been saved from destruction had not the gods perished, but rather that the gods would have perished long ago had not Rome made every effort to save them.

For, who does not see, if only he stops to consider, how futile it is to presume that Rome could not be conquered when protected by conquered custodians, and that the reason it fell was that it lost its tutelary deities? Surely, the only possible

---

[2] Virgil, *Aeneid* 1.67.

[3] *Ibid.* 2.319ff.

[4] *Ibid.* 2.293.

[5] ... *tenere non numina bona, sed nomina mala. Nomina mala* (if that is the correct reading and not *omina mala*) should be translated as 'bad debtors,' in the sense that the pagan gods do not pay back salvation in return for the worship given them; but for the sake of imitating the paronomasia, *numina ... nomina,* 'gods' and 'odds' have been used. See note in *De civitate Dei,* ed. Emanuel Hoffman, *CSEL* XXXX (Vienna 1899) 8.

reason why Rome should fall was that it wanted vincible protectors. Hence, when all these things were written and sung about the fallen gods, it was not because the poets took pleasure in lying, but because truth compelled intelligent men to avow them. However, this matter will be more fitly and more fully treated in subsequent chapters. Here I shall do my best to wind up in few words what I began to say about men's ingratitude.

These men, I say, hold Christ responsible for the evils which they deservedly suffer for their wicked lives. They have not the slightest appreciation of the fact, that, when they deserved to be punished, they were spared for Christ's sake. On the contrary, with impious perversity and bitterness, they attack His Name with those very tongues which falsely invoked that Name to save them. The very tongues which, like cowards, they held in check in the sacred places when safe, protected and unharmed by the enemy for Christ's sake, they now use to hurl malicious curses against Him.

Chapters 4–6

References to Virgil, Sallust, and Livy indicate that it was never customary for the temples or statues of the gods, in ancient Greece and Rome, to be spared in time of war.

Chapter 7

All the destruction, slaughter, plundering, burning, and distress visited upon Rome in its latest calamity were but the normal aftermath of war. It was something entirely new that fierce barbarians, by an unprecedented turn of events, showed such clemency that vast basilicas were designated as places where refugees might assemble with assurance of immunity. There, no one was to be slain or raped; many destined for liberation were to be led there by the compassionate enemy; from there, none was to be dragged away into captivity by a cruel foe. That this was in honor of the Name of Christ and to the credit of Christian civilization is manifest to all. To see this and not acknowledge it with praise is ingratitude. To impugn those who give us credit is utterly unreasonable. Let no man with sense ascribe this to the savage ways of the barbarians. It was God who struck awe into ruthless and bloodthirsty hearts, who curbed and wondrously tamed them. God who long ago spoke these words by the mouth of the Prophet; 'I will visit their iniquities with a rod: and their sins with stripes. But My mercy I will not take away from them.'[1]

Chapter 8

But, someone will say: 'How, then, is it that this divine mercy was bestowed on impious and ungrateful man?' Surely, the answer is that mercy was shown by the One who, day by day, 'maketh His sun to rise upon the good and bad, and raineth upon the just and the unjust.'[1] For, although some who reflect on these truths repent and are converted from their wickedness, others, according to the words of the Apostle, despise 'the riches of His goodness and long-suffering, in the hardness of their heart and impenitence' and treasure up to themselves 'wrath against the day of wrath and revelation of the just judgment of God Who will render to every man according to his works.'[2] Nevertheless, God's patience is an invitation to the wicked to do penance, just as God's scourge is a school of patience for the good. In like manner, God's mercy embraces the good with love, just as His severity corrects the wicked with punishment. It has pleased Divine Providence to prepare for the just joys in the world to come in which the unjust will have no part; and for the impious, pains which will not afflict the virtuous. But, as for the paltry goods and evils of this transitory world, these He allotted alike to just and unjust, in order that men might not seek too eagerly after those goods which they see even the wicked to possess, or shrink too readily from those ills which commonly afflict the just.

However, there is a vast difference between the manner in which men use what we call prosperity and adversity. A good man is neither puffed up by fleeting success nor broken by adversity; whereas, a bad man is chastised by failure of this

---

[1] Ps. 88.33.34.

[1] Matt. 5.45.   [2] Rom. 2.4ff.

sort because he is corrupted by success. God often shows His intervention more clearly by the way He apportions the sweet and the bitter. For, if He visited every sin here below with manifest penalty, it might be thought that no score remained to be settled at the Last Judgment. On the other hand, if God did not plainly enough punish sin on earth, people might conclude that there is no such thing as Divine Providence. So, too, in regard to the good things of life. If God did not bestow them with patent liberality on some who ask Him, we could possibly argue that such things did not depend on His power. On the other hand, if He lavished them on all who asked, we might have the impression that God is to be served only for the gifts He bestows. In that case, the service of God would not make us religious, but rather covetous and greedy. In view of all that, when good and bad men suffer alike, they are not, for that reason indistinguishable because what they suffer is similar. The sufferers are different even though the sufferings are the same trials; though what they endure is the same, their virtue and vice are different.

For, in the same fire, gold gleams and straw smokes; under the same flail the stalk is crushed and the grain threshed; the lees are not mistaken for oil because they have issued from the same press. So, too, the tide of trouble will test, purify, and improve the good, but beat, crush, and wash away the wicked. So it is that, under the weight of the same affliction, the wicked deny and blaspheme God, and the good pray to Him and praise Him. The difference is not in what people suffer but in the way they suffer. The same shaking that makes fetid water stink makes perfume issue a more pleasant odor.

Chapter 9

What, then, did the Christians suffer in the great devastation of Rome which, if taken in a spirit of faith, would not have served for their greater good? For one thing, if they humbly called to mind the sins for which God in His anger filled the world with calamities, they will not judge themselves to be so little responsible for these sins as not to have deserved some measure of temporal affliction—even though they were far from being criminals and godless men. The fact is that everyone, however exemplary, yields to some promptings of concupiscence: if not to monstrous crimes, abysmal villainy, and abominable impiety, at least to some sins, however rarely or—if frequently—however venially. Apart from this fact, I say, is it easy to find anyone who treats as he should those whose horrible pride, lust, avarice, damnable depravity, and scoffing impiety caused God to lay desolate the earth, as was threatened in prophecy? For the most part, we hesitate to instruct, to admonish, and, as occasion demands, to correct, and even to reprehend them. This we do either because the effort wearies us, or we fear offending them, or we avoid antagonizing them lest they thwart or harm us in those temporal matters where our cupidity ever seeks to acquire or our faint hearts fear to lose.

Thus, good men shun the wicked and hence will not share in their damnation beyond the grave. Nevertheless, because they wink at their worse sins and fear to frown even on their minor transgressions, the good must in justice suffer temporal afflictions in common with the rest—even though they will escape the eternal. Thus, when God's hand falls as heavily on them as on the others, it is just that they should taste the bitter things of this earthly life, because they loved the sweet things and refused to feel compunction while others sinned. At times, one hesitates to reprove or admonish evil-doers, either because one seeks a more favorable moment or fears that his rebuke may make them worse, and further, discourage weak brethren from striving to lead a good and holy life, or turn them aside from the faith. In such circumstance, forbearance is not prompted by selfish considerations, but by well-advised charity. What is reprehensible, however, is that, while leading good lives themselves and abhorring those of wicked men, some, fearing to offend, shut their eyes to evil deeds instead of condemning them and pointing out their malice. To be sure, the motive behind their tolerance is that they may suffer no hurt in the possession of those temporal goods which virtuous and blameless men may lawfully enjoy; still, there is more self-seeking here than becomes men who are mere sojourners in this world and who profess the hope of a home in heaven.

In truth, it is not only people of less lofty virtue, who live in the married state, having (or seeking to have) children, and possessing a home and household of their own—people such as St. Paul, in the first churches, instructed and admonished how to live:[1] wives with husbands and husbands with wives; children with parents and parents with children; servants with masters and masters with servants—it is not only such people who acquire transitory and earthly goods with zest and lose them with chagrin, and, because of that, dare not offend men whose immoral and vicious life revolts them. Even those who profess a more perfect life and are free from conjugal bonds and content with poorer food and dress are also over-solicitous for their good name and security and frequently forbear to reprehend the wicked, because they fear their snares and violence. Though the good do not fear the wicked to the point of stooping, under intimidation, to their villainies and knavery, they often are unwilling to denounce such things, even when they might convert some souls thereby. Here again they fear that a possible failure to effect reform might jeopardize their security and reputation. It is not that they are convinced that these latter are an indispensable means for the instruction of men. They are merely victims of that human infirmity which loves the flattering tongue and earthly life, and which dreads the censure of the crowd and the anguish and death of the body. In other words, they shirk this duty of fraternal correction because of a certain slavishness to avarice, not because of the obligations of charity.

Hence, this seems to me sufficient enough reason why the good are scourged with the wicked as often as it pleases God to punish degenerate morals with temporal sufferings. Both are scourged, not because both lead a bad life, but because both love an earthly life; not, indeed, to the same extent, but yet both together—a life which the good should think little of in order that the bad, by being admonished and reformed, may attain to eternal life. If the wicked refuse to join in the blessed endeavor, they should be suffered withal and loved as enemies are loved in Christian charity, since, as long as they live, there is always the possibility that they may come to a better mind. In this respect, the good men to whom the Prophet addresses these words, 'He is indeed taken away in his iniquity, but I will require his blood at the hand of the

[1] Col. 3.18–25; Eph. 5.22; 6.9.

watchman,'[2] have not merely an equal but a far graver reason for concern or reflection. For this reason, overseers[3] or rulers are set over the churches, to reprimand sin, not to spare it. Nor is a man fully free from blame who is not in authority, but who notices in those persons he meets in social life many faults he should censure and admonish. He is blameworthy if he fails to do this out of fear of hurting feelings or of losing such things as he may licitly enjoy in this life, but to which he is unduly attached. Finally, there is another reason, well known to Job, why even good men must drink the bitter cup of temporal adversity: in order that the human spirit may test its mettle and come to know whether it loves God with the virtue of religion and for His own sake.

Chapters 10–13

Amplifying his contention that physical sufferings and the loss of earthly possessions may be turned to spiritual advantage, Augustine cites the Old and New Testaments to this effect. Massacres and failures to bury the dead are regrettable but are not spiritual evils.

Chapter 14

Again, it is complained, many Christians have been led into captivity. This would be lamentable, indeed, if they had been led to a place where they could not find their God. But, Holy Scripture gives us instances of great consolations bestowed even in such calamity. There were the three boys, Daniel, and other Prophets who suffered captivity, but in no case was God's comfort lacking.

In like manner, the same God who did not abandon the Prophet Jonas even in the belly of a monster did not desert His faithful ones in the power of a barbarous people, who were, at least, human.

Those with whom I am at issue will prefer to jest at, rather

2 Ezech. 33.6.
3 St. Augustine's word is *speculatores,* possibly a Latin equivalent for *episkopoi* (bishops) or for *skopoi* (lay guardians of discipline).

than to believe, these accounts; yet they will swallow the tale of Orion of Methymna, the celebrated harper, thrown overboard from a ship, then taken up on a dolphin's back and brought to shore. Our account of Jonas the Prophet is more incredible. It is more incredible because more wonderful. It is more wonderful because it reveals a greater power.

Chapter 15

Yet, our detractors have, in the person of one of their eminent men, a striking example of captivity willingly borne for religion's sake. Marcus Aurelius Regulus, a Roman general, was held in captivity by the Carthaginians. As they preferred to have their own men liberated from Roman bondage rather than to hold Romans in their prisons, they despatched to Rome no less a man than Regulus, accompanied by their own legates to negotiate the exchange. At the same time, they bound him under oath to return to Carthage, in case he failed to accomplish what they proposed. Regulus set out on his mission, but, on reaching Rome, he persuaded the Senate not to accede, urging his view that the exchange of prisoners would not be to the advantage of the Roman republic. Having made his plea, he did not have to be compelled to return to the enemy. Of his own accord, Regulus kept the word he had sworn and returned to Carthage. There, Rome's enemies slew him, after subjecting him to fiendish torture. They packed him into a tight wooden box, spiked with sharp nails on all sides, so that he could not lean in any direction without being pierced. The agony of pain, together with privation of sleep, snuffed out his life. Deservedly, indeed, may one extol a courage that proved itself greater than such a frightful ordeal. He had sworn by those gods to return—the gods the banning of whose worship, if you believe the cavilers, brought this terrible disaster upon mankind. Yet, if those gods who were honored that they might make life prosperous here below willed or permitted a horrible fate to overtake one who scrupulously kept his oath, imagine what more frightful infliction they would, if angered, bring down upon the head of a perjured man.

Why do I not confirm my argument with a double proof? Regulus, no doubt, worshiped the gods so sincerely that to keep his oath inviolate he was absolutely resolved not to remain in his own country nor to betake himself anywhere except back into the hands of his bitterest enemies. On the one hand, if he regarded this obligation to the gods as profitable for his life on earth, which had so tragic an end, he was surely deluded. For, his example shows that the gods are utterly useless to secure temporal felicity for their worshipers. Devoted as Regulus was to their worship, he was, notwithstanding, led into captivity, and for being unwilling to violate the oath he swore to them he was slain by being put through the agony of a newly-devised instrument of torture that for devilry has no precedent in the memory of man.

If, on the other hand, the worship of the gods bestows felicity as a reward in the life to come, why do the calumniators of Christian civilization affirm that disaster came upon Rome because she ceased to honor her deities? Honor them as devotedly as she might, could she have tasted the waters of bitterness to the extent that Regulus did? To deny this, one would have to be so incredibly blind as to fly in the face of the plain truth and to contend that the entire city could not taste misery if she worshiped the gods, but that one man could, or, in other words, that the power of their gods is more adapted to preserve a multitude than to preserve individuals. Yet, do not individuals make up the multitude? If they retort that, by reason of his strength of spirit, Marcus Regulus could have found happiness even in his captivity and amid those frightful torments, then I say to them: Go and look rather for the true strength of spirit that can bring happiness to the city also.

The happiness of a city and the happiness of individual men spring from the same source, since a city is nothing else than a multitude of men in harmonius association. I do not, therefore, discuss what kind of virtue inspired Regulus. It suffices, for the moment, that in view of his magnificent gesture the pagans are compelled to admit that the gods are honored not for material advantages or goods which are external and incidental to man. Regulus preferred to forego all such things rather than to offend the gods by whom he swore. But what are we to do with people who boast of having such a fellow citizen, but dread to have a whole city of like quality? If they have no such dread, then let them avow that the very evil which befell Regulus might befall the city also, though it honor the gods no less conscientiously than he did. What is more, let them cease heaping calumny on the Christian era.

But, since this discussion started on the subject of Christian captives, let those who are impudent and stupid enough to mock the most consoling of all religions reflect on the example of Regulus and hold their peace. For, if it was no discredit to the gods that a most devoted servant of theirs who was faithful to his oath lost his native land and, in captivity among enemies, suffered a cruel and lingering death by a new-fangled instrument of torture, then there is far less cause to slander the profession of Christianity by reason of the imprisonment of its holy followers. For, while these martyrs looked forward with certain faith to a heavenly home, they still knew that they were but pilgrims even in their own country.

Chapter 16

The pagans fancy that they are throwing a colossal crime in the face of the Christians when they put their captivity in the worst light by charging further that rapes were wrought not only on married women and marriageable maidens, but also on consecrated virgins. Here, we are not to speak of faith, or piety, or strictly of the virtue we call chastity, but are to confine our discussion to the narrow limits of sense of shame and reason. I am not so much concerned to give an answer to strangers as to offer comfort to my fellow Christians. Therefore, let this stand as a firmly established truth: The virtue which governs a good life controls from the seat of the soul every member of the body, and the body is rendered holy by the act of a holy will.

Thus, as long as the will remains unyielding, no crime, beyond the victim's power to prevent it without sin, and which is perpetrated on the body or in the body, lays any guilt on the soul. An attack on one's body may inflict not merely physical pain, but may also excite carnal pleasure. If such an act is perpetrated, it does not compromise the virtue of chastity, to which the sufferer clings with an iron will; it merely outrages the sense of shame. We must not consider as committed with the will what could not, by the very constitution of nature, occur without some fleshly satisfaction.

Chapters 17–18

Because chastity is not identical with bodily integrity but is a virtue of the soul, no woman need lose her chastity through violation. Moreover, suicide is not a proper means to use in protecting one's chastity.

Chapter 19

I affirm, therefore, that in case of violent rape and of an unshaken intention not to yield unchaste consent, the crime is attributable only to the ravisher and not at all to the ravished. To my cogent argument to this effect, some may venture to take exception. Against these I maintain the truth that not only the souls of Christian women who have been forcibly violated during their captivity, but also their bodies, remain holy.

Many recall, with high praise for her chastity, the noble and ancient Roman matron, Lucretia. Upon her body, overpowered by brute force, the son of King Tarquin inflicted his lust. She revealed the crime of the villainous youth to her husband Collatinus and her kinsman Brutus, both brave and distinguished men, and bound them to avenge it. Then, becoming deeply despondent and unable to bear the shame of the foul deed perpetrated on her body, she killed herself. What judgment is to be passed on her? Is she to be regarded as an adulterous or a chaste woman? Who will cudgel his brains in trying to resolve the question? On this point someone has declared, admirably and with truth: 'Wonderful to relate! Two persons were involved, yet only one committed the adultery!' Nobly and truly said. Seeing, in this connection, only the foul passion of the one and the chaste will of the other, and regarding not so much the union of bodies as the opposition of wills, he declared: 'Two persons, but only one adulterer.'

But, what are we to say of the heavy penalty paid by her who did not commit adultery? The adulterer was driven out of the country with his father, but she bore the extreme penalty of death. If to be the unwilling victim of violent rape is no unchastity, the punishing of a chaste woman is not justice. I appeal to you, laws and judges of Rome. After the commission of a crime, you have never wanted a criminal put to death without sentence of condemnation. If, therefore, anyone brought this crime before you for judgment and it were proved that the woman was slain not only unheard, but also chaste and innocent, would you not impose a duly severe penalty upon the perpetrator of such a deed?

This is the case of Lucretia. Yes, the much-lauded Lucretia took the life of the guiltless, chaste, coerced Lucretia. Pronounce your sentence. If you cannot, because the guilty party is not present in court, why do you shower so much praise on the slayer of a pure and innocent woman? In any case, you can in no way defend her before the judges of the lower regions; if they be of the kind of whom your poets sing, since she is to be placed among those

   . . . who guiltless spoiled themselves through black despite,
  And threw their souls to hell through hate of light.[1]

And, should she crave to return to the upper world, 'Justice and loveless fens forbid the passage thence.'[2] Could it be that she is not in the upper world because she slew herself, not without guilt, and with a bad conscience? What if—only she could know—notwithstanding the young villain's violent advances, she was lured by her own lust to acquiesce and, stung with self-reproach, chose death as the way of atonement? Not even then should she have made an end to herself, if she could possibly do penance acceptable to the false gods.

However, if such be the case, and if the verdict, 'two persons, but only one adulterer,' be false—the truth being that both committed adultery, one by open aggression and the other by secret agreement—then, she did not kill herself with a clean conscience. That being so, her learned champions cannot affirm that in the lower regions she is not ranged with those 'who guiltless spoiled themselves.' Thus, the case is pinned down by both horns of a dilemma: If the suicide is condoned, the adultery is clear; if the adultery is disproved, the suicide is doubly clear. There is no way out of the dilemma. If she

[1] Virgil, *Aeneid* 6.434–436.
[2] *Ibid.* 6.438.

is an adulteress, why all the praise? If chaste, why did she kill herself?

In connection with the noble example of Lucretia, and to refute those who are incapable of grasping the idea of sanctity and make sport of the Christian women forcibly violated in captivity, I need only repeat what was said in her praise: 'Two persons, but only one adulterer.' In their eyes, she could not have stained her name with an adulterous consent. The fact is that, though free from adulterous intent, she killed herself because she suffered an adulterer. She was not in love with chastity; she was a victim of her sense of shame. The act committed on her without her consent filled her with shame. Being a Roman with a passion for praise, she was afraid that, if she lived, men might think she did willingly what she had endured by violence. Hence, as witness of her intention, she decided to put that punishment before the eyes of men who could not read her conscience. She was ashamed to be thought a party to the deed if she bore with resignation the foul thing done to her by another.

It was not in this way that women acted who endured similar violation, yet are still alive. They did not avenge on themselves others' wrongs, lest they add sins of their own to the crimes of others. This they would have done had they murdered themselves for shame because lustful enemies had made them victims of violence. They bear within them the glory of chastity, in the testimony of their conscience, and this they have in the eyes of their God. They ask for nothing more, since this is the best way not to depart from the authority of God's law by any ill-advised attempt to avoid the humiliation of human suspicion.

Chapter 20

It is significant that in Holy Scripture no passage can be found enjoining or permitting suicide either in order to hasten our entry into immortality or to void or avoid temporal evils. God's command, 'Thou shalt not kill,'[1] is to be taken as forbidding self-destruction, especially as it does not add 'thy neighbor,' as it does when it forbids false witness, 'Thou shalt

[1] Exod. 20.13,16.

not bear false witness against thy neighbor.' However, no one should think he is guiltless when he bears false witness against himself, since the duty to love one's neighbor is measured by the love of oneself, as it is written, 'Thou shalt love thy neighbor as thyself.'[2]

To be sure, the commandment forbidding false witness has another directly in view, and by misunderstanding the matter some may judge that no one is obliged to be truthful to himself. But, the fact is that a man who lies against himself is no less guilty of false witness than if he lied against another. All the more must we realize that no man may take his own life, for, in the command, 'Thou shalt not kill,' there are no limitations; hence, no one, not even the one who is commanded, is to be excepted.

Indeed, some people try to stretch the prohibition to cover beasts and cattle, and make it unlawful to kill any such animals. But, then, why not include plants and anything rooted in and feeding on the soil? After all, things like this, though devoid of feeling, are said to have life, and, therefore, can die, and so be killed by violent treatment. St. Paul himself, speaking of seeds, says, 'That which thou sowest is not quickened, except it die first,'[3] while the Psalmist writes: 'And he destroyed their vineyards with hail.'[4] Must we, then, when we read, 'Thou shalt not kill,' understand that it is a crime to pull up a shrub, and foolishly subscribe to the error of the Manichaeans?

Putting this nonsense aside, we do not apply 'Thou shalt not kill' to plants, because they have no sensation; or to irrational animals that fly, swim, walk, or creep, because they are linked to us by no association or common bond. By the Creator's wise ordinance they are meant for our use, dead or alive. It only remains for us to apply the commandment, 'Thou shalt not kill,' to man alone, oneself and others. And, of course, one who kills himself kills a man.

[2] Matt. 22.39.
[3] 1 Cor. 15.36.
[4] Ps. 77.47.

Chapter 21

The same divine law which forbids the killing of a human being allows certain exceptions, as when God authorizes killing by a general law or when He gives an explicit commission to an individual for a limited time. Since the agent of authority is but a sword in the hand, and is not responsible for the killing, it is in no way contrary to the commandment, 'Thou shalt not kill,' to wage war at God's bidding, or for the representatives of the State's authority to put criminals to death, according to law or the rule of rational justice.

Thus, Abraham was not only free from the guilt of criminal cruelty, but even commended for his piety, when he consented to sacrifice his son, not, indeed, with criminal intent but in obedience to God.[1] One may well ask, also, whether it was not at God's command that Jephte killed his daughter when she met him after he had vowed that he would sacrifice to God the first thing he encountered, if he returned victorious from battle.[2] Samson crushed himself and his enemies to death beneath the ruins of a building. He can only be excused on the grounds that the Spirit of the Lord, who wrought miracles through him, had bidden him to do so. But, apart from such men excepted by the command of a just law in general or of God, the very Source of justice, in a special case, anyone who kills a human being, himself or another, is guilty of murder.

Chapters 22–26

Neither in the Bible nor in the pagan moral works is suicide approved. The suicides of Lucretia and of Cato are examples of pseudo-courage. The story of Regulus shows the nobility of a pagan who preferred captivity to suicide. To kill oneself at God's command is not suicide, but one should be absolutely certain about the divine command.

[1] Gen. 22.1–13.
[2] Judges 11.30–39.

Chapter 27

There remains one argument for suicide, which I have
touched on already. It is to the effect that taking one's own
life is expedient in order to ward off falling into sin, either
through the allurements of pleasure or the violence of pain.
If we admit this argument, it will logically lead us to the fan-
tastic conclusion that men should prefer to end their lives as
soon as they have been cleansed by the 'laver of regeneration,'[1] and have received pardon for all their sins. That is the
proper moment for averting all future sins, when all past sins
are blotted out.

For, if self-inflicted death be morally right, why should not
that moment be chosen above all others? Why should any
baptized man hesitate to end his life? Why should a liberated
spirit enmesh itself again in the manifold hazards of this life,
when it is the easiest thing in the world for him to stave off
everything by snuffing out his life? It is written: 'He that lov-
eth danger shall perish in it.'[2] Why, then, does a man love
so many grave dangers, or, if he does not love them, at least
lay himself open to them by clinging to a life which he may
lawfully cast off? But, what insensate folly has so perverted
the heart and blinded it to the truth that a man should fancy
that, though he must kill himself lest he be forced into sin by
one enemy who has overpowered him, he ought to keep on
living, and enduring a world, constantly beset with tempta-
tions—which come not only from one master, but from the
whole of life. Why waste time in those exhortations we address
to the newly-baptized, striving to enkindle in them a love for
virginal purity, or widowed continence, or conjugal fidelity?
We have simpler short-cuts for avoiding all danger of sin: we
can urge everyone, the moment he is cleansed of his sins at
the baptismal font, to rush himself off to death. In that way,
do we not dispatch him to the Lord sounder and purer?

Now, if there be anyone who thinks that such an exhortation should be attempted, I say he is not merely silly, he is
mad. After all, with what force could he say to a man, 'Kill

---

[1] Titus 3.5.
[2] Eccli. 3.27.

yourself, lest to your slight sins you add a mortal one by living subject to a barbarous and impure master,' when, except he cast decency to the winds, he cannot say, 'Kill yourself the moment your sins are absolved, lest you commit like and worse sins while you live in a world alluring with filthy pleasures, mad with unspeakable cruelty, arrayed against you with errors and terrors'? Since it is wicked to speak thus, it is undoubtedly wicked to kill oneself. For, if there could be any justifiable occasion for suicide, there would certainly be none more justifiable than this. Since this is not so, then there is none at all.

Chapter 28

Let not your life, then, O faithful followers of Christ be a burden to you in case your chastity was made the sport of enemies. You have ample and genuine assurance on that point so long as your conscience assures you that you gave no consent to the sins of those who were allowed the liberty of committing them against you. If you ask me why they were allowed the liberty, the answer is that the providence of the Creator and Ruler of the world transcends human reckoning, and that 'incomprehensible are His judgments and . . . unsearchable His ways.'[1] Nevertheless, carefully scrutinize your own souls and see whether you were not unduly puffed up about your virtue of purity, or continence, or chastity, and whether you have not been led to envy others by reason of the human praise bestowed on them for these virtues.

I make no accusation about what I do not know, nor do I hear what answer your consciences make to the questions you ask. But, if they reply that the case is as I have supposed it might be, then do not wonder that you have lost that chastity which you displayed to win men's praises and retained that love of chastity which cannot be displayed before men's eyes. If you did not yield consent to the sin of your oppressors, it was because God's grace came to your aid that you might not lose it, whereas shame before men followed the praise of men in order that your heart might not pour itself out on this. In

[1] Rom. 11.33.

either case you may find solace, faint-hearted ones, tested as you have been by the one experience, and chastened by the other.

Then, there are those faithful women whose consciences, when interrogated, reply that they have never been puffed up with pride by reason of their virginity or continence or conjugal chastity, but that 'consenting to the humble,'[2] that is, in a spirit of humility, they rejoiced with fear and trembling in the gift of God and envied no one who enjoyed the treasure of like holiness and chastity. Far from that, they held in little regard that human praise which, as a rule, is lavished in greater measure the rarer the virtue that elicits the applause. They desired that the number of the pure should increase rather than that they themselves should stand out as more conspicuous among the few. Even those virtuous women who are both chaste and unenvious, if they have been outraged by the barbarians, must not complain that this was allowed; nor must they think that God is indifferent to such outrages because He permits to happen what no man can commit without punishment.

For, like an avalanche, some evil desires are let loose by the secret judgment of God on earth, and are reserved for His final and open judgment. Moreover, as regards those Christian women whose conscience assures them that they were not puffed up by their virtue of chastity, and who, nevertheless, had suffered the enemy's outrages in their flesh, it may possibly be that they had in them some latent weakness which could have swollen to overwhelming pride had they escaped this humiliation in the sack of the city. Hence, just as death snatched some away, 'lest wickedness should alter their understanding,'[3] so violence snatched something away from them lest prosperity should endanger their chastity.

Hence, neither the women who were already puffed up because they had suffered no immodest contact, nor those who might possibly have been puffed up had not contact been forced on them by the enemy, were robbed of their chastity, but they learned humility. The former were delivered from a

2 Rom. 12.16.
3 Wisd. 4.11.

pride that had already overtaken them; the latter, from a pride that threatened them.

There is yet another point I should not fail to mention. Some who suffered violence to their chastity might conceive of this virtue as belonging to these qualities of the body which endure so long as the body remains inviolate. Others might think that sanctity of body and soul does not depend solely on strength of will sustained by God's help. Still others might conclude that it is not a blessing which cannot be taken away from a person against his will. From such an error they are probably now delivered. For, when they reflect on how conscientiously they have served God, and when with unshaken faith they believe that He would by no means abandon those who have served Him and invoked His aid so faithfully, and when they further consider how pleasing is chastity in His sight, then they can draw only one conclusion: that He would never have permitted these evils if they could destroy in His saints that purity of soul which He had bestowed on them and delights to see in them.

Chapters 29–31

The reward for good Christians is not the possession of earthly things. Even the pagan pontifex, Scipio Nasica, counseled moderation in the attack on Carthage, denounced the Roman lust for power, and frowned on the presentation of obscene stage plays.

Chapter 32

Learn, then, you who pretend ignorance, and mark well the facts while you grumble against the One who delivered you from such masters. The stage plays, those exhibitions of depravity and unbounded license, were not introduced in Rome by men's vices, but by the command of your gods. Far more justifiably might you have paid divine honors to your Scipio than worshiped gods such as those, for they were not more virtuous than their high priest. And now mark further, if your mind, besotted as it is with long draughts of error, is still able to entertain a sane thought. Your gods, in order to allay a plague that seized upon your bodies, ordered stage plays in their honor, but your pontifex forbade the construction of the stage in order to keep a plague from seizing your souls. If your mind retains enough sense to esteem the soul more than the body, then choose whom you should worship.

Moreover, the plague did not abate when the wanton madness of the stage plays took possession of a warlike people, once accustomed only to the sports of the arena. It was the work of wicked spirits crafty enough to know that that pestilence would soon run its course. They seized the occasion, to their great delight, to inject a more deadly contagion, not into men's bodies, but into their souls. This contagion so beclouded the wits of those wretches, so befouled and deranged them, that even now—for, future generations will scarcely believe the story if it reaches them—after the City of Rome has been laid waste, those who were so infected by the plague and were able to flee from Rome to Carthage were day after day stampeding one another in a mad rush after the clowns in the theaters.

Chapter 33

Are your minds bereft of reason? You are not merely mistaken; this is madness. Here are people in the East bewailing Rome's humiliation, and great states in remote regions of the earth holding public mourning and lamentation—and you Romans are searching for theaters, pouring into them, filling them, behaving more irresponsibly than ever before. It is this spiritual disease, degeneration, decline into immorality and indecency that Scipio feared when he opposed the erection of theaters. He saw how easily ease and plenty would soften and ruin you. He did not wish you to be free from fear.

He did not think that the republic could be happy while walls were standing, yet morals were collapsing. But, you were more attached to the seductions of foul spirits than to the wisdom of men with foresight. That is why you take no blame for the evil you do, but blame Christianity for the evil you suffer. Depraved by prosperity and unchastened by adversity, you desire, in your security, not the peace of the State but liberty for license. Scipio wanted you to have a salutary fear of the enemy, lest you should rot in debauchery. Though crushed by the enemy, you put no check on immorality, you learned no lessons from calamity; in the depths of sorrows you still wallow in sin.

Chapter 34

Yet, you owe your survival to that God who, in sparing you, warned you to amend your lives by penance. Despite your ingratitude, He made it possible for you to escape from the hands of the enemy—either by professing to be His followers or by taking refuge in the churches of the martyrs.

Romulus and Remus, we are told, with a view to increasing the population of their city, opened an asylum where refugees were to be immune from every molestation. That admirable example redounded to the honor of Christ. The destroyers of the city re-established the institution of its founders. But, what is remarkable is that what the founders did to increase the number of their citizens the destroyers did to save a number of their enemies.

Chapter 35

This—or something fuller and fitter, if it can be found—is the core of the reply that the redeemed followers of Christ the Lord and the pilgrim City of Christ the King should give to their enemies. But, our city must remember that, in the ranks of its enemies, lie hid fellow citizens to be, and that it is well to bear with them as enemies until we can reach them in their profession of faith. In like manner, the City of God itself, so long as it is a wayfarer on earth, harbors within its ranks a number of those who, though externally associated in the common bond of the sacraments, will not be associated in the eternal felicity of the saints. Some there are who, covertly or overtly, join the enemy in abusing the God whom they have promised to serve. They are to be seen flocking sometimes to the theaters with the godless, and at other times to the churches with us.

There is little reason to abandon hope of reclaiming some of these persons, for among our most notorious adversaries are men destined to be friends, however little they know it. On earth, these two cities are linked and fused together, only to be separated at the Last Judgment. And now, with God's help, I must turn to what I think ought to be said about the origin, progress, and respective destinations of the two cities, in order to exalt the glory of the City of God, which by contrast with other cities will gleam the more brightly.

Chapter 36

I still have something to say against those who hold our religion responsible for the disaster to the Roman state, because it has forbidden them to sacrifice to their gods. Here, I must remind you of all the grave calamities which have occurred (or of as many as will suffice for my purpose), and which the city itself, or the provinces subject to its rule, had to endure long before their sacrifices were banned. For, beyond all doubt, they would have laid at our door all of those miseries, if at that time our religion had enlightened their minds, and had forbidden their sacrilegious rites.

Then, I must show on account of what virtues and for what reason the true God, in whose power are all kingdoms, vouchsafed His help to spread the empire, while those fictions they call gods gave no help at all, but, on the contrary, worked untold harm by their deceptions and frauds. Lastly, I shall argue against those who, though the ground is taken from under their feet by the plainest possible proofs, attempt to maintain that the gods are to be worshiped, not for the benefit they could bestow in this life, but for the sake of the life beyond the grave. The discussion of this question is, I believe, a much more difficult task, calling for more subtle reasoning. For, on this point, we are at issue, not with the common run of philosophers, but with those who stand very high in the esteem of our adversaries and who see eye to eye with us on many things, such as the immortality of the soul, the creation of the world by the true God, and His providence governing the world He created.[1] Since these same philosophers must be set right on those points in which they differ with us, we cannot evade the duty of pointing out their errors, so that, after disposing of the objections of the impious, with the ability God will vouchsafe, we may vindicate the City of God, and the true piety toward and worship of that God who alone holds out the infallible promise of eternal happiness. Here, we may bring the present book to a close, and begin to take up the points next in order in a new Book.

[1] An allusion to Platonists and Neo-platonists.

BOOK II

Pagan Gods Never Protected Men's Souls

Chapter 1

IF MAN's sickly understanding would not set plain truth at defiance, but humbly submit this common infirmity to the tonic of wholesome doctrine until, by filial trust in God's help, it regained its strength, those who think straight and express their thoughts in well-chosen speech would have no need of many words to correct the errors of baseless assumption. Unfortunately, however, there prevails a major and malignant malady of fools, the victims of which mistake their irrational impulses for truth and reason, even when confronted with as much evidence as any man has a right to expect from another. It may be an excess of blindness which prevents them from seeing the most glaring facts, or a perverse obstinacy which prevents them from accepting the facts when seen. This compels me to present more diffusely, not for their closed eyes to see, but, so to speak, for their hands to touch and feel, some obvious points.

Yet, if we always felt obliged to reply to counterstatements, when would there be an end to the argument or a limit to discussion? For, those who cannot grasp what is said, or, if they understand the truth, are too obdurate to accept it, keep on replying and, according to Holy Writ, 'speak iniquity'[1] and never weary of empty words. You can easily see what an endless, wearisome, and fruitless task it would be, if I were to refute all the unconsidered objections of people who pigheadedly contradict everything I say.

And so, my dear Marcellinus, I hope that neither you nor any others,[2] for whose profit and pleasure this work is offered

---

[1] Ps. 93.4.

[2] This is the same Marcellinus mentioned in the Preface to Book I; among the 'others,' St. Augustine no doubt included the pagan Volusianus, the proconsul of Africa, whose conversion to Christianity was so close to the heart of Marcellinus.

in the love of Christ, will read what I write in the spirit of men who demand an answer every time they hear any objections and act like those silly women whom St. Paul describes as 'ever learning and never attaining to the knowledge of the truth.'[3]

Chapter 2

When I began in the previous Book to speak of the City of God—which moved me to undertake, with God's help, this entire work—my first plan was to challenge the view of those who hold that the Christian religion is responsible for all the wars desolating this miserable world and, in particular, for the recent barbarian sack of the City of Rome.[1] It is true that the Christian religion forbids pagans to honor demons with unspeakable sacrifices; but, as I pointed out, they should thank Christ for the boon that, out of regard for His Name and in disregard of the traditional usages of war, the barbarians gave them immunity in spacious Christian buildings. What is more, they treated both the genuine followers of Christ and many who through fear pretended to be such with great concern. They refused to take measures against them which the laws of war permitted.

Thence arose the question: Why did God, on the one hand, bestow His good things upon the impious and the thankless, while, on the other, the enemy's hard blows fell with equal weight upon the good and the wicked alike? In order to answer this all-embracing question as fully as the scope of my work demanded, I lingered on it for various reasons. First, because many are disturbed in mind when they observe how, in the daily round of life, God's gifts and man's brutalities oftentimes fall indifferently and indiscriminately to the lot of both the good and the bad; but, above all, because I wanted to offer to those pure and holy women whose modesty had been outraged by the barbarian soldiery, but whose purity of soul had stood adamant, the consoling assurance that they have no reason to bewail their lives, since there is no personal guilt for them to bewail.

[3] 2 Tim. 3.7.

---

[1] By Alaric in A.D. 410.

Then, I proceeded to address a few remarks to those who shamelessly seek to defame Christian victims of calamity, and especially the virtue of outraged women who have remained undefiled and saintly. These calumniators, I pointed out, are wicked, impious, and degenerate descendants—not to say, the worst enemies—of those sturdier Romans whose many noble deeds are on the lips of men and live in the pages of history. The Rome founded and made great by the toil of their ancestors these men made even lower while it was still standing than when it fell. In the sack by the enemy only its stones and timbers fell, but in the lives of these despicable creatures everything collapsed, not merely the ramparts and armaments of their walls, but likewise of their wills. The fire of their base passions burned more fiercely in their hearts than the flames that devoured the city's roofs.

With these observations, I brought the first Book to a close. Now, I propose to speak of the calamities that befell the city from the beginning of its history, both at home and in its provinces—all of which our calumniators would have attributed to the Christian religion, if at that time the Gospel teaching had been freely bearing witness against their false and deceiving gods.

Chapter 3

Bear in mind that, in recounting these things, I am still dealing with those ignorant dupes who gave birth and popular currency to the saying: 'If there is a drought, blame the Christians.' As for those among them who have received a liberal education and appreciate the value of history, they can very easily inform themselves. In order to arouse popular hatred against us, they pretend ignorance and strive to instill into people's minds the common notion that the misfortunes which afflict the human race are due to the expansion of Christianity and to the eclipse of the pagan gods by the bright glory of its reputation and renown.

Let them, therefore, recall with me the calamities which so often and in so many ways set back the prosperity of Rome, and remember, too, that all this happened long before Christ came in the flesh, long before His Name shone before men with that glory which they vainly begrudge Him. In the face of those disasters, let them defend their gods if they can, remembering that they were worshiped precisely to prevent the evils recorded. Yet, if any of those evils befall them now, we Christians must bear the blame. Why, then, did the gods permit the misfortunes I shall mention to fall on their devotees before the promulgation of Christ's teaching provoked their wrath and proscribed their sacrifices?

Chapter 4

In the first place, why were the gods so negligent as to allow the morals of their worshipers to sink to so low a depth? The true God leaves those who do not worship Him to their own devices, but why did not those gods (whose worship, so thankless men complain, is forbidden) lay down moral precepts that would help their devotees to lead a decent life? They should have had as much concern for their worshipers' conduct as these had for their cult. But, some one will reply, each man is bad by his own will. No one ever denied this! Nevertheless, it was incumbent on protecting deities, not to conceal from their worshipers the laws of a good life, but to proclaim such laws from the housetops. It was for them to seek out and call sinners to task through the medium of prophets whose duty it was to threaten evil-doers with the punishment awaiting them, and to hold out the promise of reward for virtuous living.

Who ever heard such a thing proclaimed, fearlessly and authoritatively, in the temples of the gods? I myself, in my younger days, used to frequent the sacrilegious stage plays and comedies. I used to watch the demoniacal fanatics and listen to the choruses, and take delight in the obscene shows in honor of their gods and goddesses, of the virgin Caelestis and the Berecynthian Cybele, mother of the gods. Before the latter's couch on the day of her solemn bathing, ribald refrains were publicly sung about her by lewd actors that were unfit for the ear of the mother of the gods, and of the mother of any Senator or decent man—so unspeakably bestial, in fact, that even the mothers óf the players themselves would have been ashamed to listen. For, there is in human modesty an inborn respect for parents which wickedness itself cannot efface. Surely, the comedians themselves would have blushed to rehearse at home before their mothers the obscene words and actions which they uttered and performed in public before the mother of the gods and in the presence of a vast assemblage of both sexes. If curiosity could entice such numbers to come, a shocked sense of decency surely should have hurried them home. If these enormities are religious service, what can sacrilege be? If that bathing is purification, what is pollution? And these were called dishes, or 'courses,' as though a banquet were being celebrated at which the unclean demons were regaled with their favorite tidbits. If any one does not realize what kind of spirits find pleasure in such obscenities, then he is either unaware that there are unclean spirits wearing the deceptive masks of gods, or else he is leading the sort of life that prefers the demons, rather than the true God, as gracious masters and angry foes.

Chapters 5–6

If it is asserted that the Roman deities actually commanded indecent plays to be presented in their honor, then these gods are unworthy and no proper protectors of the morals of the people.

Chapter 7

Perhaps they will venture to refer to the schools and discussions of the philosophers. To begin with, these are not products of Rome, but of Greece. If they are to be termed Roman because Greece became a Roman province, then they are not the ordinances of deities, but the creations of human imagination. By the keenness of mind with which they are endowed, these men have striven to fathom the secrets of nature, what is to be aimed at and what avoided in the domain of morals, and in the domain of logic what conclusions are to be drawn with the rigorous sequence demanded by the laws of reasoning, what conclusions do not follow or even contradict their premises.

Some of them, so far as they were guided from on high, made great discoveries; but, as far as they were hindered by human nature, fell into error, especially when Divine Providence justly thwarted their pride in order to show them, even by opposition, that the path of virtue starts from humility and rises to higher things. I shall enquire into and discuss this matter later, the true God and Lord willing. Meanwhile, I may here observe that if the philosophers have discovered anything that can aid one to lead a good life and attain eternal happiness, how much more fitting would it be to adjudge divine honors to such men!

How much more sensible and proper would it be to have Plato's writings read in a temple dedicated to him than to have the mutilation of the priests of Cybele, the consecration of eunuchs, the slashing of insane men, in the temples of the demons, the perpetration of every cruel and foul, or foully cruel and cruelly foul, abomination that is wont to pass for a religious rite. Far more profitable would it be, for instructing the young in justice, to read the laws of the gods publicly than to give sham praise to the laws and institutions of our ancestors. For, all the worshipers of such gods, when once they are possessed by what Persius calls 'the burning poison of lust,'[1] are more captivated by what Jupiter did than by what Plato taught or Cato censured.

Thus, we read in Terence how a dissolute youth looks upon a wall painting, 'in which the tale was told how Jove sent down a shower of gold into the lap of Danaë.'[2] He appeals to the authority of this weighty example to justify his own lust, with a boast that he did but imitate a god. 'And what god?' he continues. 'Even he that shakes the loftiest temples with thunder. Since he did thus, should a wretch of a man like me not do the same? Why! I did it with all my heart.'[3]

Chapters 8–20

In a lengthy analysis of Roman writings, featuring the works of Cicero and Sallust, Augustine argues that the pagan fables and theatrical presentations corrupted the virtues of the early Romans and their contemporaries. Their gods provided no useful laws and no moral code of life. Plato recognized this when

[1] *Ibid.* 3.37,38, *dira libido . . . ferventi tincta veneno.*
[2] *Eunuchus* 3.5.36ff.
[3] *Ibid.* 42,43.

he excluded the fables of the classical religious poets from his ideal Republic.

Chapter 21

If no heed be paid to the one who declared the Roman state a 'sink of iniquity,' and if my opponents, content if it can but endure, are not moved by the shame and ignominy of utter degeneration that floods it, let them note that it has not merely become the 'sink of iniquity' described by Sallust, but that, as Cicero maintains, it had long since perished, and no longer endured as a state. Cicero lets that same Scipio who had destroyed Carthage voice his opinion of the state at a time when men felt a presentiment that it would soon be brought low by the rottenness which Sallust describes. Cicero's comments belong to that dramatic time of the murder of Tiberias Gracchus,[1] who, as Sallust writes, stirred up dangerous revolts. His death is mentioned in the same work of Cicero.

Scipio, then, had said: 'In playing the lute, or the flute, or even in vocal music, the different notes should be kept in harmony. If they are changed into discord, the trained ear cannot endure it. That agreeable harmony, however, is produced by the modulation of tones that are very dissimilar. In like manner, as in music, out of the highest and the lowest classes, and of those that lie between, by a reasonable control, the State is fashioned into a concordant whole by the consent of very diverse elements. What musicians call harmony in music, in the State is known as concord, the closest and strongest bond of security in any commonwealth, and which can in no way exist without justice.'[2] Then, further on, after he had discussed more fully how much the State has to gain from justice and how much to lose from the lack of it, Philus,[3] one of the

[1] Tiberius Sempronius Gracchus, as tribune of the people in 133 B.C., proposed a land-distribution law and produced the crisis which led to his murder by the conservatives led by P. Cornelius Scipio Nasica, who had married Sempronia, the sister of the Gracchi. Scipio was found dead in his bed in 129; and it is in this year that the dialogue of *De re publica* is placed.

[2] *De re publica* 2.42.

[3] L. Fabius Philus belonged to the literary circle of Scipio and his friend Laelius.

participants in the discussion, took up the discourse and earnestly begged that the question be treated more thoroughly, and that more be said about justice, especially as the common opinion was that the State could not be governed without justice. Scipio also agreed that the question must be thrashed out and elucidated. His answer was that nothing had as yet been said about the State that could serve as a basis for further discussion until two facts were established: first of all, the falsity of the view that the State cannot be governed without injustice, and secondly, the solidity of the truth that it cannot be governed without absolute justice.

The consideration of that question was put off to the following day, and in the third Book the matter is introduced amid a clash of opinions. Philus himself championed the stand of those who held that the State could not be governed without injustice being done, after he had solemnly disclaimed any share in such opinion. With earnestness, he advocated the case of injustice against justice, and by specious arguments and illustrations he strove to prove that injustice was an advantage to the State, while justice served no useful purpose. Then Laelius, in his turn, and at the instance of the whole company, undertook to vindicate the claims of justice. With all the emphasis he could command, he declared that the State could have no greater enemy than injustice, and that no commonwealth could either be governed or endure if justice did not dominate.

After the pros and cons of this question had been examined, Scipio again took up the broken threads of the discussion, and, going back to his definition of the republic, he endorsed in a few words the stand that 'the commonwealth is the weal of the people.' He defines the people as 'not any mass gathering, but a multitude bound together by a mutual recognition of rights and a mutual cooperation for the common good.'[4] He then proceeds to point out the advantage of defining terms when engaged in a discussion, and from principles accurately stated he concludes that you have a true commonwealth, that is, the weal of the people, when it is rightly and

---

[4] *Populum autem non omnem coetum multitudinis, sed coetum iuris consensu et utilitatis communione sociatum esse determinat* (*De re publica* 1.25).

justly administered either by one monarch, or by a few men of rank, or by all the people.

But, if the prince is unjust, or a tyrant (to use the Greek word), or if the aristocrats are unjust (in which case their group is merely a faction), or if the people themselves are unjust (and must be called, for lack of a better word, a tyrant also), then the commonwealth is not merely bad, as it was described in the discussion of the previous day, but is no commonwealth at all. The reason for that is that there is no longer the welfare of the people, once a tyrant or a faction seizes it; nor would the people, if unjust, be any longer a people, because they would not then be regarded as a multitude bound together by a common recognition of rights, and a mutual co-operation for the common good, as the standard definition of a people demands.

When, therefore, the Roman republic was such as Sallust describes it, it was not only 'very wicked and corrupt'—'a sink of iniquity,' as he puts it—it was no republic at all, if measured by the criterion established by its ablest representatives when they met to debate the nature of a republic.

Tullius himself, at the beginning of his fifth book, quotes the verse of the poet Ennius declaring: 'The Roman state rests on the men and the morals of old,' and in his own words, not those of Scipio or any other, remarks: 'That line for its conciseness and truth sounds to me like the utterance of an oracle. For, had not the state been blessed with a wholesome body of citizens, and had not those men stood at the head, neither men nor morals could have availed to found or so long maintain a republic of such might to rule so far and wide and so justly. Indeed, long before our time, it was the custom of the land to appoint distinguished men who held fast to the ancient traditions and the institutions of our forefathers. Our own generation inherited the republic, an exquisite masterpiece, indeed, though faded with age; but it failed to restore its original colors. Worse, alas; it did not even move a finger to preserve as much as its form, or its barest outlines.

What is there left of the ancient virtue which the illustrious poet Ennius declared was the mainstay of the Roman state? We are aware only that it has been so utterly cast to the winds that morals are not merely unobserved, but are positively ignored. What can we say of the men? Precisely for want of men the good old customs have been lost, and for so great an evil not only are we responsible but we should face judgment, like culprits fearing the penalty of death. By our own vices, not by chance, we have lost the republic, though we retain the name.'

All this, Cicero avowed many years after the death of Africanus, one of the disputants in the *Republic*, and before the coming of Christ.[5] If such reproaches were expressed or entertained after the triumphant advance of the Christian religion, there is not a pagan who would not think of charging them to the Christians. Why, then, did their gods not save from disaster that republic which, long before Christ appeared in the flesh, Cicero mournfully deplores as lost?

Let its panegyrists really take a look at the republic in the day of those ancient men and customs. Let them ask whether true justice flourished and inspired morality or was merely a colored painting of justice, as Cicero himself unwittingly suggests, while meaning to praise it.

We shall consider this later,[6] God willing. In its proper place I shall endeavor to show that that ancient creation was never a true republic, because in it true justice was never practiced. I shall base my position on Cicero's own definitions, in the light of which he briefly determined, through the mouth of Scipio, what was a republic and what was a people. There are many confirmatory opinions expressed in that discussion both by himself and by the interlocutors he introduced.

However, according to some definitions that are nearer the truth, it was a commonwealth of a sort, and it was better governed by the earlier Romans than by those who came later. But, true justice is not to be found save in that commonwealth, if we may so call it, whose Founder and Ruler is Jesus Christ —for, no one can deny that this is the weal of the people. This name, with its varied meanings, is perhaps not quite in tune with our language, but this at least is certain: True justice reigns in that state of which Holy Scripture says: 'Glorious things are said of thee, O City of God.'[7]

---

[5] The publication of *De re publica* is usually dated 54 B.C.
[6] The promise is fulfilled in Book XIX, Chapter 21.
[7] Ps. 86.3.

Chapters 22–28

The degeneration of Roman morals accompanied the increasing craving for worldly power and for the enjoyment of obscene ceremonies in honor of divinities such as the goddess Caelestis and the lewd Mother Flora.

Chapter 29

Why, then, do not you Romans with your noble character, you sons of the Reguli, Scaevolae, Scipii, and Fabricii, let your hearts go out to these better things. Look at the difference between these things and the base arrogance and deceiving wickedness of the demons. However great and good your natural gifts may be, it takes true piety to make them pure and perfect; with impiety, they merely end in loss and pain. Choose now your course, not to seek glory in yourself, but to find it infallibly in the true God. At one time, you could enjoy the applause of your people, but by God's mysterious providence the true religion was not there for you to choose.

But, it is now day; awake as you awoke in the persons of those men in whose sterling virtue and sufferings for the faith we glory. They battled on all sides against hostile powers and, conquering by their fearless death, 'have purchased this country for us with their blood.'[1] To this Country we pleadingly invite you. Join its citizens, for it offers more than mere sanctuary, it offers the true remission of your sins.

Give no heed to the degenerate progeny who blame Christ and Christians for what they call bad times, and long for times which assure them, not a peaceful life, but undisturbed wickedness. Such times were never to your liking, not even for an earthly fatherland. Reach out now for the heavenly country. You will have very little to suffer for it, and in it you will reign in very truth, and forever. In that land there is no Vestal altar, no statue of Jupiter on the Capitol, but the one true God, who 'will not limit you in space or time, but will give an empire universal and eternal.'[2] Seek no false and lying gods; rather, cast them from you with scorn and shine forth in

[1] *Aeneid* 11.24,25.
[2] *Ibid.* 1.278,279.

true freedom. They are not gods, but fiendish spirits, to whom your eternal happiness is a torment. Never did Juno so intensely begrudge the Trojans, your ancestors in the flesh, the battlements of Rome, as do those demons, whom you still fancy to be gods, begrudge an everlasting home to the whole human race.

You have already, in part, passed judgment on these spirits, for, while you placated them with stage plays, you branded with infamy the actors who performed them. Let your freedom assert its rights against the unclean spirits who have placed upon you the obligation of solemnly exhibiting their shame as though it were a holy thing.

You took civic rights away from performers of Olympian scandals. Now, beseech the true God to take away from you those gods who delight in immoralities—in lust, if the sins are facts; in lying, if they are feigned. You did well to ostracize the mimes and mummers from civil society. Keep a sharper watch now. Divine majesty is in no way appeased by arts which dishonor man's dignity. How, then, can you place in the ranks of the holy powers of heaven gods who delight in homage so unclean, while you banned from the lowest ranks of Roman citizens the men who enacted such homage?

Glorious beyond compare is the heavenly city. There, victory is truth, dignity is holiness, peace is happiness, life is eternity. If you blushed to tolerate that sort of men among your citizens, how much less will the heavenly city tolerate that sort of gods? Wherefore, if you long to reach that blessed country, shun the company of demons. Gods who are propitiated by infamous rites are unworthy of the worship of decent men. Deny religious rites to the gods, by a Christian reform, just as you denied civil dignity to the actors, by the censor's decree.

As regards earthly happiness and physical evils which alone the wicked wish to enjoy or refuse to endure, I shall show in the sequel that not even over these have those demons the control people imagine. Indeed, even if they did have, then we should scorn those things rather than, for their sake, worship those gods and so fail to attain the blessings they begrudge us. However, not even over those things have demons the power attributed to them by those who maintain that they must on that account be propitiated. But, as I said, more of this later. Here, I bring this Book to a close.

BOOK III

Physical Evils Were Not Prevented by the Gods

Chapter 1

IT SEEMS TO ME I have already said enough about the evils which work havoc on men's souls and morals, and which they must shun at all costs. I have shown that, far from having done aught to save their worshipers from the miseries that lay heavy upon them, the false gods did their utmost to increase the burden beyond endurance.

I must now turn to those calamities which are the only things our accusers have no wish to endure. Such are hunger, disease, war, plunder, imprisonment, massacre, and horrors such as I have mentioned in Book I. Though these do not make men evil, evildoers regard them as the only evil. Yet, they feel no shame that they themselves are evil amid the things they praise as good. They are more pained if their villa is poor than if their life is bad, as though man's greatest good were to have everything good except himself.

The fact is that the gods did not ward off the evils which pagans dread, even at a time when they were freely worshiped. At various times and in different places before the coming of our Redeemer, calamities beyond counting and description were scourging mankind. Yet, what others besides your recreant gods did the world worship? I except, of course, the Hebrew nation, and a few individuals beyond its pale, wherever by God's grace and His secret and righteous judgment they were found worthy.

Not to enlarge too much, I shall say nothing of the dreadful afflictions which other people have everywhere suffered. Confining myself to Rome alone and to the Roman Empire, that is, to the city itself and to the people linked with it either by alliance or by subjection, I shall speak of the visitations they experienced before the coming of Christ, but after their incorporation into the Roman body politic.

Chapter 2

To begin with, there is the case of Troy, or Ilium, the cradle of the Roman people. Though I alluded to this in the first Book, I must not omit it or ignore it here. Troy had and worshiped the Roman gods. Why, then, was it conquered, captured, and destroyed by the Greeks? Pagans, of course, will reply that Priam had to pay the price for his father Laomedon's perjury.[1] If so, Apollo and Neptune must have given mercenary aid to Laomedon. He pledged them pay, so it is said, and then went back on his word. That is most remarkable! To think that Apollo, who is called the Seer, should engage in so vast a venture and not know that Laomedon would default in his promise! Nor does it reflect credit on Neptune himself, his uncle, Jupiter's brother, and King of the Sea, to have been in the dark about the future. Yet, Homer, the poet who is said to have lived before Rome's foundation, represents this divinity to us as uttering a momentous prophecy about the race of Aeneas, whose progeny founded Rome, and whom Neptune, as Homer tells us, snatched up in a cloud to save him from the murderous sword of Achilles, although, as Virgil avows,

> All his will was to destroy
> His own creation, perjured Troy.[2]

So, we have the spectacle of two mighty divinities, Neptune and Apollo, unable to tell that Laomedon was going to cheat them of their pay, building up the walls of Troy—and all for nothing but ingratitude. Pagans should reflect whether it is really not more criminal to believe in such gods than to violate one's oath to them. Homer himself has not given easy credence to the fable, for, while on the one hand he represents Neptune battling against the Trojans, on the other he has Apollo fighting for them, in spite of the fact that, as the fable runs, both took offense at the perjury. Hence, if they so swallow the fables, they should blush for worshiping that sort of deities; if they do not swallow them, then they should not ap-

---

[1] Priam's father, Laomedon, violated a pledge he had given to Poseidon (or Neptune) and Apollo, and this perjury was reckoned the real cause of Troy's fall. Cf. *Iliad* 21.441–460; Horace, *Odes* 4.3.18–24; *Aeneid* 4.542; *Georgics* 1.502.

[2] *Aeneid* 5.810,811.

peal to the Trojans' perjury, or should at least find it strange
that the gods should punish perjury on the part of the Trojans
and welcome it with pleasure on the part of the Romans.

How could it possibly happen that, 'in a state so great and
so sunk in corruption,' Catiline's conspiracy could count a
large number of those 'who made their living by hand and
tongue plying perjury and murder of their fellow citizens'?[3]
How else can you explain the fact that bribery so often stole
the decisions of Senators, and so often the vote of the citizens,
both at the polls and in certain cases that were tried before
them in public assemblies, except that they, too, resorted to
the crime of perjury? For, even when, amid the general let-
down of morals, the ancient custom of taking oath was retained, that was not to restrain people from wrong-doing
through religious awe, but in order to add perjury to their
other crimes.

Chapter 3

In view of all this, there is no basis for thinking that the
gods—allegedly the 'pillars of the empire'[1] but manifestly
beaten by the greater might of the Greeks—were aroused to
anger by the Trojans' perjury. Nor did the adultery of Paris—
sometimes alleged to justify their abandoning Troy—kindle
their wrath. For, as a rule, they are the perpetrators and
teachers of evil, not its avengers. 'As I have learned the story,'
writes Sallust, 'in the beginning the city of Rome was founded
and possessed by the Trojans, who, led by Aeneas, wandered
about as refugees with no fixed home.'[2] If, therefore, the gods
thought fit to avenge the adultery of Paris, they should have
visited their penalties more on the Romans, or at least equally
on them, since it was the mother of Aeneas who committed
that crime.

But, how could they detest the misdeed in Paris when they
did not detest the adultery of his associate Venus with Anchises
(to mention no others) by whom she begot Aeneas? Was it
because the former was committed in the face of Menelaus'

---

[3] Sallust, *Catilina* 14.1.

[1] Cf. *Aeneid* 2.352.   [2] *Catilina* 6.

wrath; the latter, with Vulcan's connivance? I suppose the gods are not jealous of their wives to the extent of not deigning to share them with men! But, perhaps I may seem to be scoffing at these fables, and not treating so weighty a matter with due seriousness.

Well, then, if you please, let us suppose that Aeneas was not the son of Venus. I agree to that, provided it be also admitted that neither was Romulus the son of Mars. If the one be true, why not the other? Or is it licit for gods to consort casually with the wives of mortals and illicit for mortal men to do the same with goddesses? Those are hard, or rather incredible, terms: that what was lawful to Mars by Venus' law should not be lawful to Venus by her own law. But, both have the support of Roman authority, for, in times nearer to us, Caesar was no less convinced that he was descended from Venus than was Romulus that Mars was his father.

Chapter 4

Someone may say to me: 'Do you believe all that stuff?' My answer is that I do not. Even one of the most learned pagans, Varro, if not with outright decisiveness and confidence, still cautiously avows that all this is sheer nonsense. For all that, he affirms that it is expedient for states that men of valor should claim divine lineage, however shallow the pretence. This is on the theory that, by that sublime fiction, the human spirit, urged on by the self-assurance of being divinely born, will venture into great exploits and, by the confidence such illusion inspires, achieve more signal success.

You cannot but observe how wide a door this view, which I have summarized in my own words, would open to sham and false pretence. This is especially so where lies even about the gods are regarded as advantageous to the people. Endless fictions will be invented, and invested with a so-called sacred and religious character.

Chapters 5–30

A long survey of Greek and Roman history follows, illustrating the failure of the gods to prevent physical evils. The ar-

gument refers to incidents such as the adultery of Paris, the fratricide of Romulus, the destruction of Troy, the growing use of offensive war by the Romans, the degeneration of the social position of Roman women, the violent deaths of several Roman kings. The discussion turns to the evils suffered by the Romans during the Punic Wars. Further Roman catastrophes are presented in great detail: reprisals against the Romans in Asia, madness among the Roman domestic animals, late civil wars. All were pre-Christian evils.

Chapter 31

Let the pagans blame their own gods for all their woes, instead of repaying our Christ with ingratitude for all His good gifts. Certain it is that, when calamities rained upon them, 'the altars streamed with Sabaean incense and were fresh with fragrance of chaplets.'[1] While Romans were shedding Roman blood, not only in ordinary places, but before the very altars of the gods, the pagan priesthood was held in honor, the shrines were bright, all was sacrifices, plays and orgies in the temples. Note that Cicero sought no temple for sanctuary, because that had been of no avail for Mucius. But, the pagans of our day, while they have far less reason to decry the era, have either fled for sanctuary to the most hallowed Christian places, or have been taken there by the barbarians to save their lives.

I need not repeat what I have already said or mention anything I had to omit, but one thing is certain, and anyone whose mind is free from bias will readily admit it: If mankind had embraced Christ's teaching before the Punic Wars, and if there had followed the terrible devastation of those wars in Europe and Africa, there is not one of those intolerable critics who would not have blamed those evils on the Christian religion.

Their outcries would have been even more intolerable, especially in what touches the Romans, if the invasion of the Gauls, or the inundation of the Tiber and the devastating fires, or, what was worse, the horrors of those civil wars of evil memory had occurred after the acceptance and spread of

1 *Aeneid* 1.416,417.

Christianity. Other calamities befell, so appalling as to seem the work of demons. Suppose that these, too, had occurred in Christian times. Against what other people but Christians would they have been charged as crimes?

I shall say nothing of the merely freakish phenomena, which caused little harm: talking cattle, unborn infants uttering words in the mother's womb, flying serpents, women and hens turned male, and the like. These things are recorded in their books, not of fables but of history, and, whether they are true or false, strike men with wonderment but do no harm. However, when earth, clay, and stones (real stones, not hail, commonly called 'stones') rained from the sky, these, indeed, could also do serious harm.

In those books we read that, when the lava poured down from the crater of Mt. Aetna to the shore, the sea became such a caldron that it calcined the rocks and melted the pitch from the ships. Incredible as a marvel, this was also harmful as an occurrence. On another occasion, the writers tell us, a similar eruption poured such a deluge of ashes upon Sicily that the houses of Catania were overwhelmed by it and collapsed under the weight. Moved with pity by that disaster, the Romans remitted the tribute for that year. It is also written that Africa was already a Roman province when a swarm of locusts of monstrous proportions swooped down on the land, devoured the fruit and leaves on the trees, and then plunged into the sea in an enormous cloud. When the dead insects were washed ashore, infecting the air by their corruption, a pestilence set in, so violent that in the kingdom of Masinissa alone 800,000 men are reported to have perished, and many more in the regions that lay close to the coast.

We are further assured that in Utica, out of 30,000 people, only 10,000 were left alive. Now, if the half-wits we have to endure and must answer were to witness all these catastrophes occurring in Christian times, there is not one of them who would not saddle them on Christianity. But, they will blame their gods for none of those misfortunes. Indeed, they demand the restoration of their worship, so that they may be preserved from these and lesser evils, despite the fact that when their forebears worshiped the gods, they suffered greater calamities by far.

BOOK IV

Divine Justice and the Growth of the Roman Empire

Chapter 1

IN THE FIRST PAGES of this work on the City of God, I saw fit to give an answer to its enemies. Running mad after the pleasures of earth and eagerly grasping at fleeting goods, they denounce the Christian religion, the only salutary and true one, for any hardship they suffer rather through God's merciful admonition than through the severity of His punishment.

Among our accusers there is an ignorant rabble, incited by the authority of the learned to cast greater odium upon us. These simple souls imagine that the abnormal calamities that have occurred in our own day were entirely unknown in the past. This foolish opinion is encouraged even by those who know it to be false, but who pretend ignorance in order to give an air of truth to their grumblings. Hence, I have gone to the books in which their own historians have recorded, for men's information, the things that happened in the past, and from these I have proved two important facts: first, that the actual events were far different from what these people imagined; second, that the false gods which pagans then worshiped in the open, and now worship under cover, were unclean spirits, malignant and lying demons. The truth of this is clear from the fact that these demons go so far as to take delight in their own villainies, to the extent of wanting them exhibited, either as facts or as fictions, in the festivals celebrated in their honor. I have also pointed out that, as long as these villainies are exhibited for imitation under divine sanction, so to speak, it is impossible to restrain weak humans from actually reproducing in their own lives the abominable acts committed by the gods.

My proofs were not guesses. I have drawn them partly from my own recent recollection, for I have seen with my own eyes those indecent dramas, performed in homage to such divinities. I have drawn them also from the writings of those who left accounts of these mythological exploits, not with the intention of casting disgrace upon the gods, but of doing them honor. Thus, Varro, one of their most learned and authoritative scholars, wrote various books on human and divine institutions. But, when he arranged his topics in the order of their importance, grouping human affairs in one book, and divine in another, he by no means classed stage plays under human, but under divine institutions. He was certain that, if none but good and decent men lived in Rome, stage plays would have found no place among human institutions. Nor did Varro so classify things on his own authority. Since he was born and educated in Rome, he simply found stage plays a part of the pagan religious rites.

At the end of Book I, I briefly sketched what I had in mind to say in the sequel. Part of that I have told in the two Books that followed, but I realize what I still owe to my expectant readers.

Chapter 2

I promised to advance some facts that would show the error of those who blame our religion for the woes of the Roman state, and to recall, as they occurred to me according to their gravity and in sufficient number, the calamities which Rome and the provinces of the Empire had to endure in times before their sacrifices were forbidden. All these calamities they would certainly have blamed on us, if our faith had by then shed its light on them or banned their sacrifices. These matters I have sufficiently described, I think, in Books II and III. In the second, I dealt with the moral evils which must be regarded as the only real and serious calamities. In Book III, I treated of those calamities which alone foolish people dread to face, those evils which affect the body and material goods, and which ordinarily even the good have to suffer. As for their own moral evils, our pagan accusers accept them not only patiently, but gladly. I have spoken only of the city of Rome and its imperial possessions, and have not even extended my discussion to Caesar Augustus, and I covered very few evils.

What if I had chosen to review and to emphasize, not the kind of evils which men inflict on one another, such as the ravages and devastations brought on by wars, but those which the elements of nature let loose upon the earth? To these Apuleius briefly refers in a passage of his treatise, *De mundo*, where he says that all earthly things are subject to change, to transformation, and to annihilation.[1] To use his own words, he relates that tremendous earthquakes made yawning chasms in the ground, swallowing cities with their inhabitants. Cloudbursts deluged entire regions; what had been continents were turned into islands by the onrush of near and distant waters. Other places became accessible as the surrounding waters withdrew, and men could reach them on foot. Cities were beaten to the ground by windstorms and hurricanes. Conflagrations kindled by lightning swallowed up in flames whole regions in the East, while on the coasts of the West waterspouts and floods caused similar devastation. So, also, on one occasion the craters overflowed from the summit of Mt. Aetna and down the slopes rushed torrents of flaming lava ignited by divine power.

If I had wished to gather these and similar occurrences from history and other sources, I could never finish the tragic story of all that came to pass before the Name of Christ had put bounds to all the follies so dangerous to true salvation.

I also promised to point out the Roman virtues, and the reasons why the true God—to whose power all kingdoms are subject—deigned to bless the Empire with increase. I also proposed to show how those beings the pagans imagine to be gods contributed nothing, and how, on the contrary, they worked immense harm by their frauds and deceptions. That, I take it, is the topic I must now discuss, and, in particular, the growth of the Roman Empire. On the wicked deceits of the demons whom the Romans worshiped as gods, and on the incalculable harm those demons did to Roman morals, I have already commented at some length, principally in Book II.

On the other hand, in the three completed Books, wherever it seemed opportune, I pointed out how much comfort, even amid the hardships of war, God brought both to the good and

---

[1] Lucius Apuleius Afer, author of *The Golden Ass, On the World, On the Philosophy of Plato,* a platonist philosopher and rhetorician who flourished in the second century and who is often alluded to by St. Augustine. He does not cite here the exact words of Apuleius, in spite of the *ut verbis eius utar.*

to the wicked. This He did through the Name of Christ, whom the barbarians reverenced counter to the ways of war. Thus, 'He maketh His sun to rise upon the good and bad and raineth upon the just and unjust.'[2]

Chapter 3

Let us now consider on what grounds our adversaries affirm that the immensity and long duration of the Roman Empire are gifts of those gods whom, they insist, they have honorably worshiped by the homage of infamous plays performed by the ministrations of infamous men. I would first like to find an answer to this question: Is it reasonable and wise to glory in the extent and greatness of the Empire when you can in no way prove that there is any real happiness in men perpetually living amid the horrors of war, perpetually wading in blood? Does it matter whether it is the blood of their fellow citizens or the blood of their enemies? It is still human blood, in men perpetually haunted by the gloomy spectre of fear and driven by murderous passions. The happiness arising from such conditions is a thing of glass, of mere glittering brittleness. One can never shake off the horrible dread that it may suddenly shiver into fragments.

In order to be perfectly clear on this point, we must not be carried away by hollow verbal blasts and allow our judgment to be confused by the high-sounding words of prattlers about nations, kingdoms, and provinces. Let us imagine two individuals—for each man, like a letter in a word, is an integral part of a city or of a kingdom, however extensive. Of these two men, let us suppose that one is poor, or, better, in moderate circumstances; the other, extremely wealthy. But, our wealthy man is haunted by fear, heavy with cares, feverish with greed, never secure, always restless, breathless from endless quarrels with his enemies. By these miseries, he adds to his possessions beyond measure, but he also piles up for himself a mountain of distressing worries. The man of modest means is content with a small and compact patrimony. He is loved by his own, enjoys the sweetness of peace in his relations with kindred,

2 Matt. 5.45.

neighbors, and friends, is religious and pious, of kindly disposition, healthy in body, self-restrained, chaste in morals, and at peace with his conscience.

I wonder if there is anyone so senseless as to hesitate over which of the two to prefer. What is true of these two individuals is likewise true of two families, two nations, two kingdoms; the analogy holds in both cases. If we apply it with care and correct our judgment accordingly, it will be easy to see on which side lies folly and on which true happiness.

Hence, if the true God is adored, and if He is given the service of true sacrifice and of an upright life, then it is beneficial for good men to extend their empire far and wide and to rule for a long time. This is beneficial, not so much for themselves as for their subjects. Fear of God, and uprightness, God's great gifts, are enough for the true happiness of rulers, since this will enable them to spend this life well and thus win life eternal. On this earth, therefore, rule by good men is a blessing bestowed, not so much on themselves as upon mankind. But the rule of wicked men brings greater harm to themselves, since they ruin their own souls by the greater ease with which they can do wrong.

As for their subjects, only their own villainy can harm them. For, whatever injury wicked masters inflict upon good men is to be regarded, not as a penalty for wrong-doing, but as a test for their virtues. Thus, a good man, though a slave, is free; but a wicked man, though a king, is a slave. For he serves, not one man alone, but, what is worse, as many masters as he has vices. For, it is in reference to vice that the Holy Scripture says: 'For by whom a man is overcome, of the same also he is the slave.'[1]

Chapter 4

In the absence of justice, what is sovereignty but organized brigandage? For, what are bands of brigands but petty kingdoms? They also are groups of men, under the rule of a leader, bound together by a common agreement, dividing their booty according to a settled principle. If this band of criminals, by

[1] 2 Pet. 2.19.

recruiting more criminals, acquires enough power to occupy regions, to capture cities, and to subdue whole populations, then it can with fuller right assume the title of kingdom, which in the public estimation is conferred upon it, not by the renunciation of greed, but by the increase of impunity.

The answer which a captured pirate gave to the celebrated Alexander the Great was perfectly accurate and correct. When that king asked the man what he meant by infesting the sea, he boldly replied: 'What you mean by warring on the whole world. I do my fighting on a tiny ship, and they call me a pirate; you do yours with a large fleet, and they call you Commander.'

Chapters 5–8

The claim that the gods fostered the remarkable extension of the Roman Empire is refuted by reference to the growth of the Assyrian Empire without help from the Roman deities. Similar arguments are based on the martial successes of the Persians and Alexander the Great. Attempts to discover what gods may have been responsible for the greatness of Rome fail. There are too many candidates and none worthy.

Chapter 9

Leaving aside the swarm of petty gods, at least for a while, let us consider the activity of the major gods, which made Rome great enough to rule for so long over so many peoples. That, no doubt, is the work of Jupiter. These people look upon him as the king of all gods and goddesses, in token of which his sceptre and his temple are set on the Capitoline hilltop. Of him they brag—though it was a poet's expression—in the words: 'Everything is full of Jove.'[1] Varro, too, believes that Jupiter is also worshiped, under another name, by those who adore one single God without making any images of him. If that be true, why have the Romans, like other pagan races, dishonored him by making a statue in his likeness? Varro himself objected to the practice, so much so that, though he had to yield to the

[1] Virgil, *Eclogues* 3.60.

force of perverse custom in so large a state, he did not hesitate to declare and write that those who introduced statues among the people 'robbed them of reverence, and put error in its place.'

Chapter 10

Why did they also provide Jupiter with a wife, Juno, and call her 'sister and spouse'? Because, they say, Jupiter represents the ether and Juno the air, and these two elements are conjoined—one as the upper and the other as the lower atmosphere. But, if Juno occupies a part of the world, the statement, 'Everything is full of Jove' is not true of Jupiter. Does each one fill both parts, and are the two mates in each and both of those elements and at the same time? Then, why is the ether assigned to Jove and the air to Juno? At any rate, these two should have been enough. Why, then, is the sea allotted to Neptune and the earth to Pluto? And, that neither might lack a consort, Salacia is given to Neptune and Proserpina to Pluto. For, as they try to explain, just as Juno occupies the lower part of the atmosphere, the air, so Salacia occupies the lower part of the sea, and Proserpina the lower part of the earth.

They seek in vain for devices on which to construct their fairy tales. If things were as they imagine, their ancient sages should have postulated three constituent elements of the world, not four, so that each of the elements might be assigned to each pair of divinities. But, in fact, they emphatically stated that ether is one thing; air, another. Yet, water, whether higher or lower, is still water. Even if you assume some difference in the levels, water is still certainly water. As for the lower earth, what else can it be but earth, however much it may differ from the upper?

You now have the physical world constituted, all complete, of four or of three elements. Where will you put Minerva? What part is she to hold and fill? There stands her temple on the Capitoline beside the others, though she is not their daughter. If they say that her domain is in the upper ether, a notion which led the poets to conceive of her as sprung from the head of Jupiter, why is she not named queen of the gods, since she is above Jupiter? Was it because it would not be proper to set the daughter above the father? Then, why was not that same rule of right relations applied to Jupiter and Saturn? Was it because Saturn was beaten in battle? But, do gods go to war? Of course not, they say, that is a mere fable. We do not believe in tales; we must think better of the gods. Then, why was not the father of Jupiter given an equal place of honor, if not a higher? Because, they allege, Saturn is only a symbol of the duration of time. Therefore, in worshiping Saturn, they worship Time, implying that Jupiter, king of the gods, has Time for his father. Why, then, is it improper to say that Jupiter and Juno are born of Time, if he is the sky and she the earth, since both heaven and earth were created? This bit of theology is also down in the books of their scholars and sages.

Virgil[1] drew his inspiration, not from poetical fancies, but from the treatises of philosophers, when he wrote: 'Then the almighty father, the ether, came down in fruitful rain, in the bosom of his joyful spouse,'[2] meaning, in the bosom of Tellus or Earth. Even here they see some difference in the earth itself. They think that Terra is one thing, Tellus another, and Tellumo still another, and give to each deity a name of its own, a function of its own, and a shrine and sacrifice of its own. Moreover, they also call this same Terra mother of the gods, so that one can have more patience with the reveries of the poets than with the sacred, but not poetical, books of the pagans, which make Juno not only 'sister and spouse,' but also mother, of Jupiter. They would also identify this same Earth with Ceres, and likewise with Vesta.

More commonly, however, they believe that Vesta is but the fire that warms the hearth—failing which, there would be no city. Hence, the custom of dedicating virgins to its service, because nothing is born of fire, just as nothing is born of virgins. Surely, a stupid notion like this deserved to be banished and abolished by the One who was born of a virgin. Who can endure to see them paying to fire even the honor due to chastity, and yet feeling no shame in giving the name Venus to Vesta?

---

[1] *Aeneid* 1.47.
[2] *Georgics* 2.325,326.

When they do this they make a mockery of the virginity which is honored in her servants. For, if Vesta is merely Venus, how could virgins minister to her without imitating Venus? Are there two Venuses; one a virgin and the other a wife? Or, rather, three—one Vesta for virgins, another for married women, and a third for harlots? To this last, the Phoenicians offered the gift of prostituting their daughters before they gave them husbands.

Which of the three is the wife of Vulcan? Surely, not the virgin, since she has a husband. Heaven forbid that we should say the prostitute, lest we seem to cast dishonor on the son of Juno and the fellow worker of Minerva. Therefore, we must take it that Vulcan's wife is the Venus of the married women. We can only hope that such women will not imitate her affair with Mars! Again, they say that I go back to the fables. But, why get angry at me for saying such things about their gods, instead of at themselves for feasting their eyes on the villainies of those gods performed on the stage? And, though it would have been impossible to believe, had it not been proved beyond all doubt, the representations of these scandals were inaugurated as a tribute to the gods themselves.

Chapter 11

On the basis of every argument drawn from physical phenomena and from their discussions, let the learned pagans maintain all they please about Jove. Now, let him be the soul of this material world, filling and moving the vast structure of the universe, formed and compounded of four elements, or of as many as they please. Now, let Jupiter yield some parts of it to his sister and brothers. Again, let him be the ether embracing the underlying air, Juno. Now, let him be the entire sky and air together, and let him with fertile rains and seeds fecundate the earth—his wife and mother at the same time, for this is no scandal among the gods. Finally, not to run through all their theories, let him be the unique god to whom, according to the thinking of many, the celebrated poet refers when he says: 'God pervades all lands and all depths of the sea, all heights of the heavens.'[1]

[1] *Georgics* 4.221,222.

Let him be Jupiter in the ether, Juno in the air, Neptune in the sea, Salacia in the depths of the sea, Pluto in the earth, Proserpina in the lower world, Vesta on domestic hearths, Vulcan in the forgers' furnace, the sun, moon and stars in the heavens, Apollo in the soothsayers, Mercury in commerce, the initiator as Janus, the terminator as Terminus. Let him be Saturn in time, Mars and Bellona in wars, Bacchus in the vineyards, Ceres in the wheatfields, Diana in the forests, Minerva in intellects. Finally, let him even be, if I may say so, in the horde of common gods. As Liber, let him preside over male seed; as Libra, over female. Let him be Dispater, who brings infants into the world; let him be the goddess Mena, appointed to supervise women's periods, and Lucina, invoked by women in childbirth. Let him come to the aid of the newly born by lifting them from the lap of the earth, and be called Ops; let him open the mouths of wailing babies, and be called the god Vaticanus; let him lift them from the ground, and be called the goddess Levana; and, by guarding the cradles, be called Cunina. Let none but himself be in those goddesses who foretell the destinies of the newly born, and are called Carmentes.

Let him preside over chance events as Fortune, and as the goddess Rumina let him nurse the suckling, for *ruma* was the ancient word for breast. As the goddess Potina, let him administer drink; as the goddess Educa, proffer food. From the terror of infants, let him be called Paventia; from sudden hope, Venilia; from lust, Volupia; from activity, Agenoria; from the impulses that drive a man to excessive activity, the goddess Stimula; by inspiring energy, the divinity Strenua; by teaching to count, Numeria; by teaching to sing, Camena.

For the counsels he gives, let him be Consus; for suggesting good judgments, the goddess Sentia. Let him be the goddess Juventas, who takes charge of the entry into youth after a boy has assumed the toga. Let him also be Fortuna Barbata, who puts a beard on those grown to manhood—although, if they really wished to honor grown men they would have addressed a male divinity by a male name, Barbatus from his beard, like Nodutus from the knots, or, least, they would not have called him Fortuna, since he had a beard, but Fortunius. As the god Jugatinus, let him join couples in marriage; when the virgin wife's girdle is loosed, let him be invoked as the goddess

Virginiensis. Let him be Mutunus, or Tutunus, known among the Greeks as Priapus.

If the pagans are not ashamed of it, let the one Jupiter be all the things I have said, and all the things I have not said—for there is much I could not say. Let him be all these gods and goddesses, whether they are all parts of him, as some would have it, or powers, as those believe who like to conceive of him as the world-soul. This latter is the view of their great and very learned men.

If this be true—I do not yet inquire just what the situation is—what could the Romans lose if, with a wiser economy, they should worship one God? What part of His creation would be despised if He himself were adored? If it is to be feared that some parts of Jupiter would be enraged for being passed over or ignored, then it is not true, as they maintain, that he is the all-embracing total life of one life-giving being, who contains all the other gods as being his powers, or members, or parts. But if one part can become angry, another be pacified, and a third be irritated—independently of one another—then, each has its own life distinct from the rest.

On the other hand, if it be maintained that all parts together, that is, the totality of Jove himself, could be angered if his parts were not worshiped also, individually, that is talking sheer nonsense. No single one of those parts would be overlooked as long as the object of worship is the very totality which contains them all. To avoid endless details, let me observe that when they assert that all the heavenly bodies are parts of Jove, that all have life and rational souls, and that all are most certainly gods, there are certain things they overlook. They do not see, for example, how many gods remain without worship, how many have no temples or altars built to them, and to how few of the heavenly bodies they thought of dedicating such things, and of offering special sacrifices. If, therefore, the stars are wrathful because each is not given its own special worship, do not the pagans dread to live under the wrath of the entire heaven, since they appeased only a few gods?

But, if their worship comprises all the gods because all are contained in the Jove they honor by that procedure, they could invoke them all in the person of the one Jove. In this way, no one would become offended, since, as part of that unity, no one would be slighted. This would be preferable to worshiping only a few, thereby giving just cause of resentment to those who are ignored, and who are far more numerous. Their resentment would be particularly justified if, among the worshiped ones shining in splendor, they saw Priapus in his obscene nakedness given a primary place.

Chapter 12

What can be said of another absurdity? It should stir men of intelligence, and even the ordinary man—for no intellectual genius is needed here—to lay aside bitter contention, and face squarely this question: Is God the soul of the world, and is the world as the body of this soul in such wise that the two together make up a living organism composed of body and soul? Does this God, like nature's womb, so to speak, contain all things in Himself, so that His soul, which vitalizes the entire mass, is the source of the life and the soul of all living things, according to the lot determined for each one at birth? Does nothing remain which is not a part of God?

If this be true, does anyone fail to see how impious and blasphemous is the conclusion that follows: When anyone tramples on anything, he tramples on God; when he kills any living thing, he kills God! I refuse to set forth all the conclusions which thinking men can draw, but which they cannot express without shame.

Chapters 13–26

Roman superstition accepted so many divinities that polytheism became ridiculous: there were deities competing with each other in every corner of the Roman home. Educated pagans, such as Varro and Cicero, saw some of the deficiencies of polytheism but failed to bring order to the chaos of Graeco-Roman mythology.

Chapter 27

We are told in pagan writings that the learned pontifex

Scaevola distinguished three classes of divinities handed down to us: the first, by the poets; the second, by the philosophers; the third, by the statesmen. According to him, the first category is useless, because the poets imagined the gods full of vices. The second is ill-suited to states, because there was in it much that was superfluous, and certain things in it would be dangerous for the people to know. As to the superfluous, that is of little importance, for even lawyers have a saying, 'What is left over does no harm.'

But, what is that which it would be harmful for the people to know? 'It would be,' he says, 'to say openly that Hercules, Aesculapius, Castor, and Pollux are not gods. For, the philosophers inform us that they were human beings, and went to their graves like human beings.' What else do they reveal? 'That the cities have no true images of those who are gods, since the true God has neither sex, nor age, nor definite bodily form.' The pontifex wishes to keep the people ignorant of this, for he considers it to be true. Yet, he judges it expedient to deceive the citizens in matters of religion. Nor does Varro himself hesitate to affirm the same thing in his work *On Divine Things.*

A glorious religion indeed! A haven of refuge for a weak man in need of liberation! When he seeks the truth that makes him free, it is thought best for him to be duped! In the same writings, Scaevola makes no secret of the reasons he had for rejecting the gods of the poets. It is because 'they so distort them that the gods cannot be compared even with decent men. One they turn into a thief, another into an adulterer, and otherwise make them talk and act like degenerates and fools, such as the three goddesses who fought among themselves for the prize of beauty, and destroyed Troy when two of them were bested by Venus. Jove himself is transformed into a bull or a swan in order to carry on amours with some wanton or other. A goddess marries a man. Saturn devours his children. In fine, no prodigy nor vice can be imagined which is not here, however, utterly irreconcilable with their divine nature.

O Scaevola, pontifex, abolish those plays if you can. Forbid the people to pay to the immortal gods honors of that sort, in which they feast their eyes on divine depravities, and imitate them, as far as possible, in their own lives. If the people retort:

'You, yourselves, high priests, brought them to us,' beg of the gods at whose instigation you imposed those horrors to exact no performance of them in their honor!

If these rites are evil, and therefore utterly incompatible with the majesty of the gods, then the wrong done to them is the greater because the tales are concocted with impunity. But, they will not listen to you; they are demons, teachers of depravity, delighting in obscenity. They take it as no affront to have such things written about them. But, they would take it as an intolerable affront if these indecencies were not exhibited in their solemn festivals. In fact, if you appeal to Jupiter against them, especially since many of his own evil deeds are acted in the plays, though you proclaim him the divine ruler and governor of the world, are you not offering him the greatest insult when you associate his worship with that of those filthy divinities, and name him their king?

Chapter 28

Gods of that sort, appeased, or rather dishonored, and thereby more vicious for taking delight in the filthy falsehoods ascribed to them than they would have taken if they were true, could never have extended and preserved the Roman Empire. Were this in their power, it is upon the Greeks they should have conferred so great a favor. For, in this kind of religious observance, in stage plays, I mean, the Greeks treated the gods with more honor and dignity. They did not themselves dodge the barbs of the poets, by which they saw the gods torn to pieces, since they gave their poets full freedom to abuse any persons they pleased, nor did they class the comedians themselves as infamous. On the contrary, they even held them worthy of high honors.

Just as the Romans could have had gold money without worshiping the god Aurinus, so they could have had silver and copper money without worshiping either Argentinus or his father Aesculanus. So with the rest, which it would be wearisome for me to repeat. So, also, they could have had their empire, though by no means against the will of the true God. But, if they had ignored and despised that mob of false gods, and, with sincere faith and right living, acknowledged and worshiped that one God alone, they would have won a better kingdom, whether large or small, here below, and, with or without one here, they would have received an eternal one hereafter.

Chapters 29–34

Further examples of the superstitious dependence of the Romans on divine auguries are given. Cicero knew that much of this was nonsense; so did Varro. Belief in the One, Supreme God of Christianity is a refreshing remedy to all this foolishness.

BOOK V

Providence and the Greatness of Rome

Preface

WE HAVE NOW SEEN, first, that happiness (or the full possession of all that the heart can long for) is not a goddess but a gift of God and, second, that the only God whom men should worship is the One who can make them happy—so that, if Felicity were in fact a goddess, she alone should claim our worship.

We must now turn to consider why God, who can give such gifts as can be shared by men who are not good and, therefore, not happy, willed that the Roman Empire should spread so widely and endure so long. Certainly, as I have already said and, if need be, shall repeat, this cannot be attributed to the multitude of false gods whom the Romans worshiped.

Chapter 1

The cause, then, of the greatness of the Roman Empire was neither fortune nor fate. (I am using these words in the sense of those who say or think that fortune, or chance, is what happens without cause or rational explanation, and that fate is what is bound to happen, in spite even of the will of God or of men.) On the contrary, Divine Providence alone explains the establishment of kingdoms among men. As for those who speak of fate, but mean by fate the will and power of God, they should keep their conception but change their expression. Surely, though, it is best to say at once what one will have to say as soon as one is asked what is meant by fate. Ordinarily, when people hear the word fate they think of nothing but the position of the stars at the moment of one's birth or conception. This position is for some independent of, and for others dependent on, the will of God. As for those who think that the stars determine, independently of God's will, what we are to do and have and suffer, they should be given no hearing by anyone—none, certainly, by those who profess the true religion, and none even by those who worship any kind of gods, however false. For the conclusion from their way of thinking is that no God at all should be either adored or implored.

For the moment, my argument is not directed against sincere pagans, but only against those who, in defense of what they call gods, attack the Christian religion. However, even those who think the stars are dependent on the will of God (in determining what human beings are to be and have and suffer) do the heavens a great wrong, if they imagine that the stars have their power so communicated to them by God's supreme power that they remain responsible for what they determine. For, how can we suppose—if I may so speak—that the unblemished justice of that brilliant Senate of the Stars could choose to have crimes committed, the like of which no state on earth could command without facing a sentence of suppression at the bar of world opinion?

God is the Lord of both stars and men. But, what kind of rule over men's actions is left to God if men are necessarily determined by the stars?

On the other hand, suppose, as many do, that the stars have their power from the supreme God, but that, in imposing necessity on men, they merely carry out God's command without any responsibility of their own. In that case, we should have to impute to the will of God what, as we have just seen, would be monstrous to impute even to the stars.

There are some men who prefer to say that the stars rather signify than cause men's fate, that a particular position is like a form of words which causes us to know, but does not cause, what happens in the future. This view was shared by men of no mean learning. However, this is not the way that astrologers usually speak. For example, they do not say: 'Such and such a position of Mars signifies a murder.' What they say is: 'makes a murderer.' Yet, even when we concede that they do not express themselves as they should and that they ought to learn from philosophers the right way to say what they think they have found in the stars, difficulties still remain. For example, they have never been able to explain why twins are so different in what they do and achieve, in their professions and skills, in the honors they receive, and in other aspects of their lives and deaths. In all such matters, twins are often less like each other than like complete strangers; yet, twins are born with practically no interval of time between their births and are conceived in precisely the same moment of a single sexual semination.

Chapter 2

Cicero tells us that the eminent doctor, Hippocrates,[1] once wrote that he suspected two brothers to be twins because they both fell sick, then reached the crisis of the sickness and finally recovered, in each case, at the same time; while Posidonius,[2] the Stoic, who was greatly interested in astrology, used to insist that such brothers must have been conceived and born with identical horoscopes. Thus, what the doctor attributed to a similar predisposition of bodily health, the philosopher-astrologer ascribed to the power and arrangement of the stars at the moment of conception and birth.

In a matter like this, the medical hypothesis is far more acceptable and obviously more credible, since the parents' condition at the time of conception could easily affect the embryos, and it would be no wonder if the twins should be born with the same kind of health, since they had developed in the same way in their mother's womb. In the same way, they would be nourished with similar food in the same house, and would share the same climate, environment, and water—all of which, according to medical science, can help or hinder health. Moreover, they would be accustomed to the same kind of exercise, and so, having their bodies in the same condition, they would be likely to get sick at the same time and for the same reason.

On the other hand, it is nothing short of impudence to pretend that the movement of the heavens and stars at the moment of conception and birth can explain such similarity in the matter of sickness. One has only to remember how many beings differing in kind, character, and consequent capacities can be conceived and born in any one time and place and under the same conditions of the heavens. I myself have known

---

[1] Hippocrates of Cos lived between 460 and 357 B.C.
[2] Posidonius of Rhodes, a teacher of Cicero, died in 50 B.C.

twins who not only acted differently and traveled in different places, but were likewise quite unlike in health. And, as far as I can see, Hippocrates could easily explain these differences of health in terms of food and exercise—factors which depend, not on the temper of one's body, but on the choice of one's will.

It would be surprising, indeed, if either Posidonius or any other advocate of sidereal influence could find any explanation unless he wanted to play on the ignorance of simple minds. I know they may try to explain differences by appealing to the tiny interval of time between the precise moments of twin's births and, hence, to the precise part of the heavens which marks the hour of birth and which is called the horoscope. But, this is either too little to explain the variety in the wills, actions, character, and fortune of twins, or else it is too much to explain their identity in lowliness or nobility of social class—since the only explanation of class distinctions is supposed to be the hour in which people happen to be born.

And so it is that, if one twin is born so quickly after the other that the same part of the horoscope remains for both, I have a right to expect to find a total likeness, which, as a fact, is never to be found in twins; or, if the delay in the birth of the second twin changes the horoscope, I should expect to find different parents—which, of course, no twins can have.

Chapters 3–7

The pretensions and unreliability of astrologers are demonstrated by various arguments, notably by a consideration of the divergent careers of twins. Hippocrates' views on the medical history of twins are criticized. It is wrong to think that fate determines the destinies of men.

Chapter 8

There are some, however, who define fate, not as the arrangement of stars at conception, birth, or other beginning-to-be, but as the total series of causes which brings about all that happens. With these there is no need to enter into a lengthy debate on the use of words, since they attribute to the will and power of God the order and dependence of causes. They are perfectly right in believing that God allows nothing to remain unordered and that He knows all things before they come to pass. He is the Cause of all causes, although not of all choices.

It is easy to prove that by Fate they mean, primarily, the will of the supreme God whose power cannot be prevented from reaching everywhere. It was Annaeus Seneca,[1] I think, who wrote in verse:

> Lead where Thou wilt, Father and Lord of the world.
> Mine to obey, boldly, without delay.
> Should e'er my will resist the right and good,
> I'll take in tears whatever ill may come.
> Fate leads or drags men—willy-nilly—on.[2]

Obviously, in the last line he means by fate the will of the 'Father and Lord' mentioned in the first line. This will he is ready to obey—to be led willingly or, if need be, dragged reluctantly. The fact is that 'Fate leads or drags men—willy-nilly —on.'

There is the same idea in some lines of Homer which Cicero, when he put them into Latin, took to mean:

> Men's minds are led by whatsoever rays
> High Jove has cast upon their earthly ways.[3]

Not, of course, that Cicero thought the poet's opinion has any authority in such matters, but he notes that the Stoic philosophers used to cite these lines of Homer when they were defending the power of fate. Thus, there is question here, not of the opinion of the poet, but of the thought of the philosopher. It is clear from these verses, which they used in their discussions, that they meant by fate the supreme divinity, whom they called Jupiter, and from whom all destinies depend.

Chapter 9

Cicero[1] attempts to refute these Stoics, but he can find no

---

[1] L. Annaeus Seneca (5 B.C.–A.D. 65), philosopher and teacher of Nero and contemporary of St. Peter and St. Paul in Rome. The verses are found in his *Letters*, No. 107.

[2] *Ducunt volentem fata, nolentem trahunt.*

[3] The original Greek lines are *Odyssey* 18.136,137. Cicero's translation appears in none of his extant works.

[1] Cicero, *De divinatione*, especially Book II.

way of doing so without getting rid of divination; this he does by denying all knowledge of what is future. He makes every effort to prove that there can be no foreknowledge, whether in God or in man, and, therefore, no possibility of prediction. Thus, he denies the foreknowledge of God and seeks to get rid even of the clearest cases of prophecy by baseless arguments and by limiting himself to such oracles as are easy to refute. The fact is that he does not confute even these. However, he makes a masterly refutation of the conjectures of the astrologers—for the simple reason that their mutual contradictions are their best refutation.

Nevertheless, for all their sidereal fates, the astrologers are nearer the truth than Cicero with his denial of all knowledge of the future, for it is plain nonsense for a man to admit that God exists and then to deny that He can know the future. Cicero realized this, but was rash enough to fulfill the words of the Scripture: 'The fool has said in his heart: There is no God.'[2] It is true, he does not do this in his own name. This, he knew, was too risky. Instead, in his work *On the Nature of the Gods* he lets Cotta[3] play the role, in arguing against the Stoics, of denying the existence of any divine nature. Cicero chose to give his vote to Lucilius Balbus,[4] who defended the Stoic position, but, in his work *On Divination*, Cicero openly and in his own name attacks all foreknowledge of the future.

It is true, he seems to do this only to save free will and to reject the necessity of fate. His point is that, once any knowledge of the future is admitted, it is logically impossible to deny fate.

But, be these tortuous strifes and disputations of the philosophers what they will, we who profess belief in the supreme and true God confess, likewise, His will, His supreme power, His foreknowledge. Nor are we dismayed by the difficulty that what we choose to do freely is done of necessity, because He whose foreknowledge cannot be deceived foreknew that we

---

[2] Ps. 13.1.

[3] C. Aurelius Cotta, consul in 75 B.C., is one of the speakers in both *De oratore* and *De natura deorum*. He represents a form of Academic skepticism in philosophy.

[4] Quintus Lucilius Balbus represents Stoic philosophy in the dialogue.

would choose to do it. This was the fear that made Cicero oppose foreknowledge. It was this fear, too, that led the Stoics to admit that not everything happened of necessity, even though they held that everything happens by fate.

Let us examine, then, this fear of foreknowledge which led Cicero to attempt to deny it in his detestable disputation. He argues thus. If all that is future is foreknown, each event will occur in the order in which it is foreknown that it will occur. But, if things happen in this order, the order of things is known for certain in the mind of God who foreknows them. But, if the order of events is known for certain, then the order of causes is known for certain—since nothing can happen without a preceding efficient cause. If, however, the order of causes, by which all that happens is known for certain, then, he says, all that happens happens by fate. But, if this is so, nothing is left to our own power and, therefore, there is no choice in our will. But, he goes on, once we admit this, all human life becomes topsy-turvy; laws are made in vain; there is no point in reproaches or in praise, in scolding or in exhortation; there is no ground in justice for rewarding the good or punishing the wicked.

Thus, his motive for rejecting foreknowledge of the future was to avoid unworthy, absurd and dangerous implications for human society. He narrows down the choices of a devout mind to one or other of these alternatives: *either* the power of choice *or* foreknowledge. It seemed to him impossible that both could exist. If one stands, the other falls. If we choose foreknowledge, we lose free choice; if we choose free choice, we must lose knowledge of the future.

Magnanimous and learned as he was, and with no thought but to save human nature as best he could, Cicero made his choice. He chose free choice. To make it certain, he denied foreknowledge. Thus, to make men free, he made them give up God.

A man of faith wants both. He professes both and with a devout faith he holds both firmly. But how, one asks? For, if there is foreknowledge of the future, logical step follows logical step until we reach a point where nothing is left in the will. On the other hand, if we start from power in the will, the steps lead in the opposite direction until we come to the conclusion that foreknowledge is non-existent. This is how the reverse argument runs. If there is free choice, not all is fixed by fate. If not all is fixed by fate, there is no certain order of all causes. If there is no certain order of causes, there is no certain order of events known in the mind of God, since events cannot happen without preceding and efficient causes. If the order of events is not certain in the foreknowledge of God, not all things happen as He foresaw they would happen. But, if all does not happen as He foresaw it would happen, then, Cicero argues, in God there is no foreknowledge of all that is to happen.

Our stand against such bold and impious attacks on God is to say that God knows all things before they happen; yet, we act by choice in all those things where we feel and know that we cannot act otherwise than willingly. And yet, so far from saying that everything happens by fate, we say that nothing happens by fate—for the simple reason that the word 'fate' means nothing. The word means nothing, since the only reality in the mind of those who use the word—namely, the arrangement of the stars at the moment of conception or birth —is, as we show, pure illusion.

We do not deny, of course, an order of causes in which the will of God is all-powerful. On the other hand, we do not give this order the name fate, except in a sense in which the word 'fate' is derived from *fari*, to speak. For, of course, we cannot reject what is written in Holy Scripture: 'God hath spoken once, these two things have I heard, that power belongeth to God and mercy to Thee, O Lord, for Thou wilt render to everyone according to his works.'[5] The 'once' here means 'once and for all.' God spoke once and for all because He knows unalterably all that is to be, all that He is to do. In this way, we might use the word 'fate' to mean what God has 'spoken' [*fatum*], except that the meaning of the word has already taken a direction in which we do not want men's minds to move.

However, our main point is that, from the fact that to God the order of all causes is certain, there is no logical deduction that there is no power in the choice of our will. The fact is that our choices fall within the order of the causes which is known for certain to God and is contained in His foreknowledge—for, human choices are the causes of human acts. It follows that He who foreknew the causes of all things could not be unaware that our choices were among those causes which were foreknown as the causes of our acts.

In this matter it is easy enough to refute Cicero by his own admission, namely, that nothing happens without a preceding efficient cause. It does not help him to admit that nothing happens without a cause and then to argue that not every cause is fated, since some causes are either fortuitous or natural or voluntary. He admits that nothing happens without a preceding cause; that is enough to refute him.

As for the causes which are called fortuitous—hence, the name of fortune—we do not say they are unreal. We say they are latent, in the sense that they are hidden in the will either of the true God or one of His spirits. And, of course, still less do we dissociate from the will of Him who is the Author and Builder of all nature, the causes which Cicero calls 'natural.' There remain the voluntary causes. They are the choices of God or of angels or of men or of certain animals—if, indeed we may call 'choices' the instinctive movements of irrational animals by which they seek or avoid what is good or bad for their nature. By the choices of angels I mean those of the good ones we call the angels of God or of the wicked ones we call demons or the angels of the Devil. So of men, there are the choices of good men and of bad men.

From this we conclude that the only efficient causes of all things are voluntary causes, that is to say, causes of the same nature as the spirit or breath of life. Of course, the air or wind can be said to breathe;[6] but, being a body, it is not the breath or spirit of life. The Spirit of Life, which gives life to all and is the Creator of all matter and of every created spirit is God, a Spirit, indeed, but uncreated. In His will is the supreme power which helps the good choices of created spirits, judges the evil ones, and orders all of them, giving powers to some and not to others.

As He is the Creator of all natures, so is He the giver of all powers—though He is not the maker of all choices.[7] Evil

[6] *Nam et aer iste seu ventus dicitiur spiritus.*

[7] . . . *omnium potestatum dator, non voluntatum.*

choices are not from Him, for they are contrary to the nature
which is from Him. Thus, bodies are subject to wills. Some
bodies are subject to our wills—to the wills of all mortal animals, but especially those of men rather than of beasts. Some
bodies are subject to the wills of angels. And absolutely all
bodies are subject to the will of God; as, indeed, are all wills,
too, since they have no power save what He gave them.

Thus, God is the Cause of all things—a cause that makes but
is not made. Other causes make, but they are themselves
made—for example, all created spirits and, especially, rational
spirits. Material causes which are rather passive than active
are not to be included among efficient causes, for their power
is limited to what the wills of spirits work through them.

It does not follow, therefore, that the order of causes,
known for certain though it is in the foreknowing mind of God,
brings it about that there is no power in our will, since our
choices themselves have an important place in the order of
causes.

And so, let Cicero argue with those who hold that this order
of causes is fixed by fate, or, rather, is the reality they call
fate. Our main objection is to the word fate, which is usually
given a false sense. As for Cicero, we object to him even more
than the Stoics do when he denies that the order of all causes
is fixed and clearly known in the foreknowledge of God. Cicero
must either deny that God exists—and this, in fact, is what he
attempts to do in the name of Cotta in his work *On the Nature
of the Gods*—or else, if he admits God's existence while denying His foreknowledge, what he says amounts to nothing more
than what 'the fool hath said in his heart: There is no God.'
The fact is that one who does not foreknow the whole of the
future is most certainly not God.

Our conclusion is that our wills have power to do all that
God wanted them to do and foresaw they could do. Their
power, such as it is, is a real power. What they are to do they
themselves will most certainly do, because God foresaw both
that they could do it and that they would do it and His knowledge cannot be mistaken. Thus, if I wanted to use the word
'fate' for anything at all, I should prefer to say that 'fate' is
the action of a weak person, while 'choice' is the act of the
stronger man who holds the weak man in his power, rather

than to admit that the choice of our will is taken away by that order of causes which the Stoics arbitrarily call fate.

Chapter 10

It follows that we need not be afraid of that necessity which frightened the Stoics into distinguishing various kinds of causes. They sought to free certain causes from necessity while others were subject to it. Among the causes which they wanted free from necessity they reckoned our wills. Obviously, wills could not be free if subject to necessity.

Now, if by necessity we mean one that is in no way in our power, but which has its way even when our will is opposed to it, as is the case with the necessity to die, then, our choices of living well or ill obviously are not subject to this kind of necessity. The fact is that we do many things which we would most certainly not do if we did not choose to do them. The most obvious case is our willing itself. For, if we will, there is an act of willing; there is none if we do not want one. We would certainly not make a choice if we did not choose to make it. On the other hand, if we take necessity to mean that in virtue of which something must be so and so or must happen in such and such a way, I do not see that we should be afraid of such necessity taking away our freedom of will. We do not put the life of God and the foreknowledge of God under any necessity when we say that God *must* live an eternal life and *must* know all things. Neither do we lessen His power when we say He cannot die or be deceived. This is the kind of inability which, if removed, would make God less powerful than He is. God is rightly called omnipotent, even though He is unable to die and be deceived. We call Him omnipotent because He does whatever He wills to do and suffers nothing that He does not will to suffer. He would not, of course, be omnipotent, if He had to suffer anything against His will. It is precisely because He is omnipotent that for Him some things are impossible.

So with us, when we say we *must* choose freely when we choose at all, what we say is true; yet, we do not subject free choice to any necessity which destroys our liberty. Our choices, therefore, are our own, and they effect, whenever we

choose to act, something that would not happen if we had not
chosen. Even when a person suffers against his will from the
will of others, there is a voluntary act—not, indeed, of the person who suffers. However, a human will prevails—although the
power which permits this is God's. (For, wherever there is a
mere will without power to carry out what it chooses, it would
be impeded by a stronger will. Even so, there would be no
will in such a condition unless there were a will, and not merely
the will of another but the will of the one choosing, even
though he is unable to carry out his choice.) Therefore, whatever a man has to suffer against his will is not to be attributed
to the choices of man or of angels or of any created spirit, but
to His choice who gives to wills whatever power they have.

It does not follow, therefore, that there is no power in our
will because God foreknew what was to be the choice in our
will. For, He who had this foreknowledge had some foreknowledge. Furthermore, if He who foresaw what was to be in our
will foresaw, not nothing, but something, it follows that there
is a power in our will, even though He foresaw it.

The conclusion is that we are by no means under compulsion to abandon free choice in favor of divine foreknowledge,
nor need we deny—God forbid!—that God knows the future,
as a condition for holding free choice. We accept both. As
Christians and philosophers, we profess both—foreknowledge,
as a part of our faith; free choice, as a condition of responsible
living. It is hard to live right if one's faith in God is wrong.

Far be it from us, then, to deny, in the interest of our freedom, the foreknowledge of God by whose power we are—or
are to be—free. It follows, too, that laws are not in vain, nor
scoldings and encouragements, nor praise and blame. He foresaw that such things should be. Such things have as much
value as He foresaw they would have. So, too, prayers are
useful in obtaining these favors which He foresaw He would
bestow on those who should pray for them. There was justice
in instituting rewards and punishments for good and wicked
deeds. For, no one sins because God foreknew that he would
sin. In fact, the very reason why a man is undoubtedly responsible for his own sin, when he sins, is because He whose
foreknowledge cannot be deceived foresaw, not the man's fate
or fortune or what not, but that the man himself would be

responsible for his own sin. No man sins unless it is his choice to sin; and his choice not to sin, that, too, God foresaw.

Chapter 11

This supreme and true God—with His Word and Holy Spirit which are one with Him—this one omnipotent God is the creator and maker of every soul and of every body. All who find their joy in truth and not in mere shadows derive their happiness from Him. He made man a rational animal, composed of soul and body. He permitted man to sin—but not with impunity—and He pursued him with His mercy. He gave men —both good and bad—their being, as He gave being to the rocks. He let men share generative life in common with the trees, and the life of the senses with the beasts of the fields, but the life of intelligence only with the angels. God is the Author of all measure, form, and order; of all size, number and weight.[1] He is the source of every nature, of whatever sort or condition; of the seed of every form and the form of every seed and the movement of both seeds and forms. He gave to all flesh its beginning, beauty, health, and power of reproduction; the arrangement of its members and the general well-being of a balanced whole. To His irrational creatures He gave memory, perception, and appetite, but to His rational creatures He added a mind with intelligence and will.

He left no part of this creation without its appropriate peace, for in the last and least of all His living things the very entrails are wonderfully ordered—not to mention the beauty of birds' wings, and the flowers of the fields and the leaves of trees. And above the beauty of sky and earth is that of angels and of man. How, then, can anyone believe that it was the will of God to exempt from the laws of His providence the rise and fall of political societies?

Chapters 12–14

The original Romans were honorable people. Their achievements sprang from a love of liberty and a desire for domination.

[1] . . . *a quo est omnis modus, omnis species, omnis ordo; a quo est mensura, numerus, pondus.*

Roman literature shows that the second urge outgrew the first.
The contrast with the peaceful tendencies and high ideals of
the early Christians is striking.

Chapter 15

For these pagan heroes there was not to be the divine grace
of everlasting life along with His holy angels in His heavenly
City, for the only road to this Society of the Blessed is true
piety, that is, that religious service or *latreía* (to use the Greek
word) which is offered to the One true God. On the other
hand, if God did not grant them at least the temporal glory
of a splendid Empire, there would have been no reward for
the praiseworthy efforts or virtues by which they strove to attain that glory. When our Lord said: 'Amen I say to you they
have received their reward,'[1] He had in mind those who do
what seems to be good in order to be glorified by men.

After all, the pagans subordinated their private property to
the common welfare, that is, to the republic and the public
treasury. They resisted the temptation to avarice. They gave
their counsel freely in the councils of the state. They indulged
in neither public crime nor private passion. They thought they
were on the right road when they strove, by all these means,
for honors, rule, and glory. Honor has come to them from almost all peoples. The rule of their laws has been imposed on
many peoples. And in our day, in literature and in history,
glory has been given them by almost everyone. They have no
right to complain of the justice of the true and supreme God.
'They have received their reward.'

Chapter 16

The reward of the saints is altogether different. They were
men who, while on earth, suffered reproaches for the City of
God which is so much hated by the lovers of this world. That
City is eternal. There, no one is born because no one dies.
There, there reigns that true and perfect happiness which is
not a goddess, but a gift of God—toward whose beauty we can

[1] Matt. 6.2,5.

sigh in our pilgrimage on earth, though we hold the
ge of it by faith. In that City, the sun does not 'rise upon
good and bad'[1] for the Sun of Justice cherishes the good
ne. There, where the Truth is a treasure shared by all, there
is no need to pinch the poor to fill the coffers of the state.

It was, then, not only to reward the Roman heroes with human glory that the Roman Empire spread. It had a purpose for
the citizens of the Eternal City during their pilgrimage on
earth. Meditating long and seriously on those great examples,
they could understand what love of their Heavenly Fatherland
should be inspired by everlasting life, since a fatherland on
earth has been so much loved by citizens inspired by human
glory.

Chapter 17

When it is considered how short is the span of human life,
does it really matter to a man whose days are numbered what
government he must obey, so long as he is not compelled to
act against God or his conscience? And, what injury did the
Romans do to those they conquered, save that they imposed
their laws by means of war and slaughter? It is true, they
would have triumphed better by compact than by conquest.
But then they would have had less glory. The fact is that the
Romans lived under the identical laws they imposed on others.
And all could have been arranged without the help of Mars,
Bellona, and Victoria. But, no war, no victor; and that would
have put the Romans on the same level with other peoples.
This would have been the case, especially, if the Romans had
done earlier what they were kind and gracious enough to do
later, namely, to make the privilege of a few a fellowship of
all, and to call all who belonged to the Roman Empire citizens
of Rome. The only exception to this was the lower class of people who had no property of their own. These lived at the
public expense. They were well off in the sense that the food
that might have been taken from them by their conquerors
was guaranteed to them by the state and provided by good
administrators.

[1] Matt. 5.45.

So far as I can see, it makes no difference at all to political security or public order to maintain the purely human distinction between conquerors and conquered peoples. It adds nothing to the state but empty pomp—fit reward for those who wage fierce battles out of lust for human glory. Do not the Romans pay taxes for their lands as others do? Are they more free to learn than others are? Are there not many Senators in foreign lands who do not even know what Rome looks like? When all the boasting is over, what is any man but just another man? And, even though a crooked world came to admit that men should be honored only according to merit, even human honor would be of no great value. It is smoke that weighs nothing.

Yet, in this matter, too, let us turn to our profit the goodness of God, our Lord. Let us reflect what good things they despised, what suffering they sustained, what passions they subdued for human glory—the sole reward such marvelous virtues merited. Let it help us to suppress our pride when we think of the difference between their city and ours and to reflect how little we can claim to have done if, to gain our City, we do a little good or endure certain ills, when they have done and suffered so much for the sake of the earthly city which is already theirs. Our City is as different from theirs as heaven from earth, as everlasting life from passing pleasure, as solid glory from empty praise, as the company of angels from the companionship of mortals, as the Light of Him who made the sun and moon is brighter than the light of sun and moon. We can learn from this, too, that the remission of sins which makes us citizens of the Eternal City was faintly adumbrated when Romulus gathered the first citizens of his city by providing a sanctuary and immunity for a multitude of criminals.

Chapters 18–19

Various outstanding men contributed to the greatness of Rome. Whatever these good men achieved was accomplished under Divine Providence.

Chapter 20

Those philosophers who regard virtue as the ultimate human good try to make those others feel ashamed of themselves who think highly enough of the virtues, but who subordinate them to physical pleasure, making pleasure an end in itself and virtues merely a means to this end. They do this by picturing Pleasure enthroned like a high-born queen, surrounded by ministering virtues who watch her every nod, ready to do whatever she bids them. Thus, she bids Prudence to examine carefully in what way Pleasure may be both supreme and safe. She commands Justice to render whatever services she can in the interest of friendships which are necessary for bodily comfort, and to avoid doing wrong, lest Pleasure might be jeopardized by the breaking of laws. She bids Fortitude keep her mistress, Pleasure, very much in mind, so that, when the body suffers some affliction, short of death, the memory of former pleasures may mitigate the pangs of present pain. She orders Temperance to take just so much of food or of other pleasant things that health may not be endangered by any excess, or Pleasure (which, for the Epicureans, is mainly a matter of bodily health) be seriously checked.

Thus, the virtues with all the glory of their dignity are made to minister to Pleasure, like the servants of an imperious but ill-famed mistress. The Stoics are right when they say that no picture could be more ugly and ignominious and difficult for good people to look at than this. But, I do not see how the picture becomes much more beautiful if we imagine the virtues ministering to human glory. For, if Glory is not exactly a lovely lady, she has a certain vanity and inanity about her. Certainly, it ill becomes the gravity and solidity of the virtues to be her servants; so that, apart from pleasing men and serving their vainglory, Prudence should make no provision, Justice should share nothing, Fortitude tolerate nothing, Temperance moderate nothing. Ugly as this picture is, it fits those self-complacent and seeming philosophers who, in the guise of despising glory, pay no heed to what others think. Their virtue, if they have any, is just as much a slave to glory, though in a different way. For what is the self-complacent man but a slave to his own self-praise.

It is different with the man who believes in, hopes in, loves, and truly worships God. He gives more attention to the defects in which he takes no pleasure than to whatever virtues he may have and which are not so much pleasing to him as to the truth. And whatever he finds that is pleasing he attributes solely to the mercy of Him whom he fears to displease, thanking God meanwhile for the defects which have been corrected and praying for the correction of the others.

Chapter 21

The conclusion from all this is that the power to give a people a kingdom or empire belongs only to the same true God who gives the Kingdom of Heaven with its happiness only to those who believe in Him, while He gives the earthly city to both believers and unbelievers alike, according to His Will which can never be unjust. This much of what I have said so far God wanted to be clear to us. However, it would be too much for me and beyond my powers to discuss men's hidden merits and to measure in an open balance those which have been rewarded by the establishment of kingdoms.

This much I know. The one true God, who never permits the human race to be without the working of His wisdom and His power, granted to the Roman people an empire, when He willed it and as large as He willed it. It was the same God who gave kingdoms to the Assyrians and even to the Persians —by whom, according to their Scriptures, only two gods are worshiped, one good and one evil. So, too, to the Hebrew people, of whom I have already said enough concerning their exclusive worship of none but the one true God and also concerning the period of their rule.

This is the God who gave corn to the Persians without regard to their worshiping the goddess of corn, Segetia. He gave other gifts of lands to peoples who gave no worship to all those gods whom the Romans assigned, sometimes singly and sometimes in groups, to the care of each particular thing. He gave the Romans their empire without regard to the worship of all those gods that seemed to them the condition of their conquests.

It was this God, too, who gave power to men, to Marius and Caesar, to Augustus and Nero, to the Vespasians, father and son, who were such kindly emperors, and also to Domitian who was so cruel; and, not to mention all the others, to Constantine the Christian and to Julian the Apostate—the man whose marvelous gifts were poisoned by his lust for power. Julian fell a victim to a silly and sacrilegious occultism. He put his trust in vain oracles and, relying on them for victory, he once burned the ships transporting his supplies. On another occasion, he let rash ardor get the better of him. He paid the price of recklessness by his death in enemy country, and his army was left in such straits that its only hope to escape was —in contradiction of the prophecy of the god, Terminus, which I mentioned above[1]—by changing the frontiers of the Roman Empire. The fact was that the god Terminus, who defied Jupiter, yielded to necessity.

All such things the one true God rules and governs according to His will. And, though His reasons may be hidden, they have never been unjust.

Chapters 22–23

The history of various ancient wars (Punic, Servile, Social, and Mithridatic) is here reviewed to show how all human events are governed by God's mercy and justice.

Chapter 24

When we say that some of the Christian emperors are blest, we do not mean they are happy because they reigned many years; or because, when they died in peace, their sons reigned in their steads; or because they conquered the enemies of the republic; or because they were warned in time to put down the rebellions of seditious citizens. Such rewards and consolations in this troubled life have been rightly bestowed even on those who have worshiped pagan gods and who did not be-

---

[1] Cf. Bk. 4.23,29, here omitted.

long, like Christians, to the Kingdom of God. The reason for this is God's mercy. He does not want those who believe in Him to look upon such favors as God's highest gifts.

We call those Christian emperors happy who govern with justice, who are not puffed up by the tongues of flatterers or the services of sychophants, but remember that they are men. We call them happy when they think of sovereignty as a ministry of God and use it for the spread of true religion; when they fear and love and worship God; when they are in love with the Kingdom in which they need fear no fellow sharers; when they are slow to punish, quick to forgive; when they punish, not out of private revenge, but only when forced by the order and security of the republic, and when they pardon, not to encourage impunity, but with the hope of reform; when they temper with mercy and generosity the inevitable harshness of their decrees.

We call those happy who are all the more disciplined in their lusts just because they are freer to indulge them; who prefer to curb the waywardness of their own passions rather than to rule the peoples of the world, and who do this not out of vainglory but out of love for everlasting bliss; men, finally, who, for their sins, do not fail to offer to the true God the sacrifice of humility, repentance, and prayer.

We say of such Christian emperors that they are, in this life, happy in their hope, but destined to be happy in reality when that day shall come for which we live in hope.

Chapters 25–26

The Christian emperors, Constantine, Jovian, Gratian, Theodosius, Valentinian, and the rest, also enjoyed the favor of divine Providence. Some readers of the preceding books are writing rebuttals claiming that the gods grant favors in a future life: Augustine will reply to this argument.

PART TWO

THE PAGAN GODS AND FUTURE HAPPINESS

BOOK VI

Eternal Life and the Inadequacy of Polytheism

Preface

IN THE five preceding Books, I have, I hope, sufficiently refuted those who think that many gods are to be venerated and worshiped. Such people hold that, in order to gain advantages for this mortal life and men's temporal affairs, the gods are to be served with an adoration which the Greeks call *latreía* and which is due to the true God alone. Christian truth makes clear that these gods are false, that they are useless idols, or unclean spirits, or dangerous demons, or, at best, mere creatures and not the Creator. Of course, as everyone knows, neither my five Books nor any five hundred books are sufficient to silence folly and pertinacity. It is the glory of vain men never to yield to the truth. Such vainglory is a deadly passion for those it dominates. It is a disease that, in spite of every effort, is never cured—not because the doctor is inept, but because the patient is incurable.

Those others, however, who reflect on what they read and judge it with little or no obstinacy in their previous error, will easily come to feel that, in the five Books which I have just finished, I have said more, rather than less, than the question in debate required. They will also agree that the ill will against the Christian religion which is stirred up by people ignorant of history and who blame on us the disasters of life and the crumbling and collapse of civilization is without foundation. It is not a conclusion of right thinking and reasoning, but the evidence of reckless and malicious animosity. The facts are clear, even though some of the scholars pretend not to know them, or, yielding to irrational hate, deliberately encourage the bigotry.

Chapter 1

My next purpose, then, as I have already indicated, will be the refutation and instruction of those who hold that the gods of the pagans, which Christianity rejects, are to be worshiped, not on account of this life, but with a view to life after death. The starting point of this discussion will be the revealed truth of the holy psalm: 'Blessed is the man whose trust is in the name of the Lord; and who hath not had regard to vanities and lying follies.'[1]

In the din of all the lying inanities and insanities of men, it is bearable enough to listen to the voice of those philosophers who scorned the erroneous opinions of the populace. But, the people themselves set up idols for their gods and then invented all sorts of discreditable fictions about their immortals, or else believed in fictions already current and mixed these fictions with their sacred rites and ceremonies.

The philosophers were not always free to speak openly, but in their academic discussions they hinted at their rejection of popular superstitions. With such men, then, I find no difficulty in debating this question: Whether it is better to worship the one God who created all spiritual and corporal realities and to worship Him with a view to life after death, or to worship the many gods whom the best and greatest of the philosophers felt to have been made and set in their lofty positions by Him?

First, a word about the gods I mentioned in Book IV as having some paltry and particular function assigned to them. No philosopher, I am sure, would dream of discussing whether such gods can give us immortal life. But, what of those men, some of them extremely learned and acute, who boast of having written useful books of instructions to help people to know why each of the different gods is to be prayed to, and what is to be asked of each, and how to avoid the unbecoming absurdity of asking, like a clown on the stage, for water from

[1] Ps. 39.5.

Bacchus or for wine from the Lymphae? Would they take responsibility for a person who, when praying the immortal gods and asking the Lymphae for wine and getting the answer: 'We have only water, ask Bacchus for wine,' should rightly say: If you have no wine, give me, at any rate, your immortal life?

Just think of the monstrous absurdity of the Lymphae answering with a laugh—for, according to Virgil,[2] they are given to laughter—'O man, do you think we have power to give you life [*vitam*], when you have just been told that we can't even give you wine [*vitem*]!' (I am supposing that, unlike the demons, they would not try to deceive him.) It is indeed monstrous and absurd to ask or hope for eternal life from gods like this. Here they are so assigned to such tiny and fragmentary adjuncts of our sad and transient life that, when you ask one of them for something in the department of another, you get a situation as ridiculous as a scurrilous embarrassment on the stage.

If we have a right to laugh in the theater where actors know their parts, we should laugh still louder at ignorant fools in real life. Yet, in regard to gods and goddesses set up by various cities, learned men have discovered and listed what each must be asked for, for example, what we should ask of Bacchus, the Lymphae, Vulcan, and the rest, many of whom—but not all that I might have done—I mentioned in Book IV. Just think. If it is a mistake to ask wine of Ceres, bread of Bacchus, water of Vulcan, fire from the Lymphae, you can imagine how crazy we ought to consider a man who should ask any of such gods for eternal life. To confirm the point, recall what was said when we were discussing the question whether any of the gods or goddesses could be thought powerful enough to confer on men an earthly kingdom. It was shown, after an exhaustive discussion, that certainly political societies could not be constituted by any of the many, false divinities. Would it, then, not be as irreligious as it would be ridiculous to think that any of the gods could confer that membership in eternal society which is most certainly incomparably better than membership in all the earthly kingdoms put together?

We saw, too, that the reason why such gods can give no kingdoms to men on earth was not the impropriety of beings

[2] *Eclogues* 3.9: . . . *sed faciles Nymphae risere.*

so great and lofty deigning to bother with anything so small and lowly. In the light of human weakness, we have a right to despise even the crumbling peaks of earthly power, yet there is not one of those gods to whom a man would not be ashamed of committing the giving and preserving of human political societies. But if, as we have seen especially from the last two Books, no one of that crowd of gods, little or lofty, was fit to give a mortal society to mortal men, how much less could they make immortal citizens out of mortal men.

Here is another argument that is valid for those who think the gods are to be worshiped, not with a view to benefits in this life, but only in the life after death. Certainly, then, the gods are not to be worshiped for the sake of those separate and particular things which are only by a stretch of imagination, and not in reality, in the power of this or that particular god. Yet, this is the position of those who think the worship of the gods is necessary for benefits in this present life. I have done the best I could in the last five Books to dispose of such people.

Let us suppose for a moment that those who worship the goddess, Youth, were always in the flower of youth, while those who neglected her always died young or suffered the listlessness of old age; or, again, suppose that Fortuna Barbata always prematurely clothed the cheeks of her worshipers with a lovely beard, while her scorners were left beardless or had nothing but down. At least we could say that, within their limited sphere, these divinities could do what they were supposed to do. But, it would follow that we should not ask Juventas for eternal life since it was not her job to give us even a beard; nor ask Fortuna Barbata for any good in the life to come, since, in this life, she has no power to give us the vigor of youth which goes with the growing of beards.

There is, then, no need to worship such gods for the sake of the benefits they are supposed to confer. The fact is that many who worship Juventas had nothing of the youthful vigor of many who paid so much worship; and many who have prayed to Fortuna Barbata had a shapeless beard or none at all, and are the laughing stock of finely bearded men who paid her no sort of service. No human intelligence is so dull as to believe that a worship of such gods can bear any fruit in eternity, when the worship with a view to temporal and passing benefits and within the sphere of their competence is seen to be silly and vain.

Such gods, then, cannot give us eternal life. Not even those who wanted them to be worshiped by the ignorant populace dared to make such a claim. They were content to divide up the occupations of earthly life, and, to keep all of their gods busy, assigned to each god a particular job.

Chapter 2

No one has investigated the gods with more care than Marcus Varro. No other scholar has discovered so much, no one has given more care to the matter, no one has made such acute distinctions, no one has written so diligently and so much as he. His style may not be remarkable, but what he has written is so replete with facts and ideas that in the sphere of secular or liberal scholarship he may be called the master of history as Cicero is the prince of style.

Cicero himself confirms what I say. In his *Academica* he speaks of his discussion with Marcus Varro as with a man 'who is easily the most brilliant of his age and, undoubtedly, the most learned.'[1] He does not say 'elegant in style' or 'most eloquent' because, in fact, Varro does not shine as a writer; but he does say that he was 'brilliant' and in the *Academica*, where he treats of skepticism in philosophy, Cicero adds that Varro was undoubtedly 'most learned.' In fact, in this instance, Cicero was so certain as to exclude his habitual skepticism. It is as though he forgot that he was a Skeptical philosopher at least in regard to this one matter, even in a defense of Skeptical philosophy. In his first book, in discussing the literary works of Varro, Cicero has this to say: 'When we had lost our way in our city, as though we were strangers, your books showed us the way home. We finally learned who and where we were. You left nothing untouched: the antiquity of our country, the periods of its history, the rules of worship, the priestly laws, our domestic and public life, the topography of our cities and the names, divisions, functions, and causes of all things human and divine.'

[1] *Acad. Post.* III, *proemium.*

The poet Terentian had this remarkable and exceptional scholarship in mind when he wrote of Varro as 'a man of universal knowledge.'[2] He had read so much that we marvel he had time to write. He wrote so much that no one man, you would think, could read it all. Now, this man, so brilliant and so learned, could not have set down things about the gods more ridiculous, offensive, and scandalous, even if he had set out as an opponent and critic of the so-called religion about which he writes, and if he had taken the view that it was not religion at all but merely superstition.

Yet, while Varro worshiped the gods and felt they should be worshiped, his very work about them indicates his fear about their survival. He was not so much afraid of foreign invaders as of the devastation by his own people's indifference, and it was to save the gods from this, he says, and to keep them alive in the memory of good men that he wrote his works. He was performing a more useful service, he felt, than Metellus in saving the Vestal Palladium from the flames and Aeneas in saving the gods from the ruins of Troy. Yet, the fact is that he has set forth things for the whole world to read which are abhorrent to philosophers and fools and are of no service at all to true religion. It looks very much as though, for all his acumen and learning, he had none of that liberty of spirit which is a gift of the Holy Spirit, and was, in fact, a slave to legalism, and tradition; yet, below his superficial commendation of pagan religion, there is a hint of his real convictions in some of his admissions.

Chapter 3

Varro wrote forty-one books under the title *Antiquities*. He divided his matter under two headings, human and divine, devoting twenty-five books to the former and sixteen to the latter. He followed the plan of devoting six books to each of four subdivisions under the heading 'Things Human': Persons, Places, Times, and Actions—dealing in the first six with persons, in the second six with places, and the third six with times, in the fourth and last six, with actions. These four sixes make twenty-

[2] *Vir doctissimus undecumque Varro* is line 2846 of Book IV of the *De metris* of Terentianus Maurus, who lived in the third century.

four. At the beginning he placed one book by itself, as a general introduction to the whole. In general, he followed a similar plan in regard to divine things, as far as the subject matter allowed.

Sacred actions are performed by persons in certain places at definite times. And these are the four topics he treats, giving three books to each. The first three deal with the persons who perform the rites, the next three with places, the third with times, the fourth with the rites. Here, too, he is careful to make the distinctions: Who, Where, When and What. The main topic he was expected to deal with was: To whom. Hence, the last three deal with the gods; the five threes making fifteen in all. To make up the total of sixteen which I mentioned, he placed one book by itself at the beginning to serve as a general introduction.

Thus, there were five main divisions. Immediately after the introduction came the three books dealing with persons. These were again subdivided, so that the first dealt with the pontiffs, the next with augurs, the third with the Sacred College of Fifteen.[1] Of the second three books dealing with places, the first was about shrines; the second, about temples; the third, about sacred places. The next four dealt with time or holy days. The first of these was concerned with festivals; the next, with circus games; the third, with theatrical performances. Of the fourth trio of books dealing with worship, one concerned consecrations; the next, private worship; the last, public rites.

At the end of this procession, so to speak, of religious observances come the gods themselves, to whom all the observances are directed. They are dealt with in three other books, of which, the first concerned the known gods; the second, the unknown gods; the third and last dealt with the select major divinities.

Chapter 4

Now, in this whole series of volumes, so beautiful in the skillful arrangement of matter, one will look in vain for any mention of eternal life. Indeed, it would be illogical to hope or to

[1] The custodians and interpreters of the Sibylline books, instituted by Tarquinius Superbus and brought up to the number fifteen by Sulla.

wish for any such mention. From what I have already said and, still more from what remains to be said, the reason for this is obvious to anyone who is not blinded by his own obstinacy. Everything here treated of is an invention either of men or of demons—not of 'good demons,' to use their own expression, but, to speak plainly, of unclean spirits and manifestly malign spirits. All of these foster the idea that the human soul has so little reality that it is incapable of reaching and finding rest in unchanging and eternal truth. These malign spirits work secretly and with incredible hatred to fill the minds of wicked people. Sometimes, they openly work on people's senses and call in lying witnesses in their favor.

Varro gives a reason for treating of human things first and of divine things later, namely, because cities came into existence first and only later instituted religious rites. But, the fact is that true religion owed its foundation to no city; it was itself the foundation of a wholly celestial city. True religion is the revelation and teaching of the true God who is the Giver of eternal life to those who worship him truly.

Varro's justification for treating first of human things and secondly of divine, on the ground that divine worship was instituted by men, is expressed as follows: 'As a painter comes before the painting and the builder before the building, so do cities come before the things which cities instituted.' He admits, however, that, if he had been writing a complete treatise on the nature of the gods, he would have treated first of the gods and then of men. He seems to imply either that he had no intention of treating of all but only of some of the gods, or that some, though not all, of the gods need not have existed before men.

But, how then, explain that when, in his last three books, he treats of known, unknown, and select gods he seems to want to include all of the gods? What can he really mean when he writes: 'If I were writing of the divine and human natures in their totality, I should have first finished the treatment of the gods before entering on a discussion of man'? Is he writing of all, or of some, or of none of the gods? If of all, then the treatment of gods certainly should come first; if of some, there still is no reason why the treatment should not come first. Is it a reproach to man that a few of the gods should be preferred to the whole of humanity? And, even if this is so in regard to the whole of humanity, is it too much of a reproach that a part of the gods should be preferred to the Romans?

His books dealing with human matters do not cover the whole world, but only the city of Rome. These books, he says, rightly came before the books dealing with divine matters, for the reason, so he says, that the painter comes before the painting and the builder before the building. His assumption is always the same, that religion, like a picture or a building, is the creation of men. We are left with the possibility that he had in mind to write of none of the gods and, without wanting to say this openly, made his intention clear enough to those who read between the lines.

Certainly, when a man says 'not all,' he is usually understood as meaning 'some' (though, of course, he might be taken to mean 'none' since 'none' is neither 'some' nor 'all'). Judging from what he says, if he had been writing of *all* of the gods, he should have treated of them before treating of human matters; even though he does not say so, truth demands that he should have treated even of some of the gods—not to insist on all of them—before treating of merely Roman matters. But, what he was dealing with came properly after the discussion of Rome. The conclusion is that he was treating of nothing divine at all.

He had no intention of putting human things before divine things, but he refused to put fictions before facts. In what he writes about human matters, he follows the historians who deal with facts. In what he writes about what he calls 'divine' matters, what does he do but give us feelings about fancies? Here, we have the subtle significance of what he did, both in writing about the 'gods' in second place and in giving an explanation of why he did it.

If he had given no explanation, it might have been possible to find some other defense of his arrangement. However, in the very explanation which Varro gives, he left no other interpretation open. He made it clear, not that he was preferring the nature of man to the nature of God, but that he was treating of men before treating of human institutions. Thus, he confesses that his books dealing with 'divine' matters were based, not on facts concerning the nature of God, but on fancy—which is another name for error. As I pointed out in Book IV, he made this clear in another place, where he says he would have written according to the rule of nature if he himself had founded a new city, but that, since he was dealing with an old city, he could do nothing but follow the tradition he found there.

Chapter 5

What are we to think of his division of theology, or the systematic treatment of the divine, into three kinds, of which the first is called mythical, the second physical, and the third political? In Latin, we should call the first (if the word were in use) 'fabular'; but, let us call it fabulous, since the Greek *mythos* is the same as the Latin *fabula*. We may call the second 'natural,' for that word is in common use. The third was given the Latin name 'political' by Varro himself. His own explanation runs as follows: 'What they call "mythical" is what is especially in use among the poets; "physical" theology is used by the philosophers; and "political" by ordinary citizens. In the first of these theologies are found many fictions unworthy of the dignity and nature of immortal beings. For, in this kind of theology one divinity [Minerva] was born from another's head, a second [Bacchus] from a thigh, a third [Pegasus] from drops of blood; some gods [e.g., Mercury] were thieves, others [e.g., Jupiter] adulterers, and still others [e.g., Apollo] slaves of men, and in general deeds are attributed to gods which are not merely human but abnormal.'

Here he could speak boldly and with impunity—and he did so without a shadow of ambiguity—of the wrong done to divinity by lying fables. He was talking of 'fabulous' theology, not of natural or political theology, and he felt free to attack it. But, listen to what he says of the second kind of theology. It is the kind, he says, 'about which the philosophers have left many books discussing such questions as: Who are the gods? Where are they to be found? Of what kind and character are they? When did they begin? Are they eternal? Do they originate in fire (as Heraclitus thought), or from numbers (according to Pythagoras), or from atoms (as Epicurus said)? There is much else—all of which is more tolerable to listen to inside a classroom than out in the streets.'

He found nothing to blame in this theology of the philosophers—the *genus physicon* as they call it—save that he mentions the controversies which have made the philosophers the
fathers of many dissident sects. He wants the people in the
street to have none of this theology. He locks it behind the
walls of the schoolrooms. Yet, he did not remove from the man
in the street the filthy fancies of the poets!

Oh! how pious are the ears of the people—and, among
them, the Roman people! They are too sensitive to listen to
what philosophers have to say about the immortal gods, but
they listen, and listen gladly, to what poets fancy (because
this is counter to the dignity and nature of immortal beings)
or to what the actors perform (because on the stage, the gods
are not merely men but cads.) And what is worse, to believe
the poets and players, such things not merely please, but placate, the gods!

'Very well,' someone will say, 'but let us hear how Varro explains political theology. We want to separate, as Varro himself did, fabulous and natural theology—the *genus mythicon*
and the *genus physicon*—from political theology which is now
in question.' Well, I can see why we should separate the fabulous—for the simple reason that it is false, filthy, and unfit for
discussion. But, why should we separate the natural from the
political? Would that not be to admit that the political itself
is in need of correction? If a thing is natural, what can be
wrong with it, and why should we exclude it? And, if what
we call political is not natural, what can make it worth our
discussion?

It was, in fact, Varro's own reason for putting this discussion of human things before the discussion of divine things that,
in what he called 'divine' things, he was following, not nature,
but human conventions. Let us take a look at his 'political
theology.' 'There is,' he says, 'a third kind, which the people,
and particularly the priests, in the cities ought to know and
practice. It belongs to this theology to explain what gods
should be worshiped in public and by what rites and sacrifices
each one should do this.' What follows is noteworthy. 'The
first kind of theology is suitable for the theater; the second,
for the world; the third, for the city.' It is easy to see to what
kind he gives the palm. Obviously, to the second, the theology

of the philosopher, as he himself calls it. When he says this belongs to the world, he is relating it to that which, in the Stoic view, is the highest of realities. The other two theologies, the first and third, those of the theater and the city, he does not distinguish, but rather lumps together.

It does not at once follow that what belongs to a city can belong to the world, although cities are part of the world. For, it can happen that in a city, by reason of false opinions, things can be believed or worshiped which have no real existence either in the world or outside of it. But the theater and city go together. Whoever saw a theater except in a city? It was the city that started the theater, and its only purpose was the representation of plays on the stage. But, what are such representations apart from the gods? This brings us back to the beings which are described with such skill in Varro's books.

Chapter 6

Marcus Varro, you may be 'the most brilliant' man of your age and 'undoubtedly the most learned.' Still, you are a man, not God. You have not even been raised by the Spirit of God to see truly and to tell freely the nature of the divine. Nevertheless, you see clearly enough to separate what is divine from the silly imaginings of men. Yet, you are afraid to denounce popular opinions which are false, and official traditions which are shams, even though you know in your heart that they are repugnant to what is divine and even to such divinity as our poor human intelligence discerns in the elements of the world. This is clear from your own constant references to these opinions and from the tone of all the writings of your friends.

Your human gifts, however remarkable, do not help you here. In straits like these, human learning, however broad and deep, is of no avail. Your heart is with the God of nature, but your head bows where the state wills. You pour out revenge by openly attacking the gods of mythology but, willy-nilly, what you spill falls on the state divinities, too. You say that the mythical and political gods are at home on the stage and in the cities, while the natural gods are at home in the world. But, your point is that the world was made by God, but theaters and cities by men, and that the same gods who are adored in the temples are derided on the stage, and the same gods to whom sacrifice is offered have plays written in their honor.

It would have been more like a gentleman and a scholar to have divided the gods into those which are natural and those which were introduced by men, and to say of these latter that the account given by the poets differs from that of the priests, but that both accounts are so close in the fellowship of falsehood as to delight the demons whose only battle is with the teaching of truth.

I shall discuss 'natural' theology later; omitting it for the moment, I merely ask: Is anyone willing to ask or hope for eternal life from the mythical gods on the stage or the civic gods in the comic shows?

God forbid—may the true God save men from so gross and insane a sacrilege! Just imagine asking eternal life from gods who are pleased and placated by plays which rehearse their own sins. I should think that no one is so irrational and so irreligious as to dance on the edge of such madness. No, neither by mythical nor by political theology does anyone obtain eternal life. The former sows filthy fancies about the gods; the latter reaps by keeping them alive. The one spreads lies, and the other gathers them up; the one belittles divinity with imaginary sins and the other represents this wickedness and calls it public worship; the one puts into song the unmentionable imaginings of men and the other consecrates such things for the festivals of the gods; the one sings sins and crimes and the other loves them; whatever the one discovers or invents the other approves and enjoys.

Both theologies are a disgrace and both should be condemned, but, while the theatrical theology merely teaches turpitude in public, the popular theology wears it like a jewel. Imagine looking for eternal life in places where our brief and passing life is so polluted! If the company of wicked men can so poison our life, once they have won a way into our hearts and minds, what should we say of fellowship with devils who are worshiped by their own wickedness? The truer the wickedness, the worse for the devils; and, the more it is slanderous, the worse for our worship.

I know that some who read what I am writing and are ignorant of things as they are will imagine that only those things in the celebration of such gods are shocking, ridiculous, and unworthy of the divine majesty which are sung by poets and acted on the stage, while the worship of the priests, unlike that of the actors, is pure and free from impropriety. If this were so, no one would ever have thought that dirty plays should be used to honor the gods, and still less would the gods themselves have ordered them to be played. The fact is that no one is ashamed to worship the gods by such plays in the theaters, because the very same things take place in the temples.

The conclusion is that when Varro tried to distinguish political theology from the mythical and natural, he merely meant that it was something fashioned out of the other two rather than a third, distinct, and separate thing. It was a saying of his that what the poets write is too low for the people to follow and that what the philosophers think is too high for the people to pry into. 'Although they are different, much has been borrowed from both and put to the account of the people. Hence,' he says, 'I shall describe what is common to both along with what is proper to political theology—although this should rely more on the alliance of the philosophers than on that of the poets.' Is there, then, no alliance with the poets? The fact is that in another place he says that, in regard to the genealogies of the gods, the people lean more to the poets than to the philosophers. In the one place he is talking of what ought to be; in the other, of what actually is. He makes the point that philosophers write for our instructions, while poets write for our amusement. He implies that the people ought not to follow the poets when they write about the crimes of the gods —although they amuse both the people and the gods. He insists that the poets write to amuse, not to instruct. They write such things as the gods like and the people like to look at.

Chapters 7-10

The poetical and political theologies described by Varro are further outlined and compared. Both types are subject to criticism. Even Varro and Seneca offer frank criticisms of sacrilegious pagan practices.

Chapter 11

Seneca included among the other reprehensible superstitions of political theology the sacred institutions of the Hebrews, especially their Sabbaths. The Jews, he said, served no good purpose by resting every seventh day, since they lost nearly a seventh part of their whole lives and must neglect many matters calling for immediate attention. His attitude toward the Christians was neutral, although they were then much hated by the Jews. He did not dare to praise them counter to the established tradition of his country, or, so it would seem, to condemn them counter to his conscience.

He writes as follows in regard to the Hebrews: 'The ways of those dreadful people have taken deeper and deeper root and are spreading throughout the whole world. They have imposed their customs on their conquerors.' There is a note of wonder in these words, and, little as he knew it, a movement of grace inspired him to add, in plain words, what he thought of the true character of those institutions. He says: 'The Jewish people know the reason for all their rites, but most of our people merely go through the motions, without knowing why.'

In regard to the tradition of the Jews, I must discuss, in a later part of this work certain points which I have touched on elsewhere, particularly in my debates with the Manichaeans: why and how far these rites were instituted by divine authority, and, later, after the people of God had been given the revelation of the mystery of eternal life, at the proper time and by the same authority, why they were abrogated.

Chapter 12

We have now seen that there are three kinds of theology, called by the Greeks mythical, physical, and political, and which may be called in Latin fabulous, natural, and civil. And we have seen that there is no hope of eternal life to be derived either from the fabulous system, which even the worshipers of the many false gods openly criticize, or from the civil, which includes the fabulous as one of its parts and which is like, or even worse than, the part. If any reader feels that enough has not been said on these points in the present Book, let him read what has been written above, particularly in Book IV on God as the Giver of happiness.

For, to whom—if not to Felicity alone—should men who want eternal life dedicate themselves, if, indeed, Felicity were divine. But, since happiness is not a goddess, but a gift of God, to what God save the Giver of happiness should we consecrate ourselves? For, we love with religious charity that eternal life where there is a true and complete beatitude. I think, from what I have said so far, that no one can imagine that the Giver of happiness is any of those gods who are worshiped with such indecent rites, and are more indecently angry when they are not so worshiped, and who thus show themselves to be nothing but unclean spirits.

Further, how could anyone give us eternal life who cannot even make us happy? And, by eternal life I mean a life where there is happiness without end. For, if a soul lives in eternal pains, in which those unclean spirits are to be punished, that is eternal death rather than eternal life. There can be no greater or worse death than where death itself never dies. Since it is the nature of the soul that it cannot be without some sort of life, having been created immortal, it is the depth of death for it to be alienated from the life of God in an eternity of pain. Of eternal life, that is to say, of life that is happy without end, only He is the Giver who gives genuine beatitude. This is something which, as has been shown, those gods who are worshiped in accordance with the theology of the state cannot give. And, therefore, it is useless to worship them with a view to temporal and terrestrial benefits (as I have shown in the previous five Books) and still more useless to worship them with a view to eternal life which begins after death (as I have shown in this Book—with supporting arguments from the others). However, old habits have deep roots, and there may be some who feel I have said too little to convince them to disavow and give up this way of worship. I must commend to their attention a subsequent Book which, with the help of God, I hope to join to this one.

BOOK VII

Criticisms of Pagan Natural Theology

Preface

I HAVE BEEN TRYING to the best of my power to root out and
get rid of those depraved and inveterate opinions which, by a
long-lasting error of mankind, have taken such deep and tena-
cious roots in unenlightened minds, and which are so opposed
to religious truth. Only the true God can effect such a purpose;
I have been trying to cooperate, in however small a degree,
with Him and with His grace. I know that many whose minds
are keener will feel that what I have written is more than
enough for the purpose, but I must ask them to bear with me
a little longer and, for the sake of others, not to think superfluous what they do not need themselves.

The issue at stake is very great. What I want to bring out
is that, although we depend on the true and truly holy Divinity
for such things as are needed to support our weakness in this
present life, nevertheless, we should not seek and worship God
for the sake of the passing cloud of this mortal life, but for
the sake of that happy life which cannot be other than everlasting.

Chapters 1-4

*The functions of twenty 'select' gods, in Varro's theology,
are here discussed. Their duties and prerogatives are confused
and mutually antagonistic. The whole teaching is ridiculous.*

Chapter 5

We must now turn to those naturalist interpretations by
which the pagans seek to hide the disgrace of their low error
under the appearance of a high doctrine. Varro's first intimation of these interpretations is when he says that the ancients
made images, insignia, and ornaments of the gods so that those

who looked at them in the light of a doctrine for initiates[1] could see with their mind and contemplate the soul of the world and all its parts, that is to say, the true gods. When pagans made images of the gods that looked like men their idea was that the spirit of mortals which is in the human body is very like the spirit which is immortal. It is much the same as when vessels are set out to symbolize gods and when a wine jug is placed in the temple of Bacchus to signify wine. The container symbolizes what it contained. So, too, by means of an image with a human form, the rational soul can be symbolized, since by nature it is contained in a body as in a vessel, and they imply that god (or the gods) is of the same nature as a rational soul. Such are the mysteries (or the doctrines of the initiates) which our learned Varro penetrated and which he brings out into the light for the rest of men.

But, surely, we must appeal from the intelligence of Varro, intoxicated by esotericism, to the sober prudence of his ordinary insight,[2] as when he admits, first, that those who first set up images of the gods for the people 'took away their fear but added to their error,'[3] and, second, that the ancient Romans had a purer reverence for the gods when they had no images. These were his authorities for daring to speak against the later Romans. For, likely enough, if the early Romans had worshiped images, Varro would have been too afraid to mention the feeling against setting up images—true as that fact was—and his account of the dangerous and empty figments of this esoteric doctrine would have been more lengthy and lofty than ever.

Poor man! His spirit so acute and cultivated failed to pierce through the esoteric doctrines to the true God, by whom, and not with whom, that spirit was made, and of whom it was a creature, not a part. That God is not the soul of all things but the maker of all souls; by His light alone the soul can be happy, if it is not ungrateful for His grace.

The following pages reveal what those esoteric doctrines are and what they are worth. In the meantime, this great scholar

[1] *Doctrinae mysteria.*
[2] *Sed, o homo acutissime, num in istis doctrinae mysteriis illam prudentiam perdidisti, qua tibi sobrie visum est . . .*
[3] Cf. Bk. 4.31, here omitted.

professes to believe that the soul and the elements of the universe are the true gods. Thus, it is clear that within the scope of his theology, that is to say, the natural theology to which he gives the palm, a place could be found for the nature of the rational soul. Actually, he says very little about natural theology in his last book dealing with the select gods; but from it we shall be able to see whether it is possible, by means of naturalist interpretations, to bring the state religion into accord with natural theology. For, if that should be possible, all theology will be natural. In that case, why all the need to distinguish with such care political theology from natural theology? If, however, the distinction is valid, not even the natural theology, which he likes so much, is true, for the reason that it reaches only as far as the soul, but not as far as the true God, who made the soul. And, if natural theology is not true, then the political is of still less value and even falser, since it deals more with merely corporeal natures. This is clear from the interpretations which were so beautifully and clearly elaborated. Some of these I must deal with now.

Chapter 6

In his preface on natural theology, Varro says that he holds that God is the soul of the universe or cosmos (to use the Greek word) and that the cosmos itself is God. Yet, just as we call a wise man wise in virtue of his soul, although he is composed of both body and soul, so Varro calls the universe divine in virtue of its soul, although the cosmos is made up of a body and soul.

Here, Varro seems, in some way, to admit that there is one God, but, in order to bring in many gods, he adds that the cosmos is divided into two parts—the heavens and the earth—and that the heavens, in turn, are divided into two parts—the ether and the air. So, too, the earth is divided into two parts —water and land. The highest of all these parts is the ether; the next is the air; the third is water; the lowest is the earth. All these four parts are permeated with souls, which are immortal souls in the ether and the air, and are mortal souls in water and land.

From the highest circle of the heavens down to the circle

of the moon, the planets, and stars are ethereal souls. These celestial gods are objects, not merely of thought, but of our eyes. Between the circle of the moon and that of the highest cloud and the winds, the soul is aerial, and it can be seen with the mind only, not with the eyes. These souls are called heroes, lares, genii. This is a brief summary of his preface on natural theology. It satisfied many other philosophers besides Varro. All this I must discuss at some length as soon as, with God's help, I shall have finished dealing with the select gods—which still are a part of political theology.

Chapter 7

Varro begins with Janus. Who is Janus? Janus is the cosmos. No one can complain of the brevity and clarity of that answer. But, why are all beginnings said to belong to Janus and all endings to another god whose name is Terminus? It was to these two gods that the months of January and February were dedicated, when they were added to the original ten, beginning in March and ending in December. Hence, they say, the festival Terminalia[1] is celebrated in February, which gets its name from Februm, the sacred purification.

Are we to say, then, that the beginnings of things belong to the universe or to Janus and that the endings do not belong to him, so that a second god has to be put in charge of these? Why, then, do we admit that all the things that are said to begin in the cosmos end there also? And, if only half the work is done by Janus, what is the use of giving him two faces on his statues? Surely, they would have a neater interpretation of the two-faced god if they called him both Janus and Terminus and linked one of the faces with beginnings and the other with endings. Anyone who has a work to do must keep these both in view. Wherever there is motion, one must look to the beginnings of the action if one is to foresee the end. That is why an intention looking to the future must be connected with a memory looking to the past. For, no one can finish what he has forgotten that he began.

It is possible that they gave to Janus only the power over

[1] Celebrated on February 23.

beginnings because they held that the happy life began in this world but could only be perfected beyond it. But, in that case, they would have put Terminus before Janus and would not have excluded him from the select gods. In any case, even as things are, with the beginnings and endings of purely temporal things being represented by these two gods, more honor was due to Terminus. There is more joy whenever a thing is finished; whereas beginnings are fraught with worry until the end is reached. When we make a beginning, it is the ending which we seek, intend, expect, and long for. There is never joy until a thing begun is ended.

Chapters 8–28

Further precisions are given concerning the worship of divinities such as Janus, Jupiter, Pecunia, Saturn, Mercury, Mars, and Apollo. Obscene rites in honor of Bacchus and the Great Mother are described in some detail. Attempts at a naturalistic revision of paganism are not successful. Varro produced a theology full of learned errors.

Chapter 29

There is nothing which the philosophical theories of pagan theology referred to natural phenomena which could not, without a shadow of sacrilege, have been better referred to the true God, the Author of nature, the Creator of every soul and of every body. It could have been done in some such formula as the following. We worship God. We do not adore heaven and earth, the two essential parts of the universe; nor do we adore any world-spirit nor any spirits diffused throughout any kind of living beings. We adore God who made heaven and earth and all that they contain, God who made every kind of soul, from the lowest that lives without sensation and intellection through the sentient up to the soul that can think.

Chapter 30

At this point, I must mention various operations of the one true God. It was because of these that the pagan philosophers, who were making a serious effort to interpret the indecent and immoral mysteries, made for themselves so many false gods. First, then, it is the God we worship who constituted, for each of the natures He created, an origin and purpose of its being and powers of action. He holds in His hands the causes of things, knowing them all and connecting them all. It is He who is the source of all energy in seeds, and He who put rational souls, or spirits, into the living beings He selected, and He who gave us the gifts of speech and language.

The God we worship chose certain spirits and gave them the power of foresight, and through them He makes prophecies. To others He gave the gift of healing. He controls the beginnings, progress, and endings of wars, when they are needed for the punishment or reformation of mankind. He rules the universal element of fire, so vehement and violent, yet so necessary for the equilibrium of nature. He is the Creator and Ruler of all the water of the universe. He made the sun, the brightest of all luminous bodies, and He gave it an appropriate energy and motion.

His sovereignty and power reach to the lowest things. All things that grow and sustain animal life, both liquids and solids, He produced and made appropriate for different natures. He gave us the earth, the fertility of soil, and foods for men and beasts. All causes, primary and secondary, come within His knowledge and control. He gave to the moon its phases, and in the air and on the ground He provided ways for traveling. He endowed the human intelligences which He created with a knowledge of the arts and sciences which help both life and nature. He instituted mating and marriage for the propagation of life, and to communities of men He gave the boon of fire, to keep them warm and give them light and make their efforts easier.

Such, at least, are the activities which the acute and learned Varro sought to distribute among the select gods, by appealing to those so-called natural interpretations, some of which are traditional and some of which he made up out of his own head. The truth is that all these actions and energies belong to the one true God, who is really a God, who is wholly present everywhere, is confined by no frontiers and bound by no hindrances, is indivisible and immutable, and, though His nature has no need of either heaven or of earth, He fills them both with His presence and His power.

Yet, the Creator of every nature has so ordained that each of His creatures is permitted to have and to exercise powers of its own. Although without Him they could not exist, their essence is different from His. He does many things by the ministry of angels, but their only source of beatitude is God Himself. And He Himself, and not the angels, is the source of men's beatitude, even though He sometimes uses angels as messengers to men. It is from this one true God that we look for everlasting life.

Chapter 31

I have already said something of the general blessings of God, which, in the natural course of things, come to the good and the bad alike. However, beyond this bounty, He has reserved for the good a special sign of His great love. We can never sufficiently thank Him for the gifts of nature: that we exist and are alive, that we can enjoy the sight of earth and sky, that we have a reasoning mind by which we can seek Him who has made all these things. Yet, for the greater gifts of grace there are not hearts enough or tongues enough in all the world even to try to thank Him. For, when we were burdened and broken by our sins, and our minds were turned from His light and blinded by the love of the darkness of iniquity, He did not leave us to ourselves, but sent to us His Word, who is His only Son, so that, by His birth and passion in the flesh He assumed for our salvation, we might learn how highly God esteemed our human nature, and that we might be cleansed from all our sins by His unique Sacrifice and, by His Spirit, have Love poured into our hearts, so that, with all our warring over, we might come to everlasting rest in the supreme blessedness of gazing on His face.

Chapter 32

This mystery of eternal life, from the beginnings of the human race, has been announced to all whom it concerned by messengers of God, using outward signs and sacred symbols appropriate to particular periods. A little later, as though to enact this sacred Mystery, the Hebrew people were gathered into a single community in which all that was to happen from the coming of Christ until our day and beyond our day was foretold by men, some of whom had knowledge and some of whom had not. Still later, this nation was dispersed among the Gentiles to carry with them the witness of the Scriptures in which the future Redemption in Christ was foretold.

Thus, all that was fulfilled in Christ is being fulfilled before our eyes, and all that remains still to be fulfilled was not only preannounced in spoken prophecies and in the precepts of moral and religious life as contained in Holy Scripture, but was likewise symbolized by the Jewish rites, priesthood, tabernacle or temple, altars, sacrifices, ceremonies, festivals, and all the rest that belongs to the service which is due to God and which in Greek is properly called *latreía*—and all was with a view to the eternal life of those who believe in Christ.

Chapter 33

It was by means of the true religion alone that it could be made manifest that the gods of the pagans were nothing but unclean spirits who used the memory of people departed or the images of earthly creatures to get themselves reckoned as gods and who then rejoiced with proud impurity that divine honors should be paid to such disgusting and indecent things, all the while hating to see men's souls turn to the true God. From their horrible and hateful domination a man is delivered by faith in Him who showed us the way to rise by going to a depth of humility as great as the height of pride from which they fell.

To this category of unclean spirits belong not only the lesser gods of which I have said so much, and many, many other gods of the same sort among the various peoples of the world, but likewise those gods who were selected to form a sort of Senate of the gods. From what I have just been reporting, they were obviously chosen more for the notoriety of their wickedness than for the nobility of their virtues. By trying to give a meaning to their mysteries in terms of the phenomena of nature, Varro seeks to lend dignity to indecency. But, of course, the facts of nature do not square with the fictions of the gods, and Varro fails to make the realities and the rites agree, for the simple reason that the phenomena of nature are not, as he thinks—or wants to have thought—the real source from which the rites were drawn.

The best that can be said of Varro's interpretations or of any interpretations of this sort is that, although they have nothing to do with the true God and with the eternal life which is the very purpose of religion, they do help to mitigate the offense given by the mysteries, by suggesting that some ill-understood indecency or absurdity becomes clear in the light of some correlative phenomenon in nature. And this is what Varro did in regard to some of the stage plays and temple mysteries, though he succeeded rather in damning the temples for being like the theaters than in absolving the theaters for copying the temples. However, Varro tried as best he could to temper the outrage done to men's sense of decency by interpreting disgusting scenes as symbols of causes at work in nature.

Chapters 34–35

Varro's unedifying story of the origin of pagan ceremonies and its eventual concealment by the Roman Senate show the inferiority of polytheism as a religion.

BOOK VIII

Classical Philosophy and Refined Paganism

Chapter 1

I MUST NOW TURN to a matter which calls for much deeper thought than was needed to resolve the issues raised in the previous Books. I mean natural theology. Unlike the poetical theology of the stage which flaunts the crimes of the gods and the political theology of the city which publicizes their evil desires, and both of which reveal them as dangerous demons rather than deities, natural theology cannot be discussed with men in the street but only with philosophers, that is, as the name implies, with lovers of wisdom.[1]

I may add that, since divine truth and scripture clearly teach us that God, the Creator of all things, is Wisdom, a true philosopher will be a lover of God. That does not mean that all who answer to the name are really in love with genuine wisdom, for it is one thing to be and another to be called a philosopher. And, therefore, from all the philosophers whose teachings I have learned from books I shall select only those with whom it would not be improper to discuss this subject.

I shall not bother in this work to refute all the errors of all the philosophers, but only such as pertain to theology—which term from its Greek derivation I take to mean a study of the divine nature. My only purpose is to challenge the opinions of those philosophers who, while admitting that there is a God who concerns himself with human affairs, claim that, since the worship of this one unchangeable God is not sufficient to attain happiness even after death, lesser gods, admittedly created and directed by this supreme God, should also be reverenced.

I must say that such philosophers were nearer to the truth than Varro was.[2] His idea of natural theology embraced at most the universe and the world-soul. They, on the contrary, acknowledged a God who transcends the nature of every kind

[1] Cf. Cicero, *Tusculan Disputations* 5.3,8,9.
[2] Marcus Terentius Varro (116–27 B.C.); cf. *City of God* 6.2.

of soul, a God who created the visible cosmos of heaven and earth, and the spirit of every living creature, and who, by the communication of His own immutable and immaterial light, makes blessed the kind of rational and intellectual soul which man possesses.

Even the most superficial student will recognize in these men the Platonic philosophers, so named after their master, Plato.[3] I shall speak briefly about Plato's ideas, in so far as they are relevant to the matter in hand, but first I must review the opinions of his predecessors in the field of philosophy.

Chapter 2

The legacy of literature written in the universally admired Greek language records two schools of philosophy. They are, first, the Italian, established in that part of Italy formerly known as Magna Graecia; and second, the Ionian, in that country which is now called Greece. Pythagoras of Samos[1] is said to be the founder of the Italian school and also the originator of the word philosophy. Before his time, any person of outstanding achievement was called a sage. But when Pythagoras, who considered it arrogance to call one's self wise, was asked his profession, he replied that he was a philosopher, that is to say, a man in pursuit of, or in love with, wisdom.

Thales of Miletus,[2] who initiated the Ionian School, was one of the celebrated Seven Wise Men. While the remaining six were distinguished by balanced lives and moral teachings, Thales took up the study of nature and committed the results of his researches to writing. He won particular applause by his mastery of astronomical calculations and by his predictions of solar and lunar eclipses.[3] His deliberate purpose in this was to found a school that would survive him. His main theory was that the primary stuff of all things is water, and that from this principle originated the elements, the cosmos and everything which the world produced. As far as he was concerned,

---

[3] c.428–c.348 B.C.

[1] 582–c.507 B.C.   [2] c.624–c.548 B.C.
[3] Thales' knowledge of astronomy is recorded by Aristotle, *Politics* 1.11.8–10, and by Cicero, *De divinatione* 1.49,111.

nothing of all this universe, so marvelous to gaze upon, was directed by divine intelligence.

His disciple and successor, Anaximander,[4] proposed a new cosmological theory. For him, there could be no one ultimate element of all things such as water; rather, each thing is derived from principles of its own. Hence, he held, the number of principles is infinite, and from these arise uncounted worlds and all that they produce. And, in an endless succession of dissolution and becoming, no one world endures longer than its period permits. Like Thales, he found no place for any divine direction in the processes of nature.

Anaximander's disciple, Anaximenes,[5] believed that all cosmic energy is derived from air, which he considered infinite. He neither denied nor ignored the gods; nevertheless, he taught that they were creatures of the air and not its creators. His pupil, Anaxagoras,[6] realizing that divine spirit was the cause of all visible things, held that the divine mind, using infinite matter, consisting of unlike particles, made each particular thing out of its own kind of like particles.

Diogenes,[7] another follower of Anaximenes, held that air was the ultimate element of all things, but that nothing could be produced from it without the agency of the divine reason, which permeated it. Anaxagoras was followed by his pupil Archelaus.[8] He, too, asserted that everything in the universe was composed of like particles, which, however, were informed by intelligence. This mind, by causing the conjunction and dissolution of the eternal bodies or particles, was the source of all movements. Archelaus is said to have taught Socrates,[9] the master of Plato. This brief review has been but a preparation for the discussion of Plato's philosophy.

Chapter 3

To Socrates goes the credit of being the first one to channel the whole of philosophy into an ethical system for the reforma-

---

[4] c.611–547 B.C.

[6] c.500–428 B.C.

[8] 5th cent. B.C.

[5] 6th cent. B.C.

[7] 5th cent. B.C.

[9] 469–399 B.C.

tion and regulation of morals.[1] His predecessors without exception had applied themselves particularly to physics or natural science. I do not think that it can be definitely decided just why Socrates chose to follow this course. It has been suggested that he did so because he had become wearied of obscure and uncertain investigations, and preferred to turn his mind to a clean-cut objective, to that secret of human happiness which seems to have been the sole purpose of all philosophical research. Others have claimed, more kindly, that he did not think it right for minds darkened with earthly desires to reach out beyond their limits to the realm of the divine.

Socrates realized that his predecessors had been seeking the origin of all things, but he believed that these first and highest causes could be found only in the will of the single and supreme Divinity and, therefore, could be comprehended only by a mind purified from passion. Hence his conclusion, that he must apply himself to the acquisition of virtue, so that his mind, freed from the weight of earthly desires, might, by its own natural vigor, lift itself up to eternal realities and, with purified intelligence, contemplate the very nature of that immaterial and immutable light in which the causes[2] of all created natures abidingly dwell. Nevertheless, with his marvelous combination of wit and words, pungency and politeness, and with his trick of confessing ignorance and concealing knowledge he used to tease and poke fun at the folly of ignoramuses who talked as though they knew the answers to those moral problems in which he seemed wholly absorbed.

The result was that he incurred their enmity. He was falsely accused and condemned to death. However, the very city of Athens that had publicly condemned him began publicly to mourn his loss, and the wrath of the people was so turned against his two accusers that one[3] of them was killed by an angry mob and the other[4] escaped a similar death only by voluntary and perpetual exile.

Socrates was thus so highly distinguished both in life and

---

[1] Cf. Cicero, *Tusculan Disputations* 5.4,10.

[2] Plato speaks of his 'ideas' as causes; cf., e.g., *Phaedo,* p. 100.

[3] Meletus, prosecutor in the trial of Socrates.

[4] Anytus, the politician who remained in the background but instigated Meletus to carry on the prosecution.

in death that he left behind him numerous disciples. They
rivaled one another in zealous discussions of those ethical problems where there is question of the supreme good and, hence,
of human happiness.

In his discussions, Socrates had a way of proposing and defending his theories and then demolishing them. No one could
make out exactly what he believed. Consequently, each of his
followers picked what he preferred and sought the supreme
good in his heart's desire.

Now the truth is that the supreme good is that which, when
attained, makes all men happy. Yet, so varied in regard to
this good were the views of the Socratics that it seems hardly
credible that all of them were followers of one and the same
master. Some, like Aristippus,[5] claimed that pleasure was
the highest good; others, like Antisthenes,[6] virtue. The men
and their views are so numerous and varied that it would be
irksome to mention them all.

Chapter 4

Of the pupils of Socrates, Plato was so remarkable for his
brilliance that he has deservedly outshone all the rest. He was
born in Athens of a good family and by his marvelous ability
easily surpassed all his fellow disciples. Realizing, however,
that neither his own genius nor Socratic training was adequate
to evolve a perfect system of philosophy, he traveled far and
wide to wherever there was any hope of gaining some valuable
addition to knowledge. Thus, in Egypt he mastered the lore
which was there esteemed. From there he went to lower Italy,
famous for the Pythagorean School, and there successfully im-
bibed from eminent teachers all that was then in vogue in
Italian philosophy.

However, Plato's special affection was for his old master—
so much so that in practically all the Dialogues he makes
Socrates, with all his charm, the mouthpiece not only of his
own moral arguments but of all that Plato learned from others
or managed to discover himself.

Now, the pursuit of wisdom follows two avenues—action

[5] *c.*435–*c.*366 B.C.
[6] *c.*445–*c.*365 B.C.

and contemplation. Thus, one division of philosophy may be called active; the other part, contemplative. The former deals with the conduct of life; that is to say, with the cultivation of morals. Contemplative philosophy considers natural causality and truth as such. Socrates excelled in practical wisdom; Pythagoras favored contemplation, and to this he applied his whole intelligence.

It is to Plato's praise that he combined both in a more perfect philosophy, and then divided the whole into three parts: first, moral philosophy which pertains to action; second, natural philosophy whose purpose is contemplation; third, rational philosophy which discriminates between truth and error.[1] Although this last is necessary for both action and contemplation, it is contemplation especially which claims to reach a vision of the truth. Hence, this threefold division in no way invalidates the distinction whereby action and contemplation are considered the constituent elements of the whole of philosophy. Just what Plato's position was in each of these three divisions—that is to say, just what he knew or believed to be the end of all action, the cause of all nature, the light of all reason—I think it would be rash to affirm and would take too long to discuss at length.

Plato was so fond of following the well-known habit of his master of dissimulating his knowledge or opinions that in Plato's own works (where Socrates appears as a speaker) it is difficult to determine just what views he held even on important questions. However, of the views which are set forth in his writings, whether his own or those of others which seemed to have pleased him, a few must be recalled and included here. In some places, Plato is on the side of the true religion which our faith accepts and defends. At other times he seems opposed; for example, on the respective merits of monotheism and polytheism in relation to genuine beatitude after death.

Perhaps this may be said of the best disciples of Plato—of those who followed most closely and understood most clearly the teachings of a master rightly esteemed above all other pagan philosophers—that they have perceived, at least, these truths about God: that in Him is to be found the cause of

[1] Cf. Cicero, *Acad. Post.* 1.5,19–21.

all being, the reason of all thinking, the rule of all living. The first of these truths belongs to natural, the second to rational, the third to moral philosophy.

Now, if man was created so that by his highest faculty he might attain to the highest of all realities, that is, to the one, true and supreme God, apart from whom no nature exists, no teaching is true, no conduct is good, then let us seek Him in whom all we find is real, know Him in whom all we contemplate is true, love Him in whom all things for us are good.

Chapter 5

If, then, Plato defined a philosopher as one who knows, loves and imitates the God in whom he finds his happiness, there is little need to examine further. For, none of the other philosophers has come so close to us as the Platonists have,[1] and, therefore, we may neglect the others. Take for example, the theology of the stage. It beguiles the minds of the pagans with the crimes of the gods. Or, take political theology, according to which impure demons under the name of gods seduce the populace who are slaves of earthly pleasures, and demand human errors as divine honors for themselves. They excite in their worshipers an impure passion to watch the demons sinning on the stage as though this were an act of worship, and they are even more satisfied than the spectators with the plays that exhibit their human passions. Proper as such rites may seem in places of worship, they are debased by connection with the obscenity of the theaters; while the filth of the stage loses its foulness by comparison with the rites that take place in the temples.

Nor is the theology of Varro any better in its interpretation of these rites as symbolic of heaven and earth and the origins and movements of mortal affairs. The fact is, they do not denote what he tries to insinuate. His fancy gets the better of the truth. And, even were he right, it would still be wrong for a rational soul to worship as a god something which, in the order of nature, is in a lower category or to submit as to gods to those very things over which the true God has put men in charge.

[1] Cf. St. Augustine, *De vera religione* 7.

Finally, the Platonic theology is superior to those revealing writings about the sacred rites which Numa Pompilius[2] had buried with himself in order to hide them and which, when turned up by a plough, the Senate ordered to be burned. And to do justice to Numa, we should include in this class the letter that Alexander of Macedon[3] wrote to his mother, telling her what had been revealed to him by Leo, an Egyptian high priest, to the effect that all the gods, major as well as minor, were nothing more than mortal men—not only Picus and Faunus, Aeneas and Romulus, Hercules and Aesculapius, Bacchus, son of Semele, the twin sons of Tyndareus,[4] and such like mortals who are reckoned as gods, but even the greater gods whom Cicero in his *Tusculan Disputations*[5] alludes to without mentioning their names; that is, Jupiter, Juno, Saturn, Vulcan, Vesta, and many others whom Varro attempts to identify with the parts or elements of the world. Fearful that he had revealed a great mystery, Leo begged Alexander to have his mother burn the message conveyed to her.

Certainly, all such fancies of both the mythical and civil theologies should yield to the Platonists who acknowledged the true God as the author of being, the light of truth and the giver of blessedness. So, too, those philosophers, the materialists who believe that the ultimate principles of nature are corporeal, should yield to those great men who had knowledge of so great a God. Such were Thales, who found the cause and principle of things in water, Anaximenes in air, the Stoics in fire, Epicurus[6] in atoms, that is, minute indivisible and imperceptible corpuscles. And so of the rest, whose names it is needless to mention, who maintained that bodies, simple or compound, animate or inanimate, but nevertheless material, were the root of all reality.

The Epicureans, for example, believed that life could be produced from lifeless matter. Others taught that both animate and inanimate things derive from a living principle but that this principle must be as material as the things themselves. The Stoics claimed that fire, one of the four material

[2] Cf. Bk. 7.34, here omitted.   [3] Cf. below, 8.27; 12.11.
[4] Castor and Pollux.   [5] 1.13,29.
[6] 341–270 B.C.

elements of this visible world, had life and intelligence, that it was the creator of the universe and all within it; in fact, that it was God.

Now, philosophers of this type could think only about such matters as their sense-bound minds suggested to them. Yet they have within themselves something they have never seen and they can see in their imagination, without looking at it, an external object which they have previously seen. Now, whatever can be so imagined in the mind's eye is certainly not a body but only the likeness of a body, and that power of the mind which can perceive this likeness is itself neither a body nor an image of a body. Moreover, that faculty which perceives and judges whether this likeness is beautiful or ugly is certainly superior to the object judged.

Now, this faculty is a man's reason, the essence of his rational soul, which is certainly not material, since the likeness of a body which is seen and judged in the mind of a thinking person is not material. The soul, then, cannot be one of the four elements out of which the visible, material cosmos is composed—earth, water, air, and fire. And if our mind is not material, how can God the Creator of the soul be material?

As I said before, let all such philosophers give place to the Platonists. That goes for those, too, who were ashamed to acknowledge a material god, yet thought that men's souls were of the same nature as His—so little were they moved by the fact of a mutability in the soul that it would be unthinkable to attribute to the nature of God. Their answer to this difficulty was that the soul is unalterable in itself but is affected by the body. They might as well have said that the flesh is wounded because of the body, but in itself is invulnerable. The fact is that what is immutable can be changed by nothing. But, if a thing can be changed by a body, it can be changed by something and, therefore, cannot rightly be called immutable.

Chapter 6

The Platonic philosophers, then, so deservedly considered superior to all the others in reputation and achievement, well understood that no body could be God and, therefore, in order to find Him, they rose beyond all material things. Convinced that no mutable reality could be the Most High, they transcended every soul and spirit subject to change in their search for God. They perceived that no determining form by which any mutable being is what it is—whatever be the reality, mode or nature of that form—could have any existence apart from Him who truly exists because His existence is immutable.

From this it follows that neither the whole universe, with its frame, figures, qualities and ordered movement, all the elements and bodies arranged in the heavens and on earth, nor any life—whether merely nourishing and preserving as in trees, or both vegetative and sensitive as in animals, or which is also intellectual as in man, or which needs no nourishment but merely preserves, feels and knows as in angels—can have existence apart from Him whose existence is simple and indivisible. For, in God, being is not one thing and living another—as though He could be and not be living. Nor in God is it one thing to live and another to understand—as though He could live without understanding. Nor in Him is it one thing to know and another to be blessed—as though He could know and not be blessed. For, in God, to live, to know, to be blessed is one and the same as to be.

The Platonists have understood that God, by reason of His immutability and simplicity, could not have been produced from any existing thing, but that He Himself made all those things that are. They argued that whatever exists is either matter or life; that life is superior to matter; that the appearance of a body is sensible, whereas the form of life is intelligible. Hence, they preferred intelligible form to sensible appearance. We call things sensible which can be perceived by sight and bodily touch.

If there is any loveliness discerned in the lineaments of the body, or beauty in the movement of music and song, it is the mind that makes this judgment. This means that there must be within the mind a superior form, one that is immaterial and independent of sound and space and time. However, the mind itself is not immutable, for, if it were, all minds would judge alike concerning sensible forms. Actually, a clever mind judges more aptly than the stupid one; a skilled one better than one unskilled; an experienced one better than one inexperienced. Even the same mind, once it improves, judges better than it did before.

Undoubtedly, anything susceptible of degrees is mutable, and for this reason, the most able, learned and experienced philosophers readily concluded that the first form of all could not be in any of these things in which the form was clearly mutable. Once they perceived various degrees of beauty in both body and mind, they realized that, if all form were lacking, their very existence would end. Thus, they argued that there must be some reality in which the form was ultimate, immutable and, therefore, not susceptible of degrees. They rightly concluded that only a reality unmade from which all other realities originate could be the ultimate principle of things.

So that what is known about God, God Himself manifested to them, since 'his invisible attributes are clearly seen by them —his everlasting power also and divinity—being understood through the things that are made.'[1] By Him, also all visible and temporal things were created. Enough has been said, I think, concerning what the Platonists call physical or natural philosophy.

Chapter 7

As for the second part of philosophy, logic or rational philosophy, the Platonists are beyond all comparison with those who taught that the criterion of truth is in the bodily senses, and who would have us believe that all knowledge is to be measured and ruled by such doubtful and deceitful testimony. I mean the Epicureans and even the Stoics. For all their passion for adroitness in disputation or, as they would say, dialectics, even this was reckoned a matter of sense perception. They maintained that it was by sensation that the mind conceived those notions (or *ennoiai* as they would say) which are needed for clear definitions and, hence, for the unification and communication of the whole system of learning and teaching.

When these philosophers quote their famous dictum that only the wise are beautiful, I often wonder by just what bodily

[1] Rom. 1.19–20.

senses they have perceived that beauty, by what kind of fleshy eyes they could have possibly beheld the form and fairness of wisdom.

Certainly, the Platonists, whom we rightly prefer to all others, were able to distinguish what is apprehended by the mind from what is experienced by the senses, without either denying or exaggerating the faculties of sense. As for that light of our minds by which all can be learned, that, they declared, was the very God by whom all things were made.

Chapter 8

The final division is moral philosophy or, to use the Greek name, ethics. It deals with the supreme good, by reference to which all our actions are directed. It is the good we seek for itself and not because of something else and, once it is attained, we seek nothing further to make us happy. This, in fact, is why we call it our end, because other things are desired on account of this *summum bonum*, while it is desired purely for itself.

Now, some philosophers maintained that this happiness-giving good for man arises from the body; others claimed that it has its source in the soul; while a third group held that it derives from both.

All philosophers have realized that man is made up of body and soul and, therefore, that the possibility of his well-being must proceed either from one of these constituents or from both together, the final good, whereby man would be happy, being the one to which all human actions would be referred and beyond which they would seek nothing to which it might be referred.

Hence, those who are said to have added to the list of goods the 'extrinsic' good—such as honor, glory, wealth and so on—did not mean this as though it were a supreme good to be sought for its own sake, but merely as a relative good and one that was good for good men but bad for the wicked.

Thus, those who sought for human good either in man's body or in his mind or in both did not think they had to search outside of man himself to find it. Only those who looked to the body sought it in man's lower nature; those who looked to the soul, in man's higher nature; and the others, in man as a whole; but in every case they sought it only in man himself.

This threefold division of opinion concerning the *summum bonum* resulted, not in three, but in a multitude of philosophical sects and dissensions because of the varying views as to what constituted the good of the body, the good of the soul and the good of the whole man.

The definers of all these defective conclusions should yield to those philosophers who taught that man is never fully blessed, in the enjoyment of either corporal or spiritual good, but only by a fruition in God. This joy in God is not like any pleasure found in physical or intellectual satisfaction. Nor is it such as a friend experiences in the presence of a friend. But, if we are to use any such analogy, it is more like the eye rejoicing in light. Elsewhere, with God's help I shall try to explain the nature of this analogy. For the moment, let it suffice to recall the doctrine of Plato that a virtuous life is the ultimate end of man and that only those attain to it who know and imitate God and find their blessedness wholly in this. Consequently, Plato did not hesitate to say that to philosophize is to love that God whose nature is incorporeal.

From this we infer that the pursuer of wisdom, that is, the philosopher, will only be truly happy when he begins to rejoice in God. Certainly, not every one who delights in what he loves is always blessed, for many are unhappy in loving things they should not love and still more wretched once they begin to enjoy them. On the other hand, no one is really happy until his love ends in fruition. For, even those who love what they should not love do not consider loving but only fruition as the source of their satisfaction.

Who, then, but the very sorriest of persons would deny that a man is really happy who finds fruition in what he loves when what he loves is his true and highest good? Now, for Plato, this true and highest good was God, and, therefore, he calls a philosopher a lover of God, implying that philosophy is a hunt for happiness which ends only when a lover of God reaches fruition in God.

Chapter 9

Philosophers, therefore, of whatever sort who have believed that the true and supreme God is the cause of created things, and the light by which they are known and the good toward which our actions are directed, and that He is the source from which our nature has its origin, our learning truth, our life its happiness—all these we prefer to others and recognize them as our neighbors. It does not matter whether they call themselves —as, perhaps, they should—Platonists, or whether they give their school some other name. Nor need we enquire whether it was only the leaders of the Ionian School—like Plato and his best disciples—who were teachers of these truths, or whether we should include the Italians on account of Pythagoras and the Pythagoreans and, perhaps, others of similar views. For all I know, there may have been men reckoned as wise men or philosophers in other parts of the world who shared these views and doctrines—Atlantic Libyans, Egyptians, Indians, Persians, Chaldeans, Scythians, Gauls, and Spaniards.

Chapter 10

Doubtless, it could happen that a Christian, well versed in ecclesiastical literature, might not be familiar with the name of Platonists nor even know that among Greek-speaking people two distinct schools of philosophy have flourished: the Ionian and the Italian. Nevertheless, he is not so naive as not to know that philosophers look upon themselves as the lovers, if not the possessors, of wisdom; and he is on his guard against materialistic philosophers, who give no thought to the Creator of the world.

The Christian heeds carefully the apostolic admonition which says: 'See to it that no one deceives you by philosophy and vain deceit . . . according to the elements of the world.'[1] But the same Apostle tells him not to decry all as materialistic philosophers, for of some he says: 'What may be known about God is manifest to them. For God has manifested it to them.

[1] Col. 2.8.

For since the creation of the world his invisible attributes are clearly seen—his everlasting power also and divinity—being understood through the things that are made.'[2] And again, speaking to the Athenians, after the magnificent remark about God which so few can appreciate, namely, that 'in Him we live and move and have our being,' he went on to add: 'as indeed some of your own [poets] have said.'[3]

The Christian knows, of course, how to distrust the doctrines of even these latter where they are wrong. Thus, the very Scripture which says that God manifested His invisible attributes to be seen and understood also says that they failed to worship the true God rightly because they rendered to creatures divine honors that were due to Him alone. 'Although they knew God, they did not glorify him as God or give thanks, but became vain in their reasonings, and their senseless minds have been darkened. For while professing to be wise, they have become fools, and they have changed the glory of the incorruptible God for an image made like to corruptible man and to birds and four-footed beasts and creeping things.'[4] Here the Apostle has in mind the Romans, Greeks and Egyptians, all boastful of their renown for wisdom.

This is a matter that I intend to debate with these philosophers later on.[5] Yet we prefer them to all others inasmuch as they agree with us concerning one God, the Creator of the universe, who is not only incorporeal, transcending all corporeal beings, but also incorruptible, surpassing every kind of soul—our source, our light, our goal.

Now, it may happen that the Christian has not studied the works of these philosophers, nor learned to use their terms in disputation. He may not designate that part of philosophy which treats of the investigation of nature as natural (if he speaks Latin) or as physical (if Greek); nor that part which seeks the ways by which truth may be perceived as rational or logical; nor that part which treats of conduct, with the highest good which is to be sought and the supreme evil to be avoided, as moral or ethics. Nevertheless, he knows that from the one, true and infinitely good God we have a nature by

---

[2] Rom. 1.19–20.   [3] Acts 17.28.
[4] Rom. 1.21–23.   [5] Cf. below, 8.26.

which we were made in His image,[6] faith by which we know
God and ourselves, and grace whereby we reach beatitude in
union with God.

This, then, is the reason for preferring the Platonists to all
other philosophers. While the others consumed time and talent
in seeking the causes of things, and the right ways of learning
and living, the Platonists, once they knew God, discovered
where to find the cause by which the universe was made, the
light by which all truth is seen, the fountain from which true
happiness flows.

If philosophers, then, whether Platonists or wise men of any
nation whatsoever, hold these truths concerning God, they
agree with us. However, I have preferred to plead this cause
with the Platonists because I know their writings better. The
Greeks, whose language is universally esteemed, have elo-
quently eulogized these writings. The Latins, captivated either by their fascination or their fame, have gladly studied
them, and, by translating them into our own language, have
added to them new light and luster.

Chapter 11

Some of our fellow Christians are astonished to learn that
Plato had such ideas about God and to realize how close they
are to the truths of our faith. Some even have been led to suppose that he was influenced by the Prophet Jeremias during
his travels in Egypt or, at least, that he had access to the
scriptural prophecies; and this opinion I followed in some of
my writings.[1]

However, a careful calculation of dates according to historical chronology shows that Plato was born almost one hundred
years after Jeremias prophesied, and that nearly sixty years
intervened between Plato's death at the age of eighty-one and
the time when the Septuagint translation was begun. Ptolemy,
King of Egypt,[2] it will be remembered, asked that the Hebraic

[6] Gen. 1.26–27.

[1] De doctrina Christiana 2.43. Augustine revokes his opinion as
a slip of memory, Retractationes 2.4.

[2] Ptolemy II (309–246 B.C.).

prophecies be sent to him from Judea and he arranged to have them translated and safeguarded by seventy Hebrew scholars who were also experts in Greek.

Therefore, it follows that, while journeying in Egypt, Plato could not have seen Jeremias who was long since dead, nor could he have read the Scriptures which had not yet been rendered into Greek, his native tongue. Of course, it is just possible that Plato, who was an indefatigable student and who used an interpreter to delve into Egyptian literature, may have done the same with the Scriptures. I do not mean to suggest that he undertook a translation of them. That was a feat which Ptolemy alone could accomplish by virtue of his liberality and of others' respect for his kingly power. But Plato could have learned from conversation the content of the Scriptures, without fully understanding their meaning.

Certain evidence favors this belief. For example, the first book of Genesis begins: 'In the beginning God created the heavens and the earth; the earth was waste and void; darkness covered the abyss, and the spirit of God was stirring above the waters.'[3] Plato in the *Timaeus*,[4] which deals with the origin of the world, says that in this work God first united earth and fire. Now it is clear that Plato locates fire in the heavens. His statement, therefore, bears a certain resemblance to the words: 'In the beginning God created the heavens and the earth.'

Plato also mentions two intermediary elements, water and air, by means of which the extremes, earth and fire, were united.[5] This idea, perhaps, originated from his interpretation of the verse: 'the spirit of God was stirring above the waters.' Paying little attention to the meaning which Scripture habitually ascribes to spirit and remembering that air is often called breath or spirit, Plato could easily have assumed that all four elements were mentioned in this text.

Then, too, Plato's definition of a philosopher—one who loves God—contains an idea which shines forth everywhere in Scripture. But the most palpable proof to my mind that he was conversant with the sacred books is this, that when Moses, informed by an angel that God wished him to deliver the Hebrews from Egypt, questioned the angel concerning the name

---

[3] Gen. 1.1–2.   [4] *Timaeus*, 31B.   [5] *Ibid.*, 32B.

of the one who had sent him, the answer received was this: 'I AM WHO AM. Thus shalt thou say to the children of Israel: He who is, hath sent me to you,'[6] as though, in comparison with Him who, being immutable, truly is, all mutable things are as if they were not. Now, Plato had a passionate perception of this truth and was never tired of teaching it. Yet, I doubt whether this idea can be found in any of the works of Plato's predecessors except in the text: 'I AM WHO AM, and you shall say to them: He who is hath sent me to you.'

Chapter 12

Whether, then, Plato got his ideas from the works of earlier writers or, as seems more likely, in the way described in the words of the Apostle: 'Because that which is known of God is manifest in them. For God hath manifested it unto them. For the invisible things of him, from the creation of the world, are clearly seen, being understood by the things that are made: His eternal power also and divinity,'[1] it seems to me that I have sufficiently justified my choice of the Platonic philosophers for the purpose of discussing this present problem in natural theology. The question is this: In order to secure happiness after death, should man worship a single God or many?

The main reason for selecting the Platonists is the superiority of their conceptions concerning one God, Creator of heaven and earth, and, hence, their greater reputation in the judgment of posterity. It is true that Aristotle, a disciple of Plato, was a man of extraordinary genius and wide reputation (though in literary style inferior to Plato) who easily surpassed many others, and no less true that the Peripatetic school (so called from Aristotle's custom of teaching while walking) attracted many disciples even while his teacher, Plato, was alive. So, too, after the death of Plato, a son of his sister, Speusippus, and Xenocrates, Plato's favorite pupil, succeeded him in his Academy and, for this reason, they and their successors are called Academics. Nevertheless, the very best of the Platonists are those relatively recent philosophers who, refusing to be

[6] Exod. 3.14.

[1] Rom. 1.19–20.

styled either Peripatetics or Academics, have called themselves Platonists.

Among these last are those highly distinguished Greek scholars, Plotinus,[2] Iamblichus[3] and Porphyry.[4] A hardly less notable Platonist was the African Apuleius,[5] who was a master of both Greek and Latin. All of these and many others of the same school, not to mention Plato himself, believed in polytheistic worship.

Chapter 13

In many other significant ways, these Platonists contradict our own convictions. However, I mean to cross-examine them concerning critical matter which I have just now mentioned. My question is: In their opinion, to which gods should worship be offered, to the good, or to the evil, or to both the good and evil alike? We know what Plato thought regarding this.[1] He taught that all divinities are good and that none at all is bad. This being true, it follows that worship should be offered only to the good. This is another way of saying that rites should be rendered to the gods, for they would not be gods if they were not good.

If this be so—and what else can be seriously believed?— there is no foundation for the view of those who say that we should placate evil gods lest they harm us and invoke the good ones that they may help us. But malicious gods are non-existent. Therefore, as they say, only to beneficent ones should the due honor of worship be paid. What kind of deities, then, are those who love theatrical plays and demand them as a part of worship in their honor? Their power proves that they exist and this passion shows that they are evil. We know how Plato regarded these scenic exhibitions,[2] since he considered that poets, for composing songs unworthy of the majesty and goodness of the gods, should be banished from the state.

---

[2] *c.*205–270; cf. below, 9.10. [3] Died *c.*330.
[4] 233–304. [5] Born *c.*125; cf. above, 4.2.

[1] In such passages as *Republic* 2, 379, and *Laws* 10, 885.
[2] *Republic* 3; cf. above, 2.14.

Who, then, are these deities who defend the plays in opposition to Plato himself? While he cannot endure to have the divinities defamed, they demand that falsely imputed depravities be enacted in their honor! Finally, when they commanded that plays should be re-established, they added to the turpitude of desire malignity in deeds. When Titus Latinius[3] refused to obey, they snatched away his son and plagued him with disease, and then removed the malady as soon as he complied with their command. However, though these gods were thoroughly evil, Plato did not think that they should be feared. With robust constancy, he kept to his opinion and had no hesitation in removing from a well-ordered state all those sacrilegious frivolities of the poets which delighted the demons in their fellowship of filth.

Labeo, however, as I have already mentioned in Book II,[4] placed Plato himself among the demigods. This Labeo maintained that malignant divinities should be appeased by bloody victims and appropriate supplications, while the good gods should be reverenced by plays and the like which one associates with joy. How is it, then, that the demigod Plato constantly dared to deprive not only the inferior deities but the full gods and, therefore, the good gods of those pleasures which he considered base? Certainly, the facts about these gods refute the opinion of Labeo. In regard to Latinius, they showed themselves not only sportive and frolicsome but even cruel and terrible. Therefore, we shall ask the Platonists to give us their answer to this problem. For, following the conclusions of their master, they agree that all the gods are good and honorable and are in sympathy with the virtues of the wise. They consider it a grave offense to think otherwise concerning any of their gods. Since they are ready to explain their views, let us listen with attention.

Chapter 14

Certain philosophers have declared that of all living beings possessed of rational souls there is a threefold division into gods, men, and demons. The gods, who hold the highest place,

[3] Cf. *ibid.* 4.26. [4] Cf. *ibid.* 2.14.

reside in heaven; men, who hold the lowest, sojourn on earth; demons, in the middle, inhabit the air. As the dignity of their abode is diverse, so, also, is that of their nature. The gods are superior to both men and demons. Men, both in the order of nature and the scale of values, are inferior to both gods and demons. The demons, therefore, are in the middle. As they are lower than the gods in place and dignity, so they are higher than men. They have immortality of the body in common with the gods, but passions of the mind in common with men.

Therefore, we should not wonder, it is said, if these demons delight in the obscenities of the stage and in the fables of poetry. The reason is that they are subject to human emotions which are far removed from and altogether foreign to the gods. From this it follows that, when Plato prohibited these poetical fictions, which he detested, he did not deprive the gods but the demons of the pleasure of these theatrical plays. For the gods themselves are absolutely good and noble.

These ideas are to be found in many writings, but it was left for the Platonist, Apuleius of Madaura, to devote to this subject an entire book, entitled *The God of Socrates*. In it he discusses at length the nature of that spirit which Socrates kept near him as a sort of friend and familiar. This spirit was in the habit of warning Socrates whenever he attempted any action that would not accrue to his advantage. Apuleius says openly and proves convincingly that this companion was not a god but a demon. And, continuing the discussion, he deals with the opinions of Plato concerning the sublimity of the gods, the lowliness of men, and the intermediate state of the demons.

Now, if this be true, how did Plato dare to deprive even these demons of their theatrical dissipations by expelling the poets from the city? The gods themselves, of course, he left untouched, since he makes them inaccessible to human infirmities. Perhaps this is the answer. Plato wished to admonish man that his soul, even while imprisoned in mortal members, should for the sake of the splendor of virtue, despise the seductive demands of the demons and detest their uncleanness. At any rate, if Plato deserves esteem for banishing and flouting such defilements, then certainly the demons were disreputable for decreeing and exacting them.

Therefore, either Apuleius was wrong and Socrates' spirit

did not belong to this class of divinities; or, Plato contradicted himself by first honoring the demons and then, later, removing their festivals from a self-respecting state; or, Socrates is not to be congratulated on the friendship of a demon which so embarrassed even Apuleius that he gave the title, *Concerning the God of Socrates,* to a book which, according to its own careful and thorough distinction between gods and demons, should not have been called *Concerning the God* but *Concerning the Demon of Socrates.* He preferred, evidently, to admit this distinction in the contents rather than in the title of his book. Fortunately, our sound philosophy has so illumined the world that nearly everyone now has a horror of the name, 'demon,' so that anyone seeing the title, *Concerning the Demon of Socrates,* before reading Apuleius on the dignity of these spirits, would jump to the conclusion that Apuleius was insane.

But, just exactly what did Apuleius find to praise in these demons? Nothing but their subtlety, strength of body, and lofty habitation. When he spoke in a general way about their behavior, he had nothing good but much evil to report. In fine, no one who has read this book is at all astonished that the demons should wish to include the obscenities of the stage among their sacred rites and, desiring to be deemed as gods, should be delighted with the vices of the deities. Nor is the reader surprised that everything in their sacred rites, whether it evokes laughter by its lewd solemnity or horror by its shameless inhumanity, is in accord with their passions.

Chapters 15–22

Pagan teachings on demons, as beings with souls and bodies superior to those of men, are criticized at length. Apuleius is the chief source of this strange teaching, with which the practice of magic is closely associated. Augustine condemns demonolatry and magic.

Chapter 23

The writings[1] of Hermes, the Egyptian, called Trismegistus,

[1] One of them, *Asclepius,* the dialogue between Hermes and Asclepius was translated into Latin by Apuleius.

reveal a very different idea about these demons. It is true that
Apuleius denied that they are gods. Nevertheless, on the
ground that, as mediators between men and gods, the demons
are indispensable to mortals in their relation to gods, he does
not distinguish their cult from the worship of the superior gods.
The Egyptian, however, admits two categories of gods: some
made by the supreme God; others by men.

A reader might suppose that I refer to images, the work
of men's hands. But Hermes maintains that these visible and
tangible representations are, as it were, the bodies of gods.
He claims that they are animated by spirits who have been
invited to dwell within them and have power either to harm
or to favor those who render them reverence and divine honor.
Thus, by some kind of art, invisible spirits are united with
visible and material things, which then become animated
bodies dedicated and devoted to the spirits that inhabit them.
This, says Hermes, is what it means 'to make gods,' and this
great and amazing gift has been entrusted to men.

The words of the Egyptian, in translation, are as follows:
'Since you and I have decided to discuss the question of kinship and fellowship between men and gods, I want you to
realize, Asclepius, the power and force of man. Just as the
Lord and Father, or the supreme reality, God, is the creator
of celestial gods, so is man the maker of deities who dwell in
temples, satisfied to stay with mortals.'[2] Later, he says: 'Humanity, ever mindful of its nature and origin, persists in imitating divinity. As the Lord and Father has fashioned eternal
gods to be like himself, so man has modeled his own deities
according to the likeness of his own countenance.'

When Asclepius, to whom he was especially addressing
himself, asked: 'Are you speaking of statues, Trismegistus?'
Hermes replied: 'Statues! Asclepius, what an unbeliever you
are! I mean living statues endowed with sense and spirit able
to do all sorts of things, statues with a vision of the future
and capable of divination by lot, prophecy, dreams and many
other means, causing human maladies and then curing them,
punishing and rewarding man with grief and gladness. Do you
not know, Asclepius, that Egypt is an image of heaven? Or,
to express myself more accurately, I should say that whatso-

[2] *Asclepius* 23.

ever is directed and effected by the gods above descends and is transported here. Indeed, it may even more truly be said that our land is the temple of the whole world. However, since it is good for a wise man to know the whole future, it would be wrong for you not to realize that a time will come when it will be manifest that the Egyptians, for all their pious purpose and careful conscientiousness, have paid homage to the gods in vain.'[3]

Hermes then expands this passage into what seems to be a prediction of the present period in which Christianity is destroying all such deceitful images with a decision and freedom in proportion to the truth and holiness of our religion, and with the hope that the grace of our Saviour may save men from his self-made gods and subject him to that true God by whom he was created. However, in this prediction, Hermes speaks sympathetically of these demoniacal tricks without making any overt mention of the name of Christianity. Instead, he deplores the future as though he were witnessing the removal and destruction of rites which guaranteed to Egypt its likeness to heaven, and he speaks, as it were, like a prophet of woe.

Hermes, in fact, was one of those whom the Apostle had in mind when he said that 'although they knew God, they did not glorify him as God or give thanks, but became vain in their reasonings, and their senseless minds have been darkened. For while professing to be wise, they became fools, and they changed the glory of the incorruptible God for an image made like to corruptible man'[4]—and the rest which is too long to quote.

Much of what Hermes says about the one true God, Creator of the world, contains an element of truth, and I cannot understand by what blindness of heart he could wish men to be always subject to gods made, as he admits, by men and how he could deplore the future disappearance of these idols. For, what could be more hapless than a man controlled by his own creations? It is surely easier for a man to cease to be a man by worshiping man-made gods than for idols to become divine by being adored. For it is easier to compare a man to

[3] *Ibid.* 24.
[4] Rom. 1.21–23.

cattle if, for all his human dignity, he lacks understanding than
to prefer a work of man to a creation of God, made to His
own image—that is, to man himself. It is right, therefore, to
reckon a man a recreant to his Creator when he hands himself over to a creation of his own hands.[5]

Hermes Trismegistus lamented these vain, deceptive, pernicious, sacrilegious things because he foresaw that the time
was coming when they would be abolished. He was as impudent in his grief as imprudent in his prophecy,[6] since the
Holy Spirit had made no revelation to him as to the holy
prophets who exultantly proclaimed their inspired visions:
'Shall a man make gods unto himself, and they are no gods?'[7]
and again: 'And it shall come to pass in that day, saith the
Lord of hosts, that I will destroy the names of idols out of
the earth, and they shall be remembered no more.'[8] It is
relevant to recall that holy Isaias uttered a particular prophecy
concerning Egypt: 'And the idols of Egypt shall be moved at
his presence, and the heart of Egypt shall melt in the midst
thereof'[9] and the rest.

In the same class with these prophets were those who rejoiced because they knew He had come whom they had been
expecting. Such were Simeon and Anna, who recognized Jesus
when He was born, and Elizabeth, who, in the Spirit, realized
that He had been conceived, and Peter, who, by revelation of
the Father, affirmed: 'Thou art the Christ, the Son of the living
God.'[10] But the spirits who indicated the time of their own future destruction to this Egyptian were the same as those who
said to the Lord now present in the flesh: 'Hast thou come
here to destroy us before the time?'[11]—either trembling because predestined destruction was come sooner than they expected, or trembling with shame because it was torment
enough to be found out and despised.

It was, indeed, 'before the time,' that is, before the day of
judgment when they are to be punished by eternal damna-

---

[5] . . . *homo deficit ab illo qui eum fecit, cum sibi praeficit ipse
quod fecit.*

[6] . . . *tam inpudenter dolebat, quam inprudenter sciebat.*

[7] Jer. 16.20.   [8] Zach. 13.2.
[9] Isa. 19.1.   [10] Matt. 16.16.
[11] Matt. 8.29.

tion together with all—including men—who sought their society. Such is the teaching of that religion which neither deceives nor can be deceived—unlike this Hermes Trismegistus
blown this way and that by every wind of doctrine, mingling
truth with error and grieving for a perishing religion which
he latter confesses to be wrong.

Chapters 24-26

*Further details on Hermes' criticism of man-made gods and
the worship of idols are presented here. Paganism eventually
degenerated into ancestor worship.*

Chapter 27

Nevertheless, we do not construct shrines, consecrate priests
and render rites and sacrifices for these martyrs. The simple
reason is that it is not they but God who is our God. It is true
that we honor their shrines because they were holy men of
God who fought for truth, even unto death, so that true religion might be made known and falsehoods and fictions be
overcome. Others before them who knew the truth were too
afraid to express their convictions.

Certainly, no Christian ever heard a priest, standing before
an altar built for the honor and service of God over the holy
body of a martyr, say in his prayers: 'I offer this Sacrifice to
thee, Peter, or Paul, or Cyprian.' No! Before the monuments
of these martyrs, the Sacrifice is offered to God alone, who
made them first men and then martyrs and finally associated
them with His holy angels in heavenly honor. In celebrating
this Sacrifice we thank this true God for their victories and,
while renewing our memory of them and calling on God to
help us, we encourage ourselves to imitate them in seeking like
crowns and palms.

Thus, any signs of veneration paid by pious people at the
tombs of martyrs are mere tributes to their memory, not sacred ceremonies nor sacrifices offered to the dead, as to gods.
This is true, even of the custom of bringing food to these places
—something, by the way, which is not done by more enlight-

ened Christians and in most countries is entirely unknown. However, those who do it bring their food to the tombs and pray that it be sanctified by the merits of the martyrs in the name of the Lord of martyrs. Afterwards, they carry it away, either to eat it themselves or to distribute it to the needy. Anyone who knows that there is only one Sacrifice offered by Christians, here or elsewhere, knows that this custom is not a sacrifice to the martyrs.

We revere our martyrs, therefore, with neither divine homage nor the human vices which the pagans offer to their gods. We neither offer them sacrifices nor do we convert their sins into sacred rites. Consider, for example, Isis, the wife of Osiris, the Egyptian goddess and her ancestors, all of whom were kings according to tradition. (While offering a sacrifice to her forebears, she discovered a field of barley and carried some of the ears to the king, her husband, and to his councilor, Mercury, and so she has come to be identified with Ceres.) Now, anyone who wants to find out how many and monstrous were their wickednesses, as reported by poets and the mystic writings of the Egyptians, can get an idea from the letter which Alexander wrote to his mother, Olympias, describing the facts as revealed to him by the priest Leo.[1] Let anyone who likes it and can stand it read it, but then let him pause and reflect in honor of what kind of man, guilty of what monstrous sins, sacred rites were offered to the dead as to gods. It is unthinkable that the pagans, even though they hold such men to be divine, should be rash enough to compare them in any way with our holy martyrs whom we do not consider gods.

If, then, we do not ordain priests for the purpose of offering sacrifices to our martyrs, for that would be incongruous, improper, and unlawful, since worship is due to God alone, still less do we regale our martyrs with their crimes or with disgraceful plays as the pagans do when they commemorate the sins of their gods—either real sins committed by their deities when they were men or, if their gods were never human, fabricated for the delight of wicked demons. The god of Socrates, if he had one, could never have belonged to this class of evil spirits, unless, perhaps, some magicians, desiring to excel in

---

[1] Cf. Bk. 12.11, here omitted.

this kind of art, may have managed to impose such a deity on a man who was an utter stranger to and innocent of this art of making gods.

What more need I say? Can anyone, however slight his intelligence, imagine that such demons are to be worshiped in order that we may attain to an eternal felicity after death? Perhaps objectors, however, will answer with a distinction: As for the gods, all are good; as for the demons, some are benign and some are bad; but it is only the benevolent ones whom we should supplicate for assistance toward an eternal beatitude. This matter will be treated in the following Book.

BOOK IX

Pagan Deities, Demons, and Christian Angels

Chapter 1

SOME PHILOSOPHERS have held that there are both good and evil gods. Others, with more respect for the deities, honored and praised them to the point of believing that no god could be bad. The former (who divided the gods into good and bad) often called demons by the name of 'gods,' and sometimes, though more rarely, gods by the name of 'demons.' Thus, they acknowledge that Jupiter himself, supreme ruler of all divinities, was referred to by Homer as a 'demon.'[1]

The latter (who assert that all gods must be good and with a goodness superior to any known human excellence) are compelled by the undeniable deeds of demons to distinguish between demons and gods—since the gods, all of whom are good, are incapable of committing such acts. Thus, they attribute to demons and not to gods anything that rightly displeases them in those depraved actions or passions by which unseen spirits disclose their influence.

Persuaded, moreover, that no god mingles with man, they believe that demons have been designated as mediators between men and deities, presenting the petitions of mortals and returning with gifts from the gods. This opinion is held by the Platonists, the best and best known of all philosophers, and it is by reason of their superiority that I chose to discuss with them the question whether polytheistic worship is of any advantage in the quest for eternal happiness beyond the grave.[2]

In the preceding Book, I raised the question whether demons could possibly mediate, as neighbors and favorites, between the good gods and good men, considering that demons delight in doings that good and wise men are obliged to detest and condemn, as, for example, encouraging sacrilegious fables in which poets impute monstrous immoralities not to

[1] Cf. *Iliad* 1.22.
[2] Cf. above, 8.5.

this or that man but to the very gods; not to mention the culpable and criminal violence of magical arts. The answer was: utterly and demonstrably impossible.

Chapter 2

The present Book is to deal (according to the promise at the close of the preceding one) with the pertinent question of the differences between the demons themselves, rather than with the possible dissimilarities among the gods (who are all supposed to be good) or with the disparities between gods and demons—the former being high above and remote from mortals; the latter, in Platonic theory, being intermediaries between men and gods.

It is commonly said that there are both good and wicked spirits among the demons, and this is an opinion that calls for discussion regardless of whether it is that of the Platonists or of anyone else. For, no one should think it was his duty to gain the friendship of supposedly good demons in order to become through their mediation more acceptable to the gods (all of them good) so that, after death, he may enjoy their society. The danger for such a man is that, deceived by the wiles of malignant spirits and caught in their trap, he may never reach the true God, with whom and in whom and by whom alone the rational, intellectual, and human soul can attain its blessedness.

Chapter 3

How, then, do the good differ from the bad demons, since Apuleius the Platonist, in his general description of demons,[1] makes much of aerial bodies but says nothing of any virtues of the souls—without which there could be no good demons? Thus, he has nothing to say about any foundation of felicity, but he had to mention the evidence of their misery. In declaring them rational beings, he confesses that their minds are not merely not sufficiently imbued and fortified with virtue to protect them against the irrational passions of the soul, but,

[1] *De Deo Socratis* 8.

on the contrary, that they are tossed by the storms of emotion like the hearts of senseless mortals.

Apuleius discusses the matter as follows: 'It is, in general, of this class of demons that the poets are accustomed to write; nor are their fictions far from the truth when they represent the demons as gods who bestow prosperity and prestige on men they love and adversities and humiliations on those they hate. Hence, they experience pity, indignation, anguish, joy, and every other form of human emotion, and their minds and hearts, like those of men, are continually tossing on all the surge and tide of passionate disquietude. All such turmoil and tempests remove them far from the tranquility of celestial gods.'

Is there any doubt as to his meaning? It is evident that Apuleius is referring not to the inferior part of the soul, but to the very minds of the demons which make them rational beings, when he says that their minds are like an angry sea tossed about by the tempests of passion. Thus, they are not to be compared to those philosophers who, in spite of the inescapable weakness of human nature and the painful vicissitudes of life, face the perturbations of passion with an imperturbable mind. Wise men do not yield to passion when they are tempted either to approve or to perpetuate any action that runs counter to the way of wisdom and the law of justice. The demons are, rather, to be compared to foolish and wicked men whom they resemble, if not in body at least in character.

In fact, they are inveterately and incorrigibly worse, punished as they are by being tossed, as Apuleius says, on the high sea of their hearts, with no rock of truth or virtue to save them from the waves of their wild and depraved affections.

Chapter 4

Two opinions prevail among philosophers concerning those movements of the soul which the Greeks call *páthē* and certain Latin philosophers, like Cicero, call 'perturbations,' others 'affections' and still others, like Apuleius who keeps closer to the Greek, 'passions.' Some contend that these perturbations, affections, or passions affect even a philosopher, tempered,

however, and even tamed, by reason, so that the lordship of
the mind imposes law upon them to keep them within proper
bounds.

This view is shared by both Platonists and Aristotelians,
since Aristotle, who founded the Peripatetic school, was the
disciple of Plato. Others, such as the Stoics, hold that no wise
man should be in any way influenced by passions. However,
in his treatise, *De finibus*,[1] Cicero proves that the battle between the Stoics, on one hand, and the Platonists and Peripatetics, on the other, is one of words rather than of ideas.
While the Stoics refuse to apply the word 'goods' to external,
bodily advantages and maintain that virtue, the art of living
well and the only good, resides wholly in the mind, the other
philosophers, using simple and ordinary language, call even
external advantages 'goods,' slight as they may be in comparison with virtue, which guides good living. Thus, in spite of
their respective words, 'goods' and 'advantages,' there is but
one idea of the value of these things. The Stoics, in this case,
are merely indulging in a novelty of expression. And even in
the question whether the wise man is subject to passions or
entirely free from them, the controversy, so it seems to me,
is one rather of words than of meaning. In so far as the point
at issue is the sense and not just the sound of words, in my
opinion, the Stoics are at one with the Platonists and Peripatetics.

For the sake of brevity, I shall omit other illustrations and
mention just one which I consider cogent. In his work, *Noctes
Atticae*, the erudite and eloquent Aulus Gellius[2] tells a lengthy
and detailed story of a voyage with an eminent Stoic philosopher, the main point of which is that, when a terrific storm
arose and their ship was endangered by the wind and the
waves, the philosopher turned pale with fear.[3] The others on
board noticed this fact and, despite the danger of proximate
death, were filled with curiosity to see whether or not a philosopher would betray agitation. When the tempest subsided
and it was safe enough for talk and even for banter, a rich and

[1] Books 3 and 4.
[2] 125-175 A.D.
[3] The story occurs in *Noctes Atticae* 19.1.

voluptuous Asiatic who was among the passengers laughed and jeered at the philosopher for his panic and his pallor. He himself, he boasted, had remained fearless in the face of the impending destruction. Then the philosopher, availing himself of the reply of Aristippus,[4] the Socratic philosopher, who was taunted in similar circumstances by the same kind of person, answered: 'A rogue need not worry about losing his worthless life, but Aristippus has a duty to care for a life like his.'

This reply put the rich man in his place. Thereupon, Aulus Gellius, with no thought of teasing but only of learning, asked the philosopher the cause of his fear. The latter, willing to instruct a man so zealous for knowledge, took from his bag a book of Epictetus,[5] the Stoic, containing a faithful exposition of the doctrines of Zeno[6] and Chrysippus,[7] founders of the Stoic school. Aulus Gellius tells us that he read in this book the Stoic theory of *phantasiae,* namely, that certain impressions made on the mind are involuntary and beyond control, and that when these impressions are provoked by alarming and formidable external causes, even a philosopher is bound to yield momentarily to a movement of either fear or depression. Thus, such emotions may seem to anticipate the proper function of intellect and reason, yet no judgment is made concerning the evil of the exterior cause nor is any approval or consent given to the emotions.

This consent, the Stoics hold, lies in man's power, this being the difference between a wise man and a fool, that the mind of the latter yields and consents to such passions, while a philosopher, though forced to feel them, remains unshaken in soul with a true and solid judgment as to what he is rationally obliged to seek or avoid.

That, as briefly as I can summarize it—more clearly than Gellius but without his elegance of style—is his account of what he found in the book of Epictetus concerning the teachings and sentiments of the Stoics.[8]

This being so, there is no difference, or almost none, between the Stoics and other philosophers on the passions and emotions of the soul, since both schools defend the opinion

[4] Cf. above, 8.3.
[5] *c.*50–138 A.D.
[6] *c.*342–*c.*270 B.C.
[7] *c.*281–*c.*208 B.C.
[8] *Enchiridion* 20–22.

that the mind and reason of the wise man are free from their domination. What, perhaps, the Stoics mean, in saying that passions do not disturb the wise man, is that the wisdom by which he is wise is never clouded by error or sullied by stain because of his passions. In spite of incidental emotions arising from what they insist on calling advantages and disadvantages rather than goods and evils, the Stoic soul remains serenely wise.

For, of course, if our philosopher put no value whatever on things like life and bodily safety, which he was in danger of losing in the shipwreck, he would not have been as terrified as his pallor indicated. But the fact remains that he could suffer such emotions and, at the same time, be firmly convinced that life and security, threatened by the severity of the tempest, were not good in the sense that justice is good, that is, they could not make their possessors good.

When the Stoics insist that such things must not be called goods but advantages, this is a fight over words, not an insight into things.[9] What difference does it make whether a Stoic calls a thing a good or an advantage if he fears to lose it with the same trembling and pallor as a Peripatetic? A difference in name; the emotions are the same.[10] In reality, if they were faced with the choice of losing these 'goods' or 'advantages' or of committing some sin or crime to save them, both would prefer to give up what is necessary for bodily safety and security rather than give in to a violation of justice.[11]

Even though passions may disturb the inferior part of the soul, a mind thus firmly convinced never permits passion to prevail over rational resolve. On the contrary, the mind is the master and, by refusing consent and by positive resistance, it maintains the sovereignity of virtue. Such a man, as Virgil describes him, was Aeneas:

> 'With mind unmoved he doth remain,
> While tender tears run down in vain.'[12]

---

9 . . . *verborum certamini, non rerum examini deputandum est.*
10 . . . *ea non aequaliter appellando, sed aequaliter aestimando.*
11 . . . *amittere, quibus natura corporis salva et incolumis habetur, quam illa committere.*
12 Virgil, *Aeneid* 4.449.

Chapter 5

At present, there is no need to develop at length and in detail the doctrine contained in Sacred Scripture—fount of Christian faith—concerning passions, namely, that the mind is subject to God to be ruled and aided while the passions are subject to the mind to be tempered, tamed, and turned to the uses of righteousness. For us the important question is not whether a religious soul is subject to anger, but why this is so; not the fact of sadness, but the source of sadness; not whether a man fears, but what he fears. I hope that no one with common sense will find fault with being angry with a sinner to correct him, being sad with a sufferer to relieve him, being afraid lest a man in danger die. The Stoics, it is true, are accustomed to condemn even compassion; but how much better our Stoic would have been if he had been more moved with compassion for a man in peril than afraid of his own shipwreck.

Cicero sounds better, more like a man, more like a Christian, when he says in praising Caesar: 'Of all your virtues none is more admirable and pleasing than your mercy.'[1] Now, what is mercy but a certain feeling of compassion in our hearts, evoked by the misery of another and compelling us to offer all possible aid? An emotion of this kind is a servant to reason whenever it tenders mercy without injuring justice, as in giving to the poor and forgiving the penitent.

Cicero, so discriminating in the use of words, boldly called this compassion a virtue, while the Stoics were not ashamed in numbering it among the vices. Nevertheless, as the famous Stoic, Epictetus, has shown in his work[2] based upon the doctrines of Zeno and Chrysippus, the founders of the school, the Stoics admit that passions of this kind affect the soul even of the wise man who, as they hold, must be above all evil. We must, therefore, conclude, first, that Stoics do not, in fact, consider emotions vices, since the wise man meets them in such a way that they can do nothing to change his mind or mar his virtue; and second, that the opinion of the Peripatetics or Platonists and that of the Stoics themselves turn out to be one

[1] *Pro Ligurio* 12.37.
[2] *Enchiridion.*

and the same, in spite of the battle of words which, as Cicero tells us,[3] has been so long torturing the Greeks, those lovers of contention rather than of truth.

However, we may well ask the further question whether our liability to passion even in the performance of duty is not a part of the infirmity of our present life. For the holy angels punish without anger those whom the eternal law of God has delivered to them for punishment,[4] succor the suffering without suffering compassion, and rescue from peril those whom they love without sharing their fear. Yet, in our human way, we speak as though the angels had all these feelings. This is done by reason of the analogy between their actions and ours, not because we attribute to them the infirmity of our own passions—much as, in Scripture, God Himself is said to be angry without implying the least movement of passion. The word 'anger' is used because God's vengeance is effective, not because His nature is affective.[5]

Chapter 6

For the time being, I shall defer this question of the holy angels in order to examine the opinion of the Platonists that the demons established as intermediaries between gods and men are seething in a surge of passions. For if, under the assaults of these emotions, their minds remained free and masters of the situation, Apuleius could not say that their hearts and minds, like those of men, are tossed on all the surge and tide of passionate disquietude.[1] Notice that it is their very mind, that is, the higher part of the soul by which they are rational and in which their virtue and wisdom, if they had any, would dominate the turbulent passions of the inferior part of the soul —I repeat, it is their very mind which, according to our Platonist, is tossed on a sea of passions.

And so, the mind of demons is a slave to the passions of lust, fear, anger, and all the rest. What part of them, then, can be free and wise enough either to please the gods or to

[3] *De oratore* 1.11,47.   [4] Cf. Matt. 13.14.
[5] . . . *vindictae usurpavit effectus, non illius turbulentus adfectus.*

[1] *De Deo Socratis* 11.

urge men to aim at high moral standards? The fact is that their mind has been conquered and enslaved by sins of passion, and what little of natural intelligence they possess is all the more bent on lying and deception as their craving to injure others increases.

Chapters 7–8

Apuleius claimed that demons' bodies are eternal and that in this they resemble the gods, though the demons are inferior in their souls. This is why he considered the demons to be mediators between the gods and men.

Chapter 9

Now, what kind of mediators between men and gods are these demons through whom men may circuitously win the favor of the deities? For, what should be the better part of a living being, the soul, is, in their case, inferior, since they share this element with men; and what should be the worse part, the body, is, in their case, superior, because in body they are similar to the gods. For, every living creature or animal consists of both soul and body. Of these two components, the soul, assuredly, is superior to the body. Even when vicious and weak, the soul is, without doubt, better than the healthiest and strongest body, since it is higher by nature and, even though blemished by vice, is better than the body, just as gold, even when dirty, is worth more than silver or lead, however pure. Yet, the demons, mediators between men and gods, links holding together things human and divine, have an eternal body in common with gods and a sullied soul in common with men. One would think that religion, by which men are to have contact with gods through the demons, has its roots in the body rather than in the soul.

For what wickedness or punishment have these false and fallacious[1] mediators been hung, as it were, upside down, so that their lower part, the body, unites them with beings above them, and their higher part, the soul, links with beings below

---

[1] . . . *falsos adque fallaces* . . .

them? Thus, they are similar to gods in that part that serves and are miserable with men on earth by reason of the part that rules. For, the body is a slave, as Sallust says: 'We use the soul for sovereignty and the body for service.'[2] And he added: 'The one we have in common with gods, the other with beasts.' Here, he was speaking of men, who, like brute animals, have mortal bodies.

But these demons, whom the philosophers have given us as mediators between men and gods, can, indeed, say of soul and body: 'One we have in common with gods, the other with men.' But, as I have already said, they are, as it were, so upside down that it is their slave-like body which unites them with the blessed gods and their sovereign soul which joins them with unhappy men. They are exalted by their lower part and humbled by their higher. Therefore, even if one should think that their eternity is like the gods', merely because their souls are not severed from their bodies by death as is the case with beings on earth, their body should still be considered, not as an eternal chariot for their triumph, but as an eternal chain for their damnation.

Chapters 10–21

This treatise on demonology, as taught by some Neoplatonists, shows that these so-called demons could be neither happy nor unhappy. The question, whether a wise man can be happy in this life, is then briefly raised. It appears that happiness is unattainable in this life. Demons are not better beings than men, for popular usage takes demon to mean an evil being. Hence demons cannot be mediators between men and the divine.

Chapter 22

Now, to God's good angels all this knowledge of merely material and temporal reality which so inflates the demons seems of little value. It is not that they lack such knowledge; it is because they love that Love of God which makes them holy.

[2] *Catiline* 1.

They are so on fire with a holy love of God's beauty, so spiritual, unchangeable, and ineffable, that they hold in disdain all things—including themselves—which are less than divine, so that, with every grace that makes them good, they may rejoice in the Giver of all goodness, God.

Actually, their knowledge even of the world of time and change is greater than the demons' because, in the Word of God, through whom the world was made, they contemplate the ultimate reasons why, in the cosmic order, some things can be used while others are refused, and nothing is confused.[1] Demons, on the contrary, do not contemplate, in the wisdom of God, eternal causes—those hinges, as it were, on which history hangs. If they can foresee much more of the future than men, it is only because, by longer experience, they have learned to decipher signals which mean nothing to us. Often enough, their predictions are merely pre-announcements of what they are planning to do.[2]

Finally, demons are often wholly mistaken; the angels, never. It is one thing to predict historical events or scientific progress on the basis of human or physical phenomena, and even to play the part, which demons are allowed to play, of affecting such events and progress by their will and power. It is something quite different to foresee, in the living laws of God's eternal and unchangeable Wisdom, the historical future and to know, by a participation in the Divine Spirit, that most infallible of all causes, God's will. The special privilege of such knowledge God has rightly reserved to the holy angels. Thus, they are not only eternal but also blessed. And the good which gives them blessedness is God Himself who created them, for their perfect and unfailing bliss is to share in the Vision of God.

Chapter 23

If the Platonists prefer to call these angels gods rather than demons and to number them among the gods who, according to Plato, their founder and master, were created by the Su-

[1] . . . *quaedam probantur, quaedam reprobantur, cuncta ordinantur.*
[2] Cf. 10.32.

preme God,[1] they are welcome to do so, and I shall not bother them with a battle over words. And if they admit that, though blessed, they are so not intrinsically but only by their union with God by whom they were created, then they are saying what we say, whatever the name they may give to the angels.

Now, that this is the opinion of all Platonists or, at least, of the best of them can be shown by their writings. But, regarding the name itself, the fact that they give the name 'god' to such an immortal and blessed creature is hardly reason for quarreling with them, since in our own Scriptures we read: 'The God of gods, the Lord hath spoken';[2] and elsewhere: 'Praise ye the God of gods';[3] and again: 'a great King above all gods.'[4] And when it is said 'He is to be feared above all gods,'[5] the explanation is immediately added: 'For all the gods of the Gentiles are demons: but the Lord made the heavens.' Note that it says not just 'above all gods,' but adds: 'of the Gentiles.' The meaning is 'above those whom the pagans regard as gods,' that is, the demons. God is 'to be feared' with that terror which made the demons cry out to the Lord: 'Hast thou come to destroy us?'[6] But the expression, 'God of gods,' cannot be interpreted as the god of demons, and it would be absurd to take 'a great King above all gods' as meaning a great King above all demons.

Our Scripture also gives the name 'gods' to men who belong to the people of God: 'I have said: you are gods, and all of you the sons of the Most High.'[7] Hence, 'the God of gods' can be taken to mean 'the God of God's people.' So, too, with the expression, 'a great King above all gods.'

However, there is one question that calls for an answer. If men are called gods because they belong to the chosen people to whom God speaks through either angels or men, are not those immortal spirits much more worthy of that name who already enjoy that beatitude which men merely hope to attain by worshiping God? The answer is this. Sacred Scripture gives the name 'gods' more expressly to men than to the immortal and blessed angels (with whom we have been prom-

[1] *Timaeus*, 41A.
[2] Ps. 49.1.
[3] Ps. 135.2.
[4] Ps. 94.3.
[5] Ps. 95.4,5.
[6] Mark 1.24.
[7] Ps. 81.6.

ised equality after the resurrection) because the perfection of the angels is such that in the weakness of our faith we might be tempted to choose one of them as our god, whereas the temptation to make a man into a god is easily overcome.

Moreover, it is more proper that men belonging to the people of God should be called gods in order to make them certain and confident that He is *their* God who is called the 'God of gods.' The blessed and immortal angels in heaven might be called gods, but never 'gods of gods,' that is, never the gods of the men who form the people of God and to whom it was said: 'I have said: you are gods, and all of you the sons of the Most High.' That is what the Apostle writes: 'For even if there are what are called gods, whether in heaven or on earth (for indeed there are many gods and many lords), yet for us there is only one God, the Father from whom are all things, and we unto Him; and one Lord, Jesus Christ, through whom are all things, and we through Him.'[8]

Consequently, there is little need to dispute about the name, since the thing itself is so clear that not a shadow of uncertainty remains. However, what displeases the Platonists is that we give the name of angels to those immortal and blessed spirits who have been sent to announce the will of God to men. They believe that this ministry is carried on not by those whom they call gods and who are both immortal and blessed, but by demons, whom they do not care to call blessed although they believe them to be immortal, or, if they are both blessed and immortal, certainly they are no more than good demons, not gods in the sense of dwelling on high, far removed from human contact. Although this may seem mere wrangling over a name, the fact remains that demon is so detestable a word that we must, by all means, avoid connecting it with holy angels.

At any rate, let us now conclude this Book with the conviction, first, that no created spirits, however immortal and blessed and whatever they are called, can ever be constituted as mediators for the purpose of leading to immortal beatitude unhappy mortals from whom they are separated by a double dissimilarity; and, second, that those creatures who are in an intermediate position, sharing immortality with beings above

[8] 1 Cor. 8.5,6.

them and misery with beings below them—for misery is the mark of their malice—are more likely to envy than to offer us a beatitude which they do not possess. Hence the conclusion: The friends of the demons can offer us no cogent reason why we ought to honor them as protectors rather than avoid them as deceivers.

There remain those spirits who are good and, therefore, immortal and blessed, and whom, under the name of gods, the Platonists think should be reverenced by religious worship and sacrifices in order to attain happiness after death. Whatever their nature and whatever their proper name, they desire no such religious homage for themselves, but only for the one God by whom they were created and in communion with whom they are blessed. That this is so, I shall show, with God's grace, more at length in the following Book.

BOOK X

Christian Worship Contrasted with Platonic Theology

Chapter 1

THAT ALL MEN wish to be happy is a certitude for anyone who can think. But, so long as human intelligence remains incapable of deciding which men are happy and how they become so, endless controversies arise in which philosophers waste their time and toil. But it would be tedious and futile to recall and examine these battles here. The reader will remember what I said in Book VIII,[1] when making a choice of philosophers with whom to discuss the question of beatitude after death and whether it is to be attained by serving the one true God and Creator of gods, or by worshiping many gods. He will not expect to find the same things repeated here. If the reader has forgotten, he can easily refresh his memory by a second reading.

It will be recalled that I selected the Platonists, who are deservedly considered the outstanding philosophers, first, because they could see that not even the soul of man, immortal and rational (or intellectual) as it is, can attain happiness apart from the Light of that God by whom both itself and the world were made, and, second, because they hold that the blessed life which all men seek can be found only by him who, in the purity of a chaste love, embraces that one Supreme Good which is the unchangeable God.

However, even these philosophers, whether through yielding to popular superstition or, as the Apostle says, through 'growing vain in their reasonings,'[2] also believed—or wanted others to believe—in polytheism. At any rate, some of them went so far as to think that the divine honors of rites and sacrifices should be offered to demons—an opinion which I have already refuted at some length.

It is time, therefore, to take a look, as far as with God's help we may, at those immortal and blessed spirits established

---

[1] Cf. above, 8.5.   [2] Rom. 1.21.

in Heaven as Thrones, Dominations, Principalities, and Powers. The Platonists call them gods or, at least, good demons or even, like us, angels. We must ask in what sense it is credible that they should desire from us any kind of religious devotion. The precise point at issue is whether they wish for themselves or only for their God, who is also ours, the homage of our ceremonies and sacrifices and the consecration by religious rites of some of our goods or even of ourselves.

But this is the worship which we owe to the divinity, or, if I must speak more exactly, to the deity. However, since I do not find a sufficiently suitable Latin expression, I must use a Greek term to suggest in one word what I wish to say. Wherever the term *latreía* has been found in Sacred Scripture, our interpreters, I know, have translated it as service. But the service which is due to men and of which the Apostle speaks when he admonishes slaves to obey their master[3] is commonly called by another name in Greek,[4] whereas the term *latreía*, according to the usage of those who put divine revelation into human language, refers always or almost always to that service which pertains to the worship of God.

Consequently, if the service in question is called simply a cult [*cultus*], it seems that it is not reserved for God alone. For we employ a similar word [*colere*] in reference to distinguished men whose memory or whose company we 'cultivate.' The word 'cult' refers to things to which we subject ourselves in a spirit of piety and religion, but we also 'cultivate' certain things which are subject to us. From the Latin word, *colere*, are derived such words as agriculturists, colonists, and *incolae*, that is, inhabitants. The pagan gods are spoken of as *caelicolae* not in the sense of venerating heaven by a cult but of inhabiting heaven like colonists. However, they are not called *coloni*, in the technical sense of those whose condition in their native land demands that they cultivate the soil under the authority of the owner, but in the sense in which it is used in a line of a great master of the Latin language: 'There was an ancient city, inhabited by Tyrian colonists,'[5] where

[3] Eph. 6.5; Col. 3.22.   [4] *douleía*.
[5] Virgil, *Aeneid* 1.12.

'colonists' means inhabitants, not tillers of the soil. So, too, colonies mean cities founded, like new hives of bees, by larger cities.

Thus, although it is certainly true that 'cult,' in its special sense of 'worship,' is due to God alone, yet, because the Latin _cultus_ is used in many other ways, it cannot, when taken by itself, designate the worship due to God.

As for the word 'religion,' it usually means the cult which is rendered to God; hence, Latin translators render the Greek word, _thrēskeía_, by _religio_. Nevertheless, at least in Latin, not only the ignorant but the most educated persons use _religio_ to express the binding force of blood relationships and affinities and other social ties. Hence, when there is a question of the cult of the deity, the word _religio_ is ambiguous. If we make bold to say that _religio_ means nothing else but the worship of God, then we seem to be rudely contradicting those who use the word to signify the binding force of human relationships.

So, too, the word 'piety' (in Greek, _eusébeia_). In its strict sense, it ordinarily means the worship of God. However, it is also used to express a dutiful respect for parents. Moreover, in everyday speech, the word _pietas_ means pity or mercy. This has come about, I think, because God commands us especially to practice mercy, declaring that it pleases Him as much as or even more than sacrifices. Hence, God himself is spoken of as _pius_, in the sense of merciful. However, the Greeks never call Him _eusebēs_, although ordinary people employ the word _eusébeia_ in the sense of mercy. In certain passages of the Greek text of Scripture, to mark the distinction, _eusébeia_ (reverence in general) is replaced by _theosébeia_ (reverence to God). In Latin, there is no single word which expresses either one or the other of these ideas.

My point is that what in Greek is called _latreía_ and in Latin _servitus_ in the sense of the service of worshiping God; or what in Greek is called _thrēskeía_ and in Latin _religio_, in the sense of religion binding us to God; or what the Greeks call _theosébeia_, meaning 'piety toward God' and for which there is no Latin equivalent—this is due exclusively to God who is the true God and who makes those who worship Him sharers in His divinity.[6]

Therefore, whoever they are, these immortal and blessed beings who dwell in heaven, if they do not love us and desire us to be happy, then, undoubtedly, we owe them no service; but, if they love us and desire our happiness, then, indeed, they will wish our happiness to flow from the same source as theirs. For, how could our happiness have any other source than theirs?

Chapter 2

But, on this point, we have no dispute with these excellent philosophers. For they have borne manifold and abundant witness in their writings to their belief that these beings receive their happiness from the same source as we do—from the ray of a certain Intelligible Light which is the God of angels and is distinct from them, for only by this Light are they resplendent and only by participation in God are they established in perfection and beatitude.

Often, and with much insistence, Plotinus, developing the thought of Plato, asserts that even that being which they believe to be the soul of the universe receives its happiness from the same source as we do, namely, the Light which created the universal soul and is distinct from it and by reason of whose 'intelligible' illumination this soul is alight with intelligence. And to help us rise from the vast and visible bodies in the sky to the celestial 'intelligences,' he notices the analogy of the moon made luminous—in Platonic theory—by rays from the sun, as the spheres are alight with intelligence.[1]

This great Platonist, therefore, says that the rational (or, perhaps, better, the intellectual) soul—in which genus he includes the souls of those immortal and blessed spirits who are believed to inhabit the celestial dwellings—has no nature above it except that of God who fashioned the universe and created the soul itself, and that these heavenly beings receive their beatitude and their light for the understanding of truth from

---

[6] . . . *facitque suos cultores deos.*

[1] *Enneads* 2.9,2,3; 5.1,3.

the same source as we do. In this belief, he is in agreement with the Gospel: 'There was a man, one sent from God, whose name was John. This man came as a witness, to bear witness concerning the Light, that all might believe through him. He was not himself the Light, but was to bear witness to the Light. It was the true Light that enlightens every man who comes into the world.'[2]

The distinction here made sufficiently shows that a rational or intellectual soul such as John's cannot be a light to itself but needs to be illumined by participation in the true Light. This is what John himself confesses in his witness to the Word: 'And of his fullness we have all received, grace for grace.'[3]

Chapter 3

Since this is the case, if the Platonists and others like them who have a knowledge of God would only glorify Him as such and render Him thanks and not become vain in their thoughts, whether by starting errors among the people or by failing to correct them, surely they would acknowledge that, in order to be immortal and blessed, both immortal and blessed spirits and we miserable mortals must worship the one God of gods who is our God as well as theirs.

Both in outward signs and inner devotion, we owe to Him that service which the Greeks call *latreía*. Indeed, all of us together, and each one in particular, constitute His temple because He deigns to take for a dwelling both the community of all and the person of each individual. Nor is He greater in all than in each, since He cannot be extended by numbers nor diminished by being shared. When raised to Him, our heart becomes His altar; His only Son is the priest who wins for us His favor. It is only by the shedding of our blood in fighting for His truth that we offer Him bloody victims. We burn the sweetest incense in His sight when we are aflame with holy piety and love. As the best gifts we consecrate and surrender to Him our very selves which He has given us. We dedicate and consecrate to Him the memory of His bounties by establishing appointed days as solemn feasts, lest, by the

[2] John 1.6–9.   [3] John 1.16.

lapse of time, ingratitude and forgetfulness should steal upon us. On the altar of our heart, we offer to Him a sacrifice of humility and praise, aglow with the fire of charity.

In order to see Him as, one day, it will be possible to see and to cling to Him, we cleanse ourselves from every stain of sin and evil desire, sanctifying ourselves by His name. For He is the source of our happiness and the very end of all our aspirations. We elect Him, whom, by neglect, we lost. We offer Him our allegiance—for 'allegiance' and 'religion' are at root, the same.[1] We pursue Him with our love so that when we reach Him we may rest in perfect happiness in Him who is our goal. For our goal (or, as the philosophers in their endless disputes have termed it, our end or good) is nothing else than union with Him whose spiritual embrace, if I may so speak, can alone fecundate the intellectual soul and fill it with true virtue.

It is this Good which we are commanded to love with our whole heart, with our whole mind, and with all our strength. It is toward this Good that we should be led by those who love us, and toward this Good we should lead those whom we love. In this way, we fulfill the commandments on which depend the whole Law and the Prophets: 'Thou shalt love the Lord Thy God with thy whole heart, and thy whole soul, and with thy whole mind'; and 'Thou shalt love thy neighbor as thyself.'[2] For, in order that a man might learn how to love himself, a standard was set to regulate all his actions on which his happiness depends. For, to love one's own self is nothing but to wish to be happy, and the standard is union with God. When, therefore, a person who knows how to love himself is bidden to love his neighbor as himself, is he not, in effect, commanded to persuade others, as far as he can, to love God?

This, then, is the worship of God; this is true religion and the right kind of piety; this is the service that is due only to God. It follows, therefore, that if any immortal power, however highly endowed with virtue, loves us as itself, it must wish us to be subject, for our own happiness, to Him in submission to whom it finds its happiness. If, then, this spirit does

[1] *Hunc eligentes vel potius religentes (amiseramus enim negligentes)—hunc ergo religentes, unde et religio dicta perhibetur . . .*
[2] Matt. 22.37,39.

not worship God, it is unhappy because deprived of God, and if it worships God, it cannot wish to be worshiped in place of Him. Rather will such a spirit acknowledge, in loving allegiance, that divine decision which runs: 'He that sacrificeth to gods, shall be put to death, save only to the Lord.'[3]

Chapters 4-5

Sacrifice has always been associated with the worship of God. Augustine explains that God is not benefited by sacrifice but accepts such offerings as evidences of a contrite heart.

Chapter 6

There is, then, a true sacrifice in every work which unites us in a holy communion with God, that is, in every work that is aimed at that final Good in which alone we can be truly blessed. That is why even mercy shown to our fellow men is not a sacrifice unless it is done for God. A sacrifice, even though it is done or offered by man, is something divine—which is what the ancient Latins meant by the word *sacrificium*. For this reason, a man himself who is consecrated in the name of God and vowed to God is a sacrifice, inasmuch as he dies to the world that he may live for God. For, this is a part of that mercy which each one has on himself, according to the text: 'Have pity on thy own soul, pleasing God.'[1]

Our body, too, is a sacrifice when, for God's sake, we chasten it, as we ought, by temperance, that is when we do not yield our members as 'instruments of iniquity unto sin,'[2] but as means of holiness to God. The Apostle exhorts us to this when he says: 'I exhort you, therefore, brethren, by the mercy of God to present your bodies as a sacrifice, living, holy, pleasing to God—your spiritual service.'[3] If, then, the body, which is less than the soul and which the soul uses as a servant or a tool, is a sacrifice when it is used well and rightly for

[3] Exod. 22.20.

[1] Eccli. 30.24. [2] Rom. 6.13.
[3] Rom. 21.1.

the service of God, how much more so is the soul when it offers itself to God so that, aflame in the fire of divine Love, and with the dross of worldly desire melted away, it is re-molded into the unchangeable form of God and becomes beautiful in His sight by reason of the bounty of beauty which He has bestowed upon it. This is what the Apostle implies in the following verse: 'And be not conformed to this world, but be transformed in the newness of your mind, that you may discern what is the good and acceptable and perfect will of God.'[4]

Since, therefore, true sacrifices are works of mercy done to ourselves or our neighbor and directed to God, and since works of mercy are performed that we may be freed from misery and, thereby, be happy, and since happiness is only to be found in that Good of which it is said: 'But it is good for me to adhere to my God,'[5] it follows that the whole of that redeemed city, that is, the congregation or communion of saints, is offered as a universal sacrifice to God through the High Priest who, 'taking the form of a servant,' offered Himself in His passion for us that we might be the body of so glorious a Head. For it was this 'form of a servant'[6] which He offered, it was in this form that He was the victim, since it is in 'the form of a servant' that He is Mediator, Priest and Sacrifice.

When, therefore, the Apostle had exhorted us to present our bodies as a sacrifice, living, holy, pleasing to God—our spiritual service—and not to be conformed to this world but be transformed in the newness of our minds, that we might discern what is the good and acceptable and perfect will of God, he went on to remind us that it is we ourselves who constitute the whole sacrifice: 'By the grace that has been given to me, I say to each one among you: Let no one rate himself more than he ought, but let him rate himself according to moderation, and according as God has apportioned to each one the measure of faith. For just as in one body we have many members, yet all the members have not the same function, so we, the many, are one body in Christ, but severally members one of

4 Rom. 12.2.
5 Ps. 72.28.
6 Cf. Phil. 2.7.

another. But we have gifts differing according to the grace that has been given us.'[7]

Such is the sacrifice of Christians: 'We, the many, are one body in Christ.' This is the Sacrifice, as the faithful understand, which the Church continues to celebrate in the sacrament of the altar, in which it is clear to the Church that she herself is offered in the very offering she makes to God.

Chapter 7

The immortal and blessed spirits who are deservedly established in heavenly abodes and rejoice in communion with their Creator are rooted in His eternity, certain in His truth, and sanctified by His grace. In their compassion they love us unhappy mortals and long for us to become both immortal and happy, and, therefore, they do not wish us to offer sacrifice to them but to God, knowing as they do that, along with us, they are His sacrifice. For we and they together form the one City of God to which the psalmist addressed the words: 'Glorious things are said of thee, O city of God,'[1] and of which our part is still on pilgrimage while the other part, the angels, help to guide us. It is from that city on high, where the will of God is the intelligible and immutable law, it is, if I may so speak, from that heavenly court where our case is in good hands that the angelic couriers carry down to us the Sacred Scripture, in which it is written: 'He that sacrificeth to gods, shall be put to death, save only to the Lord.'[2]

Such miracles have confirmed this Scripture, this law and these precepts, that there can be no doubt to whom these immortal and blessed spirits (who wish us to share what they possess) would have us offer sacrifice.

Chapters 8–18

Old Testament miracles are obviously different from the 'wonders' wrought by pagan magic. Porphyry's views on theurgy are described and condemned. Augustine insists that

[7] Rom. 12.3–6.

[1] Ps. 86.3.   [2] Exod. 22.20.

God uses the angels to work true miracles but that magic is
the work of bad spirits or demons. It is not reasonable for
pagans to reject the testimony of authentic miracles.

Chapter 19

There are some who think that, though these visible sacrifices may be suitable for other gods, for the God who is invisible, greater and better, only invisible, greater and better sacrifices, such as the offering of a pure mind and upright will, are
appropriate. Such people are evidently ignorant of the fact
that these visible sacrifices are mere symbols of invisible sacrifice just as truly as audible words are mere signs of realities.
For example, when we direct our prayers and praise to Him,
we use words which have meaning and, at the same time, we
offer in our hearts the things that our words signify. So, too,
when we offer sacrifice, we know that visible sacrifice should
be offered to no one but Him to whom we ourselves, in our
hearts, should be the invisible sacrifice. It is when we are offering such sacrifice that all the angels and the higher powers
who, outstanding especially in goodness and piety, look with
favor upon us, rejoice with us, and aid us with all their strength
to make this sacrifice. Even if we should wish to offer this
homage to them, they are unwilling to receive it. And when,
under a visible form, they are sent to men, they openly forbid it, as the examples in Scripture show. When some people
thought that the honor of adoration or sacrifice which is due
to God should be given to the angels, too, these spirits admonished them and forbade it, ordering that this homage be
conferred on Him to whom alone they knew that it was rightly
due.[1]

Even saintly men of God have imitated the holy angels. In
Lycaonia, Paul and Barnabas, having worked a miraculous
cure, were taken for gods and the Lycaonians wished to sacrifice victims to them. But the humble and virtuous Apostles
remonstrated, announcing to them that God in whom they
should believe.[2]

[1] Judges 13.15,16; Apoc. 8,9.
[2] Acts 14.8–18.

The deceitful spirits, on the other hand, in their pride exact this worship for themselves precisely because they know that it is due to God. For, contrary to what Porphyry says and some fancy, it is not the odors of dead victims that these spirits love but divine honors. For, certainly, of such odors they have a great supply everywhere and, if they wish more, they are able to provide them for themselves.

The spirits, then, who claim divinity for themselves take pleasure not in the fumes of bodies but in the soul of any suppliant whom they dominate, once they have deceived and seduced him; and they bar from him the way to the true God, so that, while rendering homage to some being other than God, he is unable to offer himself in sacrifice to Him.

Chapter 20

Christ Jesus, Himself man, is the true Mediator, for, inasmuch as He took the 'form of a slave,'[1] He became the 'Mediator between God and men.'[2] In His character as God, He receives sacrifices in union with the Father, with whom He is one God; yet He chose, in His character as a slave, to be Himself the Sacrifice rather than to receive it, lest any one might take occasion to think that sacrifice could be rendered to a creature. Thus it is that He is both the Priest who offers and the Oblation that is offered.[3] And it was His will that as a sacrament of this reality there should be the daily sacrifice of the Church, which, being the Body of Him, her Head, learns to offer itself through Him. This is the true sacrifice of which the ancient sacrifices of the saints were but many and manifold symbols. This one sacrifice was prefigured, in a variety of ways, as though one idea were being expressed in many words to drive in the truth without boring the reader. It is the supreme and true sacrifice to which all false sacrifices have given place.

---

[1] Phil. 2.7.
[2] 1 Tim. 2.5.
[3] *Per hoc et sacerdos est, ipse offerens, ipse et oblatio.*

Chapters 21–30

After further comparison of the power of demons with that of holy men, Augustine addresses Porphyry directly and accuses him of failing to assent to the truth which he knew about the One God. He was intellectually dishonest in teaching theurgy. This apostrophe is not to convince the dead Porphyry but to convert his living followers. Augustine almost begs the Neoplatonists to accept Christ.

Chapter 31

Surely, in matters which the mind of man cannot penetrate it is better simply to believe what God tells us, namely, that the soul is not co-eternal with God but was created out of nothing. To justify their refusal to believe this, the Platonists have been content with the argument that nothing can be everlasting unless it has existed eternally. What, however, Plato himself expressly stated[1] is that the world and those gods whom God put in the world began to be and had a beginning, although they will have no end, since the will of the all-powerful Creator will keep them in existence forever.

However, the Platonists have invented a way of interpreting this, saying that beginning means causal subordination, not an order in time. They say: 'If from all eternity a foot were standing in dust, there would always be a footprint beneath it. No one would doubt that this footprint was caused by the pressure of the foot, but no one would think that the impression came after the foot even though it was caused by the foot. In the same way, the world and the gods created in it have always existed, just as their Maker has always existed; yet they were made.'

Let us suppose that the soul has always existed. Must we say, therefore, that its misery, also, has always existed? If not, then there is something in the soul which was not there from all eternity, but began its existence in time. If this be so, why is it not possible for the soul itself to have begun its existence in time and not to have existed eternally? Or, take the happi-

[1] *Timaeus*, 41.

ness of the soul. After the experience of evil, it will be secure for all eternity. As Porphyry himself confesses, happiness undoubtedly begins in time, although it is to continue forever, in spite of having had no previous existence.

Thus, that whole argument falls to the ground which supposes that nothing can be without an end in time unless it was without a beginning in time. It was enough to show that the happiness of the soul, which had a beginning in time, will have no end in time.

Human weakness, therefore, should yield to divine authority. In regard to true religion, let us believe those holy and immortal angels who do not claim for themselves honors which they know are due to their God, who is also ours, and who command us to offer sacrifice only to Him whose sacrifice, as I have said before[2] and must often repeat, we and they together ought to be. I mean the sacrifice offered by Him as Priest who, in the humanity which He assumed and according to which He wished to be our Priest, deigned to become a sacrifice for us even unto death.

Chapter 32

This religion constitutes the single way for the liberation of all souls, for souls can be saved by no way but this. This is, if I may so speak, the King's highway which alone leads to a kingdom, not tottering on some temporal height, but secure on the firm foundations of eternity. Porphyry, however, says, toward the end of the first book of his 'Return of the Soul,' that he has not yet come across the claim, made by any school of thought, to embrace a universal way for the liberation of the soul—certainly, not one taken from any genuine philosophy, or from the code or creed of India, or from the initiation rite of the Chaldaeans, or from any other religion. And so far, he adds, no historical research has brought any such universal way of his attention.

There is here, surely, an admission that there is such a way even though, so far, he has no knowledge of it. Thus, nothing which he had learned with so much application concerning

[2] E.g., Bk. 10.16, here omitted.

the liberation of the soul, nothing that he thought—or, at least, others thought—that he knew and believed satisfied him. He still felt that he needed a supreme authority which should be followed in this important matter. Notice that he says that not even in any of the genuine philosophies has he yet discovered a school that embodies a universal way for the liberation of the soul. This sufficiently proves, so it seems to me, either that the philosophy which he himself professed was not the truest or else that it did not constitute such a way.

How, in fact, can it be the truest philosophy if it does not include this way? For, what does a universal way for the liberation of the soul mean except a way by which all souls are liberated and without which, therefore, no soul is liberated? When he adds: 'Or from the code or creed of India, or from the initiation rite of the Chaldaeans, or from any other religion,' he testifies explicitly that neither in what he learned from the Indians nor in what he learned from the Chaldaeans did he find this universal way for the liberation of the soul; yet he had to tell us that it was from the Chaldaeans that he got those divine oracles which he keeps mentioning so frequently.

Now, what does he want us to understand by a universal way for the liberation of the soul which has not yet been accepted either by any genuine philosophy or by the doctrines of those pagan people who were considered outstanding in divine affairs, as being especially curious concerning the knowledge and worship of the angels, and which he has not yet come across in his historical reading?

What can be meant by this universal way except one which is not the particular property of any one nation, but which has been divinely bestowed and is common to all nations? That such a way exists Porphyry, who was a man endowed with no mediocre talent, does not doubt. He does not believe that Divine Providence could have left the human race without this universal way for the liberation of the soul. For he does not say that this immense good and wonderful aid does not exist, but that he had not yet come across it, that it had not yet come to his notice.

No one need be surprised at this. For, Porphyry lived at a time when this universal way for the liberation of the soul

—which is none other than the Christian religion—was, by divine permission, attacked by idolaters, demon worshipers, and earthly rulers in order that the number of martyrs might be completed and consecrated—and by martyrs I mean witnesses of the truth whose mission it was to show that all bodily sufferings must be endured when it is a question of remaining faithful to religion and of offering testimony to the truth. Porphyry, then, saw all this and thought that such persecutions would soon effect the destruction of this way and that, therefore, it could not be the universal way for the liberation of the soul. He did not understand that these persecutions, which impressed him and which he feared to suffer if he chose this way, tended rather to establish this religion more solidly and to commend it to others.

This way for the liberation of souls is universal, that is, a way granted to all nations by divine mercy and, therefore, such that no one at all to whom knowledge of it has come or is to come should have asked or should ever ask: 'Why so soon' or 'Why so late?' For, the design of Him who reveals it is impenetrable to human intelligence. This is what Porphyry himself understood when he said that this gift of God had not yet been experienced nor had even come to his knowledge. But he did not deny that this gift was a real gift just because it had not yet been experienced by faith nor had come to his attention as a piece of knowledge.

This way, I repeat, is the universal way for the salvation of believers, the way referred to in the divine promise received by the faithful Abraham: 'In your descendants all the nations of the earth shall be blessed.'[1] Abraham was, in fact, a Chaldaean by birth, but, in order that he might receive such promises and that from him might be propagated a people 'delivered by angels through a mediator,'[2] a people among whom we find this universal way for the liberation of souls—a way given to all nations—he was ordered to depart from his own country and kindred and from his father's house.[3] And, as soon as he was liberated from the superstitions of the Chaldaeans,

[1] Gen. 22.18.
[2] Gal. 3.19.
[3] Cf. Gen. 12.1.

he adored and followed the one true God and faithfully believed in the promises that had been made to him.

This universal way is the one of which it had been said in holy prophecy: 'May God have mercy on us, and bless us: may he cause the light of his countenance to shine upon us, and may he have mercy on us. That we may know thy way upon earth: thy salvation in all nations.'[4] Hence, long after, when the Saviour had taken flesh from the descendants of Abraham, He said of Himself: 'I am the way, and the truth, and the life.'[5]

This is the universal way which had been prophesied a long time before: 'And in the last days the mountain of the house of the Lord shall be prepared on the top of mountains, and it shall be exalted above the hills, and all nations shall flow unto it. And many people shall go, and say: Come and let us go up to the mountain of the Lord, and to the house of the God of Jacob, and he will teach us his ways, and we will walk in his paths: for the law shall come forth from Sion, and the word of the Lord from Jerusalem.'[6]

This way does not belong, then, to one but to all nations; and the Law and the Word of the Lord did not remain in Sion and Jerusalem, but went forth that it might spread throughout the world. For this reason, the Mediator Himself, after His resurrection, said to His alarmed disciples: 'All things must be fulfilled that are written in the Law of Moses and the Prophets and the Psalms concerning me. Then he opened their minds that they might understand the Scriptures. And he said to them, Thus it is written; and thus the Christ should suffer, and should rise again from the dead on the third day; and that repentance and remission of sins should be preached in His name to all the nations, beginning from Jerusalem.'[7]

This universal way for the liberation of souls is the one which the holy angels and holy prophets formerly disclosed to the few who, by the grace of God, could understand. This was especially so among the Hebrew people whose commonwealth was consecrated, as it were, into a prophecy and prediction of the City of God which is to be gathered from all nations. This way was symbolized by the tabernacle, temple,

[4] Ps. 66.1–3.   [5] John 14.6.
[6] Isa. 2.2,3.   [7] Luke 24.44–47.

priesthood, and sacrifices; and it was predicted sometimes in explicit statements and more often by mystical intimations. But the Mediator Himself, dwelling among us in the flesh, and His blessed Apostles have revealed the grace of the New Testament and have overtly explained what, in former ages, had been covertly symbolized, according as it has pleased the wisdom of God to make revelations to the successive ages of the human race. And at all times there has been confirmation by divine miracles, a few of which I have already mentioned.

Not only have visions of angels been seen and the words of celestial messengers been heard, but holy men of God, actuated by sincere piety, have cast out unclean spirits from the bodies and senses of men, have healed the diseases and infirmities of the body; moreover, wild beasts of the earth, the waters, birds of the heavens, trees, the elements, and stars have all obeyed their divine commands; even the infernal powers have yielded to them, and the dead have arisen from the grave. I shall not speak of the miracles which belong to the Saviour Himself—those especially of His birth and resurrection. In the former, He made known to us the mystery of His Mother's virginity; in the latter, He presented to us an example of that state which will be the privilege of those who will be resurrected on the last day.

This way purifies the whole man, preparing for immortality every mortal part of which man is composed; and it was to obviate the necessity of special purifications, one for the part which Porphyry calls the intellectual soul, another for what he calls the spiritual soul, and still another for the body that our true and all-powerful Purifier and Saviour assumed an entire human nature. This way has never been lacking to the human race, whether at the time when these mysteries were being prophesied or when they were announced as already accomplished. Thus, no one has ever been liberated, nor is being liberated, nor ever will be liberated, except by this way.

When, therefore, Porphyry says that no universal way for the liberation of souls has yet come to his knowledge by the study of history, we must point out that nothing can be more obvious than this story which has convinced the whole world of its transcendent authenticity. For, what story can be more authentic than one which not only relates past events but includes so many prophecies which have already been accomplished that we can firmly trust that all the others will likewise be fulfilled?

Neither Porphyry nor any other Platonist can discover in our way of salvation the kind of divination and prophecy relating to earthly affairs and mortal life which they discover in soothsaying and magical prognostications and rightly despise. They are right when they say that such predictions are not made by great men and are of little value. For, in some cases, such guesses are based on obscure causes, as when a doctor foresees by certain symptoms a future condition of health. In other instances, unclean demons predict deeds which they have already decided upon, thus creating the impression of having a kind of right to lead the minds and hearts of wicked men to imitate their example, and this on the lowest level of human frailty.

But, it was not such unimportant things that holy men walking in the universal way of salvation were preoccupied about prophesying, except, of course, in cases where it helped to strengthen people's faith in realities which cannot be perceived by human senses nor understood easily by experience. But, there were other really great and divine events which they foretold, in so far as it was given to them to know the will of God.

The following are some of the predictions and promises revealed in our Scriptures: the coming of Christ in the flesh with all that was fulfilled in His Person and accomplished in His Name; the repentance of men and the conversion of their wills to God; the remission of sins, the grace which justifies, the faith of the saints, and the multitude of men throughout the whole world who believe in His true divinity; the collapse of the worship of idols and demons; the trials of persecutions, the purification of those who persevered and their deliverance from every evil; the day of judgment, the resurrection of the dead, the eternal damnation of the wicked, and the eternal kingdom of the glorious City of God whose citizens will everlastingly rejoice in the vision of God. And we have seen so many of these promises already accomplished that we are sure with the confidence of faith that the rest will follow.

Those who do not believe and, therefore, do not understand

that the right way to the vision of God and eternal union with Him is that which is proclaimed and proved in the Holy Scripture can continue to debate but can never disprove our position.[8]

In these ten Books, perhaps, I may not have lived up to the expectations of all, but, to the extent that the true God and Lord has deigned to help me, I have satisfied some, at least, by my refutation of the objections of the pagans who prefer their own gods to the Founder of that holy City, which I undertook to discuss. The first five of these ten Books were directed against those who think that the gods should be worshiped for the sake of the goods of this life, and the following five against those who believe that the gods should be worshiped for the sake of the life after death. My next task is to keep the promise made in Book I and, with God's help, to discuss all that seems necessary concerning the origin, progress, and appropriate ends of these two cities which are inextricably intermingled, as I have said, in the concrete reality of history.

[8] . . . *obpugnare possunt, sed expugnare non possunt.*

PART THREE

THE ORIGIN OF THE TWO CITIES

BOOK XI

Creation and the Two Societies of Angels

Chapter 1

THE EXPRESSION, 'City of God,' which I have been using is
justified by that Scripture whose divine authority puts it above
the literature of all other people and brings under its sway
every type of human genius—and that, not by some casual intellectual reaction, but by a disposition of Divine Providence.
For, in this Scripture, we read: 'Glorious things are said of
thee, O city of God';[1] and, in another psalm: 'Great is the
Lord, and exceedingly to be praised in the city of our God,
in His holy mountain, increasing the joy of the whole earth';
and, a little later in the same psalm: 'As we have heard, so
have we seen, in the city of the Lord of hosts, in the city of
our God: God hath founded it for ever';[2] and in another text:
'The stream of the river maketh the city of God joyful: the
most High hath sanctified his own tabernacle. God is in the
midst thereof, it shall not be moved.'[3]

Through these and similar passages too numerous to quote,
we learn of the existence of a City of God whose Founder has
inspired us with a love and longing to become its citizens. The
inhabitants of the earthly city who prefer their own gods to
the Founder of the holy City do not realize that He is the
God of gods—though not, of course, of those false, wicked and
proud gods who, because they have been deprived of that unchangeable light which was meant for all, are reduced to a

[1] Ps. 86.3. [2] Ps. 47.1,2,9.
[3] Ps. 45.5,6.

pitiful power and, therefore, are eager for some sort of influence and demand divine honors from their deluded subjects. He is the God of those reverent and holy gods who prefer to obey and worship one God rather than to have many others obeying and worshiping them.

In the ten preceding Books, I have done my best, with the help of our Lord and King, to refute the enemies of this City. Now, however, realizing what is expected of me and recalling what I promised, I shall begin to discuss, as well as I can, the origin, history, and destiny of the respective cities, earthly and heavenly, which, as I have said, are at present inextricably intermingled, one with the other. First, I shall explain how these two cities originated when the angels took opposing sides.

Chapter 2

Rarely and only with great effort does a mind, which has contemplated both the material and spiritual creation of the universe and discovered the mutability of all things, soar to the unchangeable substance of God and there learn that He is the sole Creator of every nature that is not divine. For, God does not speak with man through the medium of matter, with vibrations of air causing His voice to be heard by the ears of the body, nor does He use apparitions resembling bodies such as we see in dreams or in some such way—for in this latter case the speaking is to seeming ears, through a seeming medium with a seeming material space intervening, since such apparitions are very similar to material objects. But He speaks by means of the truth itself, and to all who can hear with the mind rather than with the body.

For, He speaks to that part of man which is most excellent and which has nothing superior to it except God Himself. Now, since it is right to think or, if that is impossible, to believe that man was created to the image of God, surely man comes closer to God by that part of him which transcends those lower faculties which he has in common even with the beasts. But, since the mind, which was meant to be reasonable and intelligent, has, by dark and inveterate vices, become too

weak to adhere joyously to His unchangeable light (or even
to bear it) until, by gradual renewal and healing, it is made
fit for such happiness, its first need was to be instructed by
faith and purified.

It was in order to make the mind able to advance more
confidently toward the truth that Truth itself, the divine Son
of God, put on humanity without putting off His divinity[1] and
built this firm path of faith so that man, by means of the God-
man, could find his way to man's God. I speak of the 'Mediator between God and men, himself man, Christ Jesus.'[2] For it
is as man that He is the Mediator and as man that He is the
way. Where there is a way between a traveler and his destination, he can hope to reach it, but, if there is no way or if
he does not know which way to take, what is the good of
knowing the destination? Now, there is one way and one way
alone that can save us from all aberrations, the Way which
is both God and man—God as the goal and man as the means
to reach it.[3]

Chapter 3

This Mediator, first through the Prophets, then by His own
lips, afterwards through the Apostles, revealed whatever He
considered necessary. He also inspired the Scripture, which is
regarded as canonical and of supreme authority and to which
we give credence concerning all those truths we ought to know
and yet, of ourselves, are unable to learn. We can know by
our own witness things which are presented to our senses, either interior or exterior. In fact, we say a thing is 'present'
because it is 'presented' to our senses. For example, anything
before our very eyes is said to be present. But, when things
are not present to our senses, we cannot know them on our
own authority. So we seek out and believe witnesses to whose
senses, we believe, these things are or were present.

Thus, in the case of visible objects which we have not seen,
we trust those who have seen them. The same is true of things
known by the other senses. So, too, in the case of realities per-

[1] . . . homine adsumto, non Deo consumto . . .
[2] 1 Tim. 2.5.
[3] . . . quo itur Deus, qua itur homo.

ceived by the mind and spirit, the mind is an interior sense and we speak of a man of 'good sense.' If our perceptions are of invisible things remote from our own interior sense, we ought to believe either those who have learned these truths as revealed in the Incorporeal Light or those who contemplate these truths in an abiding Vision of God.

Chapter 4

Of all visible things, the universe is the greatest; of all invisible realities, the greatest is God. That the world exists we can see; we believe in the existence of God. But there is no one we can more safely trust than God Himself in regard to the fact that it was He who made the world. Where has He told us so? Nowhere more distinctly than in the Holy Scriptures where His Prophet said: 'In the beginning God created the heavens and the earth.'[1] Well, but was the Prophet present when God made heaven and earth? No; but the Wisdom of God by whom all things were made was there. And this Wisdom, entering into holy souls, makes of them the friends and prophets of God[2] and reveals to them, silently and interiorly, what God has done.

They are taught, also, by the angels of God who 'always behold the face of the Father'[3] and are commissioned to announce His will to others. Among these Prophets was the one who announced in writing: 'In the beginning God created the heavens and the earth.' And it was so fitting that faith in God should come through such a witness that he was inspired by the same Spirit of God, who had revealed these truths to him, to predict, far in advance, our own future faith.

But, why did it please the eternal God to create heaven and earth at that special time, seeing that He had not done so earlier? If the purpose of those who pose this question is to protest that the world is eternal, without beginning, and, therefore, not created by God, then they are far from the truth and are raving with the deadly disease of irreligion. For, quite apart from the voice of the Prophets, the very order, changes,

[1] Gen. 1.1. [2] Cf. Wisd. 7.27.
[3] Matt. 18.10.

and movements in the universe, the very beauty of form in all that is visible, proclaim, however silently, both that the world was created and also that its Creator could be none other than God whose greatness and beauty are both ineffable and invisible.

There are those who say that the universe was, indeed, created by God, denying a 'temporal' but admitting a 'creational' beginning, as though, in some hardly comprehensible way, the world was made, but máde from all eternity. Their purpose seems to be to save God from the charge of arbitrary rashness. They would not have us believe that a completely new idea of creating the world suddenly occurred to Him or that a change of mind took place in Him in whom there can be no change.

I do not see, however, how this position is consistent with their stand in other matters, especially in regard to the soul. For, if, as they must hold, the soul is co-eternal with God, they have no way to explain how a completely new misery can begin in an eternally existing soul.

For, if they say that its misery and happiness ceaselessly alternate, then they are obliged to conclude that this alternation will go on forever. Thus, an absurdity follows: though the soul is called blessed, it will not be so in fact, since it foresees its future misery and disgrace; and, even if it does not foresee its future disgrace or misery but thinks that it will be happy forever, its happiness will depend upon deception. And this is as foolish a statement as could possibly be made.

But, if they suppose that the soul has been alternately happy and unhappy through infinite ages but that, from now on, being set free, it will never return to its former misery, they are, in fact, convinced that the soul was never truly blessed but that at last it begins to enjoy a new and genuine happiness. Thus, they admit that something new, important, and remarkable happens within the soul which had never occurred to it before from all eternity. And, if they deny that God's eternal providence included the cause of this new experience of the soul, they likewise deny that He is the Author of its beatitude—which is an abominable piece of impiety. If, on the other hand, they claim that by a new decree God determined that the soul should be eternally blessed, how can they show that He is free from that mutability which even they repudiate?

Finally, if they say that the soul was created in time but will not perish in any future time, like numbers which begin with 'one' but never end, and, therefore, that having experienced misery, it will be freed from it, never again to return to it, they will surely have no hesitation in admitting that this is compatible with the immutability of God's decision. This being so, they should also believe that the world could be made in time without God who made it having to change the eternal decision of His will.

Chapter 5

Before attempting to reply to those who, while agreeing with us that God is the Creator of the world, question us about the time at which it was created, we must see what response they make when we ask them about the space in which it was created. For, just as they ask why it was made then and not earlier, we may ask why it was made here and not elsewhere. Because, if they excogitate infinite periods of time before the world, in which they cannot see how God could have had nothing to do, they ought to conceive of infinite reaches of space beyond the visible universe. And, if they maintain that the Omnipotent can never be inactive, will they not logically be forced to dream wth Epicurus of innumerable universes? (There will be merely this difference, that, while he asserts that these worlds originate and disintegrate by the fortuitous movements of atoms, they will hold that they are created by the work of God.) This is the conclusion if they insist on the premise that there is an interminable immensity of space stretching in all directions in which God cannot remain passive and that those imaginary worlds, like this visible one, are indestructible.

The present discussion is limited to those who believe with us that God is spiritual and the Creator of all existences except Himself, first, because there is something improper in inviting materialists to discuss a religious question; and second, because even in pagan circles the Platonists have gained a prestige and authority beyond that of other philosophers—for the simple reason that, however far they are from the truth, they are much nearer to it than any of the others.

Now, the Platonists hold that the divine substance is neither confined nor limited nor distributed in space; they acknowledge very properly that He is spiritually and completely present everywhere. Will they then say that He is absent from the infinitely immense spaces out beyond and is occupied only in the relatively tiny space that contains this cosmos? I do not think that they will be foolish enough to go this far.

Let us agree, then, that they admit a single cosmos of immense material bulk, indeed, yet, finite and determined in its own place, and created by the work of God. Now, whatever reason they can give for God's cessation from work in the infinite spaces outside the world, let them offer the same solution to their problem of God ceasing from activity during the infinite stretches of time before the creation of the world.

Now, it does not follow that it was by chance rather than by a divine reason that God localized the world in this spot instead of in another, even though no human reason can comprehend the divine reason and although this particular place has no special merit that it should be chosen in preference to an infinite number of others. Nor, in the same way, does it follow that we should suppose that it was by accident that God created the world at that specific time rather than before, even though previous times had been uniformly passing by throughout an infinite past and there was no difference which would cause this time to be chosen in preference to another.

Of course, they may admit that it is silly to imagine infinite space since there is no such thing as space beyond the cosmos. In that case, let this be the answer: It is silly for them to excogitate a past time during which God was unoccupied, for the simple reason that there was no such thing as time before the universe was made.

Chapter 6

The distinguishing mark between time and eternity is that the former does not exist without some movement and change, while in the latter there is no change at all. Obviously, then, there could have been no time had not a creature been made whose movement would effect some change. It is because the parts of this motion and change cannot be simultaneous, since one part must follow another, that, in these shorter or longer intervals of duration, time begins. Now, since God, in whose eternity there is absolutely no change, is the Creator and Ruler of time, I do not see how we can say that He created the world after a space of time had elapsed unless we admit, also, that previously some creature had existed whose movements would mark the course of time.

Again, sacred and infallible Scripture tells us that in the beginning God created heaven and earth in order. Now, unless this meant that nothing had been made before, it would have been stated that whatever else God had made before was created in the beginning. Undoubtedly, then, the world was made not in time but together with time. For, what is made in time is made after one period of time and before another, namely, after a past and before a future time. But, there could have been no past time, since there was nothing created by whose movements and change time could be measured.

The fact is that the world was made simultaneously with time, if, with creation, motion and change began. Now this seems evident from the order of the first six or seven days. For, the morning and evening of each of these days are counted until on the sixth day all that had been created during this time was complete. Then, on the seventh day, in a mysterious revelation, we are told that God ceased from work. As for these 'days,' it is difficult, perhaps impossible to think —let alone to explain in words—what they mean.

Chapter 7

Of course, what we mean by the 'days' we know in experience are those that have a morning because the sun rises and an evening because the sun sets. But the first three 'days' of creation passed without benefit of sun, since, according to Scripture, the sun was made on the fourth day. Of course, there is mention in the beginning that 'light' was made by the Word of God, and that God separated it from darkness, calling the light day and the darkness night. But no experience of our senses can tell us just what kind of 'light' it was and by what kind of alternating movement it caused 'morning' and 'evening.' Not even our intellects can comprehend what is meant, yet we can have no hesitation in believing the fact.

Perhaps there is a material light in the far reaches of the universe which are out of sight. Or it may mean the light from which the sun was afterwards kindled. Or, perhaps, under the name of light, there is signified that holy City composed of blessed angels and saints of which the Apostle speaks: 'That Jerusalem which is above, our eternal mother in heaven.'[1] Compare what he says elsewhere: 'For you are all children of the light and children of the day. We are not of night, nor of darkness.'[2] The only question is whether we can find an appropriate meaning for the 'morning' and 'evening' of such a day.

At any rate, the creature's knowledge in comparison with that of the Creator might be said to be dim as twilight. Yet, it breaks into dawn and brightens to morning when it is employed in the praise and love of God. Nor does the darkness of night ever fall so long as the Creator is not abandoned for love of the creature. Note that Scripture never mentions the word 'night' when speaking of those days one after the other. Nowhere does it say: 'There was night,' but: 'There was evening and morning, the first day.'[3] And so of the second day and the rest. It is as though the meaning were: The knowledge of a created thing, seen just as it is, is dimmer, so to speak, than when the thing is contemplated in the wisdom of God, as in the art by which it was made. Therefore, evening is a more suitable term than night. However, as I said, this evening twilight turns into morning as soon as knowledge turns to the praise and love of its Creator.

When the creature does this in the knowledge of itself, this is the first day; when it does so in the knowledge of the firmament—the heavens between the waters above and the waters below—this is the second day. So, too, in the knowledge of the earth and sea and of all vegetation on the earth, this is the third day; in the knowledge of the sun and moon and of

[1] Cf. Gal. 4.26; St. Augustine's text, unlike the Vulgate, has *aeterna* (eternal), not *libera* (free).
[2] Thess. 5.5.   [3] Gen. 1.5.

all the stars, this is the fourth day; in the knowledge of all the fish of the sea and the birds of the air, this is the fifth day; in the knowledge of all terrestrial animals and, lastly, of man himself, this is the sixth day.

Chapter 8

The statement that God rested from all His works on the seventh day and sanctified it should not be interpreted in a childish way, as if God had labored in His operations. For He 'spoke and they were made,'[1] not, indeed, by an audible and fleeting word, but by a spiritual and eternal one. But, the rest of God signifies the repose of those who rest in Him, just as the joy of a home means the gladness of those in a home who rejoice, although it is not the house but something else that makes them rejoice.

This is all the more so if the beauty of the house itself makes those who dwell in it rejoice. For here we are not merely using the figure of speech in which what is contained is signified by what contains—as when we say the theater applauded or speak of the mooing meadows, meaning the spectators in the one case and the oxen in the other. Here we are using a second figure of speech in which the cause is described in terms of the effect—as when a letter is said to be joyful because it makes its readers rejoice.

And so, when the inspired writer states that God rested, his words are most appropriately interpreted to mean the rest of those who rest in God and of whose rest God is the cause. And the prophecy also promises to those to whom it speaks and for whom it was written that, if by faith they have drawn as close to God as is possible in this life, then, after doing the good works which God operates in and through them, they shall enjoy in Him eternal rest. This promise was symbolized, for the chosen people of God, by the sabbath rest prescribed in their law. I shall speak more in detail about this in its proper place.[2]

[1] Ps. 148.5.
[2] Cf. below, 22.30.

Chapter 9

Since my present intention is to say something about the origin of the holy City, I must first deal with the holy angels who form such a large and, indeed, the most blessed part of that City, since they have never departed from it. With God's grace I shall interpret those passages of Holy Scripture which seem to me relevant to this subject. When Scripture speaks of the creation of the world, it does not indicate clearly whether, or in what order, the angels were created. But, if they are alluded to at all, it is perhaps under the name of the heavens in the words: 'In the beginning God created the heavens and the earth,'[1] or, more likely, under the term light, about which I was just speaking. My reason for thinking that they were not omitted is because it is written that God rested on the seventh day from all the works which He had made, although the first line of Holy Scripture, 'In the beginning God created the heavens and the earth,' implies that before the creation of heaven and earth God had made nothing. He began, then, with heaven and earth. Now, the earth, as Scripture adds, was at first invisible and formless and, since light was not yet created, darkness covered the abyss. By 'abyss' is meant a conglomeration of earth and water; and, of course, with no light, there is necessarily darkness. But if, as we are told, all things were created and ordered and the work was completed in six days, how could the angels be omitted as if they were not included in the works of God from which He rested on the seventh day?

Actually, the fact that the angels are the work of God is not omitted in the account of creation, yet it is not expressly mentioned. Elsewhere, however, Holy Scripture bears luminous witness to the fact. Thus, the canticle of the three children in the furnace, after saying, 'All ye works of the Lord, bless the Lord,' enumerates these works and includes the angels.[2] Again, the Psalmist sings: 'Praise ye the Lord from the heavens: praise ye Him in the high places. Praise ye Him, all His angels, praise ye Him, all His hosts. Praise ye Him, O sun and moon: praise Him, all ye stars and light. Praise Him, ye heavens of heavens, praise the name of the Lord. For He

[1] Gen. 1.1.   [2] Dan. 3.57–58.

spoke, and they were made: He commanded, and they were created.'[3]

Here, unmistakably and by divine inspiration the angels are said to have been created by God, since they are included among all the other celestial things of which Scripture declares: 'He commanded, and they were created.' And, surely, no one would be rash enough to hold that the angels were created after all the other things mentioned in the six days of creation. If so, his folly can be refuted by the equally authoritative Scriptural passage where God says: 'When the stars were made all my angels loudly praised me.'[4] The angels, therefore, existed before the stars; and the stars were created on the fourth day. Must we say, then, that they were made on the third day? By no means. For it is clear what was created on that day: the earth was separated from the water, the two elements each taking its proper form, while earth brought forth its vegetation.

Perhaps, then, on the second day? The answer is again 'no.' For, on that day, between the waters above and those below, a firmament was formed and was called the heavens; and in this the stars were created on the fourth day. There is, then, no doubt that, if the angels are included in the works of God during these six days, they are that light which was called day; and their unity is stressed by the fact that the day is called not the 'first day' but 'one day.' Nor are the second, third, and so on really other days. They are all the same 'one day,' repeated to complete the number six or seven, and to signify that knowledge which is six or sevenfold, namely, the sixfold knowledge of the works of God and the seventh knowledge of His rest.

If, in the passage of Scripture where God says: 'Let there be light and there was light,' we are right in taking this light to mean the angels, then we are sure that they are made participators of His eternal light, which is nothing other than the unchangeable Wisdom by which all things were made, and which we call the only-begotten Son of God. Thus, the angels, illumined by that Light which created them, became light and were called 'day' because they participated in that unchangea-

---

[3] Ps. 148. 1–5.   [4] Cf. Job 38.7.

ble Light and Day which is the Word of God, by whom they and all things were made.

For, 'the true light that enlightens every man who comes into the world'[5] illumines every pure angel that he may be light not in himself but in God. And, once an angel rejects this Light, he becomes impure. Thus, all those who are called unclean spirits are no longer light in the Lord but darkness in themselves, being deprived of a participation in His eternal light. For, evil has no positive nature; what we call evil is merely the lack of something that is good.

Chapter 10

There is, accordingly, a good which alone is simple and, therefore, which alone is unchangeable—and this is God. This good has created all goods; but these are not simple and, therefore, they are mutable. They were created, I repeat, that is, they were made, not begotten. For, what is begotten of the simple good is likewise simple and is what the Begetter is. These two we call the Father and the Son and, together with their Spirit, are one God. This Spirit of the Father and of the Son is called in Sacred Scripture, in a very special sense, the Holy Spirit.

The Spirit is other than the Father and the Son because He is neither the Father nor the Son. I say 'other than,' not 'different from,' because, equally with them, He is the simple, unchangeable, co-eternal Good. This Trinity is one God. And, although it is a Trinity, it is none the less simple. For, we do not say that the nature of this good is simple because the Father alone shares in it, or the Son alone, or the Holy Spirit alone. Nor do we say with the Sabellian heretics that it is but a nominal Trinity without subsistent Persons. Our reason for calling it simple is because it is what it has—with the exception of the real relations in which the Persons stand to each other.

For, it is true that the Father *has* a Son, yet He *is* not the Son. And the Son *has* a Father, yet *is* not the Father. Therefore, as regards Himself, without reference to His relation with the others, the Father is what He has. Thus, when He is said to be living, we mean that He has life and is the very life He has.

When a nature is called simple we mean that it can have nothing that it can lose; that it cannot be different from what it has, as a cup is different from the wine it holds, a body from its color, the air from its light or warmth, the mind from its wisdom. None of these is what it has; the cup is not the liquid, nor the body its color, nor the air its light or warmth, nor the mind its wisdom. All of these, therefore, can be deprived of what they have; they can be converted into other states or qualities: for example, the cup may be emptied of the contents of which it was full; the body may lose its color; the air may darken and grow cold; and the mind may lose its sanity.

Although the incorruptible body which is promised to the saints in the resurrection cannot, indeed, lose the quality of its incorruption, yet its permanent bodily substance and its quality of incorruptibility are not one and the same thing. For the quality of incorruptibility is entire and uniform throughout the separate parts of the body. It is not greater in one member and less in another, since there is no part that is more incorruptible than another. The body, indeed, is greater in its totality than in each part, and, although one part is larger, another smaller, the former is not more incorruptible than the latter. The body, therefore, which is not entire in each of its parts is one thing; incorruptibility which is complete throughout is another thing, since every part of the incorruptible body, though unequal to the rest, is equally incorrupt. For example, the finger, though less than the whole hand, is not, therefore, less incorruptible; although unequal in size, they are both equal in incorruptibility. Thus, although incorruptibility is inseparable from an incorruptible body, the substance by which it is a body is one thing and the quality by which it is incorruptible is another. The body is not, in spite of this inseparability, identical with what it has.

So, too, with the soul. Although it will be forever wise when redeemed in eternity, yet it will be wise only by participating in the unchangeable Wisdom, which is not the soul itself. So with the air. If it were never to be deprived of its infused light, it would still not be identical with that light by which it is illuminated. I am not suggesting that the soul is air, as some have supposed who were unable to conceive of a spiritual nature, although, for all their dissimilarity, there is here a kind of analogy which makes it reasonable to say that the immaterial soul is made luminous by the immaterial light of the simple Wisdom of God, much as we say that the material air is made luminous by the material light. And, as air grows dark when dispossessed of this light—for what is called darkness in this place or that is nothing else than air lacking light—so we may say that the soul grows dark when deprived of the light of Wisdom.

Accordingly, whatever is authentically[1] and truly divine is said to be simple because its qualities and its substance are one and the same, and because it is not by participation that it is divine, or wise or holy. It is true that in Sacred Scripture the spirit of wisdom is said to be manifold by reason of its fullness. However, what the Holy Spirit is and what it has are one, and all that it has is one.

There are not many wisdoms but only one. And in this Wisdom there is an infinite and inexhaustible treasury of intelligible realities containing all the invisible and unchangeable ideas[2] of all the visible and changeable existences which were made by this Wisdom. For, God has made nothing unknowingly; not even a human craftsman can be said to do so. But, if He knew all that He created, He created only those things which He knew. This conclusion suggests a striking but true idea: that this world could not be known by us unless it first existed; but it could not have existed unless it had first been known to God.[3]

Chapter 11

This being so, the spirits called angels were never, in any sense, at any time, partakers of darkness, but, from the moment of their creation, they were made beings of light. They were not merely created in order to exist and to live, but they were also illumined, so that they might live in wisdom and happiness. Some angels, however, turned away from this il-

---

[1] *principaliter.*   [2] *rationes.*
[3] . . . *iste mundus nobis notus esse non posset, nisi esset; Deo autem nisi notus esset, esse non posset.*

lumination and failed to attain this eminence of wisdom and blessedness which is unthinkable apart from the possession and assurance of everlastingness. These angels, however, even if they wished, could not lose their nature in so far as it is a life of reason—although not of wisdom.

Although no one can define the precise measure of their wisdom before their fall, one thing is certain. We cannot presume that they shared in wisdom equally with the angels who enjoy a plenitude of true happiness precisely because they were never deceived concerning its eternity. For, if they had participated in equal measure, then, because they were equally certain, they would have remained equally and eternally blessed. For, no matter how long a life may last, we cannot, in truth, call it eternal if at length it must have an end, since life merely implies living, whereas eternal means having no end.

It does not follow that every thing that is eternal is, therefore, blessed—for the pain of Hell is called eternal. However, if no life is truly and perfectly happy unless it is eternally so, it follows that the life of the fallen angels was not blessed since, whether they knew it or not, their blessedness was destined to end and, therefore, was not eternal. If they knew this, it was fear, and, if they did not, then it was error that prevented them from being blessed. Even if they were not so completely ignorant as to believe in a false expectation but were in doubt whether or not their happiness would be eternal, then this very uncertainty itself concerning such a blessed destiny would be at variance with the plenitude of beatitude which we believe the holy angels enjoyed.

Here we do not restrict the term 'blessed life' to so narrow a meaning that we ascribe it to God alone. His beatitude is so truly perfect that there can be none greater. In comparison, what does even the beatitude of the blessed angels amount to, although they are completely happy according to their capacity?

Chapter 12

The angels are not the only rational or intellectual creatures who we think should be called blessed. For no one will dare to deny that the first human beings in Paradise were blessed before their sin, although they were uncertain about the duration or eternity of their happiness—which, in fact, would have been eternal if they had not sinned. And even today we rightly regard as happy all those whom we see leading a good and holy life in the hope of future immortality, untroubled in conscience and with easy access to God's forgiveness for the sins which are due to the frailty of human nature.

These saints, however, although certain of their reward if they persevere, can never be sure of their perseverance. For, no man can be sure that he will continue to the end to act and advance in grace unless this fact is revealed to him by God. In His just and secret counsel, God, although He never deceives anyone, gives but few assurances in this matter.

Consequently, as regards the enjoyment of present happiness, the first man in Paradise was more fortunate than any saint now subject to weakness and mortality. But, as regards the hope of a future reward, any man who does not merely suppose but who knows, on the authority of infallible Truth, that he will enjoy, beyond the reach of evil and in the company of angels, union with the most high God is far happier in whatever state of physical sufferings he may be than the man who, even in the great delight of Paradise, was uncertain of his fall.

Chapter 13

From what has been said, the obvious conclusion is that the beatitude desired by an intelligent being as its proper end will result only from the combination of an uninterrupted enjoyment of that immutable good which is God with deliverance from any doubt or deception concerning the eternity of its continuance. With holy confidence, we believe that the angels of light possess this kind of blessedness. By a process of reasoning, we gather that the bad angels, who were deprived of this light by their own perverseness, did not have this beatitude even before their fall. However, if they lived some time before they sinned, we must believe that they were endowed with a measure of happiness lacking in any foreknowledge of its continuance.

I know it may seem difficult to believe that, while the angels were so created that some were in ignorance concerning their perseverance or defection and others were infallibly assured of the eternity of their bliss, yet all were created from the beginning equally blessed and remained so until the angels who are now evil fell voluntarily from their light and love. Nevertheless, it is much more difficult to suppose that the holy angels are uncertain of their eternal happiness and so are ignorant of a truth about themselves which we have been able to learn from Holy Scripture.

For, there is no Catholic who does not know that a good angel can no more turn into a devil than a bad one can return to the ranks of the angels who are good. For, in the Gospel, the Truth promises the saints and the faithful that they will be 'as angels of God in heaven'[1] and that they will go 'into everlasting life.'[2] Now, if we are assured that we shall never lose that immortal blessedness, whereas the angels are not sure, then we shall be better off than they and not their equals. However, since the Truth cannot deceive and since we are to be their equals, the deduction is that the angels have the certain assurance that their happiness is eternal.

Now the evil angels could not have had this same assurance. Since their happiness was destined to end, there was for them no eternal happiness about which to be certain. Thus, we are left with the conclusion that the angels were unequal at the time of creation, or, if equal, that the holy angels were given foreknowledge of their eternal blessedness after the fall of the others. Of course, it might be objected that our Lord's words in the Gospel concerning the Devil, 'He was a murderer from the beginning, and has not stood in the truth,'[3] should be interpreted to mean not only that he was a murderer from the beginning of the human race—when a man was created whom he could destroy by deception—but, also, that he did not stand in the truth even from the beginning of his own creation. Consequently, according to this interpretation, he could never have been blessed together with the other holy angels, since, refusing to be subject to his Creator, he took an arrogant joy in his own private sovereignty, thereby becoming a most

[1] Matt. 22.31.   [2] Matt. 25.46.
[3] John 8.44.

deceitful liar. But, the power of the Almighty cannot be evaded. And anyone who refuses to hold to the truth by a holy subjection strives by a proud elevation of himself to make pretense of being what he is not in reality. Thus, the words of St. John the Apostle, 'The devil sins from the beginning,'[4] may be taken to mean that from the moment of his creation the Devil refused the grace which only a will devoutly obedient to God can receive.

Whoever holds this opinion at least disagrees with the Manichaeans and similar poisonous heretics who hold that the Devil derived his peculiarly evil nature from some Principle opposed to God. Such heretics are both foolish and futile, for they believe in the authority of this Scriptural text, but have not noticed that our Lord did not say: 'He was a stranger to the truth' but that 'He has not stood in the truth.' Our Lord meant that the Devil had fallen from the truth, in which, if he had stood firm, he would have so participated as to remain forever happy with the holy angels.

Chapters 14–15

The Devil was not evil by nature; he was an angel who abandoned his original truth and goodness.

Chapter 16

Among all things which somehow exist and which can be distinguished from God who made them, those that live are ranked higher than those that do not, that is to say, those that have the power of reproduction or even of appetite are above those which lack this faculty. In that order of living things, the sentient are superior to the non-sentient, for example, animals to trees. Among sentient beings, the intelligent are higher than the non-intelligent, as with men and cattle. Among the intelligent, the immortal are superior to the mortal, as angels to men.

This is the hierarchy according to the order of nature. However, we have another and variable standard of values which

[4] 1 John 3.8.

is based on utility. By this standard, sometimes we so prefer certain non-sentient things to others which are sentient that, had we the power, we would annihilate these latter, reckless of the place they hold in the pattern of nature or wilfully sacrificing them to our own convenience. For, who would not rather have food in his house than mice, money than fleas? This is less astonishing when we recall that, in spite of the great dignity of human nature, the price for a horse is often more than that for a slave and the price for a jewel more than that for a maid.

Thus, a person who evaluates according to reason has far more freedom of choice than one who is driven by want or drawn by passion. For, reason can see the gradation of things in an objective hierarchy of values, while necessity must consider them as means to an end. Reason seeks for what seems true in the light of the intellect, while passion craves for what seems pleasant to the senses.

So, too, in evaluating rational natures, the weight, so to speak, of will and love is so great that, although in the order of nature angels are higher than men, in the scale of morality good men outweigh bad angels.

Chapters 17–18

God providentially foresaw the Devil's turn to wickedness, and also that of evil men, but permitted this for the good of the whole of creation.

Chapter 19

Even the obscurity of divine Scripture is of value in this that, when one man thinks this and another that, many interpretations of the truth are conceived and brought forth into the light of knowledge. Thus, an obscure passage can be construed in the light either of proved and manifested facts or of other passages where the meaning is not in doubt. Sometimes, after much debate, the very meaning of the author himself is at length discovered; at other times, this meaning remains obscure, but at least the discussion of a profound obscurity serves on occasion for declaring other things that are true. At any rate, there is one view which does not seem to me at variance with God's works, namely, that, once we understand the creation of the angels by the making of the first light, then we should take the distinction between the good and bad angels as the meaning of the words: 'God separated the light from the darkness, calling the light Day and the darkness Night.'[1] For, the only one who could discern this distinction was He who, even before their fall, could foresee that they would fall and that, once they were deprived of the light of truth, they would remain in the darkness of pride.

As for the separation between the light of what we know as day and the darkness of night—that, God effected by commanding those lights in the sky which are most obvious to our senses: 'Let there be lights in the firmament of the heavens to separate day from night.' And a little further on, Scripture says: 'So it was. God made the two great lights, the greater light to rule the day and the smaller one to rule the night, and he made the stars. God set them in the firmament of the heavens to shed light upon the earth, to rule the day and the night and to separate the light from the darkness.'[2]

However, the same God could also divide that 'light' (which means the society of holy angels whose minds are aglow with the illumination of Truth) from that contrary 'darkness' (which means the society of evil angels whose darkened minds turned away from the light of justice), for to Him, their future evil, which was one not of nature but of choice, could be neither hidden nor uncertain.

Chapter 20

We should not fail to notice that, in the Scripture, it was immediately after recording God's words, '"Let there be light," and there was light,' that we are told: 'God saw that the light was good.'[1] This was, not said after He separated light from darkness and called the light day and the darkness night, lest it might appear that God testified to as much satisfaction in the darkness as in the light. It is different in the

[1] Gen. 1.4,5.   [2] Gen. 1.14,16–18.

[1] Gen. 1.3,4.

case of that darkness which is not evil and which is separated by the luminaries of heaven from the light we see with our eyes. The approval, 'God saw that it was good,' is here inserted, not before, but after, the division: 'God set them in the firmament of the heavens to shed light upon the earth, to rule the day and the night and to separate the light from the darkness. God saw that it was good.'[2] Both this kind of light and this kind of darkness pleased Him because both are without sin.

But, in that passage where it is recorded that God said: '"Let there be light," and there was light. God saw that the light was good,' and in the narrative following: 'God separated that light from the darkness, calling the light Day and the darkness Night,'[3] Scripture does not add the phrase, 'And God saw that it was good.' Here, it was omitted lest both should be considered good, whereas, in fact, one of them was evil—not, of course, by nature but by its own fault. Therefore, in this case, it is the light alone which pleased the Creator, while the angelic darkness was meant merely as a part of a divine pattern, not as something pleasing in itself.[4]

Chapter 21

The only meaning we can give to the constant refrain, 'God saw that it was good,' is God's approval of a work as having been fashioned in accordance with that art which is His own wisdom. So far is it from being true that God first learned that His work was good after it was made that, had He not known this already, not one of the things He made would have been created. Since, therefore, what He sees is good would not have been made unless He had seen that it was good before He made it, we must say: He teaches, He does not learn, that it is good.[1]

Plato dared to use an even stronger expression, namely, that, at the completion of creation, God was elated with delight.[2]

---

[2] Gen. 1.17,18.　　　　　　　　[3] Gen. 1.4,5.

[4] . . . *tenebrae autem angelicae, etsi fuerant ordinandae, non tamen fuerant adprobandae.*

[1] *Docet bonum esse, non discit.*

[2] *Timaeus* 37C.

Obviously, he was not foolish enough to think that God's be-atitude was increased by the novelty of His work; he merely wished to indicate that God rejoiced in His finished product, just as, like an artist, He had been pleased in designing it. Plato does not imply in any way that the knowledge of God is subject to change, as though non-existing, existing, and no-longer-existing things were known with different kinds of cognition. For, not in our way does God look forward to the future, see the present, and look back upon the past, but in a manner remotely and profoundly unlike our way of thinking.

God's mind does not pass from one thought to another. His vision is utterly unchangeable. Thus, He comprehends all that takes place in time—the not-yet-existing future, the existing present, and the no-longer-existing past—in an immutable and eternal present. He does not see differently with the eyes and the mind, for He is not composed of soul and body. Nor is there any then, now, and afterwards in His knowledge, for, unlike ours, it suffers no change with triple time—present, past, and future. With Him, 'there is no change, nor shadow of alteration.'[3]

Neither does His attention pass from thought to thought, for His knowledge embraces everything in a single spiritual contuition.[4] His knowledge of what happens in time, like His movement of what changes in time, is completely inde-pendent of time. That is why it was one and the same to God to see that what He had made was good and to see that it was good to make it. When He saw what He had made, His knowl-edge was neither doubled nor in any way increased—in the sense that it could have been less before He made what He saw. For He could not have been so perfect a Creator without so perfect a knowledge that nothing could be added to it by seeing what He created.

Hence, we can see that, if the only truth Scripture needed to tell us was *who* created the light, it would have sufficed to say: God made the light. And if there was also a reason for telling us *how* God made it, it was enough to report: 'God said, "Let there be light," and there was light.' Thus, we would know not only that God created the light but that He did so by

[3] James 1.17.
[4] . . . *incorporeo contuitu simul adsunt cuncta quae novit.*

means of the Word. But, since there are three truths concerning every creature which we needed to know—namely: Who made it? How did he make it? and Why?—Scripture relates: 'God said, "Let there be light," and there was light. God saw that the light was good.' So, if we ask, 'who made it?' the answer is 'God'; if we ask, 'how?' the answer is that God said: 'Let it be. And it was done'; if we ask, 'why?' the answer is 'Because it is good.'——

There is no Creator higher than God, no art more efficacious than the Word of God, no better reason why something good should be created than that the God who creates is good. Even Plato says that the best reason for creating the world is that good things should be made by a good God. It may be that he read this Scriptural passage or learned it from those who had, or, by his own keen insight, he clearly saw that 'the invisible things' of God are 'understood by the things that are made,'[5] or, perhaps, he learned from others who had clearly seen this.

Chapter 22

The explanation, then, of the goodness of creation is the goodness of God. It is a reasonable and sufficient explanation whether considered in the light of philosophy or of faith. It puts an end to all controversies concerning the origin of the world. Nevertheless, certain heretics remain unconvinced, on the ground that many things in creation are unsuitable and even harmful to that poor and fragile mortality of the flesh which, of course, is no more than the just penalty of sin. The heretics mention, for example, fire, cold, wild beasts, and things like that, without considering how wonderful such things are in themselves and in their proper place and how beautifully they fit into the total pattern of the universe making, as it were, their particular contributions to the commonweal of cosmic beauty. Nor have they observed how valuable they are even to us if only we use them well and wisely. Consider, for instance, poison. It is deadly when improperly used, but when properly applied it turns out to be a health-giving medicine, while, on the contrary, some of those things we like,

[5] Cf. Rom. 1.20.

such as food, drink, and sunlight, when immoderately and unwisely used are seen to be harmful.

Thus does Divine Providence teach us not to be foolish in finding fault with things but, rather, to be diligent in finding out their usefulness or, if our mind and will should fail us in the search, then to believe that there is some hidden use still to be discovered, as in so many other cases, only with great difficulty. This effort needed to discover hidden usefulness either helps our humility or hits our pride, since absolutely no natural reality is evil and the only meaning of the word 'evil' is the privation of good.

What, however, is true is that there is a hierarchy of created realities, from earthly to heavenly, from visible to invisible, some being better than others, and that the very reason of their inequality is to make possible an existence for them all. For, God is the kind of artist whose greatness in His masterpieces is not lessened in His minor works—which, of course, are not significant by reason of any sublimity in themselves, since they have none, but only by reason of the wisdom of their Designer. Take the case of the beauty of the human form. Shave off one eyebrow and the loss to the mere mass of the body is insignificant. But what a blow to beauty! For, beauty is not a matter of bulk but of the symmetry and proportion of the members.

It is no wonder that heretics, who hold that some positive evil has sprung and sprouted from an evil principle radically opposed to God, refuse to accept this explanation of creation —that a God who is good should create things that are good. They prefer to believe that God was driven, by the sheer necessity of quelling the Evil One in rebellion against Him, to build the bulwarks of a material universe, and thus mingle the goodness of His nature with evil in order to coerce and conquer evil; so that the divine nature, prostituted and oppressed, is now in shameful and cruel captivity and can be purified and emancipated only with very great difficulty. Even then, one part will remain impervious to purification, and this is to be the prison and the chains to hold the conquered enemy in subjection.

The only way for the Manichaeans to cease from such folly —not to say insanity—is to acknowledge the nature of God to be, as it is in truth, unchangeable and absolutely incorruptible and, therefore, invulnerable; and to get in line with Christian orthodoxy, by believing that the soul—which is liable to a change for the worse by its own will and to corruption by sin and, therefore, to a loss of the light of unchangeable Truth—is a part neither of God nor of the divine nature, but merely a creature and, therefore, far from equality with God.

Chapter 23

What is far more a matter of wonder is that some, who share with us the belief that there is but one principle of all things and that nothing (except the divine nature) can exist apart from creation by God, still refuse to believe, with a good and simple faith, in this good and simple explanation of the creation of the world, namely, that it is the nature of a good God to create good things, and that good things exist—other than God and inferior to Him—which only a God who was good would have created. They also claim that souls, though not parts but merely creatures of God, have sinned by withdrawing from the Creator and, according to the gravity of their sins, have been imprisoned in bodies ranging, by degrees, from heaven down to earth, and that such souls and bodies constitute the cosmos. Thus, they, too, explain creation by saying that it was not for the sake of producing things that were good but merely for imprisoning things that were sinful.

Origen has been rightly reproved for holding and expressing such views in his work, which he calls *Perì Archōn*, that is, *Of Origins*. I am inexpressibly astonished that a scholar so versed in ecclesiastical literature should have failed to observe, first, that he was contradicting the plain meaning of highly authoritative Scriptural texts. In regard to each of the works of God we are reminded that 'God saw that it was good.' And, when all creation was complete, Scripture concludes: 'God saw that all he had made was very good.'[1] Surely, this can only mean that there was no other reason for creating the world except that good creatures might be made by a good God. If no one had sinned, this beautiful world could have been

---

[1] Gen. 1.31.

filled with created natures that are good. Even now, with sin in the world, it does not follow that all things are sinful. The great majority of those in heaven preserve the integrity of their nature; and not even the sinfulness of a will refusing to preserve the order of its nature can lessen the beauty of God's total order, designed, as it is, according to the laws of His justice. For, as the beauty of a picture is not dimmed by the dark colors, in their proper place, so the beauty of the universe of creatures, if one has insight to discern it, is not marred by sins, even though sin itself is an ugly blotch.

In the second place, Origen and his followers ought to have seen that, if their opinion were true that matter was created that souls might be enclosed in bodies, as in penitentiaries for the punishment of sin, then the higher and lighter bodies should have been for those whose sins were slight and the lower and heavier ones for those whose crimes were great. Hence, logically, demons who are the worst of sinners should have been imprisoned in earthly bodies which are the lowest and heaviest of all, whereas it is men, and even good men, whose bodies are made of earthly matter.

Now, the fact is that it was precisely that we might understand that the merits of souls are not to be measured by the qualities of their bodies that the utterly wicked Devil was given an aerial body, while man—certainly before the fall and, even now, a sinner of far less malice—was given a body of clay.

Most stupid of all is the Origenist idea that what the Creator had in mind, in making a single sun for our single world, was neither to lend to it the luster of beauty nor to provide a source of corporeal well-being, but that He made it because one soul happened to sin in such a way that it had to be imprisoned in just such a body, and, if not one but two or ten or even a hundred souls had happened to sin in the same way at the same time, then the world would have had a hundred suns.

That such was not the case, they explain, was not due to any marvelous provision of the Creator in regard to the health and beauty of corporeal creatures. It just happened the way it did because the extravagance of sin in one single soul called for just such a body. The real extravagance that calls for restraint is not in the souls about which they talk so ignorantly, but in the Origenists themselves who have wandered so far from the truth.

But, to return to the three answers which, as I suggested above,[2] should be given when we are asked concerning any creature—Who made it? How? and Why?—the answers are: 'God'; 'by the Word'; and 'because it is good.' Whether or not we have here, in the mystical sense, an intimation of the Trinity Itself—Father, Son and Holy Spirit—or whether there is some objection to such an interpretation of this passage of Scripture, this is a discussion that would require many words and, surely, I cannot be expected to explain everything in one volume.

Chapter 24

We believe, maintain and faithfully teach that the Father begot the Word, that is, the only-begotten Son who is the Wisdom by which all things were created. He is one as the Father is one, eternal as the Father is eternal, and, equally with the Father, is supremely good. The Holy Spirit is, likewise, the Spirit of the Father and of the Son, consubstantial and co-eternal with both. And this whole is a Trinity because of the individuality of the Persons and, yet, a single God because of indivisible divinity and a single Almighty because of indivisible omnipotence. Yet, when we ask concerning each Person individually, the answer must be that each one is God and each is Almighty; and when we inquire concerning the three together, the reply must be that there are not three Gods or three Almighties, but a single God Almighty. Such is the indivisible unity in the Three and such is the way it should be stated.

I am not prepared to offer any premature opinion as to whether or not the Holy Spirit of the good Father and of the good Son should be called the goodness of both since He is common to both. However, I would more readily venture to say that He is the holiness of both, not in the sense that this Holy Spirit is an attribute of both but that He is a substance and is the third Person in the Trinity. I find a kind of proof

[2] Cf. above, 11.21.

for this view[1] in the fact that, although the Father and the Son are both spirits and are both holy, yet, the third Person, in a special way, is called the Holy Spirit as if He were substantial holiness and consubstantial with the other two.

Notice, however, that if the divine goodness is identical with divine holiness, then it is rational and intelligent rather than rash and presumptuous to pursue the hypothesis that each of God's creatures speaks to us in a kind of mystical code[2] in order to stimulate our curiosity and to intimate an image of the Trinity every time we ask: Who made it? How? and Why? Who? Our mind hears the answer: It was the Father of the Word who said: 'Let it be made'; and what was made when He spoke was made, without doubt, by means of the Word; and the fact that 'God saw that it was good' is sufficient proof that what God created was made solely because of His goodness, not by reason of any necessity nor of any need to use the thing for Himself. In a word, it was made because it was good. And it was called good only after it was made to intimate to our mind that each created being reflected the goodness which was the reason of its being made.

Now, if we are right in understanding this goodness to be the Holy Spirit, then there is an intimation of the whole Trinity in each of God's creations. This same Trinity is also the source, the light, the joy of the Holy City 'which is above'[3] with the holy angels. For, if we ask whence it came, the answer is: 'God created it'; whence its wisdom, 'God enlightens it'; whence its happiness, 'God is its joy.' By subsisting in Him it is what it is; by contemplating Him it receives its light; by abiding in Him it possesses beatitude. It is; it knows; it loves. Its life is in the eternity of God; its light is in the truth of God; its joy is in the goodness of God.

Chapter 25

For much the same reason, as far as one can judge, philosophers have sought or, rather, found a kind of trinity of levels in the field of philosophy. Notice that it was not an in-

[1] *Ad hoc enim me probabilius ducit quod . . .*
[2] *. . . secreto quodam loquendi modo . . .*
[3] Gal. 4.26.

vention but a discovery that one part should be physics, another logic, and a third ethics, or, as many writers in the Latin tradition would call them, natural, rational and moral philosophy. I dealt with this briefly in Book VIII.[1]

I do not mean to suggest that the philosophers who employed this threefold division had any idea of the Trinity in God. This much is true, however, that the first to discover and recommend this division seems to have been Plato; and it was he who held that God is the sole Author of all being, the Giver of intelligence, and the Inspirer of that love which makes possible a life that is both good and happy.

However much philosophers disagree concerning the nature of things, the method of investigating truth, and the supreme good or end toward which all actions should be referred, they are at one in directing their full attention to the study of these three important, general questions. In spite of the great discrepancy of opinion in regard to each of these issues, there is not one of the philosophers who hesitates to assert that there is some cause of being, some norm in knowing, some aim in living. Moreover, there are three requisites if an artist wants to produce something: natural endowment, education, and practice. The Criterion of the first is genius; of the second, knowledge; of the third, the thing produced.

I know that we ought to say that a person *enjoys* what he produces, but merely *makes use* of practice. The point of this distinction seems to be that a thing enjoyed is related directly to ourselves and not to something else, whereas a thing used is sought as a means to some other end. Thus we say that the things of time should be used (rather than enjoyed) as a means to our enjoyment of the things of eternity. It is a perversion for people to want to enjoy money, but merely to make use of God. Such people do not spend money for the sake of God, but worship God for the sake of money. However, in actual everyday speech we 'use' what we produce and we 'enjoy' what we use. For, 'what we produce' means, rightly enough, the fruits of the field which, of course, we all make use of in this present life.

It is in this popular sense that I mentioned experience or

[1] Cf. above, 8.4–8.

practice or usage as one of the three requisites to be looked for in a man, namely, natural endowment, education, and experience or use or practice.

When philosophers, as I said, developed the three aspects of philosophy which relate to a happy life, what they had in mind was that natural philosophy might serve natural endowment; rational philosophy, education; and moral philosophy, practice or behavior.

Now, if we were the cause of our own nature, then, indeed, we would be the fathers of our own wisdom and would not need to get an education from our teachers. And if we were the source and the only object of our love, we would be self-sufficient and would need enjoyment of no other good to make us happy. But, in fact, God is the Author of the existence of our nature and, therefore, He must be our Teacher if we are ever to be wise, and He must be the Source of our inmost consolation if we are ever to be happy.

Chapter 26

We ourselves can recognize in ourselves an image of God, in the sense of an image of the Trinity. Of course, it is merely an image and, in fact, a very remote one. There is no question of identity nor of co-eternity nor, in one word, of consubstantiality with Him. Nevertheless, it is an image which by nature is nearer to God than anything else in all creation, and one that by transforming grace can be perfected into a still closer resemblance.

For, we are, and we know that we are, and we love to be and to know that we are. And in this trinity of being, knowledge, and love there is not a shadow of illusion to disturb us. For, we do not reach these inner realities with our bodily senses as we do external objects, as, for example, color by seeing, sound by hearing, odor by smelling, flavor by tasting, hard or soft objects by touching. In the case of such sensible things, the best we can do is to form very close and immaterial images which help us to turn them over in our minds, to hold them in our memory, and thus to keep our love for them alive. But, without any illusion of image, fancy, or phantasm, I am certain that I am, that I know that I am, and that I love to be and to know.

In the face of these truths, the quibbles of the skeptics lose their force. If they say; 'What if you are mistaken?'—well, if I am mistaken, I am. For, if one does not exist, he can by no means be mistaken. Therefore, I am, if I am mistaken. Because, therefore, I am, if I am mistaken, how can I be mistaken that I am, since it is certain that I am, if I am mistaken? And because, if I could be mistaken, I would have to be the one who is mistaken, therefore, I am most certainly not mistaken in knowing that I am. Nor, as a consequence, am I mistaken in knowing that I know. For, just as I know that I am, I also know that I know. And when I love both to be and to know, then I add to the things I know a third and equally important knowledge, the fact that I love.

Nor am I mistaken that I love, since I am not mistaken concerning the objects of my love. For, even though these objects were false, it would still be true that I loved illusions. For, if this were not true, how could I be reproved and prohibited from loving illusions? But, since these objects are true and certain, who can doubt that, when they are loved, the loving of them is also true and certain? Further, just as there is no one who does not wish to be happy, so there is no one who does not wish to exist. For, how can anyone be happy if he does not exist?

Chapter 27

Merely to exist is, by the very nature of things, so pleasant that in itself it is enough to make even the wretched unwilling to die; for, even when they are conscious of their misery, what they want to put an end to is not themselves but the misery. This is even the case with those who not merely feel miserable but manifestly are so, men who seem fools, in the eyes of the wise, and paupers and beggars to those who consider themselves well off. For, if they had a choice between personal immortality, in which their unhappiness would never end, or complete and permanent annihilation if they objected to eternal misery, they would be delighted to choose to live forever in misery rather than not to exist at all.

If proof were needed, appeal can be made to the well-known feeling of these men. They are afraid to die, and prefer to live on in misfortune rather than to end it by death. This is proof enough that nature shrinks from annihilation. And even when they know that they must die, they beg for mercy and ask as a boon that death be delayed so that they may live a little longer in their misery. Without a doubt, they prove with what alacrity they would accept immortality—at any rate, one that involved no worse affliction than perpetual indigence.

Why, even irrational animals, with no mind to make such reflections, from the greatest serpents to the tiniest worms, show in every movement they can make that they long to live and escape destruction. Even trees and plants, that can make no conscious movement to avoid destruction, can, in some sense, be said to guard their own existence by guaranteeing sustenance. They attach their roots deep into the earth in order to thrust forth their branches safe into the air. Last of all, even material bodies, lacking sensation and every sign of life, at least rise upwards or sink downwards or remain balanced in between, as though seeking the place where they can best exist in accordance with their nature.

If proof be needed how much human nature loves to know and hates to be mistaken, recall that there is not a man who would not rather be sad but sane than glad but mad. Now, this great and marvelous light of love and hate is peculiar to men alone among all the living animals. For, although some animals have much keener sight in penetrating the light of day, they cannot penetrate that spiritual light which, as it were, illumines our mind and makes us able to judge correctly of all other things. For the faculty of judgment is in proportion to our capacity for this light.

Nevertheless, although irrational animals do not have knowledge as such in their senses, at least they have something that is like knowledge, whereas purely material things are called sensible, not because they can sense, but only because they can be sensed. Plants have something like sensation only in so far as they take nourishment and reproduce.

While the ultimate explanation of all such material things is a secret of nature, the things themselves openly reveal to our senses their forms which help to make the pattern of this visible world so beautiful. It is as though, in compensation for their own incapacity to know, they wanted to become known by us.

However, although we perceive them by our bodily senses, we do not make judgments concerning them by our senses. For, we men have another and far higher perception which is interior, and by which we distinguish what is just from what is unjust—justice by means of an intellectual conception; what is unjust by the lack of such a form. The function of this sense is not aided by a keen eye, nor by ear, nose or palate, nor by any bodily touch. By it I am certain of my existence and of the knowledge of my existence. Moreover, I love these two and, in like manner, am certain that I love them.

Chapter 28

The plan of my book does not call for further consideration of the measure of our love for our existence and knowledge, nor of the analogy to this love which can be found even on the lower levels of creation. However, nothing has been said to make clear whether the love by which our existence and the knowledge of it are loved is itself the object of love. The answer is yes; and the proof is this, that what is really loved, in men who deserve to be loved, is love itself. For, we do not call a man good because he knows what is good, but because he loves it. Why, then, do we not see that what we love in ourselves is the very love by which we love whatever is good?

There is also a love by which we love what should not be loved. And a man hates this love in himself if he loves the love of whatever is good. Both loves can exist in one and the same person. This co-existence is good for a man in that he can, by increasing in himself the love of what is right, decrease his love of what is evil until his whole life has been transformed to good and brought to perfection.

For, if we were beasts, we would love the carnal life of the senses which would be our sufficient good and, therefore, as soon as all was well with us, we would seek for nothing further. Likewise, if we were trees, we could not love by any conscious tendency; nevertheless, there would be a kind of striving for whatever would make us more abundant in our fruitfulness. Again, if we were stones or waves, winds or flames, or anything of this sort which is without sensation and life, we would nevertheless be endowed with a kind of attraction for our proper place in the order of nature. The specific gravity of a body is, as it were, its love, whether it tends upward by its lightness or downward by its weight. For, a body is borne by gravity as a spirit by love, whichever way it is moved.

It is, therefore, because we are men, created to the image of a Creator, whose eternity is true, His truth eternal, His love both eternal and true, a Creator who is the eternal, true, and lovable Trinity in whom there is neither confusion nor division, that, wherever we turn among the things which He created and conserved so wonderfully, we discover His footprints, whether lightly or plainly impressed. For, not one of all these things which are below us would either be, or belong to a particular species, or follow and observe any order, unless it has been created by Him whose existence, wisdom, and goodness are all transcendent.

When, therefore, we contemplate His image in our very selves, let us, like the younger son in the Gospel,[1] return to ourselves, rise and seek Him from whom we have departed by sin. In Him our existence will know no death, our knowledge embrace no error, our love meet no resistance. At present we are certain that we possess these three things, not by the testimony of others but by our own consciousness of their presence in our interior and unerring vision. Nevertheless, since we cannot know of ourselves how long they will last or whether they will never cease[2] and what will result from our good or bad use of them, we seek for other witnesses if we have not already found them. Not now, but later,[3] I shall carefully discuss the reasons why we should have unhesitating trust in these witnesses.

But in this Book, God helping, I shall continue to discuss, to the best of my ability, the City of God, not as it is in the pilgrimage of this mortal life but as it is in the eternity of heaven. There it consists of the holy and faithful angels who

[1] Luke 15.17,18.
[2] . . . *quamdiu futura vel utrum numquam defutura* . . .
[3] Cf. below, 22.22.

never were nor ever will be deserters from God, and who, as I have already said, were separated by God, in the very beginning, from those who rejected the eternal light and were turned into darkness.

Chapter 29

The holy angels gain a knowledge of God not by the spoken word but by the presence in their souls of that immutable Truth which is the only-begotten Word of God. They know this Word and the Father and their Holy Spirit, understanding that this Trinity is indivisible and that each of the Persons is substantial, although there are not three Gods but only one. They comprehend all this in such a way that it is better known to them than we are known to ourselves.

They also know every creature not merely in itself but, still better, in the wisdom of God, in the very art by which it was created. And, therefore, they know themselves better in God than as they are in themselves, although, of course, they have this knowledge, too. For, these angels were created and are something different from the One who created them. Therefore, in the sense I have explained above,[1] the knowledge which they have in Him is as clear as daylight, whereas what they have in themselves is like the twilight.

For, there is a great difference between knowing something in the very idea according to which it was made and knowing it as it is in itself. For example, it is one thing to understand the straightness of a line or the correctness of a figure when seen by the intellect and another when traced in the sand. So, too, to know justice in the light of immutable Truth is different from knowing justice in the soul of a just man.

It is the same with all other things—as the firmament of the heavens between the waters above and those below; the gathering of the waters below, the appearance of the dry land, and the production of plants and trees; the creation of sun, moon, and stars; of land animals, of fowl, fish, and of sea monsters; of all creatures that walk and crawl upon the earth; and of man himself who was to excel all that is upon the earth.

---

[1] Cf. above, 11.7.

All these are known by the angels in one way as the things are in the Word of God, where the angels see the unchangeable and eternal purposes and the ideas according to which all these things were created, and, in another way, as these things are in themselves. In the one case, the knowledge has the clarity of the Artist's thought; in the other, it has the shadows of the thing produced. But, when these creations are referred to the praise and adoration of the Creator Himself, it is as if the morning dawned in the minds of those who were contemplating them.

Chapter 30

It is recorded that all God's works were completed in six days (the day being repeated six times), because six is a perfect number. Of course, no prolongation of time was necessary for God. He could have at once created all things and then let them measure time by their appropriate movements. It is the perfection of God's work that is signified by the number six. For, this is the first number made up of aliquot parts, a sixth, a third and a half, respectively, one, two and three, totaling six. In this way of dealing with numbers, aliquot parts are those which exactly divide the number, that is, fractions like a half, a third, a fourth, and so on that have a whole number as denominator. For example, four is a part of the number nine, but it cannot, for that reason, be called an aliquot part, whereas one is, since it is the ninth; and three is a third. However, these last two parts—the ninth and third, that is, one and three—when added, are far from making the total nine.

In the same way, four is a part of ten, but no fraction indicates which part, whereas one is an aliquot part because it is one tenth. Ten has also a fifth part which is two and a half which is five. But these three parts—the tenth, fifth and half, that is, one, two and five—do not total ten but to eight. Again, the aliquot parts of twelve add up to more than twelve: one twelfth of it is one; one sixth, two; one fourth, three; one third, four; one half, six; but one, two, three, four, and six make more than twelve, namely, sixteen.

I considered it necessary to mention these few examples in order to illustrate the perfection of the number six. As I have said, it is the first that is exactly made up of its aliquot parts added together. And six is the number of days in which God completed His works. Thus we see that we should not underestimate the significance of numbers, since, in many passages of Sacred Scripture, numbers have a meaning for the conscientious interpreter. Not without reason has it been said in praise of God: 'Thou hast ordered all things in measure, and number, and weight.'[1]

Chapters 31–33

After a digression on the significance of the number seven in various Biblical texts, Augustine offers a miniature commentary on the opening verses of Genesis. From the mention of light and darkness, in Genesis, he is led to speculate on the separation of the good and bad angels.

Chapter 34

Some people have had the idea that angelic choirs are somehow symbolized under the name of waters and that this is the meaning of the words, 'Let there be a firmament in the midst of the waters to divide the waters.'[1] They think that waters 'above' the firmament mean the angels and those 'below' mean either the waters we can see, or the host of evil angels, or the races of mankind. If this interpretation be true, then it is not clear from this text when the angels were created, but when they were separated. However, other people are perverse and heretical enough to deny that any waters at all were created by God, alleging that it is nowhere written: 'God said, Let there be waters.'

The fact is, of course, that they might, with equal folly, say the same about the earth, for nowhere do we read: 'God said, Let there be earth.' To which they retort with the text: 'In the beginning God created the heavens and the earth.' Very well; but here water also is implied, both being included in the one word, as can be seen from the words of the psalm:

[1] Wisd. 11.20.

---

[1] Gen. 1.6,7.

'The sea is his, and he made it: and his hands formed the dry land.'[2]

As for those who claim that 'waters above the heavens' means angels, their worry is the weight of water. They do not see how anything so fluid and heavy could have been placed in the upper reaches of the cosmos. By the same logic, if they could create a man, they would not place in his head any of that pituitary secretion which the Greeks call *phlegma* and which plays the role of water in the composition of our bodies. However, according to God's plan, it is the head which was found to be the most suitable place for this *phlegma*. Now, according to the hypothesis of our opponents, this seems so absurd that, if the fact were unknown and Scripture said that God had placed a moist and cold and, therefore, heavy humor in the very highest part of the human body, these assayers of the cosmic elements[3] would refuse to believe it, or, if they accepted Scriptural authority, they would find some quite different meaning for the words.

But, now, to go on scrutinizing and discussing every detail concerning the creation of the world which Scripture has recorded would take too much space and would take me too far from the purpose of the present work. What I have already said of the two different and opposed societies of angels seems to me enough to reveal the origins of the two Cities which are in conflict in human history and which are to be the theme of the rest of this work. So, at long last, let this be the end of the present Book.

[2] Ps. 94.5.
[3] . . . *isti trutinatores elementorum* . . .

BOOK XII

Created Wills and the Distinction of Good and Evil

Chapter 1

IN THE PREVIOUS BOOK[1] we saw something of the beginning of the two cities, so far as angels are concerned. In the same way, we must now proceed to the creation of men and see the beginning of the cities so far as it concerns the kind of rational creatures who are mortal. First, however, a few remarks about the angels must be made in order to make it as clear as I can how there is no real difficulty or impropriety in speaking of a single society composed of both men and angels; and why, therefore, it is right to say that there are not four cities or societies, namely, two of angels and two of men, but only two, one of them made up of the good—both angels and men— and the other of those who are evil.

There is no reason to doubt that the contrary dispositions which have developed among these good and bad angels are due, not to different natures and origins, for God the Author and Creator of all substances has created them both, but to the dissimilar choices and desires of these angels themselves. Some, remaining faithful to God, the common good of all, have lived in the enjoyment of His eternity, truth, and love, while others, preferring the enjoyment of their own power, as though they were their own good, departed from the higher good and common blessedness for all and turned to goods of their own choosing.

Preferring the pomp of pride to this sublimity of eternity, the craftiness of vanity to the certainty of truth, and the turmoil of dissension to the union of love, they became proud, deceitful, and envious.

Since the happiness of all angels consists in union with God, it follows that their unhappiness must be found in the very contrary, that is, in not adhering to God. To the question: 'Why are the good angels happy?' the right answer is: 'Because they adhere to God.' To the question: 'Why are the others unhappy?' the answer is: 'Because they do not adhere to God.' In fact, there is no other good which can make any rational or intellectual creature happy except God. Not every creature has the potentialities for happiness. Beasts, trees, stones, and such things neither acquire nor have the capacity for this gift. However, every creature which has this capacity receives it, not from itself, since it has been created out of nothing, but from its Creator. To possess Him is to be happy; to lose Him is to be in misery. And, of course, that One whose beatitude depends upon Himself as His own good and not on any other good can never be unhappy since He can never lose Himself.

Thus, there can be no unchangeable good except our one, true, and blessed God. All things which He has made are good because made by Him, but they are subject to change because they were made, not out of Him, but out of nothing. Although they are not supremely good, since God is a greater good than they, these mutable things are, none the less, highly good by reason of their capacity for union with and, therefore, beatitude in the Immutable Good which is so completely their good that, without this good, misery is inevitable.

But it does not follow that other creatures in the universe are better off merely because they are incapable of misery. That would be like saying that other members of the body are better than the eyes because they can never become blind. A sentient nature even in pain is better than a stone that cannot suffer. In the same way, a rational nature even in misery is higher than one which, because it lacks reason or sensation, cannot suffer misery.

This being the case, it is nothing less than a perversion of the nature of the angels if they do not adhere to God. For, remember, their nature is so high in the order of creation that, mutable as it is, it can attain beatitude by adhering to the immutable and supreme Good, which is God, and that, unless it achieves beatitude, this nature fails to satisfy its inmost exigencies, and, finally, that nothing but God can satisfy these needs of the angelic nature.

Now, this perversion, like every imperfection in a nature, harms nature and, therefore, is contrary to the nature. It follows, therefore, that what makes the wicked angels differ from the good ones is not their nature but a perversion or imperfection; and this very blemish is a proof of how highly to be esteemed is the nature itself. Certainly, no blemish in a thing ought to be blamed unless we are praising the thing as a whole, for the whole point of blaming the blemish is that it mars the perfection of something we would like to see praised.

For example, when we say that blindness is a defect of the eyes, we imply that it is the very nature of the eyes to see, and when we say that deafness is a malady of the ears, we are supposing that it is their nature to hear. So, too, when we say that it is a failure in an angel not to attain union with God, we openly proclaim that they were meant by nature to be one with God.

Of course, no one can fully comprehend or properly express the ineffable union of being one with God in His life, in His wisdom, in His joy, and all this without a shadow of death or darkness or disturbance. One thing is certain. The very failure of the bad angels to cling to God—a desertion that damaged their nature like a disease—is itself proof enough that the nature God gave them was good—so good that not to be one with God was for them a disaster.

Chapter 2

This explanation just given seemed to me necessary to forestall the objection that the apostate spirits might have received from some principle other than God a nature different from that of the other angels. The malice of this mistake can be more easily and speedily removed the more clearly one grasps what God meant by the words, 'I AM WHO AM,'[1] spoken through the medium of an angel at the time when Moses was being sent to the children of Israel.

Since God is supreme being, that is, since He supremely *is* and, therefore, is immutable, it follows that He gave 'being' to all that He created out of nothing; not, however, absolute being. To some things He gave more of being and to others less and, in this way, arranged an order of natures in a hier-

---

[1] Exod. 3.14.

archy of being. (This noun, 'being,' is derived from the verb 'to be' just as 'wisdom' from the verb 'to be wise.' In Latin, *essentia,* being, is a new word, not used by the ancient writers, recently adopted in order to find an equivalent of the Greek, *ousía,* of which *essentia* is the exact translation.)

Consequently, no nature—except a non-existent one—can be contrary to the nature which is supreme and which created whatever other natures have being. In other words, nonentity stands in opposition to that which is. Therefore, there is no being opposed to God who is the Supreme Being and Source of all beings without exception.

Chapter 3

In Scripture, those who oppose God's rule, not by nature but by sin, are called His enemies. They can do no damage to Him, but only to themselves; their enmity is not a power to harm, but merely a velleity to oppose Him. In any case, God is immutable and completely invulnerable. Hence, the malice by which His so-called enemies oppose God is not a menace to Him, but merely bad for themselves—an evil because what is good in their nature is wounded. It is not their nature, but the wound in their nature, that is opposed to God—as evil is opposed to good.

No one will deny that God is supremely good. Thus, any lack of goodness is opposed to God as evil is opposed to good. At the same time, the nature itself is not less good because the lack of goodness is evil and, therefore, the evil of lacking some goodness is opposed to this good, which is the goodness of the nature. Note that in respect to God the contrast is merely that of evil to good, but in respect to the nature which suffers a lack of something good, the lack is not only evil but also harmful. No evils, of course, can be harmful to God, but only to mutable and corruptible natures—and, even then, the harm done bears witness to the goodness of the natures which suffer, for, unless they were good, they could not suffer the wounds of a lack of goodness.

Just consider the harm done by these wounds—the loss of integrity, of beauty, of health, of virtue, or of any other natural good which can be lost or lessened by sin or sickness. If a nature has nothing of goodness to lose, then there is no harm done by lacking this nothing and, consequently, there is nothing wrong. For, there is no such thing as something wrong that does no harm.[1]

The conclusion is that, although no defect can damage an unchangeable good, no nature can be damaged by a defect unless that nature itself is good—for the simple reason that a defect exists only where harm is done. To put the matter in another way: a defect can never be found in the highest good, nor ever apart from some kind of good.[2]

Thus, good things without defects can sometimes be found; absolutely bad things, never—for even those natures that were vitiated at the outset by an evil will are only evil in so far as they are defective, while they are good in so far as they are natural. And when a vitiated nature is being punished, in addition to the good of being what it is, it is a good for it not to go unpunished, since this is just and whatever is just is certainly good. No one is punished for natural defects, but only for deliberate faults. And even for a vice to develop, by force of habit and overindulgence, into a strong natural defect, the vice must have begun in the will. But here, of course, I am speaking of the vices of that nature which has a mind illumined by an immaterial light in virtue of which it can distinguish what is just from what is unjust.

Chapter 4

Of course, in the case of beasts, trees, and other mutable and mortal creatures which lack not merely an intellect, but even sensation or life itself, it would be ridiculous to condemn in them the defects which destroy their corruptible nature. For, it was by the will of the Creator that they received that measure of being whereby their comings and goings and fleeting existences should contribute to that special, if lowly, loveliness of our earthly seasons which chimes with the harmony of the universe. For, there was never any need for the things

---

[1] *Nam esse vitium et non nocere non potest.*
[2] . . . *vitium esse nec in summo posse bono nec nisi in aliquo bono.*

of earth either to rival those of heaven or to remain uncreated merely because the latter are better.

It is, in fact, the very law of transitory things that, here on earth where such things are at home, some should be born while others die, the weak should give way to the strong and the victims should nourish the life of the victors. If the beauty of this order fails to delight us, it is because we ourselves, by reason of our mortality, are so enmeshed in this corner of the cosmos that we fail to perceive the beauty of a total pattern in which the particular parts, which seem ugly to us, blend in so harmonious and beautiful a way. That is why, in those situations where it is beyond our power to understand the providence of God, we are rightly commanded to make an act of faith rather than allow the rashness of human vanity to criticize even a minute detail in the masterpiece of our Creator.

Although these defects in the things of earth are involuntary and unpunishable, yet, like voluntary ones, when properly contemplated, they reveal the excellence in the natures themselves, all of which have God for their Author and Creator. For, in both cases, what we dislike is the lack by defect of something which we like in the nature as a whole. Sometimes, of course, natures themselves are displeasing to men because they happen to be harmful. It is a case of regarding only their utility, not the things themselves, as with the plague of frogs and flies which scourged the pride of the Egyptians.[1] But, with such reasoning, fault could be found even with the sun, since criminals and debtors have sometimes been judicially condemned to solar exposure. It is not by our comfort or inconvenience, but by the nature considered in itself, that glory is given to its Creator. So, even the nature of unquenchable fire is, without doubt, worthy of praise, although it is to serve as a punishment for the damned. Is there anything, in fact, more beautiful than a leaping, luminous flame of fire? Or anything more useful, when it warms us, heals us, cooks our food? Yet, nothing is more painful when it burns us. Thus, the same thing applied in one way is harmful, but when properly used is extremely beneficial. It is all but impossible to enumerate all the good uses to which fire is put throughout the world.

[1] Exod. 8.

We should pay no attention to those who praise fire for its light but condemn its heat—on the principle that a thing should be judged not by its nature, but by our comfort or inconvenience. They like to see it, but hate to be burnt. What they forget is that the same light which they like is injurious and unsuitable for weak eyes, and that the heat which they hate is, for some animals, the proper condition for a healthy life.

Chapter 5

All natures, then, are good simply because they exist and, therefore, have each its own measure of being, its own beauty, even, in a way, its own peace.[1] And when each is in the place assigned by the order of nature, it best preserves the full measure of being that was given to it. Beings not made for eternal life, changing for better or for worse according as they promote the good and improvement of things to which, by the law of the Creator, they serve as means, follow the direction of Divine Providence and tend toward the particular end which forms a part of the general plan for governing the universe. This means that the dissolution which brings mutable and mortal things to their death is not so much a process of annihilation as a progress toward something they were designed to become.

The conclusion from all this is that God is never to be blamed for any defects that offend us, but should ever be praised for all the perfection we see in the natures He has made. For God is Absolute Being and, therefore, all other being that is relative was made by Him. No being that was made from nothing could be on a par with God, nor could it even be at all, were it not made by Him.

Chapter 6

It follows that the true cause of the good angels' beatitude lies in their union with Absolute Being. And if we seek the cause of the bad angels' misery, we are right in finding it in this, that they abandoned Him whose Being is absolute and

[1] Cf. below, 19.12, for the meaning of 'peace.'

turned to themselves whose being is relative—a sin that can have no better name than pride. 'For pride is the beginning of all sin.'[1] They refused to reserve their strength for Him.[2] They might have had more of being if they had adhered to Him whose Being is supreme, but, by preferring themselves to Him, they preferred what was less in the order of being.

Such was the first defect, the first lack, the first perversion of that nature which, being created, could not be absolute, and yet, being created for beatitude, might have rejoiced in Him who is Absolute Being; but which, having turned from Him, was doomed, not to be nothing but to have so much less of being that it was bound to be wretched.

If one seeks for the efficient cause of their evil will, none is to be found. For, what can make the will bad when it is the will itself which makes an action bad? Thus, an evil will is the efficient cause of a bad action, but there is no efficient cause of an evil will. If there is such a cause, it either has or has not a will. If it has, then that will is either good or bad. If good, one would have to be foolish enough to conclude that a good will makes a bad will. In that case, a good will becomes the cause of sin—which is utterly absurd. On the other hand, if the hypothetical cause of a bad will has itself a bad will, I would have to ask what made this will bad, and, to put an end to the inquiry: What made the first bad will bad? Now, the fact is that there was no first bad will that was made bad by any other bad will—it was made bad by itself. For, if it were preceded by a cause that made it evil, that cause came first. But, if I am told that nothing made the will evil but that it always was so, then I ask whether or not it existed in some nature.

If this evil will existed in no nature, then it did not exist at all. If it existed in some nature, then it vitiated, corrupted, injured that nature and, therefore, deprived it of some good. An evil will could not exist in an evil nature but only in a good one, mutable enough to suffer harm from this deprivation. For, if no harm were done, then there was no deprivation and, consequently, no right to call the will evil. But, if harm was done, it was done by destroying or diminishing what was good. Thus,

[1] Eccli. 10.15.   [2] Cf. Ps. 58.10.

an evil will could not have existed from all eternity in a nature in which a previously existing good had to be eliminated before the evil will could harm the nature. But, if it did not exist from all eternity, who, then, caused this evil will?

The only remaining suggestion is that the cause of the evil will was something which had no will. My next question is whether this 'something' was superior, inferior, or equal to the will. If superior, then it was better. So, then, how can it have had no will and not rather a good will? If equal, the case is the same: for, as long as two wills are equally good, one cannot produce an evil will in the other. The supposition remains, then, that it was an inferior thing without a will which produced the evil will of the angelic nature which first sinned.

But that thing itself, whatever it was, even though it was low to the lowest point of earthliness, was, without doubt good since it was a nature and a being having its own character and species in its own genus and order. How, then, can a good thing be the efficient cause of an evil will? How, I ask, can good be the cause of evil? For, when the will, abandoning what is above it, turns itself to something lower, it becomes evil because the very turning itself and not the thing to which it turns is evil. Therefore, an inferior being does not make the will evil but the will itself, because it is a created will, wickedly and inordinately seeks the inferior being.

Take the case of two men whose physical and mental make-up is exactly the same. They are both attracted by the exterior beauty of the same person. While gazing at this loveliness, the will of one man is moved with an illicit desire; the will of the other remains firm in its purity. Why did the will become evil in one case and not in the other? What produced the evil will in the man in whom it began to be evil? The physical beauty of the person could not have been the cause, since that was seen by both in exactly the same way and yet both wills did not become evil. Was the cause the flesh of one of those who looked? Then why not the flesh of the other, also? Or was the cause the mind of one of them? Again, why not the mind of both? For the supposition is that both are equally constituted in mind and body. Must we say, then, that one was tempted by a secret suggestion of the Devil, as if it were not rather by his own will that he consented to this suggestion or enticement or whatever it was?

If so, then what was it in him that was the cause of his consent, of the evil will to follow the evil suggestion? To settle this difficulty, let us suppose that the two men are tempted equally, that one yields and consents to the temptation, that the other remains as he was before. The obvious conclusion is that one was unwilling, the other willing, to fail in chastity. And what else could be the cause of their attitudes but their own wills, since both men have the same constitution and temperament? The beauty which attracted the eyes of both was the same; the secret suggestion by which both were tempted was the same. However carefully they examine the situation, eager to learn what it was that made one of the two evil, no cause is apparent.

For, suppose we say that the man himself made his will evil. Very well, but what was the man himself before he made his will evil? He was a good nature, created by God, the immutable God.

Take a person who says that the one who consents to the temptation and enticement made his own will evil although previously he had been entirely good. Recall the facts. The one consents, while the other does not, to a sinful desire concerning a beautiful person; the beauty was seen by both equally, and before the temptation both men were absolutely alike in mind and body. Now, the person who talks of a man making his own will evil must ask why the man made his will evil, whether because he is a nature or because he is nature made out of nothing? He will learn that the evil arises not from the fact that the man is a nature, but from the fact that the nature was made out of nothing.

For, if a nature is the cause of an evil will, then we are compelled to say that evil springs from good and that good is the cause of evil—since a bad will comes from a good nature. But how can it come about that a good, though mutable, nature, even before its will is evil, can produce something evil, namely, this evil will itself?

Chapter 7

No one, therefore, need seek for an efficient cause of an evil will. Since the 'effect' is, in fact, a deficiency, the cause should be called 'deficient.' The fault of an evil will begins when one falls from Supreme Being to some being which is less than absolute.[1] Trying to discover causes of such deficiencies—causes which, as I have said, are not efficient but deficient—is like trying to see darkness or hear silence. True, we have some knowledge of both darkness and silence: of the former only by the eyes; of the latter only by the ears. Nevertheless, we have no sensation but only the privation of sensation.

So there is no point in anyone trying to learn from me what I know I do not know—unless, perhaps, he wants to know how not to know what, as he ought to know, no one can know.[2] For, things we know, not by sensation, but by the absence of sensation, are known—if the word says or means anything— by some kind of 'unknowing,' so that they are both known and not known at the same time.[3] For example, when the vision of the eye passes from sensation to sensation, it sees darkness only when it begins not to see. So, too, no other sense but the ear can perceive silence, yet silence can only be heard by not being heard.

So, too, it is only the vision of the mind that discerns the *species intellegibilis* when it understands intelligible realities. But, when the realities are no longer intelligible, the mind, too, knows by 'unknowing.' For 'who can understand sins?'[4]

Chapter 8

This I know, that the nature of God can never and nowhere be deficient in anything, while things made out of nothing can be deficient. In regard to these latter, the more they have of

[1] Deficere *namque ab eo, quod summe est, ad id, quod minus est, hoc est* incipere habere voluntatem malam.

[2] . . . *nisi forte ut nescire discat, quod sciri non posse sciendum est.*

[3] . . . *si dici aut intellegi potest quodam modo nesciendo sciuntur, ut sciendo nesciantur.*

[4] Ps. 18.13.

being and the more good things they do or make—for then
they are doing or making something positive—the more their
causes are efficient; but in so far as they fail or are defective
and, in that sense, 'do evil'—if a 'defect' can be 'done'—then
their causes are 'deficient.' I know, further, that when a will
'is made' evil, what happens would not have happened if the
will had not wanted it to happen. That is why the punishment which follows is just, since the defection was not necessary but voluntary. The will does not fall 'into sin'; it falls 'sin-
fully.'[1] Defects are not mere relations to natures that are evil;
they are evil in themselves because, contrary to the order of
natures, there is a defection from Being that is supreme to
some lesser being.

Thus, greed is not a defect in the gold that is desired but
in the man who loves it perversely by falling from justice
which he ought to esteem as incomparably superior to gold;
nor is lust a defect in bodies which are beautiful and pleasing:
it is a sin in the soul of the one who loves corporal pleasures
perversely, that is, by abandoning that temperance which
joins us in spiritual and unblemishable union with realities far
more beautiful and pleasing; nor is boastfulness a blemish in
words of praise: it is a failing in the soul of one who is so
perversely in love with other peoples' applause that he despises
the voice of his own conscience; nor is pride a vice in the one
who delegates power, still less a flaw in the power itself: it
is a passion in the soul of the one who loves his own power so
perversely as to condemn the authority of one who is still more
powerful.

In a word, anyone who loves perversely the good of any
nature whatsoever and even, perhaps, acquires this good
makes himself bad by gaining something good and sad by losing something better.[2]

Chapter 9

There is, then, no natural efficient cause of an evil will or,
if I may use the word, no essential cause. The reason for this
is that it is the evil will itself that starts that evil in mutable

---

[1] *Deficitur enim non ad mala, sed male.*
[2] . . . *ipse fit in bono malus et miser meliore privatus.*

spirits, which is nothing but a weakening and worsening of the good in their nature. What 'makes' the will evil is, in reality, an 'unmaking,' a desertion from God. The very defection is deficient—in the sense of having no cause. However, in saying that there is no efficient cause even of a good will, we must beware of believing that the good will of the good angels was uncreated and co-eternal with God. But, if good angels were created, how can we say that their good will was not created? The fact is, it was created; the only question is whether it was created simultaneously with the creation of the angels or whether they first existed without a good will. If simultaneously, then, undoubtedly, it was created by Him who created the angels, so that, as soon as they were created, they adhered to Him who created them by means of that love with which they were created. Thus, the reason why the bad were separated from the society of good angels was that the good persevered in the same good will, whereas the others changed themselves into bad angels by defection from good will. The only thing that 'made' their will bad was that they fell away from a will which was good. Nor would they have fallen away, had they not chosen to fall away.

In the hypothesis, however, that the good angels, existing at first without a good will, produced it in themselves without the help of God, they must have made themselves better than what they were when God created them. This is nonsense. For, without a good will, what could they be but evil? Or, if we may not say evil, since their will was not yet evil—for they could hardly fall away from what they had not yet begun to have—at least, they certainly were not good angels—not as good as they were to become when they came to possess a good will.

So much for the hypothesis. Since they could not make themselves better than God made them—for no one can make anything better than God can—then it follows that, without the co-operation of their Creator, they could never have come into possession of that good will which made them better.

Now, it is true that their good will was not only the cause of their turning and adhering to Him, who is Perfect Being, rather than to themselves, whose being was less than perfect, but also the reason why they had more of being than before and could live wisely and happily in union with God. Nevertheless, this merely shows that any will, however good, would have been destitute and destined to remain in hopeless desire, did not He who had created their good nature out of nothing, and had given it a capacity for union with Himself, first awaken in the will a greater longing for this union and then fill the will with some of His very Being in order to make it better.[1]

This raises another issue. For, if the good angels did something themselves to bring about their good will, did they do this with or without a will? If without, then, of course, they were not the agents. If with a will, was it an evil or a good one? If evil, how could it produce a good will? If good, well, then, they had a good will already. And who made this but God Himself who created them with a good will (that is, with the unblemished love by which they could adhere to Him) and who at the same time created their nature and enriched it with grace?

Thus, we are compelled to believe that the holy angels never existed without a good will, that is, without the love of God. But what of those angels who were created good and became evil by their own bad will for which their good nature is not responsible except in so far as there was a deliberate defection from good—for it is never good, but a defection from good, that is the cause of evil? These angels either received less grace of divine love than those who persevered in grace, or, if both were created equally good, then, while the former were falling by bad will, the latter were increasingly aided to reach that plenitude of beatitude which made them certain that they would never fall—a matter which I discussed in the preceding Book.[2]

Thus with our praise to our Creator, we should all proclaim that, not only of holy men, but also of holy angels, it may be said that 'the charity of God is poured forth' in them 'by the Holy Spirit who has been given' to them.[3] Nor is it the good only of men, but first and foremost that of angels, which is referred to in the words: 'It is good for me to adhere to my God.'[4]

---

[1] . . . *ex se ipso faceret inplendo meliorem prius faciens excitando avidiorem.*

[2] Cf. above, 11.13.   [3] Rom. 5.5.

[4] Ps. 72.28.

And they who share this common good are in a holy communion both with Him to whom they adhere and one with another, and they form a single community, one City of God, which is also His living sacrifice and His living temple.

This ends the discussion of the origin of this City in so far as it concerns the angels. I must now turn to the rise of that part of the City which is made up of mortal men, created by the same God, who will one day be united to the immortal angels and who, at present, are either sojourning on earth or, if dead, are resting in the hidden sanctuaries where the souls of the departed have their abode.

It was from one man, the first whom God created, that the whole human race took its start. This is the faith revealed in Holy Scripture, a faith that has gained marvelous and merited authority throughout the world and among all peoples—as, along with other truths, Scripture itself divinely predicted would be the case.

Chapter 10

I shall not dwell, then, on the conjectures of men who 'know not what they say' concerning the nature and origin of the human race. There are, for example, those who hold the opinion that men—like the universe—have always existed. Thus, Apuleius, in his account of the human race, observes: 'Individually they are mortal but all together as a race they are immortal.'[1]

Suppose the following questions are put to these men: If the human race has always existed, how, then, do you vindicate the truth of your own history which records the names of inventors and what they invented, the first founders of liberal education and of other arts, the first inhabitants of this or that region and of this or that island? They will answer that, at certain intervals of time, most of the land was so devastated by floods and fire that the human race was greatly reduced in size and that from this small number the former population was again restored; and that, thus, at intervals, there was a new discovery and organization of all these things, or, rather,

---

[1] *De deo Socratis* 4 (ed. Goldbacher, p. 8).

a restoration of what had been damaged or destroyed by the great devastations; and that, in any case, men could simply not exist unless they were produced from man. Of course, all this is opinion, not science.

Chapter 11

Citing a letter, supposedly from Alexander the Great to his mother, Augustine points to many discrepancies in ancient chronologies of world history and argues that Scripture is a more reliable source of such chronological information.

Chapter 12

There are others who think that our present world is not everlasting. Of these, some hold that, besides this one, there are a number of other worlds. The remainer, who admit only one world, claim that, over and over again, it periodically disintegrates and begins again. In either theory, they are forced to conclude that the human race arose without human procreation, since there is no room here for the hypothesis that a few men would always remain each time the world perished, as was the case in the previous theory where floods and fires did not affect the whole world but left a few survivors to repeople it. For they hold that, just as the world is reborn out of its previous matter, so a new human race would arise from the elements of nature and only thereafter would a progeny of mortals spring from parents. And the same would be true of the rest of the animals.[1]

Chapters 13–18

Recording a curious anticipation of modern views on the long prehistory of this world (600,000 years), Augustine admits he does not know how old it is but he is against the theory of periodic cycles. Man was created once, in time, and that is certain. In the ensuing discussion of time two points

[1] Augustine here records, without approving, an important anticipation of modern cosmological and evolutionistic theories [Ed.].

are made: no creature is co-eternal with God, and no human being preceded Adam. The problem of infinity is then introduced.

Chapter 19

The second of the fundamental positions I mentioned is that not even the knowledge of God can comprehend anything that is infinite. Very well, then, let them dare to say—from the depths of their abysmal impiety—that God does not know all numbers. Now, numbers are certainly infinite,[1] for at no matter what number you think you have reached an end, you cannot merely add one to this number, but you can multiply it by two or any other number including itself; by the very nature of mathematics it does not matter how big or all-embracing the number may be.

Moreover, by the very nature of numbers no one number can be equal to any other number. The result is that, though taken separately, each number is finite, yet, because they are all unequal and different, taken all together, they are infinite. It ought to follow, then, that God does not know all the numbers because they are infinite, and that His knowledge can reach so far and count no further. Now who in the world would be fool enough to say that?

Some of the philosophers, those at least who respect Plato's idea that God designed the cosmos on the principle of numbers, will hardly dare to despise numbers, in the sense of pretending that they are no part of the knowledge of God. And as for us, our Scripture thus addresses God: 'Thou hast ordered all things in measure, and number, and weight,'[2] and one of the Prophets refers to God as one 'who bringeth forth their world by numbers.'[3] Again, in the Gospel, our Saviour declares that 'the very hairs of your head are all numbered.'[4] We are far, then, from doubting that all numbers are known

---

[1] This text is quoted by G. Cantor (*Letter to Eulenburg* [1886] in *Abhandlungen*, Berlin 1932, pp. 401–402) as a source of modern mathematical views on infinity. Cf. D. J. Struik, *A Concise History of Mathematics*, London 1954, pp. 106 and 243 [Ed.].

[2] Wisd. 11.21.   [3] Cf. Isa. 40.26.

[4] Matt. 10.30.

to Him of whose wisdom, according to the Psalmist, 'there is no number.'[5]

Although, then, there is no definite number corresponding to an infinite number, an infinity of numbers is, nevertheless, not incomprehensible to Him of whose intelligence 'there is no number.' It follows, then, that since whatever is comprehended by knowledge is limited by the very comprehension of the one who knows, in some ineffable way, all infinity is made finite by God since in His knowledge it is not incomprehensible.

Now, if the infinity of numbers cannot be beyond the limits of the knowledge of God which comprehends it, who are we little men that we should presume to put limits to His knowledge, as is done by those who argue that, unless the same pattern of temporal events is repeated in identical cycles, God can neither foresee what He creates with a view to making it, nor know it after He has made it? The fact is that God, whose knowledge is simple in its multiplicity and one in its diversity, comprehends all incomprehensible things with an incomprehensible comprehension. And this is so true that, even if He willed to keep on endlessly creating one new and dissimilar thing after another, not one of them could possibly seem new and unexpected to Him, nor would He foresee them merely, as it were at the last moment, but by His foreknowledge He would have them before Him throughout all eternity.

Chapters 20–21

The meaning of the Biblical phrase 'ages of ages' is examined; it does not mean periodic cycles of time. Chapter 21 is a long criticism of the theory that the souls of the dead will return to live again on this earth. Augustine is clearly opposed to human reincarnation or metempsychosis.

Chapter 22

Now that I have explained, as well as I could, this difficult question of the eternal God creating new things without any change in His will, it is simple enough to see how much better

[5] Ps. 146.5.

it was for God to multiply the human race from one man whom He created rather than to develop it from many.

In regard to other animals, we see that He created some to be solitary, lone rangers, so to speak, like eagles, hawks, lions, wolves, and so on; and others to be gregarious, animals that prefer to live together in flocks, such as doves, starlings, stags, and others of the kind. However, He propagated neither of these classes from a single pair, but ordered the creation of several at the same time.

On the other hand, He created man with a nature midway between angels and beasts, so that man, provided he should remain subject to his true Lord and Creator and dutifully obey His commandments, might pass into the company of the angels, without the intervention of death, thus to attain a blessed and eternal immortality. But, should he offend his Lord and God by a proud and disobedient use of his free will, then, subject to death and a slave to his appetites, he would have to live like a beast and be destined to eternal punishment after death. Therefore, God created one sole individual, not that he was meant to remain alone deprived of human companionship, but in order that the unity of society and the bond of harmony might mean more to man, since men were to be united not only by the likeness of nature but also by the affection of kinship. God did not even wish to create the woman who was to be mated with man in the same way that He created man but, rather, out of him, in order that the whole human race might be derived entirely from one single individual.

Chapter 23

God was not unaware that man would sin and, being subjected to death, would propagate mortals destined to die; and that these mortals would go so far in the monstrousness of sin that even the beasts without power of rational choice, that had been created in numbers from the waters and the earth, would live more securely and peacefully among their own kind than men—even though the human race had been given a single progenitor for the very purpose of promoting harmony. And, in fact, neither lions nor dragons have ever waged such wars with their own kind as men have fought with one another.

However, God also foresaw that a community of saints would be called to supernatural adoption, would have their sins forgiven, be sanctified by the Holy Spirit, and finally be united with the holy angels in eternal peace, so that, at last, the enemy death will be destroyed.[1] And God knew how good it would be for this community often to recall that the human race had its roots in one man, precisely to show how pleasing it is to God that men, though many, should be one.

Chapter 24

When God made man according to His own image, He gave him a soul so endowed with reason and intelligence that it ranks man higher than all the other creatures of the earth, the sea, the air, because they lack intelligence. God, then, formed man out of the dust of the earth and, by His breath, gave man a soul such as I have described. It is not certain whether God's breathing imparted to man a soul previously created or whether God created the soul by the act of breathing, as though He wanted the soul of man to be the very breath of God. (Notice that to breathe is the same as to *make* a breathing.)

Next, He took a bone from the man's side and made of it a mate to collaborate in procreation. Of course, all this was done in a divine way. We must not imagine the process in a material way, as though God worked, as ordinary artists do, with hands, shaping, as best they can, some earthly material into a form dictated by the rules of art. The 'hand' of God means the power of God which works in an invisible way to produce even visible results. If some people take these true facts for mere fables it is because they use familiar, everyday craftsmanship to measure that power and wisdom of God which not merely can but does produce even seeds without seeds. And as for those things which God first created, they refuse to believe them on the ground that they have no way to know them. Yet, they know facts about human conception

[1] Cf. 1 Cor. 15.26.

and birth which would seem far more incredible if they were told to others who did not know them and, what is more, they often think such things can be attributed to natural, physical causes rather than to the efficacy of any divine action.

Chapter 25

In this work, I am not dealing with those who do not believe that the divine mind was a Creator and has a care for what He created, but with those who, along with Plato, distinguished between the Supreme God who created the cosmos and the lesser gods, who, so they think, were created by God and had God's consent or command to be creators themselves. These gods are supposed to have made all mortal animals and, especially, man who ranks so near to the gods themselves. Now, if these philosophers would only give up their superstitious attempt to justify the rites and sacrifice they offer to these gods as to their creators, they would easily escape from the error of believing that anyone but God can create.

Even before the nature of God is understood, it is wrong to think and say that there can be any other Creator of any nature whatsoever, however tiny and mortal it may be. Even though the angels (whom the Neo-Platonists prefer to call gods) can be ordered or permitted to aid God in producing what the earth brings forth, they can no more be called creators of animals than farmers can be called the creators of crops and trees.

Chapter 26

The word 'form' has two meanings. Every material body has an outer form shaped by a potter, or smith, or other artisan who can paint or fashion even forms that look like the shapes of animals. But there is also an inner form which is not a shape but a shaper, with an efficient causality deriving from the secret and hidden determination of some living and intelligent nature which can shape not merely the outer forms of physical bodies but the inner souls of living things. The first kind of form we may attribute to any artificer, but the second, only to the one Artificer, Creator and Maker, who is God.

It is He who created the universe and all the angels before there were any worlds or any angels there to help him.

It was by this divine creative power, which, so to speak, knows not what it is to be made but only how to make, that the form of roundness was given to the sky and to the sun when the cosmos was created. It was by this same divine creative force, which knows not what it is to be made but only how to make, that roundness was given to the eye, to the apple, and to other objects that are by nature round and which we see all about, taking on their form with no extrinsic cause but by the intrinsic power of the Creator, who said: 'Do not I fill heaven and earth?'[1] and whose wisdom 'reacheth from end to end mightily, and ordereth all things sweetly.'[2]

So, I do not see what kind of aid the angels, who were first made, could give to the Creator in the production of other things. I neither dare to attribute to them what, perhaps, they cannot do nor ought I to detract from any power they actually possess. But, as for the creation and origin of all natures as such, that I attribute solely to God, and, in this, the angels join me, since they gratefully acknowledge that they are indebted to Him for all that they are.

Not only do we deny that farmers are the creators of their crops—'neither he who plants is anything, nor he who waters, but God who gives the growth'[3]—but we refuse to the earth itself creative power, even though she seems to be the fruitful mother of all that she prompts to sprout from seeds while holding them down by roots. We remember what Scripture tells us: 'God gives it a body even as he has willed, and to each of the seeds a body of its own.'[4] Nor do we look upon a woman as the creator of the child she bears, since He is the Creator who said to one of His servants: 'Before I formed thee in the bowels of thy mother, I knew thee.'[5]

Although it is true that this or that emotion of a pregnant woman may have some effect on the child she is bearing—as Jacob's variegated staffs affected the colors of the lambs to be born—nevertheless, the mother herself no more creates the nature of her child than she creates herself.

[1] Jer. 23.24.   [2] Wisd. 8.1.
[3] 1 Cor. 3.7.   [4] 1 Cor. 15.38.
[5] Jer. 1.5.

Therefore, whatever bodily or seminal causes may play a part in reproduction, whether by the influence of angels or of men or other animals, or by the intermingling of the two sexes, and whatever longings or emotions of the mother may affect the features or the color while the fetus is still soft and pliable, nevertheless, every nature as such, however affected by circumstances, is created wholly by the Supreme God. It is the hidden and penetrating power of His irresistible presence which gives being to every creature that can be said to be, whatever its genus and species may be. For, without His creative act, a nature would not only not be in this or that genus; it simply could not have being at all.[6]

Everyone admits, even when there is question of the outward form which artisans impose on material things, that it was not the masons and architects who were the founders of Rome and Alexandria, but the kings, by whose purpose, plan, and power these cities were built. In the one case, Romulus was the founder, and, in the other, Alexander. Obviously, then, we should acknowledge that God alone is the Founder of every nature. In His creation, He uses no material and no workmen which He Himself has not made. And if He were to withdraw, so to speak, His building power from creatures, they would no more exist than they existed before they were created. The 'before,' of course, refers not to time but to eternity. For He alone could be the Creator of time who created those things whose motions are the measure of time.

Chapter 27

Of course, when Plato taught that the lesser gods, made by the Supreme God, were the makers of the mortal part of all other animals, he knew that the immortal part came from God;[1] therefore, he maintained that the lesser gods were responsible not for our souls but only for our bodies.

Now, Porphyry, who claims that the soul must free itself from all matter if it is to be purified, at the same time agrees with Plato and his followers that those who in life transgressed

[6] Cf. *De Trin.* 3.13–16.

[1] *Timaeus* 41C.

the moderation of mortality must return to mortal bodies for their purgation and punishment—not, however, to bodies of beasts, as Plato held, but only to those of men. Now, notice the conclusion. The so-called gods whom they want us to worship, as though they were our parents or makers, are, in reality, nothing more than the forgers of our fetters and our prison bars, not our creators but our incarcerators, who weigh us down with chains in wretched prisons.

So, let these Platonists, then, take their choice. Either they should stop threatening us with reincarnation as a punishment for our souls, or else they should stop telling us to worship as gods beings who are responsible for the one part of our make-up that they encourage us to avoid as much as possible. The fact is that both the reincarnation and the responsibility are equally ridiculous. As to the former, there is no such thing as a return to this life for the punishment of souls; as to the latter, the sole responsibility for all living things in heaven or on earth belongs to the God who created heaven and earth.

If punishment is the only reason why a soul should inhabit a body, how can Plato declare that the only way to make the universe so perfect and beautiful was to have it filled with every genus of animals, mortal as well as immortal?[2] And if our creation, even as mortals, is due to God, how can the return to bodies which are gifts of God be punishment? And if God, as Plato continually reminds us, contains in His eternal intelligence the forms of the entire universe and of every living creature within it, how is it that He did not create them all Himself? Could it be that He was unwilling to be Creator of some of those things, the design for whose creation He possessed within His ineffable and ineffably admirable intelligence?

Chapter 28

It follows that the true religion is right in recognizing and teaching that the Creator of the whole universe is the same as the Creator of all living things, that is, of all souls and all bodies. And of all the animals on earth the main one is man. He was made to be the image of God, and, for the reason

2 *Ibid.* 92B.

previously given or for some better one unknown to me, only one man was made—although he did not remain alone. For there is nothing so social by nature, so anti-social by sin, as man. And if any man should ever need an argument against the evil of dissension, either to prevent it breaking out or to bring it to an end, there is nothing better than to recall that single father of all our human race whom God created as a solitary individual, for the precise purpose of reminding us to preserve unity of heart in a multitude of men. And the fact that a woman was made from the side of the man shows clearly enough how highly we were meant to esteem the relationship between husband and wife.

Of course, these works of God are extraordinary because they are His first. But no one who refuses so to believe them has a right to believe in any kind of prodigies, for nothing would be even called a prodigy if it happened in the ordinary course of nature. As for that greater governance of divine providence, everything that happens has a purpose even though the causes are hidden. The inspired Psalmist sings: 'Come and behold ye the works of the Lord: what wonders [*prodigia*] he hath done upon earth.'[1] Later on,[2] with God's help, I shall explain what is prefigured by the first prodigy[3]— if I may so call it—the creation of woman from the side of man.

But now, since I must put an end to this Book, I shall merely say that, in my view, in this first man created in the beginning, there was established, not as yet, indeed, in actual appearance but in the foreknowledge of God, the origin of these two cities or societies, as far as concerns the human race. From this first man were to come all men, some to be associated with the bad angels in their punishment and others to be fellow citizens with the good angels in their reward. All this was ordered by a secret yet just judgment of God, for Scripture tells us that 'all the ways of the Lord are mercy and truth,'[4] and we know that His grace can never be unjust nor His justice ever cruel.

---

[1] Ps. 45.9.   [2] Cf. Bk. 22.17, here omitted.
[3] Through this passage there is a play on the pagan word, *prodigium*, a pointing out beforehand, a prophetic sign and, hence, any portent or marvel, and the word, *providentia*, in the Christian sense of God's foresight or foreknowledge from eternity.
[4] Ps. 25.10.

BOOK XIII

Adam's Sin and Its Consequences

Chapter 1

Now THAT I HAVE DISCUSSED the intricate problem about the origin of the world and the beginning of the human race, a proper order calls for a study of the fall of the first man, in fact, of the first parents, and of the origin and transmission of human mortality. It is true that God did not endow man with the same nature that He gave to the angels—who could not possibly die even if they sinned—yet, had our first parents complied with the obligations of obedience, they, too, would have attained, without interruption of death, an immortality like that of the angels and an everlasting happiness. However, as I have pointed out in the preceding Book,[1] God so made men that, should they disobey, death was to be a just judgment for their disobedience.

Chapter 2

It seems to me that I ought to examine more carefully the nature of death. For, although the human soul is, in a true sense, immortal, nonetheless it, too, can suffer its own sort of death. It is said to be immortal because it can never, in the least degree, cease to live and perceive. The body, on the other hand, is mortal because it can be deprived entirely of life and because, of itself, it has no power to live. Death comes to the soul when God abandons it, just as death comes to the body when the soul departs.

There is also a total death for man, a death of body and soul, namely, when a soul, abandoned by God, abandons the body. In this case, the soul has no life from God and the body no life from the soul. The consequence of such total death is the second death, so called on the authority of divine Reve-

---

[1] Cf. Bk. 12.21, here omitted.

lation.[1] This is the death which our Saviour meant when He said: 'Be afraid of him who is able to destroy both soul and body in hell.'[2]

Since this second death does not occur until soul and body are reunited, never to be separated again, you might wonder how the body is said to die by a death in which it is not deserted by the soul but rather is given a life by the soul to feel the torment it endures. For, in man's last and everlasting punishment (of which I shall have more to say in its proper place[3]) the soul is rightly said to be dead when its life from God is gone, but, since the body's life depends on the soul, how can the body be said to be dead? If the body were dead, it could not feel the bodily torments which are to be felt after the resurrection.

Perhaps it is because any sort of life is a real good, while pain is an evil that we ought not to say that a body is alive when the only purpose of its soul is not so much to give it life but rather to keep it in pain.[4] The soul takes its life from God when it lives holily, for the reason that it cannot live holily unless God is the cause of its good works.[5] The body, however, takes its life from the soul when the soul is alive in the body, whether the soul is receiving any life from God or not. Life in the bodies of the impious is not the life of their souls, but simply the life of their bodies. This life, even souls that are dead, in the sense of being deserted by God, can confer, since they do not desist from that flicker of life which they can call their own, that is, the life which makes them immortal.

It is true that, when a man is finally damned, he does not lose sensation; nevertheless, because his feelings are not gentle enough to give pleasure nor soothing enough to be restful, but are purifying to the point of pain, they can more properly be called death rather than life. The reason why this death of damnation is called a second death is that it comes after that first death which is a divorce of two natures meant to be in

---

[1] Apoc. 2.11; 20.14; 21.8.   [2] Matt. 10.28.
[3] Cf. below, 19.28.

[4] . . . ideo nec vivere corpus dicendum est, in quo anima non vivendi causa est, sed dolendi.

[5] . . . non enim potest bene vivere nisi Deo in se operante quod bonum est.

union, whether God and the soul or the soul and the body. It can be said of the first death, the death of the body, that it is good for saints and bad for sinners,[6] but of the second that it is certainly good for no one and non-existent for the saints.

Chapter 3

I know, of course, that in saying that the death which sunders soul and body is, in reality, good for the saints I have raised a difficulty which cannot be dismissed. If that be so, how can death be considered the punishment of sin? Certainly, if the first parents had not sinned, they would not have suffered this death. But, how can something that could not have happened except to sinners be good for the saints? Besides, if it could not have happened except to sinners, it should not even happen to the saints, let alone be good for them. For, why should those who deserve no punishment be punished?

The answer seems to be that, while the first parents were so created that, had they not sinned, they would have experienced no kind of death, nevertheless, these first sinners were so punished that all of their descendants were to be subject to the same penalty of death. No one was to be born of them who was less a sinner than they were. Such was the greatness of the guilt that the punishment so impaired human nature that what was originally a penal condition for the first parents who sinned became a natural consequence in all of their descendants.

Man is not produced from man in the same way that he was created from the dust. Dust was but the material out of which man was made, while a man is the parent of his child. Earth and flesh are not identical, even though the latter was made from the former, but parent and offspring are identical in having the same human nature. Hence, when the first couple were punished by the judgment of God, the whole human race, which was to become Adam's posterity through the first woman, was present in the first man. And what was born was

---

[6] . . . quod bonis bona sit, malis mala; secunda vero sine dubio sicut nullorum bonorum est, ita nulli bona.

not human nature as it was originally created but as it became after the first parents' sin and punishment—as far, at least, as concerns the origin of sin and death.

Note that sin and punishment did not reduce the first man to that infantile state of mental and physical weakness which we see in children; but God did will that human progeny should begin life much as animals do, seeing that the first parents had been lowered to the level of beasts during their life and in death, as Scripture has pointed out: 'Man when he was in honor did not understand: he is compared to senseless beasts, and is become like to them.'[1] Actually, the human infant is far weaker in the use and movement of its limbs and in its appetitive and protective sense than the most tender offspring of any other animal. It would seem that the human faculties were meant, all the more, to excel those of other animals, just because their early energies are held in check, like an arrow drawn far back by the bending of a bow.

Now, the first man's sinful presumption and just punishment did not reduce him to this infantile condition. However, in his person, human nature was so changed and vitiated that it suffers from the recalcitrance of a rebellious concupiscence and is bound by the law of death. And what the first man became by perversion and penalty, this his descendants are by birth—natures subject to sin and death.

If, through the grace of the Mediator Christ, infants are redeemed from the bondage of sin, then they can suffer only that death which separates the soul from the body; being freed from the bondage of sin, they do not pass to that second death which is both penal and eternal.

Chapter 4

If one should wonder why death, which is the punishment of sin, must be borne by those whose guilt has been annulled by grace, I must refer him to another work of mine[1] which deals with the baptism of infants and which discusses and an-

---

[1] Ps. 48.13.

[1] *De peccatorum meritis et remissione et de baptismo parvulorum* 2.39.

swers the present question. I have there offered as an explanation why the soul must endure separation from the body, in spite of the connection with sin being removed, that, were the immortality of the body to follow immediately upon the sacrament of regeneration, faith might be weakened, since faith is really faith only when, in hope, it awaits that which is not yet seen in substance.

In former ages, at least, there was need to face the fear of death with a robust and aggressive faith, as was so clear in the case of the holy martyrs. Indeed, these saints would have enjoyed no glory and no victory, since there could have been no strife, if, once they were made holy by the waters of regeneration, they could suffer no bodily death. Who would not run to join the infants about to be baptized, if the main purpose of Christ's grace were to save us from bodily death? Thus, faith would be put to no test by an invisible reward; it could not even be called faith; it would be merely a desire to receive an immediate reward of its work.

But now, by a greater and more wonderful grace of the Saviour, the punishment of sin serves the purposes of sanctity. In the beginning, the first man was warned: 'If you sin, you shall die'; now, the martyr is admonished; 'Die that you may not sin.' The first man was told: 'If you transgress, you shall die the death'; now, the martyr is reminded: 'If you refuse death, you transgress the commandment.' What before was to be feared, if a man were to keep himself from sin, is now to be faced, if he is not to sin.

Thus, by the ineffable mercy of God, the penalty of sin is transformed into the panoply of virtue and the punishment of the sinner into the testing of a saint. In the case of the first parents, death was incurred by sinning; now, sainthood is attained by dying. This is true of the holy martyrs. To them, their persecutors offered the alternative: either deny the faith or die. And the saints choose to suffer for their faith what the first sinners had no choice but to suffer for their infidelity. The sinners would not have died unless they sinned; the saints will sin unless they die. The sinners died because they sinned; the martyrs do not sin because they die. In the one case, guilt was pursued by punishment; in the other case, the punishment keeps the guilt at bay.

This does not mean that death, which before was an evil, has now become something good. But it means that God has rewarded faith with so much grace that death, which seems to be the enemy of life, becomes an ally that helps man enter into life.

Chapter 5

When the Apostle wished to express the power of sin to harm a man who is not aided by grace, he did not hesitate to say that this power lies in the very Law which prohibits sin. 'Now the sting of death is sin, and the power of sin is the Law.'[1] Nothing could be truer. For a prohibition always increases an illicit desire so long as the love of and joy in holiness is too weak to conquer the inclination to sin; and, without the aid of divine grace, it is impossible for man to love and delight in sanctity.

However, lest people might think that the Law were evil, by reason of the expression, 'the power of sin,' the Apostle, in another context, put the matter thus: 'So that the Law indeed is holy and the commandment holy and just and good. Did then that which is good become death to me? By no means! But sin, that it might be manifest as sin, worked death for me through that which is good.' Thus, a sinner or a sin, by reason of the commandment, might become immeasurably worse.[2] He says 'immeasurably' because the transgression is worse when an increasing desire of sin causes the Law itself to be despised.

Why do I consider it necessary to mention this? For the simple reason that, as the Law is not evil, though it increases the concupiscence of sinners, neither is death good, though it increases the reward of the martyrs. The Law, when defied through love of evil, produces sinners; death when suffered through love of truth produces martyrs. Thus, the Law is good because it is the prohibition of sin; death is evil because it is the penalty of sin. Wickedness makes a bad use not only of

---

[1] 1 Cor. 15.56.
[2] Rom. 7.12,13. . . . *ut fiat super modum peccator aut peccatum per mandatum.* The Vulgate reads: . . . *ut fiat supra modum peccans peccatum per mandatum.*

evil, but also of good. In the same way, holiness makes a good use not only of good, but also of evil. Thus, sinners make a bad use of the Law, although the Law is good, while saints make a good use of death, although death is an evil.

Chapter 6

Mere physical death, the separation of soul and body that the dying must endure, is not good for anyone. For, there is something harsh and unnatural in the violent sundering of what, in a living person, were so closely linked and interwoven; and the experience lasts until there is a complete loss of all feeling that depends on the union of soul and body. Sometimes, however, the body is battered or the soul is snatched away so swiftly that there is no time to feel the anguish of dying.

However painful the feeling of a dying person that all feeling is falling away, if it is suffered with faith and piety, it increases the merit of patience, without, however, forfeiting its claims to be called a punishment. Undoubtedly, death is the penalty of all who come to birth on earth as descendants of the first man; nevertheless, if the penalty is paid in the name of justice and piety, it becomes a new birth in heaven. Although death is the punishment of sin, sometimes it secures for the soul a grace that is a security against all punishment for sin.

Chapter 7

I have in mind those unbaptized persons who die confessing the name of Christ. They receive the forgiveness of their sins as completely as if they had been cleansed by the waters of baptism. For, He who said: 'Unless a man be born again of water and the Spirit, he cannot enter into the kingdom of God,'[1] made exceptions in other decisions which are no less universal: 'Everyone who acknowledges me before men, I also will acknowledge him before my Father in heaven';[2] and again: 'He who loses his life for my sake will find it.'[3]

[1] John 3.5. [2] Matt. 10.32.
[3] Matt. 16.25.

So, too, in the psalm: 'Precious in the sight of the Lord is the death of his saints.'[4] For, what could be more precious than a death which remits all sin and amasses merit? Men, unable to defer their death, who are baptized, and thus depart from life with all their sins forgiven, are not equal in merit to those who have not postponed death, although they could have done so, because they preferred to lose life by confessing Christ rather than, by denying Him, to gain time for baptism.

Of course, if through fear of death they did deny Christ, even that sin could be canceled by the baptism which washed away even the heinous outrage of those who killed Christ. But, what shall we say when, without the fullness of grace of the Spirit, that 'blows where it will,'[5] they were able to love Christ so much that they were unable to deny Him even in the face of a death from which they could so easily have escaped.

The precious death of the saints, for whom the death of Christ had already merited so much grace that they hastened to lose their own lives in order to find Him, proves that the right use of death, which originally was intended as the punishment of sin, may bring forth abundant fruits of holiness. Death itself, however, should not, on this account, be looked upon as good since it was turned to good account not by any goodness of its own, but by the help of God. Originally, death was ordained as something to be feared, to prevent sin from being committed; now, it is proposed as something to be endured, both that sin may not be committed and, if already committed, may be deleted so that the palm of sanctity may be granted for this great victory.

Chapter 8

If we look a little more closely, we shall notice that, even when a man dies out of faith and loyalty to the truth, he escapes death. His motive in facing a partial death is to escape total death and, above all, a death which is eternal. He suffers the separation of his soul from his body to prevent its separation both from God and his body—to prevent a first death of

---

[4] Ps. 115.15.   [5] John 3.8.

the whole man which would be followed by a second and eternal death.

Thus, in a word, while men are in the throes of death and death is bringing on disintegration, death is good for no one, but it may become meritorious if suffered to retain or to gain some good. However, when it is a question, not of dying, but of being dead, then death may well be said to be bad for sinners and good for saints. For, the separated souls of the saints are now in peace, while those of the wicked are in pain, and will be so until the resurrection of their bodies, when the former will enter into life everlasting and the latter into a second and eternal death.

Chapters 9–11

These chapters discuss the precise moment of death, whether it belongs to the living or the dead—and, further, whether throughout his mortal life man is dying. The gloom of the passage is lightened by an atrocious pun: the Latin verb, to die, cannot be declined regularly but the second dying, that of the soul, can be declined with the grace of God.

Chapter 12

The next question to be asked is with what death God threatened our first parents, should they disobey and transgress the command He had given them. Was it the death of the soul, or of the body, or of the entire man, or the so-called second death? The answer is: every kind of death.

The first death includes two deaths; total death includes all.[1] As the whole earth includes many lands and the whole Church many churches, so the total death embraces many deaths. The first death includes two, that of the soul and that of the body; so that the first death is a death of the whole man, in so far as the soul, deprived of both God and the body, suffers a temporal punishment. The second death is one in which the soul, deprived of God but united to the body, suffers eternal punishment.

[1] Neglecting the *secunda* which appears in many MSS and is printed within brackets in the Hoffmann text.

Therefore, when God, referring to the forbidden fruit, said to the first man whom He had established in Paradise: 'In what day soever thou shalt eat of it, thou shalt die the death,'[2] His threat included not only the first part of the first death, that is, the soul's deprivation of God; not only the second part of the first death, that is, the body's deprivation of the soul; not only the whole of the first death in which the soul, separated from both God and the body, is punished; but whatever of death there is up to and including that absolutely final and so-called second death.

Chapter 13

As soon as our first parents had disobeyed God's commandment, they were immediately deprived of divine grace, and were ashamed of their nakedness. They covered themselves with fig leaves,[1] which, perhaps, were the first things noticed by the troubled pair. The parts covered remained unchanged except that, previously, they occasioned no shame. They felt for the first time a movement of disobedience in their flesh, as though the punishment were meant to fit the crime of their own disobedience to God.

The fact is that the soul, which had taken perverse delight in its own liberty and disdained the service of God, was now deprived of its original mastery over the body; because it had deliberately deserted the Lord who was over it, it no longer bent to its will the servant below it, being unable to hold the flesh completely in subjection as would always have been the case, if only the soul had remained subject to God. From this moment, then, the flesh began to lust against the spirit.[2] With this rebellion we are born, just as we are doomed to die and, because of the first sin, to bear, in our members and vitiated nature, either the battle with or defeat by the flesh.

Chapter 14

God, the Author of all natures but not of their defects, created man good; but man, corrupt by choice and condemned

2 Gen. 2.17.

1 Cf. Gen. 3.7–10.   2 Cf. Gal. 5.17.

by justice, has produced a progeny that is both corrupt and condemned. For, we all existed in that one man, since, taken together, we were the one man who fell into sin through the woman who was made out of him before sin existed. Although the specific form by which each of us was to live was not yet created and assigned, our nature was already present in the seed from which we were to spring. And because this nature has been soiled by sin and doomed to death and justly condemned, no man was to be born of man in any other condition.

Thus, from a bad use of free choice, a sequence of misfortunes conducts the whole human race, excepting those redeemed by the grace of God, from the original canker in its root to the devastation of a second and endless death.

Chapter 15

Since there is no mention of more than one death in the Scriptural passage: 'Thou shalt die the death,'[1] we should interpret it to mean that particular death which occurs when the life of the soul (which is God) abandons it. (The soul was not first deserted by God and so deserted Him, but it first deserted God, with the result that it was deserted by Him.[2] For, as regards man's evil, it is his will that comes first, but where his good is in question, it is the Creator's will that is responsible, both for creating him out of nothing and for restoring him to life after he had fallen, and was dead.) However, although we may take it that God intimated only this one death in the words: 'In what day soever thou shalt eat of it, thou shalt die the death,'[3] by which He meant: 'In whatever day you shall leave me through disobedience I shall leave you without grace,'[4] nevertheless, the mention of this one death includes all the other deaths which were certainly to follow.

In so far as a rebellion of the flesh against the rebellious soul prompted our parents to cover their shame, they experienced one kind of death—God's desertion of the soul. It was this death which was intimated when God asked Adam, beside himself

---

[1] Gen. 2.17.
[2] . . . *non enim deserta est ut desereret, sed ut desereretur deseruit.*
[3] Gen. 2.17.   [4] . . . *deseram vos per iustitiam*

with fear and in hiding: 'Where art thou?'[5] not, of course, because God did not know the answer, but to scold Adam by reminding him that there really was nowhere that he could be, once God was not in him.

Then when the soul departed from Adam's body, wasted and worn out with old age, he experienced a second kind of death, one which God specified when He pronounced this sentence upon man: 'Dust thou art, and into dust thou shalt return.'[6] Now, what I call the first death—that of the entire man—embraces these two deaths. Ultimately, it will be followed by a second one, unless, by God's grace, man is delivered from it.

The body of man would never return to the earth out of which it was formed unless it did so by its own death, which occurs when the soul, the life of the body, abandons it. Consequently, all Christians who really hold to the Catholic faith[7] believe that it is not by a law of nature that man is subject to bodily death—since God created for man an immortal nature—but as a just punishment for sin. For, it was in retribution for sin that God said to the man, in whose existence we all shared: 'Dust thou art, and into dust thou shalt return.'

Chapter 16

Some philosophers, against whose charges I am defending the City of God, that is to say, God's Church, seem to think it right to laugh at our doctrine that the separation of the soul and body is a punishment for the soul, whose beatitude, they think, will be perfect only when it returns to God simple, solitary, and naked, as it were, stripped of every shred of its body.

Now, if I could, in their own writings, find no refutation of this hypothesis, I would have to go to all the trouble of proving that it is not the body as such but only a corruptible body that is burdensome to the soul. That is why, as I quoted in a previous Book,[1] our Scripture says: 'For the corruptible body is a load upon the soul.'[2] The additional word 'corruptible'

---

[5] Gen. 3.9.   [6] Gen. 3.19.
[7] . . . *Christianos veraciter catholicam tenentes fidem* . . .

---

[1] Cf. Bk. 12.16, here omitted.   [2] Wisd. 9.15.

makes it clear that the soul is weighed down not by the body as such, but by the body such as it has become as a consequence of sin and its punishment. And even if 'corruptible' had not been added, this text could have no other meaning.

The fact is, however, that Plato teaches, as plainly as can be, that the supreme God made the lesser gods with immortal bodies and promised to them the great boon of remaining forever in their own bodies, of which death would never deprive them. Why on earth, then, do these philosophers, for the sake of poking at the Christian faith, pretend not to know what they know full well, except that they would rather squabble and disagree among themselves than agree with us?

Just listen to the very words of Plato, as Cicero has translated them into Latin.[3] Plato is supposing that the supreme God is addressing the gods whom he has made: 'You who have sprung from seed of the gods, give ear. The works of which I am the parent and maker, these are imperishable as long as I will them to be, even though all else that has been put together can be taken apart. For, it can never be good even to think of putting asunder what reason has joined together. Since you have had a beginning, you cannot be immortal and indestructible; yet, by no means shall you ever suffer dissolution nor shall any decree of death destroy you, nor prevail over my determination which is a stronger pledge of your perpetuity than those bodies with which you were joined when you were brought into being.'

Thus, as you see, Plato teaches that the gods are mortal by virtue of their union of body and soul, and immortal by the will and decree of the God who made them. If it is a punishment for the soul to be bound to any body whatsoever, why does the supreme God speak to the inferior gods as if they were afraid they might die and be separated from their bodies? And why does He assure them of their immortality, promising it not as due to their nature (which is not simple), but as dependent on His unconquerable will which can save from any setting what has had a rising, from dissolution what was put together, and make what is corruptible continue forever?

Note that it is beside the point whether or not Plato is right in this conjecture about the stars. I shall merely say that we

<hr>

[3] *Timaeus* 41A (in Cicero's *De universo* 11).

need not take his word for it, insistent as he is, that these globes or disks of physical light, whose rays illumine the earth whether by day or night, are animated by souls which are capable of thought and happiness, and that the entire universe is but one vast living mass containing within itself all other living creatures. As I have said, this is another question, and I have no intention of discussing it at present.

This much, however, I think needed to be said in the face of those who are so proud of being, or of being called, Platonists that they are ashamed to be Christians, afraid that to share this name with ordinary people might taint the title of philosopher which they are so proud to share with a coterie so exclusive. Ever on the lookout for something to tilt at in Christian doctrine, they violently assail our belief in the immortality of the body, pretending to see a contradiction in our double desire for the happiness of the soul and its permanence in a body to which, they imagine, it is bound by a chain of grief. They forget that their very founder and master, Plato, has taught that the supreme God had granted to the lesser gods, whom he had made, the favor of never dying, in the sense of never being separated from the bodies which he had united to them.

Chapter 17

Such Platonists, while protesting that no earthly body can be eternal, have no hesitation in proclaiming that our globe, which is the midmost member of their great though not supreme god, namely the god which is the universe, is itself eternal. Their supreme God, then, has made for them another god which they suppose divine, namely, this universe, which is superior to all other lesser gods, and which is a living creature, so they say, with a rational or intellectual soul, enclosed in its enormous and bulky body, the properly placed and distributed members of which are the four elements, indissolubly and eternally united, so that this great god, in their theory, may never die.

If, then, it is true that this earth—the central member in the body of a greater living creature—is eternal, why cannot the bodies of other earthly living beings also be eternal, if God should so will it? Their answer is that earth must return to the earth from which the material bodies of all living creatures have been taken.[1] They explain that this is the reason why such creatures must necessarily die and be dissolved and so return to the solid and eternal earth from which they were created.

If anyone should use like logic in regard to the element of fire, arguing that bodies created from fire, in order to become celestial animals, must first be restored to the universal fire, then would not that immortality which Plato represents the supreme God as promising to such gods[2] vanish in the violence of this debate? Or is it that God's will alone—invincible, in Plato's theory—prevents this restoration to universal fire? If so, then what hinders God from acting in like manner with terrestrial bodies? For, Plato himself admits that God can bring it about that things which have a rising need not set, nor things bound together fall asunder, nor what is formed of the elements disintegrate, nor souls once established in bodies ever desert them—and, thus in union with their bodies, they can enjoy immortality and perpetual beatitude.

Why, then, cannot God see to it that terrestrial things do not die? Does His power not extend as far as the Christians believe it does, or does it end where the Platonists want it to end? Must we, really, assume that philosophers have been able to penetrate into the purpose and power of God, while the Prophets could not? The truth is just the opposite. While the Spirit of God taught His Prophets to declare His will, in so far as He deigned to reveal it, the philosophers, in search of this will, were deceived by human surmises.

Yet, even philosophers should not have been so misled by obstinacy added to ignorance as to fall into the open contradiction of first vehemently arguing that no soul can be blessed unless it escapes both the earthly and every other kind of a body, and then declaring there are gods whose souls are blessed and yet are bound to their eternal bodies—the gods in the sky with bodies of fire—while the soul of Jove—their name for the whole cosmos—is enclosed in every single element of

[1] Cf. Cicero, *Tusc. Disp.* 3.25,29.
[2] *Timaeus* 41A.

matter in the cosmic mass which stretches from earth to heaven.[3]

Plato teaches that this soul of the universe flows, as it were, in rhythmic waves, and reaches from the middlemost point of the earth (its geometrical center) up through all space to the highest and farthest limits of heaven. Thus, for the Platonists, the cosmos is an immense, eternal, and utterly blessed living creature, whose soul, without abandoning its own body, enjoys the perfect happiness of wisdom, while its body is eternally alive by reason of the soul, and yet, in spite of being complex and composed of so many great masses of matter it cannot dull the soul or slow it down.

Since, then, these Platonists are so indulgent to their own suppositions, why do they refuse to believe that, by the will and power of God, even earthly bodies can be made immortal and that in these bodies, souls never separated by death nor ever burdened by their weight may live forever and in all felicity at least as well as their own gods can live in the bodies of fire and Jove, their king, in all the elements of matter. And if souls, in order to be blessed, must flee from every kind of body, then let their own gods flee from the starry spheres and let Jupiter escape from heaven and earth. Or, if that is beyond their powers, then let them be held to be unhappy.

Our philosophers, however, do not want to face either of these alternatives: they do not dare to grant to their gods a separation from their bodies, for then it would seem that they were merely worshiping mortals; nor will they admit a privation of blessedness, for then they would have to acknowledge that their gods are miserable. To attain to blessedness, then, there is no need to be free of every kind of a body but only of those which are corruptible and irksome, burdensome and moribund, not such bodies as God, in His goodness, created for our first parents but only such as were imposed as a punishment for sin.

Chapter 18

Gravity, we are told, either holds earthly bodies on earth or compels them to fall, and, therefore, they cannot be in

[3] *Timaeus* 34B; 36E.

heaven. It is true that our first parents lived on earth in a wooded and fruitful land called Paradise. Nevertheless, the philosophers might well examine again the question of earthly gravity in the light either of the body of Christ with which He ascended into heaven or of the bodies of the saints as they will be in their resurrection.

If it is not beyond human skill to fashion floating vessels out of metals which sink as soon as they are put in water, can we not readily believe that the power of God, in some more effectual, if secret, manner, can free the earthly bodies of the saints in heaven from the law of gravity which pulls them toward earth and can give to the souls of the saints the power to rest or move their bodies, earthly as ever but now incorruptible, wherever they wish and with the utmost ease? After all, even Plato admits that the all-powerful will of God can save what is born from dying and what is composite from disintegration, and it is much more wonderful than any combination of bodies that spiritual realities can be united to material substances.

Again, when we read of angels carrying off creatures, of any kind, anywhere on earth, and depositing them wherever they please, have we no choice but to be skeptical, or else to believe that the angels feel the burden?[1] And since we have, why should we doubt that the souls in heaven, made perfect and blessed by the grace of the Divine Spirit, can carry and rest their own bodies wherever they choose and without a shadow of difficulty? In this connection, it may be observed that, although in general the greater the bulk of any material object we are carrying happens to be, the heavier it is, and though more things weigh heavier than fewer, nevertheless, when the body is our own and in good health, our soul carries it as though it were lighter than when it has been reduced by illness. To anyone else who is carrying him, a stout and healthy man seems heavier than one who is thin and ailing, yet the man himself who carries and moves his own body does so with much more agility when, in good health, he weighs more than when his frame is weakened by disease or hunger. Thus,

1 . . . *aut eos non posse aut onera sentire credendum est?* The suggested translation avoids the necessity of introducing *sine labore*, as the Maurists proposed.

even when we have ea...ly bodies which are still mortal and corruptible, it is not so much the size and weight that matter but rather the condition of health. Now, just think of the inexpressible difference between what we now call health and our future immortality.

The philosophers, then, have no argument against our faith on the basis of the weight of the body. If I do not ask them why they deny that an earthly body can be in heaven when, as a matter of fact, the whole universe has nothing to hold it up, it is because they have a semblance of an answer by saying that, perhaps, the same law which attracts all heavy beings to the center holds the cosmic center in position. The point I want to make is this. If the lesser gods, in Plato's theory, the creators of all terrestrial animals including man, were able to remove from fire, as he says, its quality of burning, leaving only its brightness to shine through the eyes,[2] and, if the supreme God, by His power and will, can save things created from death, and things composed of such distinct and dissimilar parts as a material and spiritual substance from disintegration, then why should we hesitate to acknowledge that God can remove from the body of man, to which He has given immortality, its corruption, leaving its nature, harmonious form and features, but removing the hindrance of weight? However, at the end of this work,[3] God willing, I intend to discuss more fully our faith in the resurrection of the dead and their immortal bodies.

Chapters 19–20

Whether death would ever have been experienced by men, had not Adam sinned, is a difficult question. The Platonic view, that souls are immortal but human bodies cannot be resurrected, is criticized.

Chapter 21

For this reason, there are some who have allegorized the entire Garden of Eden where, according to Holy Scripture,

---

[2] *Timaeus* 42D; 45B.   [3] Cf. Bk. 22.12, here omitted.

the first parents of the human race actually lived. The trees
and fruit-bearing shrubs are turned into symbols of virtues
and ways of living, as though they had no visible and material
reality and as if Scripture had no purpose but to express meanings for our minds. The assumption here is that the possibility
of a spiritual meaning rules out the reality of a physical Paradise. That is like saying that Agar and Sara, the mothers of
the two sons of Abraham, 'the one by a slave-girl and the other
by a free woman,'[1] had no historical existence simply because
the Apostle has said that 'by way of allegory . . . these are
the two covenants';[2] or that Moses struck no rock nor did water actually flow[3] simply because the story can also be read
as an allegory of Christ, as the same Apostle does read it: 'but
the rock was Christ.'[4]

There is no reason, then, for anyone forbidding us to see
in the Garden, symbolically, the life of the blessed; in its four
rivers, the four virtues of prudence, fortitude, temperance, and
justice; in its trees, all useful knowledge; in the fruits of the
trees, the holy lives of the faithful; in the tree of life, that
wisdom which is the mother of all good; and in the tree of the
knowledge of good and evil, the experience that results from
disobedience to a command of God. The punishment which
God imposed on the sinners was just and, therefore, good in
itself, but not for man who experienced the taste of it.

This account can be even better read as an allegory of the
Church, prophetical of what was to happen in the future.
Thus, the Garden is the Church itself, as we can see from the
Canticle of Canticles;[5] the four rivers are the four Gospels;
the fruit-bearing trees are the saints, as the fruits are their
works; and the tree of life is, of course, the Saint of saints,
Christ; and the tree of the knowledge of good and evil is the
free choice of our own will. For, if a man disdains the divine
will, he can only use his own to his own destruction, and, thus,
he comes to the knowledge of the difference between obedience to the good common to all and indulgence in a good
proper to oneself. For, anyone who loves himself is left to himself until, filled with fears and tears, he cries out, if he has any

[1] Gal. 4.22.   [2] Gal. 4.24.
[3] Exod. 17.6; Num. 20.11.   [4] 1 Cor. 10.4.
[5] Cant. 4.12.

sensitivity to his own sufferings, like the psalmist: 'My soul is troubled within myself,'[6] so that, when he has learned his lesson, he may cry: 'I will keep my strength to thee.'[7]

No one should object to such reflections and others even more appropriate that might be made concerning the allegorical interpretation of the Garden of Eden, so long as we believe in the historical truth manifest in the faithful narrative of these events.

Chapters 22–23

Speculating on whether the bodies of the blessed will consume food, Augustine dwells on the difference between Adam's body in the original state and the spiritualized bodies of the saints. He then begins to explain the Biblical expression: 'a living soul.'

Chapter 24

By not reflecting sufficiently on the text: 'God breathed into his face the breath of life, and man became a living soul,'[1] some have supposed that it means, not that a soul was then bestowed on the first man, but that the soul which he already possessed was vivified by the Holy Spirit. Their argument is that, after He had risen from the dead, the Lord Jesus breathed upon His disciples, saying: 'Receive the Holy Spirit,'[2] and that what took place in one case took place in the other; so that the Evangelist might well have gone on to say: 'And they became living souls.'

But, even if the Evangelist had said this, we certainly would have interpreted his words to mean that the Spirit of God is that kind of life of the soul without which rational souls must be considered dead although their living bodies are present before us. This, however, is not what took place when man was created, as the words of Scripture clearly prove: 'Then the Lord God formed man out of the dust of the ground.'[3]

---

[6] Ps. 58.10.　　　　　　　　[7] *Ibid.*
[1] Gen. 2.7.　　　　　　　　[2] John 20.22.
[3] Gen. 2.7.

Hoping to make the meaning clearer, some have thought that the words should be translated: 'And God fashioned man from the slime of the earth,' since the preceding verse in the text reads: 'A mist rose from the earth and watered all the surface of the ground.'[4] Their point is that 'slime' must here be understood, since it is a mixture of moisture and soil.

This text, according to the Greek manuscripts from which it has been translated into Latin, is followed immediately by the words: 'Then the Lord God formed man out of the dust of the ground.' Whether *formavit* or *finxit* is the better Latin rendering for the Greek, *éplasen*, makes no real difference, although *finxit* is, in fact, the better word. It was to avoid any ambiguity that some preferred *formavit*. The only trouble with *fingere* is that, as the word is commonly used, it means rather to 'make up a fiction' than to make something real.

This first man, then, who was formed from the dust of the earth or from slime (since the dust was moistened dust), this 'dust of the earth,' to use the exact expression of Scripture, became a living body when he received a soul, according to the Apostle's words: 'And this man became a living soul.'

But, it is objected, Adam had a soul already for, otherwise, he would not have been called a man, since a man is not a body only nor a soul only but a being consisting of the two. Now, it is true that the soul is not the entire man, but only his better part; nor is the body the entire man, but merely his inferior part. Only when body and soul are in union can we speak of a man. However, either part, even when it is mentioned separately, can be used for a man, for in everyday speech no one can be blamed for saying 'That man is dead and is now in peace or in pain'—although this can be said strictly only of his soul. We also say: 'That man is buried in such or such a place'—although this applies only to his body. Perhaps they will protest that such a manner of speaking is contrary to the usage of Holy Scripture. On the contrary, Scripture is so much on our side in this matter that, even when referring to a man who is still alive with body and soul united, it calls either part a man, meaning by 'the inner man' his soul and by 'the outer man' his body,[5] almost as if there were two men, although both together make but one man.

[4] Gen. 2.6.   [5] Cf. 2 Cor. 4.16.

What we need to understand is how a man can be called, on the one hand, the image of God and, on the other, is dust and will return to dust. The former relates to the rational soul which God by His breathing or, better, by His inspiration communicated to man, meaning to the body of man; but the latter refers to the body such as God formed it from dust into the man to whom a soul was given that it might become a living body, that is, that man might become a living soul. But, what our Lord wanted us to understand when He breathed on His disciples, saying: 'Receive the Holy Spirit,' was that the Holy Spirit is the Spirit not only of the Father but also the Spirit of the Only-begotten Son Himself. For, in fact, one and the same Spirit is the Spirit of both the Father and the Son —not a creature but the Creator, and forming with them the Trinity: Father, Son and Holy Spirit. Not, of course, that the physical breath issuing from His actual mouth was the very substance and nature of the Holy Spirit; rather, it was a sign by which we are to understand, as I have said, that the Holy Spirit is common to both the Father and the Son, since neither has His own individual Spirit but both have the same Spirit.

However, the Greek text of Holy Scripture always calls this Spirit *pneuma,* the name our Lord here used in giving Him to His disciples under the symbol of the breath which issued from His mouth. And throughout Holy Scripture I have not seen the Spirit called by any other name. Certainly, in the verse: 'And God formed man out of the dust of the ground and blew or breathed into his face the breath of life,' the Greek text does not give *pneuma,* the usual word for the Holy Spirit, but *pnoé,* a word used more frequently of the creature than of the Creator. Because of this distinction, some have preferred to translate this word not by the Latin *spiritus* but by *flatus.*

This word, *pnoé,* occurs also in the Greek text of Isaias in which God says: 'I have made every breathing,'[6] meaning, undoubtedly, every soul. And so our translators have rendered the Greek *pnoé* in various ways: sometimes as breathing, sometimes as spirit, and sometimes as inspiration or aspiration even when it refers to God. However, their only interpretation for *pneuma* is spirit, whether it is the spirit of man of which the Apostle says: 'For who among men knows the things of a man

[6] Cf. Isa. 57.16.

save the spirit of the man which is in him?'[7] or the 'spirit of beasts' referred to in the Book of Solomon: 'Who knoweth if the spirit of the children of Adam ascend upward, and if the spirit of the beasts descend downward?'[8] or that material spirit, the wind, as it is called in the psalm: 'Fire, hail, snow, ice, stormy winds,'[9] or, finally, the Spirit which is uncreated, the Creator-Spirit indicated by our Lord in the following words of the Gospel: 'Receive the Holy Spirit' (the Spirit being symbolized by the breath which issued from our Lord's mouth); 'Go, baptize all nations in the name of the Father, and of the Son, and of the Holy Spirit'[10]—a clear and perfect expression of the Trinity itself; and in the phrase, 'God is Spirit,'[11] and many other places in Holy Scripture. In fact, in all these Scriptural texts we find, in Greek, *pneuma* not *pnoé*, and, in Latin, *spiritus* not *flatus*.

And so, even if in the verse, 'He blew' or better 'He breathed into his face the breath of life,' the Greek text had not used *pnoé*, as it has, but *pneuma*, it would not follow that we would have to interpret it as the Creator-Spirit, who in respect to the Trinity is properly called the Holy Spirit, since, as I have already said, it is manifest that *pneuma* is often used to indicate the spirit of the creature as well as that of the Creator.

The objection, however, is raised that, since Sacred Scripture used the word 'spirit,' the expression 'of life' would not have been added except to indicate the Holy Spirit, nor in the text, 'man became a soul,' would Scripture have inserted 'living' save to signify that life of the soul which is a divine gift bestowed by the Spirit of God. For, since the soul, so the argument runs, lives by its own mode of life, there was no necessity of supplying the word 'living' unless the life meant were the life which is imparted to the soul by the Holy Spirit. Now, what does such reasoning reveal but a careful contention for the notions of man and a careless attention to the words of God.[12]

---

[7] 1 Cor. 2.11.   [8] Eccle. 3.21.
[9] Ps. 148.8.   [10] Cf. Matt. 28.19.
[11] John 4.24.
[12] *Hoc quid est aliud nisi* diligenter *pro humana suspicione* contendere *et scripturas sanctas* neglegenter adtendere.

In the very same book, without too much trouble, anyone could have read a previous text: 'Let the earth bring forth the living soul,'[13] which refers to all the terrestrial animals that were then created. Then, a little further on in the same book, one could just as easily have noticed the verse: 'And all things wherein there is the breath of life on the earth, died,'[14] which means that everything which lived on the earth perished in the flood.

Thus we find that Holy Scripture is accustomed to use both phrases—'living soul' and 'the breath of life'—in regard even to beasts, and in the verse, 'All things wherein there is the breath of life,' the Greek text does not use the word *pneuma* but *pnoé*. Hence, the only real question here is: What need was there to add 'living,' since the soul cannot exist without being alive? Or what need was there to add 'of life' after the word 'breath'? The answer to this question is that Scripture regularly uses the terms 'living soul' and 'breath of life' to signify animals or animated bodies that are clearly capable of sensation on account of a soul, but, on the contrary, when there was a question of the creation of man, the ordinary usage of Holy Scripture is forgotten. There is now an altogether special mode of expression which is meant to imply that when man was created he received in addition a rational soul not produced from water and earth like the souls of other animals, but created by the breath of God, and that, nevertheless, man was so made as to live, just like the other animals, in an animal body, but in one which is animated by a human soul. It was of the other animals that Scripture says: 'Let the earth bring forth the living soul,' and likewise says of this animal soul that it has the 'breath of life.' That is why the Greek text does not use the word *pneuma* but *pnoé*, the word that was needed to make clear that it was not the Holy Spirit that was meant, but an animal soul.

Another objection is that what issued from the mouth of God must be understood as the breath of God and that, if we take this breath to be the soul, then logically we must acknowledge that the soul is equal to and consubstantial with that Wisdom which says: 'I came out of the mouth of the

13 Cf. Gen. 1.24.   14 Gen. 7.22.

most High.'[15] The answer is that Wisdom does not say that it was breathed out of the mouth of God but that it proceeded therefrom. Notice that with man it is not out of our nature by which we are men that we make a breathing when we breathe but out of the surrounding air which we first inhale and then exhale, whereas with Almighty God it is neither out of His nature nor out of any creature subject to Him but out of absolutely nothing that He was able to create a breath which was so introduced into the body of man that the action is most appropriately indicated by a verb like 'inspire' or 'breathe' or 'blow into.' God, who is both immaterial and immutable, breathed a breath which was immaterial yet mutable, since the breath was created, whereas God is uncreated.

Of course, it is not only what is consubstantial with God that is said to proceed from His mouth. If those who want to discuss Scripture but have overlooked the words of Scripture care to learn this truth, let them hear or read the text in which God says: 'Because thou art lukewarm, and neither cold nor hot, I am about to vomit thee out of my mouth.'[16]

There is no reason, then, for any of us to raise such objections, since the Apostle speaks so clearly. He distinguishes the natural from the spiritual body, that is, the body in which we now are from that in which we are one day to be. His words are: 'What is sown a natural body rises a spiritual body. If there is a natural body, there is also a spiritual body. So, also, it is written: "The first man, Adam, became a living soul"; the last Adam became a life-giving spirit. But it is not the spiritual that comes first, but the physical, and then the spiritual. The first man was of the earth, earthy; the second man is from heaven, heavenly. As was the earthy man, such also are the earthy; and as is the heavenly man, such also are the heavenly. Therefore, even as we have borne the likeness of the earthy, let us bear also the likeness of the heavenly.'[17]

In a previous chapter I have discussed all these words of the Apostle.[18] We saw that the natural body, to use the Apostle's expression, in which the first man, Adam, was created was not so created that under no conditions could it die, but in

15 Eccli. 24.5.   16 Apoc. 3.16.
17 1 Cor. 15.44–49.   18 Cf. Bk. 13.23, here omitted.

such a way that it would not die unless man sinned. But the body which, by the life-giving spirit, will become spiritual and immortal will under no conditions be able to die. It will be immortal, just as a created soul is immortal, for, even though a soul can be said to be dead when sin deprives it of that special kind of life which is the Spirit of God that could have enabled the soul to live wisely and blessedly, nevertheless, even in sin the soul does not cease to live, however miserably, a life of its own, because it is immortal by creation. So, too, the rebel angels, by reason of their sin, have died in the sense that, in abandoning God, they gave up the fountain of life which had enabled them to live in wisdom and blessedness. However, they could not die in the sense of ceasing to live and to feel, since they, too, were created immortal. That is why, even when the final judgment hurls them into a second death, they will not be wholly dead, for they will never lack the sense of the pains they are to suffer.

On the other hand, men who are sharers in the grace of God and fellow citizens with the holy angels abiding in Beatitude will be so clothed with spiritual bodies as to be saved forever from sin and death. Yet, while invested with an immortality like the angels' which can never be lost by sin, the nature of their flesh will remain the same, without a trace, however, of any remnant of corruption or clumsiness.

Here, however, a question arises, which it is necessary to discuss and, with the help of the Lord, the God of truth, to solve. It is true that passion sprang up in the rebellious members of our first parents as soon as their sin of disobedience deprived them of divine grace. That is why their eyes were opened to their nakedness in the sense that they became more curious about it and more concerned to cover their shame because a shameful rebellion of the flesh was resisting the control of their will. But what, then, would have urged them to beget children had they remained sinless as they were when created?

However, it is high time to put an end to this Book; besides, the topic is too large for summary treatment. I shall, therefore, defer this discussion to the following Book.

BOOK XIV

Two Loves Originate Two Different Cities

Chapter 1

I HAVE ALREADY SAID, in previous Books, that God had two purposes in deriving all men from one man. His first purpose was to give unity to the human race by the likeness of nature. His second purpose was to bind mankind by the bond of peace, through blood relationship, into one harmonious whole. I have said further that no member of this race would ever have died had not the first two—one created from nothing and the second from the first—merited this death by disobedience. The sin which they committed was so great that it impaired all human nature—in this sense, that the nature has been transmitted to posterity with a propensity to sin and a necessity to die. Moreover, the kingdom of death so dominated men that all would have been hurled, by a just punishment, into a second and endless death had not some been saved from this by the gratuitous grace of God. This is the reason why, for all the difference of the many and very great nations throughout the world in religion and morals, language, weapons, and dress, there exist no more than the two kinds of society, which, according to our Scriptures, we have rightly called the two cities. One city is that of men who live according to the flesh. The other is of men who live according to the spirit. Each of them chooses its own kind of peace and, when they attain what they desire, each lives in the peace of its own choosing.

Chapter 2

Our immediate task, then, must be to see what it means to live, first, according to the flesh and, second, according to the spirit. It would be a mistake for anyone to take what I have said at face value and without recalling or sufficiently considering the manner of speech used in Holy Scripture, imagining that it is the Epicurean philosophers who live according to the flesh simply because they place man's highest good in material pleasure. The same might be thought of any others who, in one way or another, think that the good of the body is man's highest good. So, too, of that great mass of men who do not dogmatize or philosophize about it but who are so inclined to sensuality that they cannot enjoy anything unless they can experience it with their senses. It would be no less a mistake to imagine, because the Stoics place man's highest good in the soul (and because 'soul' and 'spirit' mean the same), that, therefore, it is the Stoics who live according to the spirit. The fact is the language of Sacred Scripture clearly proves that both of these classes live according to the flesh. Scripture uses the word flesh not only in reference to the body of an earthly and mortal animal, but also to man, that is, to human nature. We have an example of the former in the words: 'All flesh is not the same flesh, but there is one flesh of men, another of beasts, another of birds, another of fishes';[1] but it often uses the word flesh, with many other meanings, to denote man himself. In this case, the 'body' of man is used in the sense of a part for the whole, as for example: 'For by the works of the Law, no flesh shall be justified.'[2] What Scripture means here is 'no man.' In fact, a little further on, it says more plainly: 'By the Law no man is justified before God.'[3] And in the Epistle to the Galatians, we read: 'But we know that man is not justified by the works of the Law.'[4] In this sense we understand the expression, 'And the Word was made flesh'[5]—that is, man. It was a misunderstanding of the meaning here that led some to think that Christ had no human soul. In the same way, the whole is used for a part in the words of Mary Magdalene in the Gospel, when she says: 'They have taken away my Lord and I do not know where they have laid him';[6] here, Scripture was speaking only of the body of Christ, which was buried and which she thought had been taken away from the tomb. In the same way, a part is used for the whole when the entire man is understood from the term flesh, as in these extracts quoted above.

Sacred Scripture, then, uses the word flesh in so many

---

[1] 1 Cor. 15.39.
[2] Rom. 3.20.
[3] Gal. 3.11.
[4] Gal. 2.16.
[5] John 1.14.
[6] John 20.13.

meanings that it would be tedious to assemble and examine them all. However, if we wish to investigate what it means to 'live according to the flesh'—remembering that such living is sinful, although flesh is not by nature evil—we should carefully consider a passage in the Epistle which Paul the Apostle wrote to the Galatians: 'Now the works of the flesh are manifest, which are: immorality, uncleanness, licentiousness, idolatry, witchcrafts, enmities, contentions, jealousies, anger, quarrels, factions, parties, envies, murders, drunkenness, carousings, and suchlike. And concerning these I warn you, as I have warned you, that they who do such things will not attain the kingdom of God.'[7] If we reflect upon this whole text from the apostolic Epistle, in relation to the point of issue, we shall discover that it is all we need to determine what it means to live according to the flesh. In the works of the flesh which St. Paul said were manifest and which he enumerated and condemned, we find, of course, those which pertain to carnal pleasures, such as immorality, uncleanness, licentiousness, drunkenness, carousings, but we also find others, not related to the gratification of the body, which give evidence of the vices of the soul. It is clear enough to everyone that idolatry, witchcrafts, enmities, contentions, jealousies, anger, quarrels, factions, parties, envies are vices of the soul rather than of the body. For it is possible for a person to abstain from bodily indulgence by reason of idolatry or some heretical error. Such a person may seem to be subduing and curbing the desires of the flesh, yet even then he is guilty (according to this same apostolic authority) of living according to the flesh; the very fact that he is refraining from the pleasures of the flesh is the proof that he is performing detestable works of the flesh. If a man entertains enmity, does he not entertain it in his mind? No one would say to any enemy—real or imagined—'You show a bad flesh toward me.' He would say: 'Your mind is ill-disposed to me.' Finally, just as anyone who hears of sins of carnality (if I may use the word) immediately attributes them to the flesh, so no one doubts that sins of animosity belong to the mind. Why, then, does the Doctor of the Gentiles say that all such vices are, in faith and in fact, works of the flesh?

[7] Gal. 5.19–21.

His only reason is that by his figurative use of a part for the whole he wants us to interpret the word 'flesh' as meaning the whole of human nature.

Chapter 3

Should anyone say that the cause of vices and evil habits lies in the flesh because it is only when the soul is influenced by the flesh that it lives then in such a manner, he cannot have sufficiently considered the entire nature of man. It is true that 'the corruptible body is a load upon the soul.'[1] But notice that the Apostle who, in discussing the corruptible body, had used the words, 'Even though our outer man is decaying,'[2] goes on, a little further, to declare: 'For we know that if the earthly house in which we dwell be destroyed, we have a building from God, a house not made by human hands, eternal in the heavens. And indeed, in this present state we groan, yearning to be clothed over with that dwelling of ours which is from heaven; if indeed we shall be found clothed, and not naked. For we who are in this tent sigh under our burden, because we do not wish to be unclothed, but rather clothed over, that what is mortal may be swallowed up by life.'[3]

On the one hand, our corruptible body may be a burden on our soul; on the other hand, the cause of this encumbrance is not in the nature and substance of the body, and, therefore, aware as we are of its corruption, we do not desire to be divested of the body but rather to be clothed with its immortality. In immortal life we shall have a body, but it will no longer be a burden since it will no longer be corruptible. Now, however, 'the corruptible body is a load upon the soul, and the earthly habitation presseth down the mind that museth upon many things.'[4] Yet, it is an error to suppose that all the evils of the soul proceed from the body.

Virgil, it is true, seems to express a different idea, following Plato in his luminous lines:

'A fiery vigor of celestial birth
Endows these seeds so slowed by weight of earth

[1] Wisd. 9.15. [2] 2 Cor. 4.16.
[3] 2 Cor. 5.1–4. [4] Wisd. 9.15.

Or body's drag; and so they ever lie
In bondage to dull limbs that one day die.'[5]

And, as if he wanted us to believe that the four most common emotions of the soul—desire, fear, joy, and sadness—which are the causes of all sins and vices, spring from the body, he continues with the verse:

'Thus do they fear and hope, rejoice and grieve,
Blind in the gloomy jail they cannot leave.'

So Virgil. Our faith teaches something very different. For the corruption of the body, which is a burden on the soul, is not the cause but the punishment of Adam's first sin. Moreover, it was not the corruptible flesh that made the soul sinful; on the contrary, it was the sinful soul that made the flesh corruptible. Though some incitements to vice and vicious desires are attributable to the corruption of the flesh, nevertheless, we should not ascribe to the flesh all the evils of a wicked life. Else, we free the Devil from all such passions, since he has no flesh. It is true that the Devil cannot be said to be addicted to debauchery, drunkenness, or any others of the vices which pertain to bodily pleasure—much as he secretly prompts and provokes us to such sins—but he is most certainly filled with pride and envy. It is because these passions so possessed the Devil that he is doomed to eternal punishment in the prison of the gloomy air.

It is true that the Apostle attributes to the flesh (which Satan certainly does not possess) those vices which dominate the Devil. He says, in fact, that 'enmities,' 'contentions,' 'jealousies,' 'anger,' and 'quarrels' are the works of the flesh, whereas the origin of all these evils is pride—a vice which rules over the Devil who has no flesh. For, who is a worse enemy to the saints than he? Who is more contentious toward them, more wrathful, jealous, and quarrelsome?

Now, since the Devil has all of these vices but has no flesh, they can only be the works of the flesh in the sense that they are the works of man. Actually as I have mentioned, Paul often refers to man under the name of 'flesh.' It was not by reason of the flesh—which the Devil does not possess—but by reason of a man's desire to live according to himself, that is,

[5] *Aeneid* 6.730–734.

according to man, that man made himself like the Devil. For, the Devil wished to live according to himself when he did not abide in the truth. So that, when he told a lie, it was not of God's doing but of his own, for the Devil is not only a liar but is also 'the father of lies.'[6] This means that he was the first liar. Lying began with him, as all sin began with him.

Chapter 4

When a man lives 'according to man' and not 'according to God' he is like the Devil. For, even an angel had to live according to God and not according to an angel if he were to remain steadfast in the truth, speaking the truth out of God's grace and not lying out of his own weakness. The same Apostle elsewhere says of man: 'Yet if God's truth has abounded through my lie.'[1] Notice that he says 'my lie' and 'God's truth.' So, then, when a man lives according to truth, he lives not according to himself but according to God. For it was God who said: 'I am the truth.'[2]

When man lives according to himself, that is to say, according to human ways and not according to God's will, then surely he lives according to falsehood. Man himself, of course, is not a lie, since God who is his Author and Creator could not be the Author and Creator of a lie. Rather, man has been so constituted in truth that he was meant to live not according to himself but to Him who made him—that is, he was meant to do the will of God rather than his own. It is a lie not to live as a man was created to live.

Man indeed desires happiness even when he does so live as to make happiness impossible. What could be more of a lie than a desire like that? This is the reason why every sin can be called a lie. For, when we choose to sin, what we want is to get some good or get rid of something bad. The lie is in this, that what is done for our good ends in something bad, or what is done to make things better ends by making them worse. Why this paradox, except that the happiness of man can come not from himself but only from God, and that to live according

1 Cf. Rom. 3.7.　　　　　　　2 John 14.6.

to oneself is to sin, and to sin is to lose God? When, therefore, we said that two contrary and opposing cities arose because some men live according to the flesh and others live according to the spirit, we could equally well have said that they arose because some live according to man and others according to God. St. Paul says frankly to the Corinthians: 'Since there are jealousy and strife among you, are you not carnal, and walking as mere men?'[3] Thus, to walk as a mere man is the same as to be carnal, for by 'flesh,' taking a part for the whole, a man is meant.

Notice that those very men whom the Apostle designates as carnal he had previously called animal, as in the text: 'Who among men knows the things of a man save the spirit of the man which is in him? Even so, the things of God no one knows but the Spirit of God. Now we have received not the spirit of the world, but the spirit that is from God, that we may know the things that have been given us by God. These things we also speak, not in words taught by human wisdom, but in the learning of the spirit, combining spiritual with spiritual. But the animal man does not perceive the things that are of the spirit of God, for it is foolishness to him.'[4] It is to these same 'animal' men that he later says: 'And I, brethren, could not speak to you as to spiritual men but only as carnal.'[5]

In both cases we have the same figure of speech, using a part for the whole. For, either the soul or the flesh, which are the parts of man, can be used for the whole, that is, to mean man. Thus the animal man is not one thing and the carnal another, but both are one and the same, namely, man living according to man. So, too, it is men who are meant in the following texts: 'By the works of the Law no human flesh shall be justified'[6] and 'seventy-five souls went down into Egypt with Jacob.'[7] In one passage, 'no flesh' means 'no man'; in the other, 'seventy-five souls' means seventy-five men. Moreover, in the text, 'not in words taught by human wisdom,' 'carnal wisdom' could have been used, just as in the text, 'you walk according to man,' 'according to the flesh' could have been said. This fact appears more apparent as the Apostle continues:

[3] 1 Cor. 3.3.
[4] 1 Cor. 2.11–14.
[5] 1 Cor. 3.1.
[6] Cf. Rom. 3.20.
[7] Cf. Gen. 46.27.

'Whenever one says, "I am of Paul" but another "I am of Apollos," are you not mere man?'[8] What he had implied by the expressions 'you are animal' and 'you are carnal,' he now states more clearly in the words 'you are men'—that is to say, 'You are living according to the ways of men not according to the will of God, for if you lived according to Him you would be gods.'

Chapter 5

We ought not, therefore, to blame our sins and defects on the nature of the flesh, for this is to disparage the Creator. The flesh, in its own kind and order, is good. But what is not good is to abandon the Goodness of the Creator in pursuit of some created good, whether by living deliberately according to the flesh, or according to the soul, or according to the entire man, which is made up of soul and flesh and which is the reason why either 'soul' alone or 'flesh' alone can mean a man.

Anyone, then, who extols the nature of the soul as the highest good and condemns the nature of the flesh as evil is as carnal in his love for the soul as he is in his hatred for the flesh, because his thoughts flow from human vanity and not from divine Truth. However, unlike the Manichaeans, Platonists are not so senseless as to despise earthly bodies as though their nature derived from an evil principle. The Platonists attribute to God, the Maker, all the elements together with their qualities that make up this visible and tangible universe. Nevertheless, they think that our souls are so influenced by 'the earthly limbs and mortal members'[1] of our bodies that from these arise the diseases of desires and fears, of joy and sadness—the four perturbations (as Cicero calls them[2]) or passions (to use the common expression borrowed from the Greeks) which comprehend the whole defectiveness of human behavior.

---

[8] 1 Cor. 3.4.

[1] Cf. Virgil, *Aen.* 6.732. *Terrenique hebetant artus moribundaque membra.*

[2] *Tusc. Disp.* 4.6,11.

Now, if this is true, why should Virgil's Aeneas, learning from his father in the lower world that souls are to return to their bodies, cry out in surprise:

'O Father, do you mean, we must believe

That souls, for upper air, this realm would leave,

And with slow-moving bodies reunite?

Whence comes this baleful longing for the light?'[3]

Is it possible that this baleful longing, born of 'earthly limbs and mortal members,' still survives in the much vaunted purity of Platonic souls? Does not Virgil tell us that, when these souls begin to desire a return to their bodies, they have already been purged of every such kind of bodily disease?

From this it is clear that, even if the belief, which is absolutely unfounded, were true, namely, that there exists this unceasing alternation of purification and defilement in the souls which depart from and return to their bodies, no one could rightly say that all culpable and corrupt emotions of our souls have their roots in our earthly bodies. For, here we have the Platonists themselves, through the mouth of their noble spokesman, teaching that this direful desire has so little to do with the body that it compels even the soul already purified of every bodily disease and now subsisting independently of any kind of body to seek an existence in a body.

We conclude, therefore, from their own admission that it is not only because of the flesh that the soul is moved by desires and fears, by joy and sorrow, but that it can also be agitated by these same emotions welling up within the soul itself.

Chapter 6

Man's will, then, is all-important. If it is badly directed, the emotions will be perverse; if it is rightly directed, the emotions will be not merely blameless but even praiseworthy. The will is in all of these affections; indeed, they are nothing else but inclinations of the will. For, what are desire and joy but the will in harmony with things we desire? And what are fear and sadness but the will in disagreement with things we abhor?

[3] *Aeneid* 6.719–721.

The consent of the will in the search for what we want is called desire; joy is the name of the will's consent to the enjoyment of what we desire. So, too, fear is aversion from what we do not wish to happen, as sadness is a disagreement of the will with something that happened against our will. Thus, according as the will of a man is attracted or repelled by the variety of things which he either seeks or shuns, so is it changed or converted into one or other of these different emotions.

It is clear, then, that the man who does not live according to man but according to God must be a lover of the good and, therefore, a hater of evil; since no man is wicked by nature but is wicked only by some defect, a man who lives according to God owes it to wicked men that his hatred be perfect, so that, neither hating the man because of his corruption nor loving the corruption because of the man, he should hate the sin but love the sinner. For, once the corruption has been cured, then all that is left should be loved and nothing remains to be hated.

Chapters 7–10

From the main topic, the importance of the will and its act of love, Augustine digresses to examine the Stoic theory of virtue as non-disturbance from the passions. Stoic apathy is not fully possible now in this life, but before the first sin Adam and Eve were undisturbed by passions.

Chapter 11

Since God foresaw all things and, hence, that man would sin, our conception of the supernatural City of God must be based on what God foreknew and forewilled, and not on human fancies that could never come true, because it was not in God's plan that they should. Not even by his sin could man change the counsels of God, in the sense of compelling Him to alter what He had once decided. The truth is that, by His omniscience, God could foresee two future realities: how bad man whom God had created good was to become, and how much good God was to make out of this very evil.

Though we sometimes hear the expression, 'God changed His mind,' or even read in the figurative language of Scripture that 'God repented,'[1] we interpret these sayings not in reference to the decisions determined on by Almighty God but in reference to the expectations of man or to the order of natural causes. So, we believe, as Scripture tells us,[2] that God created man right and, therefore, endowed with a good will, for without a good will he would not have been 'right.'

The good will, then, is a work of God, since man was created by God with a good will. On the contrary, the first bad will, which was present in man before any of his bad deeds, was rather a falling away from the work of God into man's own works than a positive work itself; in fact, a fall into bad works, since they were 'according to man' and not 'according to God.' Thus, this bad will or, what is the same, man in so far as his will is bad is like a bad tree which brings forth these bad works like bad fruit.

A bad will, however, contrary as it is to nature and not according to nature, since it is a defect in nature, still belongs to the nature of which it is a defect, since it has no existence apart from this nature. This nature, of course, is one that God has created out of nothing, and not out of Himself, as was the case when He begot the Word through whom all things have been made.[3] Though God has fashioned man from the dust of the earth, that same dust, like all earthly matter, has been made out of nothing. And it was a soul made out of nothing which God united to the body when man was created.

In the long run, however, the good triumphs over the evil. It is true, of course, that the Creator permits evil, to prove to what good purpose His providence and justice can use even evil. Nevertheless, while good can exist without any defect, as in the true and supreme God Himself, and even in the whole of that visible and invisible creation, high in the heavens above this gloomy atmosphere, evil cannot exist without good, since the natures to which the defects belong, in as much as they are natures, are good. Moreover, we cannot remove evil by the destruction of the nature or any part of it, to which the damage has been done. We can only cure a dis-

---

[1] Gen. 6.6; Exod. 32.14; 1 Sam. 15.11.
[2] Eccle. 7.30.   [3] John 1.3.

ease or repair the damage by restoring the nature to health or wholeness.

Take the case of the will. Its choice is truly free only when it is not a slave to sin and vice. God created man with such a free will, but, once that kind of freedom was lost by man's fall from freedom, it could be given back only by Him who had the power to give it. Thus, Truth tells us: 'If therefore the Son makes you free, you will be free indeed.'[4] He might equally have said: 'If, therefore, the Son saves you, you will be saved indeed.' For the same reason that God's Son is our Saviour He is also our Liberator.

Thus, man once lived according to God in a Paradise that was both material and spiritual. Eden was not merely a place for the physical needs of the body, but had a spiritual significance as food for the soul. On the other hand, it was not so purely spiritual as to delight only the soul, and not also a place where man could get enjoyment for his bodily senses. It was both, and for both purposes.

However, the joy of Eden was short-lived because of the proud and, therefore, envious spirit who fell from the heavenly Paradise when his pride caused him to turn away from God to his own self and the pleasures and pomp of tyranny, preferring to rule over subjects than be subject himself. (His downfall and that of his companions, the former angels of God who became his angels, I have discussed, to the best of my ability, in Books XI and XII of this present work.[5])

This Lucifer, striving to insinuate his sly seductions into the minds of man whose fidelity he envied, since he himself had fallen, chose for his spokesman a serpent in the terrestrial Paradise, where all the animals of earth were living in harmless subjection to Adam and Eve. It was suited for the task because it was a slimy and slippery beast that could slither and twist on its tortuous way. So, subjecting it to his diabolical design by the powerful presence of his angelic nature and misusing it as his instrument, he, at first, parleyed cunningly with the woman as with the weaker part of that human society, hoping gradually to gain the whole. He assumed that a man is less gullible and can be more easily tricked into following a bad example than into making a mistake himself.

---

[4] John 8.36.   [5] Cf. above, 11.13. and 12.1.

This was the case with Aaron. He did not consent to the making of idols for his erring people, but he gave an unwilling assent when he was asked by the people to do so;[6] and it is not to be thought that Solomon was deceived into believing in the worship of idols, but was merely won over to this sacrilege by feminine flattery.[7] So, too, we must believe that Adam transgressed the law of God, not because he was deceived into believing that the lie was true, but because in obedience to a social compulsion he yielded to Eve, as husband to wife, as the only man in the world to the only woman. It was not without reason that the Apostle wrote: 'Adam was not deceived but the woman was deceived.'[8] He means, no doubt, that Eve accepted the serpent's word as true, whereas Adam refused to be separated from his partner even in a union of sin—not, of course, that he was, on that account, any less guilty, since he sinned knowingly and deliberately. That is why the Apostle does not say: 'He did not sin,' but 'he was not deceived.' Elsewhere, he implies that Adam did sin: 'Through one man sin entered into the world.' And a little further on, even more plainly, he adds: 'After the likeness of the transgression of Adam.'[9] The distinction is here made between those who, like Adam, sin with full knowledge and those who are deceived because they do not know that what they are doing is a sin. It is this distinction which gives meaning to the statement: 'Adam was not deceived.'

Nevertheless, in so far as he had had no experience of the divine severity, Adam could be deceived in believing that his transgression was merely venial. And, therefore, he was at least not deceived in the same way that Eve was; he was merely mistaken concerning the judgment that would follow his attempt to excuse himself: 'The woman you placed at my side gave me fruit from the tree and I ate.'[10]

To summarize briefly: though not equally deceived by believing the serpent, they equally sinned and were caught and ensnared by the Devil.

---

[6] Exod. 32.2,21–24.
[7] 3 Kings 11.4.
[8] 1 Tim. 2.14.
[9] Rom. 5.12,14.
[10] Gen. 3.12.

Chapter 12

Someone may be puzzled by the fact that other sins do not change human nature in the way that the transgression of our first parents not merely damaged theirs but had the consequence that human nature, ever since, has been subject to death, to the great corruption which we can see and experience, and to so many and such opposing passions which disturb and disorder it, which was not the case in Eden before there was sin, even though the human body was animal then as now. However, no one has a right to be puzzled, on the assumption that our first parents' sin must have been a small, venial sin, since it involved merely a matter of food—a thing good and harmless in itself apart from being forbidden, as everything else was good which God had created and planted in that place of perfect happiness.

However, what is really involved in God's prohibition is obedience, the virtue which is, so to speak, the mother and guardian of all the virtues of a rational creature. The fact is that a rational creature is so constituted that submission is good for it while yielding to its own rather than its Creator's will is, on the contrary, disastrous. Now, this command to refrain from a single kind of food when they were surrounded by an abundance of every other kind of food was so easy to obey and so simple to remember for anyone still free from passion resisting the will (as would be the case later on, in punishment for sin) that the sinfulness involved in breaking this precept was so very great precisely because the difficulty of submission was so very slight.

Chapter 13

Moreover, our first parents only fell openly into the sin of disobedience because, secretly, they had begun to be guilty. Actually, their bad deed could not have been done had not bad will preceded it; what is more, the root of their bad will was nothing else than pride. For, 'pride is the beginning of all sin.'[1] And what is pride but an appetite for inordinate ex-

[1] Eccli. 10.15.

altation? Now, exaltation is inordinate when the soul cuts it-self off from the very Source to which it should keep close and somehow makes itself and becomes an end to itself. This takes place when the soul becomes inordinately pleased with itself, and such self-pleasing occurs when the soul falls away from the unchangeable Good which ought to please the soul far more than the soul can please itself. Now, this falling away is the soul's own doing, for, if the will had merely remained firm in the love of that higher immutable Good which lighted its mind into knowledge and warmed its will into love, it would not have turned away in search of satisfaction in itself and, by so doing, have lost that light and warmth. And thus Eve would not have believed that the serpent's lie was true, nor would Adam have preferred the will of his wife to the will of God nor have supposed that his transgression of God's com-mand was venial when he refused to abandon the partner of his life even in a partnership of sin.

Our first parents, then, must already have fallen before they could do the evil deed, before they could commit the sin of eating the forbidden fruit. For such 'bad fruit' could come only from a 'bad tree.'[2] That the tree became bad was contrary to its nature, because such a condition could come about only by a defection of the will, which is contrary to nature. Notice, however, that such worsening by reason of a defect is possible only in a nature that has been created out of nothing. In a word, a nature is a nature because it is something made by God, but a nature falls away from That which Is because the nature was made out of nothing.

Yet, man did not so fall away from Being as to be absolutely nothing, but, in so far as he turned himself toward himself, he became less than he was when he was adhering to Him who is supreme Being. Thus, no longer to be in God but to be in oneself in the sense of to please oneself is not to be wholly nothing but to be approaching nothingness. For this reason, Holy Scripture gives another name to the proud. They are called 'rash' and 'self willed.'[3] Certainly, it is good for the heart to be lifted up, not to oneself, for this is the mark of pride, but to God, for this is a sign of obedience which is precisely the virtue of the humble.

[2] Cf. Matt. 7.18.   [3] Cf. 2 Pet. 2.10.

There is, then, a kind of lowliness which in some wonderful way causes the heart to be lifted up, and there is a kind of loftiness which makes the heart sink lower. This seems to be a sort of paradox, that loftiness should make something lower and lowliness lift something up. The reason for this is that holy lowliness makes us bow to what is above us and, since there is nothing above God, the kind of lowliness that makes us close to God exalts us. On the other hand, the kind of loftiness which is a defection by this very defection refuses this subjection to God and so falls down from Him who is supreme, and by falling comes to be lower. Thus it comes to pass, as Scripture says, that 'when they were lifting themselves up thou hast cast them down.'[4] Here, the Psalmist does not say: 'When they had been lifted up,' as though they first lifted themselves up and afterwards were cast down, but 'when they are lifting themselves up, at that moment they were cast down,' which means that their very lifting themselves up was itself a fall.

Hence it is that just because humility is the virtue especially esteemed in the City of God and so recommended to its citizens in their present pilgrimage on earth and because it is one that was particularly outstanding in Christ, its King, so it is that pride, the vice contrary to this virtue, is, as Holy Scripture tells us, especially dominant in Christ's adversary, the Devil. In fact, this is the main difference which distinguishes the two cities of which we are speaking. The humble City is the society of holy men and good angels; the proud city is the society of wicked men and evil angels. The one City began with the love of God; the other had its beginnings in the love of self.

The conclusion, then, is that the Devil would not have begun by an open and obvious sin to tempt man into doing something which God had forbidden, had not man already begun to seek satisfaction in himself and, consequently, to take pleasure in the words: 'You shall be as Gods.'[5] The promise of these words, however, would much more truly have come to pass if, by obedience, Adam and Eve had kept close to the ultimate and true Source of their being and had not, by pride, imagined that they were themselves the source of their being. For, created gods are gods not in virtue of their own being

[4] Cf. Ps. 72.18.   [5] Gen. 3.5.

but by a participation in the being of the true God.[6] For, whoever seeks to be more than he is becomes less, and while he aspires to be self-sufficing he retires from Him who is truly sufficient for him.[7]

Thus, there is a wickedness by which a man who is self-satisfied as if he were the light turns himself away from that true Light which, had man loved it, would have made him a sharer in the light; it was this wickedness which secretly preceded and was the cause of the bad act which was committed openly. It has been truly written that 'before destruction, the heart of a man is exalted: and before he be glorified, it is humbled.'[8] The 'destruction' which is not seen precedes the 'destruction' which is seen, though the former is not looked upon as such. For, who would think of exaltation as a ruin; yet there is a fall the moment that the will turns away from the Highest. On the other hand, everyone can recognize the ruin when a command has been openly and unmistakably violated.

Therefore, God forbade that which, when committed, could be defended by no pretense of sanctity. And I am willing to say that it is advantageous for the proud to fall into some open and manifest sin, and so become displeasing to themselves, after they had already fallen by pleasing themselves. For, when Peter wept and reproached himself, he was in a far healthier condition than when he boasted and was satisfied with himself. A verse of the psalm expresses this truth: 'Fill their faces with shame; and they shall seek thy name, O Lord,'[9] meaning, 'May those who pleased themselves in seeking their own glory find pleasure in Thee by seeking Thy name.'

Chapter 14

There is a worse and more execrable kind of pride whereby one seeks the subterfuge of an excuse even when one's sin is manifest. There was an example of this in the case of our first

[6] Cf. above, 9.23.

[7] . . . dum sibi sufficere deligit, ab illo, qui ei vere sufficit, deficit.

[8] Cf. Prov. 18.12. Augustine's text reads: Ante ruinam exaltatur . . .

[9] Ps. 82.17.

parents when the woman said: 'The serpent deceived me and I did eat,' and when Adam said: 'The woman, whom thou gavest me to be my companion, gave me of the tree and I did eat.'[1] There is not a hint here of any prayer for pardon, not a word of entreaty for any medicine to heal their wound. They do not, it is true, deny like Cain that they had sinned. Still, their pride seeks to put the blame for the sin on someone else. The pride of the woman blames the serpent; the man's pride blames the woman. But where there is a case, as here, of an open transgression of a divine command, they did more to increase their guilt than to lessen it. For, where there is a question of believing or obeying, no one can be preferred to God, and, therefore the blame was in no way lessened merely because the woman believed the suggestion of the serpent and the man obeyed the woman who gave him the fruit.

Chapter 15

For many reasons, then, the punishment meted out for disobeying God's order was just. It was God who had created man. He had made man to His own image, set man above all other animals, placed him in Paradise, and given him an abundance of goods and of well-being. God had not burdened man with many precepts that were heavy and hard, but had propped him up with a single precept that was momentary and utterly easy and that was meant merely as a medicine to make man's obedience strong, and as a reminder that it was good for man who is a creature to give his service freely to God who is his Master.

This just punishment involves many consequences. Man who was destined to become spiritual even in his flesh, if only he had kept the commandment, became, instead, fleshly even in his soul.

Man, who had pleased himself because of pride, was abandoned by divine justice to his own resources—not, that is, to his power but to his weakness. The very self that had been obeyed when he sinned now became a tyrant to torment and, in place of the liberty he longed for, he had to live in the

---

[1] Gen. 3.12,13.

misery of servitude. He had chosen freely the death of his soul; he was now condemned, unwillingly, to the death of his body. He had been a deserter from eternal life; he was now doomed to eternal death—from which nothing could save him but grace.

This punishment was neither excessive nor unjust. Anyone who thinks otherwise merely proves his inability to measure the magnitude of this sinfulness in a case where sin was so easy to avoid. For, just as the obedience of Abraham is rightly regarded as magnificent precisely because the killing of his son was a command so difficult to obey, so in Paradise the lack of obedience was so lamentable because the prohibition imposed was so easy to respect. And just as the obedience of the Second Man is so marvelous because He made Himself obedient unto death, so is the disobedience of the first man so malignant because he made himself disobedient unto death. It was the Creator Himself who commanded; the thing commanded was perfectly easy; the penalty attached was known to be great. Surely, then, the malice is incalculable when the creature defies, in a matter so simple and in the face of so fearful a penalty, the supreme authority of Omnipotence.

Actually, in the punishment for that sin the only penalty for disobedience was, to put it in a single word, more disobedience. There is nothing else that now makes a man more miserable than his own disobedience to himself. Because he would not do what he could, he can no longer do what he would.[1] It is true that even in the Garden, before man sinned, he could not do everything; but he could still do all he desired to do, since he had no desire to do what he could not do. It is different now. As Scripture says: 'Man is like to a breath of air.'[2] That is what we see in Adam's progeny. In too many ways to mention, man cannot do what he desires to do, for the simple reason that he refuses to obey himself; that is to say, neither his spirit nor even his body obeys his will. For, in spite of his will, his spirit is frequently troubled and his body feels pain, grows old, and dies. Now, if only our nature, wholly and in all its parts, would obey our will, we would not have to suffer these and all our other ills so unwillingly.

[1] . . . *ut, quoniam noluit quod potuit, quod non potest velit.*
[2] Ps. 143.4.

As for the objection that the only source of suffering that makes service impossible is the body, the first answer is that the source is of no consequence. The main fact is that we are suffering the just retribution of the omnipotent God. It is because it was to Him that we refused our obedience and our service that our body, which used to be obedient, now troubles us by its insubordination. And notice that, though our refusal of obedience to God could bring trouble on ourselves, it could do no harm to God. For He has no such need of our service as we have need of the service of our body. Thus, although His punishment can bring pain to us, our sin could inflict no suffering on Him.

A second answer is that when people talk of the sufferings of the body, what they really mean are the sufferings of the soul which are felt in, and because of, the body. For, of course, the flesh of itself, apart from the soul, can feel neither pain nor desire. When we say that 'the flesh lusts' after anything or that the body suffers pain, what is meant, as I have already explained, is that it is the man himself who lusts or suffers, or, at least, that some part of his soul is affected by what happens to his flesh, whether it is hard pressure causing pain or a soft impression producing pleasure. Pain of body is simply suffering of soul arising from the body; it is, as it were, the soul's disapproval of what is happening to the body, much as that anguish of spirit which is called sorrow is a disapproval of what is happening in opposition to our wills.

There is an important difference, however. Whereas sorrow is usually preceded by fear, an emotion which is itself in the soul and not in the body, bodily pain is never preceded by anything that could be called a fear in the flesh and that could be felt before the pain is felt. Bodily pleasure, however, is preceded by a kind of appetite, a sensation in the flesh corresponding to desire in the soul, familiar in the form of hunger and thirst, and commonly called *libido* when connected with sex—although, strictly speaking, lust is a word applicable to any kind of appetite, as in the classical definition of anger as a lust for revenge. In connection with this definition, it might be objected that there are times when a man gets angry with inanimate things that cannot feel his revenge, as when a man smashes a pen or crushes a quill that is writing badly. However, even here there is a kind of lust for revenge, a subconscious projection, if I may use the expression, of that law of retribution which runs: Ill betide him who evil does.[3] But, to return to the word 'lust.' As lust for revenge is called anger, so lust for money is avarice, lust to win at any price is obstinacy, lust for bragging is vanity. And there are still many other kinds of lust, some with names and some without. For example, it would be difficult to find a specific name for that lust for domination which plays such havoc with the souls of ambitious soldiers and comes to light in every civil war.

Chapter 16

There are, then, many kinds of lusts for this or that, but when the word is used by itself without specification it suggests to most people the lust for sexual excitement. Such lust does not merely invade the whole body and outward members; it takes such complete and passionate possession of the whole man, both physically and emotionally, that what results is the keenest of all pleasures on the level of sensation; and, at the crisis of excitement, it practically paralyzes all power of deliberate thought.

This is so true that it creates a problem for every lover of wisdom and holy joys who is both committed to a married life and also conscious of the apostolic ideal, that everyone should 'learn how to possess his vessel in holiness and honor, not in the passion of lust like the Gentiles who do not know God.'[1] Any such person would prefer, if this were possible, to beget his children without suffering this passion. He could wish that, just as all his other members obey his reason in the performance of their appointed tasks, so the organs of parenthood, too, might function in obedience to the orders of will and not be excited by the ardors of lust.

Curiously enough, not even those who love this pleasure most—whether legitimately or illegitimately indulged—can con-

---

[3] *Verum et ista licet inrationabilior, tamen quaedam ulciscendi libido est, ut nescio qua, ut ita dixerim quasi umbra retributionis, ut qui male faciunt mala patiantur.*

[1] Thess. 4.4.

trol their own indulgences. Sometimes, their lust is most importunate when they least desire it; at other times, the feelings fail them when they crave them most, their bodies remaining frigid when lust is blazing in their souls. Thus, lust itself, lascivious and legitimate, refuses to obey, and the very passion that so often joins forces to resist the soul is sometimes so divided against itself that, after it has roused the soul to passion, it refuses to awaken the feelings of the flesh.

Chapter 17

An explanation is offered for Genesis 2:25, 'they were naked but they felt no shame.'

Chapter 18

Wherever sexual passion is at work, it feels ashamed of itself. This is so not only in the case of rape, which seeks dark corners to escape the law, but even where worldly society has legalized prostitution. Even when there is no fear of the law and passion is indulged with impunity, it shrinks from the public gaze. There is a natural shame which forces even houses of ill fame to make provision for secrecy, because, easy as it was for lust to get rid of legal restrictions, it was far too difficult ever to remove the darkness from the dens of indecency. The most shameless of men know that what they are doing is shameful; much as they love this pleasure, they hate publicity.

Even the parental duty, done as it is in accordance with Roman law for the procreation of children,[1] and, therefore, both legally right and morally good, looks for a room from which all witnesses have been carefully removed. It is only after the best-man and bridesmaids, the friends and the servants, have gone from the room that the bridegroom even begins to show any signs of intimate affection. It may be true in

[1] *Concubitus coniugalis, qui secundum matrimonialium praescripta tabularum procreandorum fit causa liberorum* . . . Both Roman and early ecclesiastical law required a written marriage contract (*tabulae nuptiales*), indicating procreation of children as the purpose of marriage, and signed by ten witnesses.

general, as the 'greatest master of the Roman language'[2] once
put it, that deeds well done like to come into the light,[3] in the
sense that they want to become known; but this deed, well
done as it is, may seek to be known when done but it is certainly ashamed to be seen in the doing. What is done by parents so that children may be born comes to be known to all the
world; in fact, it is to get this action done that marriages are
made with such pomp. But when it is being done, it is different. Not even the children who have been born because it
was done are allowed to be witnesses while it is being done.
Yes, it is a good deed; but it is one that seeks to be known
only after it is done, and is ashamed to be seen while it is
being done. The reason can only be that what, by nature, has
a purpose that everyone praises involves, by penalty, a passion
that makes everyone ashamed.

Chapters 19–25

*The shame now associated with procreation is noted, to-
gether with the view of the Cynic school that the marital act
is good and so might well be performed in public. Criticizing
this, Augustine speculates on the possibility of procreation
without lust, on the peculiar things some people can do with
their bodies (such as wiggling both ears), and on the ability
of a man named Restitutus to assume a state of suspended
animation. The point is made again that no man can be perfectly happy in this life.*

Chapter 26

Now, the point about Eden was that a man could live there
as a man longs to live, but only so long as he longed to live
as God willed him to live. Man in Eden lived in the enjoyment
of God and he was good by a communication of the goodness
of God. His life was free from want, and he was free to pro-
long his life as long as he chose. There were food and drink
to keep away hunger and thirst and the tree of life to stave off
death from senescence. There was not a sign or a seed of decay

---

[2] Lucan, *Pharsalia* 7.62.   [3] Cicero, *Tusc. Disp.* 2.26,64.

in man's body that could be a source of any physical pain.
Not a sickness assailed him from within, and he feared no
harm from without. His body was perfectly healthy and his
soul completely at peace. And as in Eden itself there was never
a day too hot or too cold, so in Adam, who lived there, no
fear or desire was ever so passionate as to worry his will. Of
sorrows there was none at all and of joys none that was vain,
although a perpetual joy that was genuine flowed from the
presence of God, because God was loved with a 'charity from
a pure heart and a good conscience and faith unfeigned.'[1]
Family affection was ensured by purity of love; body and mind
worked in perfect accord; and there was an effortless observance of the law of God. Finally, neither leisure nor labor had
ever to suffer from boredom or sloth.

How in the world, then, can anyone believe that, in a life
so happy and with men so blessed, parenthood was impossible without the passion of lust? Surely, every member of the
body was equally submissive to the mind and, surely, a man
and his wife could play their active and passive roles in the
drama of conception without the lecherous promptings of lust,
with perfect serenity of soul and with no sense of disintegration between body and soul. Merely because we have no
present experience to prove it, we have no right to reject the
possibility that, at a time when there was no unruly lust to
excite the organs of generation and when all that was needed
was done by deliberate choice, the seminal flow could have
reached the womb with as little rupture of the hymen and
by the same vaginal ducts as is at present the case, in reverse,
with the menstrual flux. And just as the maturity of the fetus
could have brought the child to birth without the moanings
of the mother in pain, so could connection and conception
have occurred by a mutually deliberate union unhurried by
the hunger of lust.

Perhaps these matters are somewhat too delicate for further
discussion. It must suffice to have done the best that I could
to suggest what was possible in the Garden of Eden, before
there was any need for the reins of reticence to bridle a discussion like this. However, as things now are, the demands
of delicacy are more imperative than those of discussion. The

[1] 1 Tim. 1.5.

trouble with the hypothesis of a passionless procreation controlled by will, as I am here suggesting it, is that it has never been verified in experience, not even in the experience of those who could have proved that it was possible. Actually, they sinned too soon and brought on themselves exile from Eden. Hence, today it is practically impossible even to discuss the hypothesis of voluntary control without the imagination being filled with the realities of rebellious lust. It is this last fact which explains my reticence; not, certainly, any lack of proof for the conclusion my mind has reached.

What, in any case, is certain is this, that God Almighty the ultimate and supremely good Creator and Ruler of all living creatures, the Giver of grace and glory to all good wills, and the God who abandons bad wills to the doom they deserve, was not without His own definite plan of populating the City of God with that fixed number of saints which His divine wisdom had ordained, even though the City had to be filled with citizens chosen from the ranks of a fallen human race. Of course, once the whole mass of mankind was, as it were, cankered in its roots,[2] there was no question of men meriting a place in His City. They could only be marked out by His grace; and how great that grace was they could see not only in their own deliverance but in the doom meted out to those who were not delivered from damnation. For, no one can help but acknowledge how gratuitous and undeserved is the grace which delivers him when he sees so clearly the contrast between his privileged, personal immunity and the fate of the penalized community whose punishment he was justly condemned to share.

Here we have an answer to the problem why God should have created men whom He foresaw would sin. It was because both in them and by means of them He could reveal how much was deserved by their guilt and condoned by His grace, and, also, because the harmony of the whole of reality which God has created and controls cannot be marred by the perverse discordancy of those who sin.

[2] . . . *universa massa tamquam in vitiata radice damnata.*

Chapter 27

What I have just said applies to both angelic and human sinners. They can do nothing to interfere with 'the great works of God which are accomplished according to His will.'[1] God who both foresees all things and can do all things, when He distributes to each of His creatures their appropriate endowments, knows how to turn to good account both good and evil. Hence, there was no reason why God should not make a good use even of the bad angel who was so doomed to obduracy, in punishment of the sin that issued from the primal bad will, that a return to good will became for him impossible. This God did by permitting the bad angel to tempt the first man who had been created good, in the sense of having a will that was good by nature.

The point here is that the first man had been so constituted that if, as a good man, he had relied on the help of God, he could have overcome the bad angel, whereas he was bound to be overcome if he proudly relied on his own will in preference to this wisdom of his maker and helper, God; and he was destined to a merited reward if his will remained firm with the help of God, and to an equally deserved doom if his will wavered because of his desertion from God. Notice here that, whereas the reliance on the help of God was a positive act that was only possible by the help of God, the reliance on his own will was a negative falling away from favors of divine grace, and this was a possibility of his own choice.

There is an analogy to this in living. The act of living in a body is a positive act which is not a matter of choice but is only possible by the help of nourishment; whereas the choice not to live in the body is a negative act which is in our human power, as we see in the case of suicide. Thus, to remain living as one ought to live was not a matter of choice, even in Eden, but depended on the help of God, whereas to live ill, as one ought not to live, was in man's power; therefore, man was justly responsible for the cutting short of his happiness and the incurring of the penalty that followed.

Since, then, God was not without knowledge of man's future

1 Cf. Ps. 110.2.

fall, He could well allow man to be tempted by the angel who hated and envied man. God was in no uncertainty regarding the defeat which man would suffer; but, what matters more, God foresaw the defeat which the Devil would suffer at the hands of a descendant of Adam, and with the help of divine grace, and that this would be to the greater glory of the saints. Now, all this was so accomplished that nothing in the future escaped the foreknowledge of God, yet nothing in the foreknowledge compelled anyone to sin. God's further purpose was to reveal to all rational creatures, angelic and human, in the light of their own experience, the difference between the fruits of presumption, angelic or human, and the protection of God. For, of course, no one would dare to believe or declare that it was beyond God's power to prevent the fall of either angel or man. But, in fact, God preferred not to use His own power, but to leave success or failure to the creature's choice. In this way, God could show both the immense evil that flows from the creature's pride and also the even greater good that comes from His grace.

Chapter 28

What we see, then, is that two societies have issued from two kinds of love. Worldly society has flowered from a selfish love which dared to despise even God, whereas the communion of saints is rooted in a love of God that is ready to trample on self. In a word, this latter relies on the Lord, whereas the other boasts that it can get along by itself. The city of man seeks the praise of men, whereas the height of glory for the other is to hear God in the witness of conscience. The one lifts up its head in its own boasting; the other says to God: 'Thou art my glory, thou liftest up my head.'[1]

In the city of the world both the rulers themselves and the people they dominate are dominated by the lust for domination; whereas in the City of God all citizens serve one another in charity, whether they serve by the responsibilities of office or by the duties of obedience. The one city loves its leaders as symbols of its own strength; the other says to its God: 'I

[1] Ps. 3.4.

love thee, O Lord, my strength.'[2] Hence, even the wise men
in the city of man live according to man, and their only goal
has been the goods of their bodies or of the mind or of both;
though some of them have reached a knowledge of God, 'they
did not glorify him as God or give thanks but became vain in
their reasonings, and their senseless minds have been darkened.
For while professing to be wise' (that is to say, while glorying
in their own wisdom, under the domination of pride), 'they
have become fools, and they have changed the glory of the
incorruptible God for an image made like to corruptible man
and to birds and four-footed beasts and creeping things'
(meaning that they either led their people, or imitated them,
in adoring idols shaped like these things), 'and they wor-
shipped and served the creature rather than the Creator who
is blessed forever.'[3] In the City of God, on the contrary, there
is no merely human wisdom, but there is a piety which worships the true God as He should be worshiped and has as its
goal that reward of all holiness whether in the society of saints
on earth or in that of angels of heaven, which is 'that God may
be all in all.'[4]

[2] Ps. 17.2.
[3] Rom. 1.21–25.
[4] 1 Cor. 15.28.

PART FOUR

THE DEVELOPMENT OF THE TWO CITIES

BOOK XV

The Two Cities in Early Biblical History

Chapter 1

REGARDING THE Garden of Eden, the happiness that was possible there, the life of our first parents, their sin and their punishment, a great deal has been thought, said, and written. In the foregoing Books I myself have said something on these subjects, setting forth what can be found in the text of Scripture and adding only such reflections as seemed in harmony with its authority. The discussion could be pursued in greater detail, but it would raise so many and such varied problems that I would need for their solution more books than our present purpose calls for; nor is there so much time at my disposal that I feel obliged to waste it in satisfying the curiosity of those persons with nothing to do who are more captious in putting their questions than capable of grasping the answers.

Actually, I think I have said enough on the really great and difficult problems concerning the origin of the world, the soul, and the human race. In regard to mankind I have made a division. On the one side are those who live according to man; on the other, those who live according to God. And I have said that, in a deeper sense, we may speak of two cities or two human societies, the destiny of the one being an eternal kingdom under God while the doom of the other is eternal punishment along with the Devil.

Of the final consummation of the two cities I shall have to speak later. Of their original cause among the angels whose number no man knows and then in the first two human beings, I have already spoken. For the moment, therefore, I must deal with the course of the history of the two cities from the

time when children were born to the first couple until the day
when men shall beget no more. By the course of their history,
as distinguished from their original cause and final consummation, I mean the whole time of world history in which men
are born and take the place of those who die and depart.

Now, the first man born of the two parents of the human
race was Cain. He belonged to the city of man. The next born
was Abel, and he was of the City of God. Notice here a parallel
between the individual man and the whole race. We all experience as individuals what the Apostle says: 'It is not the
spiritual that comes first, but the physical, and then the spiritual.'[1] The fact is that every individual springs from a condemned stock and, because of Adam, must be first cankered
and carnal,[2] only later to become sound and spiritual by the
process of rebirth in Christ. So, too, with the human race as
a whole, as soon as human birth and death began the historical
course of the two cities, the first to be born was a citizen of
this world and only later came the one who was an alien in
the city of men but at home in the City of God, a man predestined by grace and elected by grace. By grace an alien on
earth, by grace he was a citizen of heaven. In and of himself,
he springs from the common clay, all of which was under
condemnation from the beginning,[3] but which God held in
His hands like a potter, to borrow the metaphor which the
Apostle so wisely and deliberately uses. For, God could make
'from the same mass one vessel for honorable, another for
ignoble use.'[4] The first vessel to be made was 'for ignoble use.'
Only later was there made a vessel for honorable use. And as
with the race, so, as I have said, with the individual. First
comes the clay that is only fit to be thrown away, with which
we must begin, but in which we need not remain. Afterwards
comes what is fit for use, that into which we can be gradually
molded and in which, when molded, we may remain.[5] This
does not mean that everyone who is wicked is to become

---

[1] 1 Cor. 15.46.
[2] . . . *ex damnata propagine exoritur . . . primo . . . malus
adque carnalis.*
[3] . . . *massa . . . quae originaliter est tota damnata.*
[4] Rom. 9.21.
[5] . . . *prius est reprobum . . . posterius vero probum.*

good, but that no one becomes good who was not once wicked. What is true is that the sooner a man makes a change in himself for the better the sooner he has a right to be called what he has become. The second name hides the first.

Now, it is recorded of Cain that he built a city,[6] while Abel, as though he were merely a pilgrim on earth, built none. For, the true City of the saints is in heaven, though here on earth it produces citizens in whom it wanders as on a pilgrimage through time looking for the Kingdom of eternity. When that day comes it will gather together all those who, rising in their bodies, shall have that Kingdom given to them in which, along with their Prince, the King of Eternity, they shall reign for ever and ever.

Chapter 2

A shadow, as it were, of this eternal City has been cast on earth, a prophetic representation of something to come rather than a real presentation in time. Yet this shadow, merely symbolic as it is and not the reality that is to be, is properly called the holy City. It was of these two cities, the one, as it were, in bondage to symbolic purpose and the other free, that the Apostle writes in the Epistle to the Galatians: 'Tell me, you who desire to be under the Law, have you not read the Law? For it is written that Abraham had two sons, the one by a slave-girl and the other by a free woman. And the son of the slave-girl was born according to the flesh, but the son of the free woman in virtue of the promise. This is said by way of allegory. For these are the two convenants: one indeed from Mount Sinai, bringing forth children unto bondage, which is Agar. For Sinai is a mountain in Arabia, which corresponds to the present Jerusalem, and is in slavery with her children. But that Jerusalem which is above is free, which is our mother. For it is written, "Rejoice thou barren, that dost not bear; break forth and cry, thou that dost not travail; for many are the children of the desolate, more than of her that has a husband." Now we, brethren, are the children of promise, as Isaac was. But as then he who was born according to

6 Gen. 4.17.

the flesh persecuted him who was born according to the spirit, so also it is now. But what does the Scripture say? "Cast out the slave-girl and her son, for the son of the slave-girl shall not be heir with the son of the free woman." Therefore, brethren, we are not children of a slave-girl, but of the free woman—in virtue of the freedom wherewith Christ has made us free.'[1]

This exegesis, which comes to us with apostolic authority, opens up for us a way to understand much that is written in both Testaments, the Old and the New. We see that one portion of the world community became a symbol of the heavenly City and was 'in bondage' in the sense that its significance was not in itself but in serving to signify the other city. It was, in fact, founded, not for its own sake, but as the shadow of another substance, a shadow that was itself foreshadowed by a previous symbol. For, the symbol of this shadow was Sara's handmaid, Agar, with her son. It was because shadows were to cease when the light came that the free woman, Sara, symbol of the free City (to which, in turn, the shadow served as another kind of prelude), uttered the words: 'Cast out this slave-girl with her son; for the son of this slave-girl shall not be heir with my son Isaac,'[2] or, to use the Apostle's expression, 'with the son of the free woman.'[3]

In the world community, then, we find two forms, one being the visible appearance of the earthly city[4] and another whose presence serves as a shadow of the heavenly City.

Notice that it is nature, flawed by sin, that begets all the citizens in the world community, whereas nothing but grace, which frees nature from sinfulness, can bring forth citizens of the heavenly City. The former are called 'vessels of wrath'; the latter, 'vessels of mercy.'[5] This distinction was symbolized in the two sons of Abraham. One, Ismael, was born of the slave-girl whose name was Agar and he was born according to the flesh. The other, Isaac, was born of the free woman,

---

[1] Gal. 4.21–31.

[2] Gen. 21.10.

[3] Gal. 4.30.

[4] It will be noticed that St. Augustine uses *civitas terrena* to mean both the community of earthly minded men and also the world community (which includes the City of God on earth).

[5] Rom. 9.22,23.

Sara, according to the promise. Of course, both were sons of Abraham, but he begot the one by a law suggesting the order of nature, while the other was born in virtue of a promise which pointed to the order of grace. What is clear in the one case is human action; in the other, divine favor.

Chapter 3

Augustine suggests a spiritual explanation of the births of Ismael and Agar.

Chapter 4

As for the city of this world, it is neither to last forever nor even to be a city, once the final doom of pain is upon it. Nevertheless, while history lasts, it has a finality of its own; it reaches such happiness by sharing a common good as is possible when there are no goods but the things of time to afford it happiness. This is not the kind of good that can give those who are content with it any freedom from fear. In fact, the city of man, for the most part, is a city of contention with opinions divided by foreign wars and domestic quarrels and by the demands for victories which either end in death or are merely momentary respites from further war. The reason is that whatever part of the city of the world raises the standard of war, it seeks to be lord of the world, when, in fact, it is enthralled in its own wickedness. Even when it conquers, its victory can be mortally poisoned by pride, and if, instead of taking pride in the success already achieved, it takes account of the nature and normal vicissitudes of life and is afraid of future failure, then the victory is merely momentary. The fact is that the power to reach domination by war is not the same as the power to remain in perpetual control.

Nevertheless, it is wrong to deny that the aims of human civilization are good, for this is the highest end that mankind of itself can achieve.[1] For, however lowly the goods of earth, the aim, such as it is, is peace. The purpose even of war is

---

[1] *Non autem recte dicitur ea bona non esse, quae concupiscit haec civitas, quando est et ipsa in suo humano genere melior.*

peace. For, where victory is not followed by resistance there is a peace that was impossible so long as rivals were competing, hungrily and unhappily, for something material too little to suffice for both. This kind of peace is a product of the work of war, and its price is a so-called glorious victory; when victory goes to the side that had a juster cause it is surely a matter for human rejoicing, and the peace is one to be welcomed.

The things of earth are not merely good; they are undoubtedly gifts from God. But, of course, if those who get such goods in the city of men are reckless about the better goods of the City of God, in which there is to be the ultimate victory of an eternal, supreme, and untroubled peace, if men so love the goods of earth as to believe that these are the only goods or if they love them more than the goods they know to be better, then the consequence is inevitable: misery and more misery.

Chapter 5

Now, the city of man was first founded by a fratricide who was moved by envy to kill his brother, a man who, in his pilgrimage on earth, was a citizen of the City of God. It need not surprise us, then, that long afterwards, in the founding of that city which was to dominate so many peoples and become the capital of that earthly city with which I am dealing, the copy, so to speak, corresponded to the original—to what the Greeks call the archetype. For, in both cases, we have the same crime. As one of the poets puts it: 'With brother's blood the earliest walls were wet.'[1] For Rome began, as Roman history records, when Remus was killed by Romulus, his brother. However, in this case, both men were citizens of the earthly city. It was the ambition of both of them to have the honor of founding the Roman republic, but that was an honor that could not be shared; it had to belong to one or the other. For, no one who had a passion to glory in domination could be fully the master if his power were diminished by a living co-regent. One of the two wanted to have the whole of the sovereignty;

---

[1] Lucan, *Pharsalia* 1.95.

therefore, his associate was removed. Without the crime, his position would have had less power, but more prestige. However, the crime made everything worse than before.

In the case of the brothers Cain and Abel, there was no rivalry in any cupidity for the things of earth, nor was there any envy or temptation to murder arising from a fear of losing the sovereignty if both were ruling together. In this case, Abel had no ambition for domination in the city that his brother was building. The root of the trouble was that diabolical envy which moves evil men to hate those who are good for no other reason than that they are good. Unlike material possessions, goodness is not diminished when it is shared, either momentarily or permanently, with others, but expands and, in fact, the more heartily each of the lovers of goodness enjoys the possession the more does goodness grow. What is more, goodness is not merely a possession that no one can maintain who is unwilling to share it, but it is one that increases the more its possessor loves to share it.

What, then, is revealed in the quarrel between Remus and Romulus is the way in which the city of man is divided against itself, whereas, in the case of Cain and Abel, what we see is the enmity between the two cities, the city of man and the City of God. Thus, we have two wars, that of the wicked at war with the wicked and that of the wicked at war with the good. For, of course, once the good are perfectly good, there can be no war between them. This much is true, however, that while a good man is still on the way to perfection one part of him can be at war with another of his parts; because of this rebellious element, two good men can be at war with each other. The fact is that in everyone 'the flesh lusts against the spirit, and the spirit against the flesh.'[2]

The spiritual longing of one good man can be at war with the fleshly passion of another just as fleshly passion in one man can resist spiritual tendencies in another. And the war here is much like that between good and wicked men. So, too, a good deal like the war of the wicked against the wicked is the rivalry of fleshly desires in two good men, and this will continue until grace wins the ultimate victory of soundness over sickness in both of them.

[2] Gal. 5.17.

Chapter 6

Of course, even good men can be sick, suffering from that disobedience (discussed in Book XIV) which is the penalty of a primal disobedience which, therefore, is a wound or weakness in a nature that is good in itself. It is because of this wound that the good who are growing in grace and living by faith during their pilgrimage on earth are given the counsels: 'Bear one another's burdens, and so you will fulfill the law of Christ,'[1] and elsewhere: 'We exhort you, brethren, reprove the irregular, comfort the fainthearted, support the weak, be patient towards all men. See that no one renders evil for evil to any man,'[2] and again: 'If a person is caught doing something wrong, you who are spiritual instruct such a one in a spirit of meekness, considering thyself, lest thou also be tempted,'[3] and elsewhere: 'Do not let the sun go down upon your anger,'[4] and in the Gospel: 'If thy brother sin against thee, go and show him his fault, between thee and him alone.'[5] So, too, the Apostle gives the command: 'When they sin, rebuke them in the presence of all, that the rest also may have fear.'[6]

These are not the only reasons for the many careful precepts which have been given us such as those concerning mutual forgiveness and the encouraging of that peace which is the very condition of our seeing God.[7] One has only to recall the fearsome command given to the servant to pay the debt of the 10,000 talents from which he had been released, because he had not released his fellow servant from the debt of one hundred pence which he owed. When the Lord had proposed this parable, He added the words: 'So also my heavenly Father will do to you, if you do not each forgive your brothers from your hearts.'[8]

It is in this way that citizens of the City of God are given medicine during their pilgrimage on earth while praying for the peace of their heavenly fatherland. And, of course, the

---

[1] Gal. 6.2.
[2] 1 Thess. 5.14,15.
[3] Gal. 6.1.
[4] Eph. 4.26.
[5] Matt. 18.15.
[6] 1 Tim. 5.20.
[7] Heb. 12.14.
[8] Matt. 18.35.

Holy Spirit is operative interiorly to give healing power to the medicine which is applied externally, for, otherwise, no preaching of the truth is of any avail. Even though God makes use of one of His obedient creatures, as when He speaks in human guise to our ears—whether to the ears of the body or to the kind of ears we have in sleep—it is only by His interior grace that He moves and rules our mind.

In doing this, God separates the vessels of wrath from the vessels of mercy. The dispensation by which He knows the one from the other is profoundly deep, yet no less just. It is He who, in His wonderful and hidden ways, helps us whenever that sin which has a home in our members and which, as the Apostle reminds us, is rather the penalty for previous sin, ceases so 'to reign in our mortal body that we obey its lust,' and whenever we 'do not yield our members to sin as weapons of iniquity.'[9] It is because God is ruling us that our soul is turned into a spirit that no longer yields to itself for its own ill but so orders us that our peace goes on increasing in this life until, when perfect health and immortality have been given us, we shall reign in utter sinlessness and in eternal peace.

Chapter 7

God spoke to Cain in the way He spoke to our first parents, namely, by using, as I have done my best to explain, a suitably created form to appear as a human companion. Yet, not even this was of any avail for Cain, for it was after he heard God's voice that he carried out his purpose of killing his brother. God made a distinction between the sacrifices of Cain and Abel, having respect for the one and disregarding the other and, undoubtedly, making the discrimination clear by some visible sign. God did so because Cain's deeds were evil and those of his brother were good. Cain was very much chagrined and ashamed. The narrative says: 'And the Lord said to him: "Why art thou angry? And why is thy countenance fallen? If thou offerest rightly but do not rightly distinguish, hast thou

---

[9] Cf. Rom. 6.12.

not sinned? Be calm for unto thee will be his turning and thou shalt rule over him." [1]

In this admonition or warning given by God to Cain, notice the clause: 'If thou offerest rightly but do not rightly distinguish, hast thou not sinned?' Its obscurity has occasioned many interpretations, because it is not clear how or why it came to be said, and thus each commentator on Scripture tries to explain the words as best he can, according to the rule of faith. Surely, a sacrifice is offered rightly when it is offered to the true God to whom alone sacrifice should be offered. One does not 'rightly distinguish' when one does not properly discriminate in the matter of place or time or victim or subject or object of the sacrifice or of those among whom what is offered up is distributed as food. Thus, 'distinguish' here means 'discriminate.' An offering can be made in a place where it should not be offered; or of a victim which should be offered in one place but not in another, or at a wrong time; or of a victim that should be offered at one time rather than at another; or an offering can be made that simply should not be offered anywhere or at any time; or there can be one in which a man keeps for himself what is choicer than what is offered to God; or a sacrifice may be indiscreet if a profane person or any other who is not entitled to participate eats of the victim.

Now, it is not easy to determine by which of these indiscretions Cain displeased God. However, a key may be found in the following words: 'not like Cain who was of the evil one, and killed his brother. And wherefore did he kill him? Because his own works were wicked but his brother's just.' [2] Here the Apostle John gives us to understand that the reason why God did not respect Cain's offering was that it was 'indiscreet' in this, that while he gave to God some possession that was his, he kept himself for himself. This, in fact, is what all those do who, following their own will rather than God's or living with a perverted rather than an upright heart, offer to God some gift by which they imagine He can be bribed to

---

[1] Cf. the quite different rendering of the Vulgate text, Gen. 4.6,7.
[2] 1 John 3.12.

help them in satisfying their passions rather than in healing their infirmities.

Here we have the very heart of the earthly city. Its God (or gods) is he or they who will help the city to victory after victory and to a reign of earthly peace; and this city worships, not because it has any love for service, but because its passion is for domination. This, in fact, is the difference between good men and bad men, that the former make use of the world in order to enjoy God, whereas the latter would like to make use of God in order to enjoy the world—if, of course, they believe in God and His providence over man, and are not so bad as those who deny even this.

Now, once Cain knew that God had welcomed the sacrifice of his brother but had no regard for his, he should have made a change in himself in order to imitate his brother, but what he did was to yield to pride and emulation. He let himself yield to sadness and 'his countenance fell.' It is this sin of regret because someone else—in this case, his brother—is good that God, in a special way, held against Cain. It was this that God accused him of in asking: 'Why art thou angry? And why is thy countenance fallen?' What God saw was the envy toward his brother and it is for this envy that God reproaches Cain. To men, however, to whom the heart of a fellow man is hidden, it might be doubtful or quite uncertain whether Cain's sadness was contrition for his own wickedness which, as he knew, was displeasing to God or whether it was envy of the goodness by which his brother was pleasing to God when God had regard for his sacrifice. God explains why He refused to accept Cain's sacrifice. It was because Cain should have been rightly displeased with himself rather than wrongly displeased with his brother; God makes clear that, unjust as Cain was in not 'distinguishing rightly' (in the sense of not living properly and of being unworthy to have his offering approved), he was far more unjust in hating his brother without provocation.

Nevertheless, God does not dismiss Cain without giving him some counsel which was holy, just, and good: 'Be calm; for unto thee will be his turning and thou shalt rule over him.' Must we suppose that 'over him' means 'over his brother'? Not at all. Surely it means 'over sin.' Notice that God had said: 'hast thou not sinned?' Then He added: 'Be calm; unto thee let *its* turning be and thou shalt rule over *it*.' There is no reason why we should not take the text to mean that the 'turning of sin' should be to the sinner in the sense that the sinner should realize that he alone, and no one else, is responsible for his sinning. And if we read 'let its turning be' rather than 'will be its turning,' we have the salutary medicine of penance and a suitable petition for pardon. We have only to suppose that the implied verb is in the imperative mood rather than in the future indicative. As for ruling over sin, each man will do that as soon as he subdues sin by his contrition and gives up defending it and so yielding to it. Otherwise, if a man offers protection to his sin, he will end as its slave.

If, on the other hand, we are to take sin to mean the kind of carnal concupiscence of which the Apostle says: 'The flesh lusts against the spirit,'[3] and of which he mentions envy as one of the fruits, then, since it was by envy that Cain was driven to kill his brother, we may well supply the verb 'will be' and read: 'Unto that will be its turning and thou shalt rule over it.' It is the movement of this carnal part of a man that the Apostle calls sin in the text: 'Now it is no longer I who do it, but the sin that dwells in me.'[4]

(It may be mentioned in passing that philosophers, too, call this part of the soul defective in the sense that it must not lead, but should be ruled by, the mind, and must be restrained by reason from doing what is wrong.) If, then, the carnal part is moved to commit some sin but is calmed into obedience to the counsel of the Apostle, 'do not yield your members to sin as a weapon of iniquity,' then it is 'turned' to the mind, it is tamed and subdued into submission to the rule of reason. It was this command which God gave to Cain when he was so enkindled in the flames of envy in regard to his brother that he longed to have the one whom he should have followed put out of the way. God said: 'Be calm,' that is, 'hold your hand from crime; let sin not reign in your mortal body and command obedience to its impulses; do not yield your members to sin as weapons of iniquity.' 'For unto thee will be its turning,' so long as you do not give it rein but bridle it, so long as you do not urge it on, but keep it calm. 'And thou shalt rule over it.' For, so long as no external action is permitted, it gets so

[3] Gal. 5.17.　　　　　　　　　[4] Rom. 7.17.

used to the authority of the mind and the benevolent power of the will that even the interior movement is calmed.

A somewhat similar expression is found in the same inspired book in connection with Eve. After her sin, God questioned her and judged and condemned the Devil in the form of the serpent, and also herself and her husband. First God said: 'I will multiply thy sorrows and thy conceptions: in sorrow shalt thou bring forth children.' Then He added: 'And to thy husband will thy turning be, and he will rule over thee.'[5] What is said to Cain concerning his sin or the concupiscences of his corrupted flesh is, in the present text, said concerning the sinful woman. Thus we must conclude that a husband is meant to rule his wife as the spirit rules the flesh. This explains what the Apostle says: 'He who loves his own wife, loves himself. For no one ever hated his own flesh.'[6] Thus, a man's flesh, like his wife, is his own and as such is meant to be healed, not treated like something alien and condemned. In Cain's case, the command of God was received in a spirit of impenitence. The sickness of his envy grew worse, and he killed his brother. Such was the founder of the city of earth.

There is a sense in which Cain is a symbol of the Jews who killed Christ the Shepherd of men, as Abel, the shepherd of sheep, is also a prefiguring of Christ. But I shall refrain from discussing this here, because the sense is allegorical and prophetical. I refer the reader to a treatment of the subject in my work, *Against Faustus the Manichaean*.[7]

Chapter 8

Before proceeding further, it seems to me necessary to offer some explanation of the apparently incredible Scriptural story of a city built by a single man at a period, just after the fratricide, when, so far as we have evidence, there were no more than four men in the world. Actually, there seem to have been only three: the first man and father of us all, Cain himself, and his son Henoch, whose name was given to the city.

[5] Gen. 3.16. The Douay translation reads: 'and thou shalt be under thy husband's power, and he shall have dominion over thee.' The Confraternity translation reads: 'your husband shall be your longing, though he have dominion over you.'
[6] Eph. 5.29.   [7] In 12.9.

Those who find a difficulty here have failed to realize that the writer of this Scriptural story was under no obligation to mention the names of all who may have been alive at the time, but only of those whom the scope of his work required him to mention. All that the writer had in mind, under the inspiration of the Holy Spirit, was to trace the succession in definite lines from Adam to Abraham and then from the children of Abraham to the people of God. The directing idea was that this people, as distinct from others, prefigured and preannounced what in the light of the divine Spirit the writer foresaw would be fulfilled in that City which is to continue eternally and in that City's king and founder, Christ. It is here that the Scripture makes some mention of that other society, the city of man as I call it, but this is only in so far as was necessary to bring the City of God into clearer light by contrast with the city opposed to it.

Now notice that, when the inspired writer sets forth the length of the lives of the men he mentions, the narrative always ends with the formula: 'and he begot sons and daughters and all the time that so and so lived were so many years, and he died.'[1] Considering that these sons and daughters are not named and remembering how long people lived in that first period of our history, can anyone refuse to believe that a multitude of men so great was born as to have been able, in groups, to build a great number of cities? But all this was beside the divine purpose which inspired these writings, namely, to summarize in a single narrative the earlier generations before the flood in the respective histories of the two cities which are so clearly interpenetrated and yet distinguished, the one peopled by men living a purely human life and the other by the sons of God, that is to say, by men obedient to the will of God. The distinction between the cities is made clear by mentioning apart the two lines of succession, one descending from the fratricide, Cain, and the other from Seth the son who was born to Adam to take the place of the one killed by his brother. The interpenetration of the cities is revealed in the fact that the good were so corrupted that at last all men had to be swept away by the flood, with the exception of one just man whose name was Noe, together with his wife and three

[1] Cf. Gen. 5.4,5.

sons and daughters-in-law. These eight souls were found worthy to be saved in the ark from the flood which destroyed all other human beings.

Consider now the text: 'And Cain knew his wife, and she conceived, and brought forth Henoch; and he built a city and called the name thereof by the name of his son Henoch.'[2] It does not at all follow from these words that we must believe Cain's first son was Henoch, as though 'Cain knew his wife' must refer to their first intercourse. You have the same expression used of the first father, Adam, but not only in reference to the conception of Cain, who seems to have been his firstborn, since a little later Scripture records: 'Adam knew his wife and she conceived and brought forth a son, and called his name Seth.'[3] What is clear is that we have here the usual Biblical expression to indicate human conception, although the expression is not always used nor is it restricted to the first marital intercourse.

Again, the fact that the city was named after Henoch does not compel us to conclude that he was his father's first-born son. Likely enough, the father had other sons, but for some reason he liked Henoch better than the rest. At any rate, Judah was not the first-born even though it was from him that Judea and the Jews get their names. But, even if we suppose that Henoch was the first-born son of the founder of the city, it does not follow that the name was given to the city at the time Henoch was born. For, of course, no city, that is, no large body of men held together by some bond of association, could have been founded at that time by a single person. However, when Cain's family so increased in number as to form a large group, there is no reason why he could not then have begun to build the city and later, when the city was finished, have given it the name of his son. We have to remember that before the flood the human life-span was so long that of all those mentioned in the early chapters of Scripture the minimum age reached 753 years.[4] No one reached 1,000 but several passed their 900th year. Thus, there is no difficulty in seeing how a single man living that long could have so large a family of

2 Gen. 4.17.   3 Cf. Gen. 4.25.
4 Gen. 5.31 in the Septuagint version gives 753 as the age of Lamech.

descendants as to people not merely one but many cities. The
simple proof of this is the case of Abraham. From their single
ancestor, in not much more than 400 years, the Hebrew people became so numerous that at the time of the exodus from
Egypt there were, we are told, 600,000 men of military age.[5]
This number does not include the Idumeans who were not
reckoned with the people of Israel, although they were descended from Israel's brother Esau, who was a grandson of
Abraham; nor does it include those other descendants of
Abraham who were not of the line of his wife Sara.[6]

Chapter 9

The conclusion reached is that no one who carefully weighs
the evidence can doubt that, in an age when the human life-
span was so long, Cain could have built not merely a city but
a large city. Of course, a skeptical unbeliever might raise a
difficulty in regard to the length of human life which our authorities attribute to the men of that period and, on this
ground, deny our conclusion. A similar skepticism prevails in
regard to the claim that men had far larger bodies then than
now. Although, in this connection, we have the noblest of the
pagan poets implying that once upon a time the earth used
to produce bigger bodies than now. Recall his lines about the
immense rock fixed in the ground as a landmark and which a
man fighting one of the mighty battles of yore snatched up as
he ran and then with a swing hurled at the enemy:

> A rock that no twelve men in modern days,
> Howe'er select, could to their shoulders raise.[1]

Surely, what is true of relatively recent times is much more
so of the days before that flood of which all the world has
heard. Actually, the size of ancient bodies has often enough
been proved to the incredulous by old sepulchers which have
been broken open by the ravages of time or torrents or otherwise and have exposed to view skeletons of immense proportions. Once, on the beach at Utica, I saw with my own eyes
—and there were others to bear me witness—a human molar

[5] Exod. 12.37.
[6] The Ismaelites and others descended from Agar and Cetura.
[1] *Aeneid* 12.899,900.

tooth so big that it could have been cut up, I think, into a hundred pieces each as big as one of our modern teeth. That tooth, however, I can well believe, was the tooth of a giant; and, of course, giants were much bigger than others even in the days when these others were bigger than we are, for there have never been lacking, then or now, specimens, however rare, of extraordinary stature. No less a scholar than Pliny the Elder holds it to be an historical law that, as progress advances, man's stature grows less.[2] He invokes the Homeric laments on declining size and, far from smiling at them as though they were poetical fancies, the historian of natural wonders accepts them as historical evidence. The real proof, as I have said, is to be found in the frequent discoveries of ancient bones of immense size, and this proof will hold good in centuries far in the future, since such bones do not easily decay.

Unfortunately, there is no such archaeological evidence to prove any particular case of longevity in the pre-flood period. This, however, is no excuse for skepticism, which in regard to the recorded facts of sacred history is particularly gratuitous, seeing how accurately and manifestly its predictions have come true. This much may be said, that it is no less an authority than Pliny who states that there exists today a people among whom the life-span is 200 years.[3] At least, no one who can believe the evidence for exceptional longevity in places too far away to be familiar should have any difficulty in regard to periods in the distant past. If it is rational to believe that what is not here may exist elsewhere, it is no less rational to believe in something in the past of which no evidence exists at present.

Chapter 10

It is true that in this matter of life-span there is some discrepancy, which I cannot explain, between what appears in the translation made directly from the Hebrew and what is given in the translations from the Greek.[1] However, these minor differences do not affect the common agreement on the

---

[2] *Natural History* 7.16.   [3] *Ibid.* 7.49.

[1] St. Augustine says *inter Hebraeos et nostros codices*, meaning St. Jerome's Vulgate and the older versions of the Septuagint Greek.

fact of very long life-spans. Take the example of the first man, Adam, at the time when his son Seth was born. The ordinary translation gives the age as 230 years; the translation from the Hebrew says 130. So, too, for Adam's subsequent life. The former says he lived 700 years; the latter says 800. The sum total is the same in both cases. So, too, with the generations that followed Adam. Wherever there is mention of a birth, the age given for the father in the translation from the Hebrew is found to be 100 years short; whereas it is the number of years following the birth that is found to be 100 years short in the other versions. But, here again, the totals agree. In the sixth generation, however, there is no such discrepancy. Nevertheless, it reappears in the seventh in connection with Henoch, the man who was born but suffered no death because he was so pleasing to God. As in the first five generations, his age at the time the son who is mentioned was born differs by 100 years in the different translations, yet at the time he was translated he was, according to both translations, 365 years old. In the eighth generation, there is merely a minor discrepancy and it is of a different kind. The age of Henoch's son, Mathusala, at the time his successor was born, is given in the direct translation, not as 100 years too little, but as twenty years too much; but once more, in the popular version, the difference is adjusted in his later years, and the total is the same in both translations. The only discrepancy in the totals, and it is a slight one, occurs in the ninth generation, in regard to the age of Lamech the son of Mathusala and father of Noe. The translation from the Hebrew gives him twenty-four more years than is the case with the current version. At the time of Noe's birth, Mathusala's age is six years less in the former than in our version, but his subsequent years are given as thirty years more. Hence, as I mentioned, there is a difference of twenty-four, that is, thirty minus six.

Chapter 11

It is from the discrepancy above described that there has arisen the famous problem of the age of Mathusala. If the calculation is correct, he must have survived the flood by fourteen years, yet Scripture does not mention his name among the eight who alone of all the inhabitants on earth escaped the flood. According to the texts in common use among us, Mathusala was 167 years old when he became the father of the son he named Lamech, and this Lamech was 188 before his son Noe was born. This gives a total of 355. Add to this 600, Noe's age in the year of the flood, and we get 955 years from Mathusala's birth to the year of the flood. Yet, by calculation, Mathusala's final age was 969. He was 167 when he became the father of Lamech, and after this he lived 802 years. This gives a total, as I mentioned, of 969. Take 955 (the number of years from Mathusala's birth to the flood) from 969 and we get fourteen, the number of years by which he is supposed to have survived the flood.

This has led some people to maintain that Mathusala did not remain on earth (where every creature that could not naturally live in water was destroyed) but that he dwelt with his father, who had been 'translated,' until the flood was over. Those who believe this do so because they are so unwilling to surrender their confidence in translations which have been accorded high authority by the Church that they are ready to believe that it must be the Hebrew texts, rather than the received translations, which are wrong. They do not admit that it is more likely that the translators have made a mistake than that there was an error in the original from which our translation has come second-hand through a Greek translation. Instead, they maintain that it is impossible to believe that the seventy translators who worked simultaneously and produced identical translations could have made a mistake or could have deliberately changed the meaning in a matter where no self-interest was at stake. On the contrary, they suppose that it was the Jews, who envy us our translation of the Law and the Prophets, who actually changed their texts in order to diminish the authority of ours.

Each of us must decide for himself whether this is an opinion or a mere suspicion. What, however, is certain is that Mathusala did not survive the flood, but died that very year, if the numbers given in the Hebrew manuscripts are true. I have my own opinion concerning the seventy translators and I must be very careful to mention it in its proper place in so far as this present work may call for it, but that will be when, please God, I come to deal with the period when the translation was made.[1] For my present purpose it is enough to say that, according to both translations, the men of that early period lived so long that, during the single life-span of the first-born son of the two parents who, at the time of his birth, were the only parents on earth, the human race could multiply sufficiently to form a whole city.

Chapter 12

There are some who hold that in the early ages the length of what was reckoned as a year was no more than one-tenth of our present year. There is, however, no foundation whatever for the view that, when we read or hear that so-and-so lived 900 years, we should take that to mean ninety, on the ground that ten of the ancient years made only one of ours, so that ten of ours would equal 100 of theirs. On this reckoning, Adam was thirty-three when Seth was born and Seth was only twenty years and six months old when Enos was born, although Scripture says 205. In the view I am discussing, the ancients are supposed to have divided the real year into ten parts and called each part a year. The number of days in each of these parts was six squared, the reason being that God finished the work of creation in six days so that He might rest on the seventh. (To this matter I gave some attention in Book XI.[1]) Now, six times six, or six squared, equals thirty-six, and thirty-six days multiplied by ten comes to 360 days or twelve lunar months. It takes five-and-a-quarter more days to make up the solar year. The quarter-days were taken care of by adding one day each fourth or leap year. The other days added were said by the Romans to be intercalated to fill out the full solar year. In the view I am discussing, Enos, son of Seth, was only nineteen years old when his son Cainan was born, though Scripture speaks of 190. So, for all the generations before the flood, hardly one of those who are mentioned

---

[1] Cf. below, 18.42–43.

[1] Cf. above, 11.8.

in our texts as having a son was then less than 100 or even 120 years old. Actually, the minimum age mentioned at the time of fatherhood is a little more than 160 years. The reason of this, so it is said, is that no boy of ten (or, in Scriptural language, 100) is capable of fatherhood, whereas at sixteen (in Biblical language, 160) puberty is reached and procreation is now possible.

To clinch their argument, those who hold that the Biblical year was reckoned differently from ours adduce the testimony of many historians to the effect, for example, that the Egyptians had a year of four months, the Acarnanians one of six, the Lavinians a year of thirteen months. So, too, when Pliny the Elder mentions that there are documents recording one man as living to be 152, a second to be 162, and others as reaching 200 or 300 or 500 or even 600 or, in rare cases, 800, he attributes this to ignorance of chronology. 'For,' says Pliny, 'there are some people who reckon summer and winter each as a full year; others, like the Arcadians, reckoned by seasons and so had years of three months.' Pliny further remarks that the Egyptians (who, as I mentioned above, ordinarily had years of four months) sometimes shortened their years to a single month. 'Thus,' he says, 'some Egyptians are said to have lived 1,000 years.'

It is by such arguments, which seem plausible enough, that certain people have persuaded themselves and have a right, they think, to persuade others that the original Biblical year was so short that it took ten of them to make one of ours, so that ten of our years would make 100 Biblical years. They have no intention, of course, of impugning the historicity of the Bible. On the contrary, what they want is to build a better case for credibility by explaining how such lengthy life-spans came to be recorded. But the simple fact is that their position can be demolished by a proof of the utmost cogency. This I shall give, but first I should like to mention that an even more plausible conjecture is possible.

One certain way of refuting the argument from puberty is to take the passage in the Hebrew text which states that Adam was not 230 but 130 years old when his third son was born. If this 130 really means thirteen, then he could not have been much more than eleven when he first became a father. Now, in the ordinary way of nature which is familiar to everyone, no one is capable of fatherhood at so early an age. This point, however, cannot be pressed, since Adam may have been capable of parenthood as soon as he was created. Certainly, no one can suppose that when he was created he was no bigger than one of our babies. Take, then, Seth, Adam's son. He was not 205 (as the current versions have it), but 105, when his son Enos was born. According to our short-year theorists, he was not even eleven years old. The case of his son Cainan is still more awkward. Where our version has 170, the Hebrew text says he was 70 when he begot Malaleel. If seventy really means seven, then we are faced with an impossibility—a boy of seven becoming a father!

Chapter 13

As soon, however, as I appeal to the Hebrew text I shall be given the old argument mentioned above that the Jews must have falsified their text, since the seventy translators were men of such high reputation that they could not possibly have been guilty of falsification. To this I must answer with a question. Which is the more credible: that the whole Jewish people scattered far and wide could have agreed to a man to transcribe this forgery and, out of envy for others, deprive themselves of the truth; or that seventy men, all of them Jews and all in the same place (to which they had been called by King Ptolemy of Egypt for the task of translation) could have been the ones who envied the Gentiles this truth and by common consent committed the forgery? Anyone can see which of these possibilities is easier and more natural to believe. But, of course, both guesses should be scorned by any man of common sense. We should refuse to believe that any Jews, however perverse and malicious, could have tampered with so many manuscripts scattered throughout the world and we should equally refuse to believe that those seventy remarkable scholars could have conspired out of envy in a single purpose to deprive the Gentiles of the truth.

A more plausible explanation would be this. When copies

first began to be made from the original in Ptolemy's library, some such misstatement may have found its way into the first transcription and from this source have spread far and wide, and this need not have arisen from any deliberate falsification on the part of the copyist. At least, this hypothesis would seem reasonable enough to solve the problem of Mathusala's life-span and would also serve to explain the case where there is a discrepancy of twenty-four years. The real difficulty is to explain the apparently systematic tampering with numbers so that, although totals agree, yet, for periods before the birth of an heir, while one version gives 100 years too much, this excess is absent from the other, and for the periods after the birth the excess is subtracted and the deficiency is made up in the respective versions. This is the case in all of the first five generations and also in the seventh. The repetition of this kind of mistake seems to be more by design than by accident.

My own conclusion is that the general discrepancy between the Greek and Latin texts on the one side and the Hebrew texts on the other—apart from this special case of the addition and subtraction of 100 years in no less than six different generations—is not to be attributed to any malice on the part of the Jews in general or to any deliberate purpose on the part of the seventy translators, but simply to the carelessness of some scribe who made the first copy from the original in the royal library. The same thing happens often enough in our day. Where mere numbers do not focus attention on something which in itself is easy to understand or useful to know, they are rarely transcribed with accuracy, and mistakes once made are still more rarely emended.

Practically no one feels any interest in knowing just how many men each of the tribes of Israel contained, for the simple reason that very few people see any use for such knowledge. In fact, very few men indeed have any awareness of the real usefulness of this knowledge.

The case is different where we find that for so many consecutive generations one text consistently adds 100 years which are missing in the other and then for the life-span after the birth of a son and heir where there was an excess of 100 years, the excess is subtracted and, where the 100 were missing, they now find a place, thus making the two totals agree. It seems to me to be likely that the scribe who added the 100 years must have been an apostle of the idea that Biblical longevity was the result of the shortness of the ancient year, and that he tried to prove his point by reference to the age of puberty at which procreation becomes possible. It was to help the incredulity of those who found a difficulty in the long life-spans that the scribe wanted to insinuate that 100 Biblical years meant ten of ours. When, however, on his own theory, he found paternity occurring before the age of puberty, all he could do was to add another 100 Biblical years. These, of course, he had to subtract from the life-span after the heir was born, so that the total age would be correct. His purpose was to find plausible ages at which fatherhood was possible, without falsifying the data in regard to total life-spans. The test comes in the sixth generation. There was here no need to make any addition and the scribe made none, which suggests that it was only when his theory called for the additional years that he put them in. In regard to the sixth generation the scribe found in the Hebrew original that Jared was already 162 years old when his son Henoch was born. Even in the theory of the shortness of Biblical years, 162 means that Jared was almost two months more than sixteen years old, and, therefore, old enough for paternity. Hence there was no need to add the 100 Biblical years which would have made Jared twenty-six in our reckoning. And, of course, since nothing was added to the age before Henoch was born, there was no need of a subsequent subtraction. Hence, in this instance, there is no discrepancy between the Hebrew original and the copy of the translation.

Another reason for suspecting this copyist is that in the eighth generation, for the period before Mathusala begot Lamech, while the Hebrew text gives us 182 years, our texts have a number twenty years less, and not, as we would have expected, 100 years more. This twenty is added to the period subsequent to the birth of Lamech to make the same total in both the original and the translation. Actually, there was here no need either to add or to subtract in order to reach an age like seventeen (170 in Biblical numbers) for puberty. The scribe in this case had before him an age sufficient for paternity, which was not so in the cases where he added his 100 years. We might well suppose, therefore, that this discrepancy of twenty years was attributable to a simple copyist's mistake, except that the twenty years subtracted are later carefully added in order to get a correct total. This suggests the possibility that there was here an astute design deliberately to cloak the previous trick of adding and subtracting 100 years, by adding and subtracting, in this case, not 100, but a random number which would keep up the appearance of a system.

All this is open to many interpretations. Whether we suppose or doubt that it happened in this way, or whether even the fact is so or not, one thing seems to me beyond all doubt. It is this. When there is any discrepancy in two versions, since both of them cannot be true to the facts, it is better to believe what we find in the original from which the translations have been made. This is confirmed when translations agree with one another, as in the case of the three Greek, one Latin, and one Syrian translations, that Mathusala died six years before the flood.

Chapter 14

It is now time to examine the evidence which proves convincingly that the Biblical years, so far from being only onetenth as long as ours, were precisely as long as the present solar years. This is true of the years used in giving those extremely long life-spans. It is said, for example, that the flood occurred in the 600th year of Noe's life. But, notice the full text: 'The waters of the flood overflowed the earth in the six hundredth year of the life of Noe, in the second month, in the twenty-seventh day of the month.'[1] Now those words are inexplicable if a year was so short that it took ten of them to make one of ours. That would mean that a year had only thirty-six days. For, so short a year (if it was actually called a year in ancient usage) either had no months at all, or, if it had twelve months, then each month could have had but three

---

[1] Gen. 7.10,11. St. Augustine has twenty-seventh for our seventeenth.

days. How, then, explain the words of the text, 'in the six hundredth year . . . in the second month, in the twenty-seventh day of the month,' unless the months then were the same as they are now. There is no other way of explaining how the flood could be said to have had a beginning on the twenty-seventh day of the second month.

So, too, when the flood was over, we are told: 'And the ark rested in the seventh month, the seven and twentieth day of the month upon the mountains of Armenia. And the waters were going and decreasing until the eleventh month; for in the eleventh month, the first day of the month, the tops of the mountains appeared.'[2] But, if the months were then the same as now, it certainly follows that the years also were the same; for, of course, a three-day month could not have a 'seven and twentieth day.' Or must we say that the thirtieth part of a three-day month was called a 'day,' in order to keep the same proportion? In that case, we would have to conclude that the tremendous deluge which is said to have lasted forty days and forty nights was all over in less than four of our days. Surely, baseless absurdity of this sort is intolerable. This kind of error, which tries to build, on a foundation of false conjecture, faith in our Scriptures only to destroy it, is an error which should have no place among us.

The truth is that the day was then just what it is now, a period measured by the twenty-four hours in the course of a single daytime and nighttime. So, too, a month then was what it is now, a period fixed by the waxing and waning of the moon. The year also was the same then as now, a period of twelve lunar months plus the five days and a quarter required to complete the solar revolution. And it was on the twenty-seventh day of the second month of this kind of a year—which was the 600th of Noe's life—that the flood began; and the forty days of continuous rain which the Scripture records were not 'days' of a little more than two hours but periods of light and darkness each lasting twenty-four hours.

The conclusion is that some men of those ancient times reached an age of more than 900 years and these years were just as long as the years that made up Abraham's age of 170,

and his son Isaac's age of 180, and then Jacob's age of nearly
150 and, some time later, Moses' age of 120, and as long as
the years that, in our time, make up the age of men who live
to be seventy or eighty or a little more and of which last years
it is said, 'most of them are labor and vanity.'[3]

Whatever the discrepancy in the numbers given in the
Hebrew original and in our translations, it does not affect their
agreement in this matter of long life-spans in the early days.
As to the discrepancy, if it is ever so great that both accounts
cannot be true, then we must look for conformity to the facts
in the original text from which our translations derive. And
this is easy enough for anyone in the world who wants to do
it. However, it is worth noticing that no one has in fact presumed to emend the version of the seventy translators in its
many variations from the Hebrew original. The reason is that
the differences have not been considered deliberate falsifica-
tions, and with this view I wholeheartedly concur. Apart
from the errors of copyists, there are discrepancies which may
conform to and even emphasize the truth. In such cases, we
may well believe that the translators were inspired by the divine Spirit to depart deliberately from the original, for along
with their duties as scholars they had rights as prophets.[4]
This explains why the Apostles rightly lend their authority not
only to the Hebrew text but also to the Septuagint, as when
they quote Scriptural texts from the latter. I have already
promised to pursue this matter more carefully, please God, on
some more appropriate occasion. But for the moment I must
draw my present argument to its conclusion. It is this: There
is no reason to doubt that, in an age when the life-span was
so long, a great city could have been built by the first-born
son of the first man, Adam. It was, indeed, merely an earthly
city; it was not that city called the City of God which it is my
main purpose to describe and which moved me to undertake
the toilsome task of writing this very big Book.

[3] For these ages see Gen. 25.7, 35.28, 47.28; Deut. 34.7; Ps. 89.10.
[4] . . . non interpretantium munere, sed prophetantium libertate
aliter dicere voluisse credendum est.

Chapter 15

Further problems of chronology for the period of Cain and Abel are raised in this chapter.

Chapter 16

The first of all marriages was that between the man made out of dust and his mate who had issued from his side. After that, the continuance and increase of the human race demanded births from the union of males and females, even though there were no other human beings except those born of the first two parents. That is why the men took their sisters for wives.

But, of course, just as this is the best thing to do when natural necessity compels it, it becomes all the more wicked when moral obligation condemns it.[1] This can be proved as follows. The supreme human law is love and this law is best respected when men, who both desire and ought to live in harmony, so bind themselves by the bonds of social relationships that no one man monopolizes more than one relationship, and many different relationships are distributed as widely as possible, so that a common social life of the greatest number may best be fostered. Take the two relationships which are implied by the words, 'father' and 'father-in-law.' Now, when a person has one man for a father and a second for his father-in-law, love can reign over a larger number. Adam, however, was obliged to monopolize in his single person this double relationship of love to his sons and daughters when, as brothers and sisters, they became husbands and wives. So, too, Eve, his wife, played the double role of mother and mother-in-law to her children of either sex, whereas, had there been two women available, one to be mother and the other to be mother-in-law, there would have been more strands in the bond of social love. So, too, a sister who had to become a wife was the bearer in her

---

[1] . . . *quod profecto quanto est antiquius conpellente necessitate, tanto postea factum est damnabilius religione prohibente.* The translation takes *antiquius* in its classical meaning of 'better' or 'preferable.'

single person of two relationships of love. If these had been borne by two different persons, one a sister and the other a wife, then a greater number of persons would have had a share in the love of kinship. But there was then no possibility for this increase, since the only human beings were the brothers and sisters born of the first two parents.

But, as soon as, with an increased population, it became possible for men to choose wives who were not their sisters, they were bound by the law of love to do so. Thus, once there was no necessity for the old arrangement, it ceased to have any moral validity. The reason is that the grandchildren of the first pair could now choose cousins for their wives, and, if they continued to marry sisters, then not merely two but three relationships of love which ought to be distributed would have been concentrated in a single person, in disregard for the duty of each to respect the right of love to have itself diffused, so that one love may hold together as many persons as possible. For, in this case, one person would be in relation to his own children—to a brother and sister become man and wife—not only as father and father-in-law but also as uncle; and his sister-wife, in relation to his and her children, would be mother and aunt and mother-in-law; and the children of a brother and sister would be in relation to one another not only as brothers and sisters, and husbands and wives, but also as cousins. Now, instead of concentrating three relationships in a single person, there could have been nine relationships of love diffused over nine persons, so that a man could have been linked in love to one person as his sister, to another as his wife, to a third as his cousin, to a fourth as his father, to a fifth as his uncle, to a sixth as his father-in-law, to a seventh as his mother, to an eighth as his aunt, and to a ninth as his mother-in-law. Thus, the love which holds kindred together, instead of being narrowed to a few, could have opened its arms to embrace a greater number of people spread over a far wider area.

Now that the human race has increased and multiplied, we find this law of love well observed even among the pagan worshipers of many and false gods. There are, indeed, occasional perversions of law which allow brothers and sisters to marry, yet by custom men's lives are so much better than these laws that such license is utterly repudiated; so that, allowable as it was in the very earliest ages to marry one's sister, the practice is today just as abominated as though it could never have been permitted. In general, custom has great power both in provoking and preventing the play of human passion. In this matter, custom keeps concupiscence in bounds and, therefore, any detraction from or destruction of custom is branded as criminal. Thus, unjust as it is to encroach, out of greed, on another's property, it is still more wicked to transgress, out of lust, the limits of established morals. In fact, I have noticed how rarely custom allows even in our days what is permissible in law, namely, marriages between first cousins, who are the nearest in consanguinity after brothers and sisters. The divine law has not forbidden this nor, so far, has human law. Nevertheless, custom has disapproved of something that is right, simply because it is too near to what is wrong. After all, a marriage with a cousin looks almost like one with a sister; because, by custom, cousins who are so closely related are called brothers and sisters; and they almost are so.

It is true that our ancestors had a religious regard for kinship and, being afraid that it might be lessened and lost in the course of successive generations, they tried to hold on to it by the bond of marriage and, as it were, to call it back before it got too far away. So it was that, when the world was fully populated and there was no more marrying of sisters or half-sisters, people still preferred to marry within their own clan. No one, however, can doubt that the modern attitude toward the marriage even of cousins is morally sounder. First, there is the argument I have already outlined, namely, that it is socially right to multiply and distribute relationships of love and wrong to have one person needlessly monopolizing two relationships which could be distributed to two persons and thus increase the community of kinship. There is also the argument from that indefinably precious modesty of our human nature which makes even the purest of parents to blush over the element of lust in the generative act and which bridles this desire when a double respect is due to a partner by reason of close consanguinity.

The union of male and female is, then, so far as mortal living goes, the seed-bed, so to speak, from which a city must grow; but, while the city of earth needs only human generation, the City of heaven demands a spiritual regeneration to escape from the taint of the generative act. Of this regeneration, whether in the period before the flood there was any material and visible sign (like the circumcision which was later enjoined on Abraham) or, if so, what that sign was, Scripture does not tell us. Scripture does say, however, that those earliest men offered sacrifice to God, and we have clear examples of this in the case of the first two brothers. It is related, too, of Noe that he offered victims to God as soon as he issued from the ark after the flood. On this matter of sacrifices, I have pointed out in some of the previous Books that the reason why the demons, who arrogate to themselves divinity and seek to be recognized as gods, demand sacrifices and delight in such worship is that they know that true sacrifice is due to the true God.

Chapter 17

Adam, then, was the ultimate father of two lines of succession, one of which was that of the earthly city and the other was that of the heavenly City. But, from the time when the death of Abel revealed itself as a marvelous symbol of the persecuted City of God, each of the two lines had its own father, Cain being father of the one and Seth of the other. It was in their sons who were to be mentioned in Scripture that we begin to see more clearly the specific characteristics of the two cities as they appear in this mortal life.

Cain became the father of Henoch and gave Henoch's name to the city he built. It was a city of earth, at home and not in exile in the world, a city satisfied with such temporal peace and joy as is possible here. Note that the name Cain means 'ownership,' which explains what was said at the time of his birth by his father or mother: 'I have come into possession of a man through God.'[1] So, too, Henoch means 'dedication'; because the city of earth is dedicated to earth, it possesses here

[1] Cf. Gen. 4.1.

the ultimate good it wants and strives to get. Seth on the other hand, means 'resurrection,' and the name of his son Enos means 'man.' The name Adam also means 'man,' but in Hebrew it can be used for any human person, either male or female, as one can see from the text: 'He created them male and female; and blessed them and called their name Adam.'[2] This text leaves no doubt that Eve was given her proper name, whereas the common noun, 'adam,' or 'human being,' applied to both Adam and Eve. It was different with the name Enos. This means 'man,' Hebrew scholars tell us, in the sense of a man as distinguished from a woman. Thus, Enos was a 'son' of 'resurrection,' and in the resurrection 'they neither marry nor take wives,'[3] for there is no generation where regeneration leads to resurrection. That is why, I think, it is not irrelevant to remark that, although 'sons and daughters' were born in the generations that sprang from Seth, no name of any woman is mentioned; whereas, among the descendants of Cain, we find that at the very end of the line, the last name mentioned is that of a woman. The text runs: 'Mathusael begot Lamech, who took two wives: the name of one was Ada, and the name of the other Sella. And Ada brought forth Jabel: who was the father of such as dwell in tents, and of herdsmen. And his brother's name was Jubal: he was the father of them that play upon the harp and the organs. Sella also brought forth Tubalcain, who was a hammerer and artificer in every work of brass and iron. And the sister of Tubalcain was Noema.'[4] This is as far as the line of descent from Cain is carried. There are eight generations in all, including Adam. The seventh is that of Lamech, who was the husband of two wives; the eighth is that of his children, among whom is the woman who is mentioned by name. What is here delicately intimated is that to the very end of its existence the earthly city will be propagated by physical births proceeding from the union of the sexes. That is why we are given the proper names of the wives of the last man mentioned as begetting children—a practice unheard of before the flood, except in the case of Eve.

There is likewise a symbolical interpretation of the fact

[2] Gen. 5.2.   [3] Luke 20.35.
[4] Gen. 4.18–22.

that Cain means 'ownership' and Henoch means 'dedication.'
'Ownership' was the originator of the city of earth and 'dedication' was the name given when the building ended—as
though to indicate that both in its oirgin and end that city is
earthly, that in the earthly city there is nothing to be hoped
for beyond the things that can be seen in the world of time.
Contrast this with the name of Seth, which means 'resurrection.' 'Resurrection' is the father of those generations which
are mentioned apart from the others. That is why we must
examine more closely what is said in sacred history of the 'son
of resurrection.'

Chapters 18–19

*These chapters suggest symbolic interpretations of the
names of Seth, Abel, Enos, and Henoch. They are of some
importance in determining the extent of Augustine's knowledge of Hebrew.*

Chapter 20

Someone will ask the question: What was the intention of
the writer of sacred history in mentioning the generations that
descended from Cain, and how far did he intend to continue
that line of succession? For, surely, his primary intention was
to follow the line of Adam through Seth as far as Noe, in
whose time the flood occurred, and then to resume the line
of succession as far as Abraham, from whom Matthew traces
the line which ends in Christ, the eternal King of the City of
God.

To one part of the question—How far did the writer intend
to continue the line of Cain?—the answer is: As far as the flood.
It was by this that the whole population of the city of earth
was destroyed, to be replaced, however, by some of the
descendants of Noe, because the city of earth, the society of
men who live according to man, cannot be completely depopu-
lated until the end of that world which our Lord had in mind
when He said: 'The children of this world marry and are given

in marriage.'[1] In contrast to this, it is by regeneration that the City of God, at the end of its pilgrimage in this world, will enter another world whose children neither marry nor are given in marriage.

In this present world, of course, marrying and being born are common to both cities. However, many thousands of those who are in the City of God on earth abstain from the function of human generation; in fact, there are some in the other city who erringly follow this example. Among these are some of the heretics who have fallen from the faith of the City of God into the city of man and now live according to man and not according to God. There are also the 'gymnosophists,' those naked philosophers in the solitudes of India who abstain both from eating food and begetting children. I said 'erringly,' because such abstention is not good in itself, but only when inspired by faith in God, who is the Supreme Good. There is no evidence that anyone before the flood practiced such continence, not even Henoch himself, who was in the seventh generation after Adam, and who was taken away to God without dying. Thus Henoch, before this 'translation,' became the father of sons and daughters and, particularly, of Mathusala who continued the series of recorded generations.

But why, then, it will be asked, if the line of Cain was meant to end with the flood and if there was none of that long period of impuberty that was supposed to make procreation impossible for a hundred years or more, why are so few generations mentioned in the line of Cain? In the case of the line of succession from Seth, the sacred writer clearly intended to trace the direct succession as far as Noe and then to resume the direct line and continue it; but, if there was no such intention in regard to the line from Cain, what need was there to pass in review the first-born sons and so come to Lamech and his children in whom the line ends? This was the eighth generation from Adam and the seventh from Cain. But, surely, there was no way for the writer to find any connecting link which could allow him to continue the line down to the time when the people of Israel in the terrestrial Jerusalem served as a prophetic type of the heavenly City; or, still less, to continue

[1] Luke 20.34.

the line as far as 'the Christ, according to the flesh, who is, over all things, God blessed forever,'[2] the Maker and Monarch of the heavenly Jerusalem. What, then, could possibly have been the writer's intention, since, as a fact, the complete posterity of Cain was destroyed in the deluge? It is evident that in this succession from Cain it is the first-born sons who are listed. Why, then, are there so few of them? There must have been more than seven generations between Cain and the flood, unless we suppose either that in those days lateness of puberty was in proportion to longevity, or that those early fathers abstained from procreation for the first hundred years. But, if we assume that, on an average, they were thirty years old when they became fathers, then the eight generations from Adam to Lamech and his children give us eight times thirty or only 240 years. Must we then suppose that, after that and until the flood, they produced no more children? And if we must not, why in the world was the writer unwilling to mention these subsequent generations? Just think, from Adam to the flood there were 2,262 years according to the calculation from the data in our versions of the Scripture; or, if we use the Hebrew original, 1,656. Even supposing the lesser number is the more accurate, and subtracting 240 from 1,656, we have more than 1,400 left before the flood. Now, can anyone believe that during all those years the whole posterity of Cain could have abstained from procreation?

If anyone is disturbed by this argumentation, let him remember what I said when I discussed the difficulty of believing that primitive men could have abstained so long from procreation. I said there are two solutions. One is to suppose that their puberty was late in proportion to their longevity. The other is that the sons mentioned in the genealogies are not the eldest sons but those in the direct line leading to the particular descendant whom the writer has in mind, as, for example, Noe in the descent from Seth. If it is a fact that the writer had no intention of reaching a particular person by substituting picked persons in the direct line for first-born sons, then, of course, we must fall back on the hypothesis of late puberty. In that case, we must suppose that the men only became capable of fatherhood at some age over 100, that the line of succession was through the first-born, and that eight generations were enough to fill the long period up to the flood.

There is, however, another possibility. There may have been some hidden reason, which escapes me, why the sacred writer should have traced the line of succession in what I have called the earthly city as far as Lamech and his children and then have left the succeeding generations down to the deluge to go unmentioned. There may be a reason, too, why the line of succession was not traced through the first-born sons, namely, that the city which Cain founded and called Henoch may have developed into a far-flung kingdom under a single king reigning for his whole life and then leaving his heir as his successor. Of these kings Cain would have been the first and his son Henoch, whose name was given to the city where he was to reign, the second; the third, Henoch's son Gaidad; the fourth, Gaidad's son Mevia; the fifth, Mevia's son Mathusael; the sixth, Mathusael's son Lamech, who was in the seventh generation from Adam through Cain.

In this supposition there is no need for the hypothesis of delayed puberty, since there was no need to have first-born sons succeeding their fathers. The successors could have been chosen on a basis of worth in terms of usefulness to the earthly city, or they could have been chosen by lot, or the best-loved son of his father may have had a kind of right of succession to the throne. There is, here, no difficulty about Lamech being alive and reigning at the time the flood occurred and destroyed him and all others, with the exception of those in the ark. Nor is there any difficulty in the fact that the number of generations in the two lines is different—seven from Cain and ten from Seth—considering the length of time from the beginning to the flood and the great variation of individual ages. Lamech, then, as I said, was in the seventh generation in his line from Adam, and Noe in the tenth in his. The reason why, in the special case of Lamech, several sons are mentioned is that it was not certain which of his sons would succeed if he had died and there was time enough before the flood for another reign.

But, whatever may have been the arrangement in regard

to the line of succession from Cain, whether it went by primogeniture or by chosen kings, there is one circumstance which seems to me so important that it must be mentioned, namely, that, besides Lamech, whose name was listed seventh after Adam, there were enough names mentioned, including the three sons and one daughter, to bring the total up to eleven, the number which is a symbol of sin. The wives, too, may have some meaning beyond the one I am at present suggesting in connection with the line of succession, but in this connection the names of the wives are irrelevant. My point is that, just as law in general, and the Decalogue in particular, is symbolized by the number ten, so the number eleven which goes beyond ten, *transgreditur denarium*, stands for a transgression of the law and, therefore, for sin. This explains why the number of haircloth curtains prescribed to cover the top of the tabernacle of the testimony, of that traveling temple, so to speak, of the people of God in their wanderings, was eleven.[3] The haircloth, made of goats' hair, was a reminder of sins because of the goats that were to be kept on the left. So, too, when we confess our sins, we kneel down in haircloth as though to express the thought in the psalm: 'And my sin is ever before me.'[4]

Thus, it is that the descendants of Adam through Cain, the transgressor, end on the number eleven, the symbol for transgression. And, as the last in that number is a woman, so was it by a woman that the first sin was committed, the one which brought death to us all. But, the first consequence that followed the committing of that sin was the concupiscence of the flesh, the pleasure which resists our spirit. Now, Noema was the daughter of Lamech, and her name means 'pleasure.'

On the contrary, it is the number ten, symbol of law, that is linked with the line from Adam through Seth to Noe. Noe had three sons and, though one of them sinned, the other two were blessed. Discounting the sinner and adding the two who were blessed to the number ten, we get twelve, the number which has been made significant by connection with both the Patriarchs and the Apostles, and also by the fact that, as you

[3] Exod. 26.7.   [4] Ps. 50.51.

get seven by adding four and three, so you get twelve by multiplying them.

That is all I need say on this point. The next matter to be mentioned and discussed is how the two lines of succession, which at first were kept distinct and so symbolized the respective cities of the worldly and the regenerate, later became so mingled and indistinguishable that the whole human race, with the exception of eight persons, deserved to perish in the deluge.

Chapter 21

The first point to notice is this. In giving the line of succession from Cain, the first name mentioned before all others is that of Henoch, the son whose name was given to the city, and then the line is continued to the last name, which I have spoken of, that is, until both Cain's direct line and all his other descendants were swept away by the flood. It is different with the line of Seth. As soon as the name of one son has been mentioned, namely, Enos, and before continuing the genealogy to the flood, the narrative interposes the following clause: 'This is the book of the generation of Adam. In the day that God created man he made him to the likeness of God. He created them male and female; and blessed them and called their name Adam in the day when they were created.'[1]

The reason for this break was, I take it, that the writer, as though bidden by God, was unwilling to have the beginning of world chronology reckoned from the earthly city, and so he deliberately went back to Adam for a new beginning.[2] If we ask why this return to recapitulate was made immediately after mentioning Seth's son, the man who hoped to call upon the name of the Lord God, the answer must be that this was the proper way to present the two cities. The one begins and ends with a murderer, for Lamech, too, as he admitted to his two wives, was a murderer. The other City begins with the

[1] Gen. 5.1,2.
[2] Taking the reading of E. Hoffmann (CSEL), *tamquam eum Deus sic commoneret, ut non conputaret,* not the reading, *tamquam eam deus sic commemoraret.*

man who hoped to call upon the name of the Lord God, for the invocation of God is the whole and the highest preoccupation of the City of God during its pilgrimage in this world and it is symbolized in the one 'man' (Enos) born of the 'resurrection' (Seth) of the man who was slain (Abel). That one man, in fact, is a symbol of the unity of the whole heavenly City, which is not yet in the fullness which it is destined to reach, and which is adumbrated in this prophetic figure.

The son of Cain, that is, the son of 'possession'—and, of course, possession means earthly possession—this son of Cain is welcome to have a name in the earthly city which was founded in his name, for that city is peopled with the kind who are spoken of in the psalm: 'They have called lands by their own names,'[3] and who, therefore, suffer the consequences mentioned in another psalm: 'Lord, in thy city thou wilt bring their image to naught.'[4] But, meanwhile, let the son of Seth, the son of 'resurrection,' hope to call on the name of the Lord God, seeing that he prefigures that human society that can say of itself: 'But I, like a blooming olive tree in the house of God have put my trust in the mercy of God.'[5] Let him not seek the empty renown of a famous name on earth, because 'Blessed is the man who has put his trust in the Lord and has no regard for vanities and lying follies.'[6]

The chronology of the two cities is begun only when both cities have been presented to the reader as issuing from that single gate of our mortality which Adam opened. One is the city of 'belongings' here in this world; the other is the City of 'longings' for God.[7] Once started on their way, they take different roads, each to the proper doom or destiny it deserves. One undated sequence of generations is given, but all generations are traced back to Adam, out of whom, as out of a single mass of damaged clay thrown on a waste-heap, God fashions two kinds of pottery: the vessels fashioned by His wrath and fit only for contempt and the vessels made by His mercy and meant to be honored. To the former He pays in punishment

---

[3] Ps. 48.12. [4] Cf. Ps. 72.20.
[5] Cf. Ps. 51.10. [6] Cf. Ps. 39.5.
[7] . . . una in re huius saeculi, altera in spe Dei.

the doom they earn; to the latter He bestows, as a gift of grace, a destiny they never could have deserved. God's purpose in this is that the heavenly City, during its exile on earth, by contrasting itself with the vessels of wrath, should learn not to expect too much from the freedom of the power of choice, but should trust in the 'hope to call upon the name of the Lord God.' It is true, indeed, that the human will resides in a nature that was created good because its Creator is good, but that nature is mutable even though its Maker is immutable, for the simple reason that it was made out of nothing. Therefore, when the will turns from the good and does evil, it does so by the freedom of its own choice, but when it turns from evil and does good, it does so only with the help of God.

Chapters 22–27

Additional problems of Old Testament interpretation are now considered. The seduction of the 'sons of God' by the beauty of women leads to a discussion of bodily beauties. They are good but can be loved both well and ill. The notion that giants are the offspring of angels and women is rejected. Certain chronological difficulties in the account of the flood and the period of Noe are then reviewed. The meaning of divine anger is explained, as is Noe's ark as a symbol of the Church.

BOOK XVI

The City of God from the Flood to King David

Chapter 1

AFTER THE FLOOD, do the traces of the holy City continue unbroken, or were they so interrupted by periods of unholiness that not a single worshiper of the true God remained? It is difficult to discover any clear answer to this question in the revelations of Holy Scripture. The fact is that in the canonical books, for the period from Noe (who was saved in the ark from the waste of waters, along with his wife, their three sons, and their wives) to Abraham, there is only one clearly revealed testimony of religious virtue. This one exception is that Noe praised his sons, Sem and Japheth, with a prophetic blessing, when he foresaw in a vision events that were to happen long afterwards. In this connection, it will be recalled that, when his second son—the one younger than the first-born but older than the other—had sinned against his father, he was not cursed in his own person but in that of his son, Noe's grandson, and in these words: 'Cursed be Chanaan, a servant of servants shall he be unto his brethren.'[1] Now, Chanaan was the son of Cham, who, instead of covering the nakedness of his sleeping father, had revealed it. There is also a prophetic sense, veiled by symbols, in the words that follow, when Noe blessed his oldest and youngest sons: 'Blessed be the Lord God of Sem, be Chanaan his servant. May God enlarge Japheth, and may he dwell in the tents of Sem.'[2] The same is true of Noe's planting of the vineyard, his inebriation from wine, his nakedness while asleep, and the rest of what happened and is recorded in this connection.

Chapters 2-6

These chapters offer a detailed treatment of the immediate descendants of Noe, of the meaning of the tower of Babel and

[1] Gen. 9.25.   [2] Gen. 9.26,27.

*the confusion of languages, and of how God 'spoke' to ancient
men.*

Chapter 7

A question arises how wild animals, propagated by ordinary
mating, like wolves and the rest, can be found on the islands
far at sea, unless those which were destroyed by the flood were
replaced by others descended from the animals, male and female, which were saved in the ark. (There is no problem in
regard to domestic animals or to those which, like frogs, spring
directly from the soil.) One hypothesis is that they swam to
the islands, but only to those that were near. But there are
some islands so far from the continental mainland that it seems
impossible that any of the animals could have swum there. Of
course, there is nothing incredible in the supposition that men
captured the animals and took them with them and bred them
for the sake of hunting. Another possibility is that, by the command or permission of God and with the help of angels, the
animals could have been transferred to the islands. Another
hypothesis would be that they sprang up from the earth, as
they sprang up in the beginning when God said: 'Let the earth
produce a living soul.'[1] In this case, if the earth produced the
many animals in islands which could not be reached, it becomes clearer than ever that the purpose of all the animals
in the ark was less for the sake of replenishing the stock of
animals than for the sake of prefiguring the mystery of the
Church which was to be composed of so many peoples.

Chapter 8

A further question arises whether it was from one of the
sons of Noe or from Adam himself that human monsters have
sprung. At any rate, the history of many peoples records that
there have been, for example, beings with one eye in the middle of their forehead, and others with feet growing backwards;
the Hermaphrodites with the left side of their chest like a

[1] Cf. Gen. 1.24.

woman's and the right side like a man's and who exercise in turn the male and female functions in begetting and bearing offsprings; others, who have no mouths, breathe only through their ears and live on air; others, no more than a few feet high, are called Pygmies, from the Greek word *pygmé* meaning an arm's length; others, whose women conceive when they are five and die before they are eight years old. They also speak of a people who have but one leg with two feet and who can run with remarkable speed without bending a knee. They are called Sciopodes because they lie on their backs in the summer and they keep the sun off with their feet. There are others who are neckless and with eyes in their shoulders; and so for the other kinds of men or near-men who are depicted in the mosaic to be seen in the square near the seafront at Carthage, all of which are taken from books dealing with the history of curiosities. I do not know whether I should mention the Cynocephalae, whose dog-like heads and barking voices prove they are more like animals than men. There is no need to believe that species like these are human, even though they are called men. What is true for a Christian beyond the shadow of a doubt is that every real man, that is, every mortal animal that is rational, however unusual to us may be the shape of his body, or the color of his skin, or the way he walks, or the sound of his voice, and whatever the strength, portion or quality of his natural endowments, is descended from the single first-created man.

What is clear, however, is that nature produces a normal type for the most part, and a thing is wonderful only because it is rare. If whole peoples have been monsters, we must explain the phenomenon as we explain the individual monsters who are born among us. God is the Creator of all; He knows best where and when and what is, or was, best for Him to create, since He deliberately fashioned the beauty of the whole out of both the similarity and dissimilarity of its parts.

The trouble with a person who does not see the whole is that he is offended by the ugliness of a part because he does not know its context or relation to the whole.

I know men who were born with more than five fingers or toes, which is one of the slightest variations from the normal, but it would be a shame for anyone to be so silly as to suppose that, because he did not know why God did this, the Creator could make a mistake in regard to the number of fingers on a man's hand. Even in cases of greater variations, God knows what He is doing and no one may rightly blame His work. Near Hippo Zaritus there is a man with feet shaped like a crescent and with only two toes on each; the same is true of his hands. If some whole race should be born like that, they would add a chapter to the history of rare curiosities. Should that be a reason, then, for saying that the race was not derived from the first created human being?

There are those who are half-men, half-women, the so-called Hermaphrodites. They are born very rarely, but there is hardly ever a period but some creature is born so like both a man and a woman that no one is sure from which sex the name should be taken, even though it is usual to call the person a man on the ground that the male is the stronger sex. Certainly, no one ever refers to them as though they were women.

Not many years ago, within living memory, a person was born in the East who had two heads, two chests, four hands, as though he were two persons, but one stomach, and two feet, as though he were one. And he lived long enough and the case was so well known that many people went to see the wonder.

It would be impossible to list all the human offspring who have been very different from the parents from whom they were certainly born. Still, all these monsters undeniably owe their origin to Adam. The same is true of whole nations. However abnormal they are in their variation from the bodily shape that all or nearly all men have, if they still fall within the definition of men as being rational and mortal animals, we have to admit that they are of the stock of the first father of all men—always supposing, of course, the truth of what is told about peoples who are so different among themselves and so different from us. For, if we did not know that apes, monkeys and baboons are not humans, but animals, historians, eager to show off the curiosity of their knowledge, might falsely and with impunity describe them as human. Let us suppose, however, that the monsters that have been reported are human.

Why could God not will so to create certain whole peoples that, when monsters are born from human parents, we should not imagine that His wisdom in making human nature had failed Him, as though His were the art of an unskilled craftsman.

It need not seem inconceivable to us, then, that, just as there are individual monsters in every nation, so there might be whole nations of monsters in the totality of mankind. However, to bring this discussion to a somewhat hesitating and cautious conclusion, I shall only say: Either the accounts of the whole nations of monsters are valueless; or, if there are such monsters, they are not human; or, if they are human, then they have sprung from Adam.

Chapter 9

As to the nonsense about there being *antipodae*, that is to say, men living on the far side of the earth, where the sun rises when it sets for us, men who have their feet facing ours when they walk—that is utterly incredible. No one pretends to have any factual information, but a hypothesis is reached by the argument that, since the earth is suspended between the celestial hemispheres and since the universe must have a similar lowest and central point, therefore the other portion of the earth which is below us cannot be without human inhabitants.

One flaw in the argument is that, even if the universe could be proved by reasoning to be shaped like a round globe—or at least believed to be so—it does not follow that the other hemisphere of the earth must appear above the surface of the ocean; or if it does, there is no immediate necessity why it should be inhabited by men. First of all, our Scriptures never deceive us, since we can test the truth of what they have told us by the fulfillment of predictions; second, it is utterly absurd to say that any men from this side of the world could sail across the immense tract of the ocean, reach the far side, and then people it with men sprung from the single father of all mankind.

Let us be content, then, to limit our search for the citizens of the pilgrim City of God on earth to those races of men which, as we have seen, were made up of the seventy-two nations, each with its own language. The City pursued this pilgrimage as far as the flood and the ark, and its progress among the sons of Noe is revealed in the blessings they were granted. Trying to find this City, if we can, we turn especially to the eldest of those sons, to Sem, seeing that the blessing given to Japheth was that he was to dwell in the houses of his brother.

Chapter 10

We must keep before our eyes, then, the succession of generations beginning with Sem if we are to follow the fortune of the City of God subsequent to the flood, as we have seen it before the flood in the series of generations beginning with Seth. That is why Holy Scripture, once it has revealed the earthly city of Babylon (that is to say, of disorder) returns to the patriarch Sem and, after a short summary, follows the generations from Sem to Abraham, indicating the year in which each heir was born and the number of years his father continued to live.

In this connection, something to which I have already alluded[1] can be certainly recognized, namely, the explanation of the expression used in connection with the sons of Heber: 'The name of the one was Phaleg, because in his days the earth was divided.'[2] For, what else are we to understand by this division of the earth if not the division effected by the diversity of tongues? The other sons of Sem are passed over as irrelevant in this connection and only those are linked to Phaleg in the series of generations who were in the direct line of succession leading to Abraham. In much the same way, before the flood, only those were mentioned who were in the direct line of succession that stretched from the son of Adam called Seth to Noe. That is why the new genealogy is introduced with the words: 'These are the generations from Sem. Sem was a son a hundred years old when he became the father of Arphaxad in the second year after the flood. And after becoming the father of Arphaxad, Sem lived 500 years, begetting sons and

[1] Bk. 16.3.　　　　　　　　[2] Gen. 10.25.

daughters, and then he died.'[3] And so with the others, Scripture mentions the age at which each one begot the son who was in the direct line to Abraham, and then how long each continued to live, adding the note that he begot other sons and daughters. The point of this is that it helps us to understand how the population could increase so greatly and saves us from childishly wondering how from the few descendants of Sem who are mentioned such large areas of whole kingdoms could be populated—in particular, the Assyrian Empire, whose ruler, the famous Ninus, conquered the Eastern peoples far and wide and reigned with immense success over a realm so broad and strong that, when he left it to his heirs, it continued for a long time to come.

Not to make our narrative too long, we shall neglect the numbers of years each lived and mention only the ages at which each begot the heir who continued the line, so that thus we may calculate the number of years from the flood to Abraham. Other matters we may touch on briefly and in passing if some special pertinence requires it.

So, then, in the second year after the flood Sem begot Arphaxad; and Arphaxad at the age of 135 begot Cainan, who was 130 when Sale was born; and Sale was the same age when he begot Heber. Heber was 134 when Phaleg was born, and its was in Phaleg's days that the earth was divided. Phaleg himself was 130 years old when he became the father of Reu, who was 130 when he begot Sarug, who was 130 when Nachor was born; and Nachor was seventy-nine when Thare was born; Thare was seventy when he begot Abram, whose name was later changed by God to Abraham.

Thus, in all, from the flood to Abraham, we have 1,072 years, according to the Latin translation of the Septuagint. It is said that in the Hebrew text, however, the number of years given is far smaller—which is very difficult, if not impossible, to explain.

When we seek for the traces of the City of God among the seventy-two nations, we cannot say that, during the time when there continued to be one tongue or way of speaking, the human race had departed so far from the worship of the true

[3] Cf. Gen. 11.10,11.

God that true religion was confined solely to those who were in the direct succession from Sem, through Arphaxad, to Abraham. What is certain is that the society of the wicked made an appearance in that overwhelming effort to reach heaven by the tower which is the very symbol of godless pride. It may have made its first appearance then; or it may have had a latent existence earlier; or the two cities may have had a continuous history from the time of Noe's sons, the one City in the sons who were blessed and their posterity, the other in the son who was cursed and his posterity, among whom was born the giant, the hunter against God. However, a decisive judgment in this matter is difficult. What seems highly credible to me is that among the sons even of the two who were blessed and even before men began to build Babylon there were, probably, those who despised God and that among the descendants of Cham there were some who worshiped God. We ought to believe that at no time was the world without both kinds of men. At any rate, on both occasions when we meet the words of the Psalmist, 'All men have failed and become useless; there is no one who does good, not one,'[4] we also read: 'Shall not all they know that work iniquity, who devour my people as they eat bread.' This proves that at that time there was a people of God. Yet, the previous words, 'There is no one who does good, not one,' are said of the sons of men, not of the sons of God. Note the preceding words: 'God looked down from heaven on the children of men, to see if there were any that did understand, or did seek God,'[5] and then the words that follow prove that all the sons of man, that is, all who belong to the city that lives according to men and not according to God are reprobate.

Chapters 11–16

Hebrew is thought to be the original language of man. The period of Abraham and the promises made to him are reviewed.

[4] Cf. Ps. 13.3,4; 52.5.   [5] Ps. 52.3.

Chapter 17

About this time, there were three famous pagan empires, the Achaian,[1] the Egyptian and the Assyrian, in which the city of the world, the society of man living with purely human purposes under the domination of the traitor-angels, played an important part. Of those empires, the Assyrian was by far the most powerful and the most prominent. In fact, the well-known ruler Ninus, son of Belus, had subdued the whole of Asia except India; and by Asia I mean, not just what is now the Roman province of Asia, but the whole continent of Asia which is sometimes reckoned as a half or, more commonly, as a third of the whole world which consists of Asia, Europe and Africa.

These three continents are not equal in size. Continental Asia stretches far to the south, to the east and to the north; Europe, to the north and west; Africa, to the west and south. Thus, Europe and Africa together take up one half of the world and Asia the other. Africa is divided from Europe by the great oceanic gulf whose waters bathe both shores and which forms our Great Sea.[2] Hence, if the great circle of land is divided into East and West, Asia occupies the one half while Europe and Africa the other.

Hence, the reason why the empire of the Achaians one of the great three, was not subject to Assyria, was because Achaia was in Europe; but it is not obvious why Egypt did not fall under the Assyrians, who are reported to have ruled over the whole of Asia except India.

It was in Assyria, then, that the domination of the godless city was at its height. The capital was Babylon—the best of all names for the city of the earth-born, since Babylon means 'confusion.' It was there that Ninus ruled after the death of his father, Belus, whose reign lasted sixty-five years. When the father died, his son, Ninus, succeeded to the empire and reigned fifty-two years in the forty-third of which Abraham

[1] The Sicyonians, as St. Augustine calls them, lived in Achaia. Cf. below, 18.2.
[2] The Mediterranean.

was born. This was about 1,200 years before the founding of Rome—which, if I may say so, was to be a second Babylon in the West.

Chapters 18–40

These chapters continue with the Biblical history of the Jews, from the period of Abraham to Jacob's journey into Egypt. Many names and events are interpreted as foreshadowing the coming of Christ and as illustrations of the course of the heavenly City.

Chapter 41

It is because the City of God in its present earthly pilgrimages is found in the people of Christ that we are tracing the genealogy of Christ. Beginning with Abraham and neglecting the sons of his concubines, we come to Isaac; in the line of Isaac, by passing over Esau (also called Edom), we reach Jacob (also called Israel); in the line of Israel, passing over other sons, we come to Juda; and it was from the tribe of Juda that Christ sprang. It is for this reason that we must hear how Israel in Egypt, when he was about to die, blessed his sons and in doing so pronounced a prophetic blessing over Juda: 'Juda thy brethren shall praise thee; thy hand shall be on the neck of thy enemies; the sons of thy father shall bow down to thee. Juda is a lion's whelp; from the prey thou hast gone up, my son. Resting thou hast couched as a lion and as a lioness; who shall rouse him? A leader shall not be taken away from Juda, nor a ruler from his thigh till those things come that are laid up for him, and he shall be the expectation of the nations. Tying his foal to the vine, and his ass's colt to the choicest vine, he shall wash his robe in wine, his garment in the blood of the grape. His eyes are red from wine, his teeth whiter than milk.'[1]

In my work *Against Faustus the Manichaean*,[2] I have commented on these words sufficiently, I think, to make the truth

[1] Gen. 49.8–12.
[2] *Contra Faustum Manichaeum.*

of this prophecy clear. In the word 'couched' we have a prediction of the death of Christ; in the expression, 'as a lion,' we see the death as being by the power of choice and not of necessity. This is the power of choice which He Himself speaks of in the Gospel: 'I lay down my life that I may take it up again. No one takes it from me, but I lay it down of myself. I have the power to lay it down, and I have the power to take it up again.'[3] And what He said, like a lion 'roused' from sleep, He fulfilled, for there is a reference to His power in the prediction of His Resurrection contained in the words: 'Who shall rouse him.' They imply the answer: 'No man, but only He Himself who said of His body: "destroy this temple, and in three days I will raise it up." '[4] In the preceding words, 'thou art gone up,' we can see foretold the kind of death He suffered high on the Cross. In the next words, 'Resting thou hast couched,' we have predicted what the Evangelist describes in the words: 'And bowing his head, he gave up his spirit.'[5] Or if not this, then certainly the reference is to His burial, for in the tomb He rested sleeping, and from it He rose as from sleep. No man raised Him, as Prophets have raised some men and as He himself raised others. 'He shall wash his robe in wine' is a prediction that He cleanses from sin in His blood, the mysterious power of which blood is known to those who are baptized. Hence, too, the words that follow: 'and his garment in the blood of the grape.' What is this 'garment' but the Church? And 'his eyes are red from wine' means that these eyes full of His spirit have been inebriated by His chalice, of which the Psalmist sings: 'And thy chalice that inebriates, how excellent it is.'[6] The following words, 'his teeth whiter than milk,' anticipate what the Apostle says of Christ: 'I fed you with milk,' meaning the nourishing words given to the 'little ones in Christ' who were not yet ready for solid food.

It is Christ, in whom the promises were made to Juda provisionally so that, 'until He came that is to be sent,' there would never be lacking in the race of Israel princes in the sense of kings of Israel. 'And he shall be the expectation of the nations' is too clear to the reader to call for any explanation.

[3] John 10.17,18.
[5] John 19.30.
[4] John 2.19.
[6] Cf. Ps. 22.5.

Chapter 42

We have seen that the two sons of Isaac, Esau and Jacob, were prophetic symbols of two peoples, the Jews and the Christians, although in terms of physical genealogy it was not the Jews but the Idumeans who were descended from Esau, and it was the Jews rather than the Christians who came from Jacob. Strictly speaking, it is only in regard to the text, 'The elder shall serve the younger,' that the symbolic application holds. Now, there is a similar symbolic foreshadowing of Jews and Christians in the two sons of Joseph, the elder being a type of the former and the younger of the latter. Jacob blessed the two boys, but in doing so he held his right hand above the younger who was at his left and his left hand over the elder who was on the right. This caused some concern to Joseph, and to correct the mistake he pointed out to Jacob which of the sons was the elder. Jacob, however, refused to change the position of his hands, but said: 'I know, my son, I know. He too shall become a people; he too shall be great; but his younger brother shall be greater than he, and his descendants shall become a multitude of nations.'[1]

What Jacob is here doing is to point to the two famous promises. For, one of the sons is to be the father of a 'people' and the other of a 'multitude of nations,' and nothing could be clearer than that these two promises refer to the people of Israel and the whole world filled with the sons of Abraham, the 'people' being sons according to the flesh and 'the multitude of nations' being sons according to the faith.

Chapter 43

Jacob died; then Joseph. During the 144 years that remained before the exodus of the people of Israel from Egypt, the population increased incredibly in spite of devastating persecutions. At one time, every male child that was born was put to death, so terrified were the astonished Egyptians by the extraordinary increase of the Jewish population. It was

[1] Gen. 48.19.

then that Moses was snatched by stealth from the hands of the executioners and found a home in the royal palace, for God's providence had great things for him to do. He was nursed and adopted by a daughter of Pharao—all kings in Egypt were named Pharao. So great a hero did Moses become that he freed his people from the yoke of slavery, or, rather, God wrought through him what He had promised to Abraham. It was a hard and heavy yoke, yet the people increased marvelously. It is true that, at first, Moses fled because, to defend an Israelite, he had killed an Egyptian and was afraid, but later God told him to return, and in the power of the Spirit of God he overcame the magicians of Pharao who attempted to oppose him. When the Egyptians continued to refuse to free the people of God, ten memorable afflictions were sent by God to afflict the Egyptians—water changed to blood, the frogs and lice and flies, the dying cattle, boils and hail storms, the locusts, darkness, and the death of first-born children. At last, the spirit of the Egyptians was broken by so many grievous afflictions and the Israelites were freed. However, some Egyptians pursued them, and these perished in the Red Sea. The waters opened to leave a path for the departing Israelites, but, when the Egyptians followed them, the waters returned and drowned the Egyptians. After this, for forty years the people wandered in the desert with Moses as their leader. The Law was promulgated in a terrifying way on the mountain, with its divine origin revealed by miraculous signs and voices. The place where God was worshiped with sacrifices prophetic of what was to come was thereupon called the Tabernacle of Testimony.

This occurred soon after the departure from Egypt, when the people were beginning their wanderings in the desert, on the fiftieth day after the Pasch was celebrated by the sacrifice of a lamb. Not only is this lamb a perfect symbolic prophecy of Christ passing, through the sacrifice of His passion, from this world to the Father—I need hardly recall that *pascha* is the Hebrew for 'passing,'—but in the period of the revelation of the New Covenant, it was on the fiftieth day after Christ our Pasch was offered up in the sacrifice that the Holy Spirit came down from heaven. Note, too, that this Spirit is called in the Gospel the Finger of God: first, because He directs us to recall to memory events first enacted in prophetic symbols, and, second, because the Tablets of the Law are said to have been written by the finger of God.

After the death of Moses, the people were ruled by Josue, son of Nun, and it was he who led them into the promised land and who divided the land among the people. Both these marvelous leaders were highly successful in war. In these there was an element of the miraculous, since, as God made clear, the victories were less in reward for any merits of the Jewish people than in punishment of the sins of the people who were conquered.

After these leaders came the Judges. The people by now were settled in the promised land and the first promise made to Abraham, which has reference to one people, namely, the Hebrews, and to the land of Chanaan began to be fulfilled. There was no question yet, of course, of the promise in reference to all peoples and the whole world, since that was to be fulfilled by the coming of Christ in the flesh and by the faith revealed in the Gospel rather than by any observances of the old Law. And it was as a foreshadowing of this that it was not by Moses (who received on Mount Sinai the Law for the people) but by Josue (whose name was changed into Jesus at God's command) that the people were brought into the promised land.

The wars that were fought while the Judges were in authority were sometimes won and sometimes lost, depending on the sins of the people and the mercy of God.

The next period is that of the Kings. The first to reign was Saul. He was deposed and defeated in battle, and his heirs were rejected as candidates for the crown. So David succeeded, and it is as Son of David that Christ is most commonly known. With David begins the period of mature manhood in the history of God's people, following the period of adolescence, so to speak, which lasted from Abraham to David. It was not without reason that Matthew in his Gospel so lists the steps in the genealogy from Abraham to David that this first period includes fourteen generations. For it is in the period of adolescence that procreation becomes possible.

Hence, the generations are made to begin with Abraham, who was declared the father of the nations when he was given his new name. Thus we may say that before Abraham the people of God were in their childhood from Noe to Abraham, the period in which they were identified by their speaking the Hebrew language.[1] For, a human being begins to speak in childhood, the age following infancy—which is derived from the Latin, *infans*, meaning unable to speak. Infancy is a period the memory of which is lost, much as all memory of the infancy of the human race was lost in the flood. For, how many persons are there who can remember their infancy?

I am here tracing the history of the City of God. Just as the previous Book dealt with one age, the first, so the present Book may be thought of as covering two ages, the second and third. In this third age the yoke of the Law was imposed (foreshadowed by the 'cow of three years'[2]); second, sin began to abound (symbolized by the 'she-goat of three years'); third, the earthly kingdom took its rise (as indicated by the 'ram of three years'). It was a period in which men living according to the spirit were not lacking (as was mysteriously foretold under the symbol of the turtle-dove and the pigeon).

---

[1] . . . *pueritia . . . populi Dei . . . in ea lingua inventa est, id est Hebraea.*

[2] Gen. 15.9. St. Augustine's handling of the symbolism of the cow, the she-goat, the ram, the turtle-dove and the pigeon in Bk. 16.24, herein omitted.

BOOK XVII

From the Age of the Prophets to Christ's Birth

Chapter 1

WE HAVE SEEN the promises which God made to Abraham—to be the father, first, of the Jewish race according to the flesh, and, second, of all nations who were to embrace the faith. The development in history of the City of God will show how these promises were kept.

The end of the preceding Book brought us up to the reign of King David. I shall now begin with his reign, and treat of what ensued in as much detail as the theme of this Book requires. There is a period which begins with the prophecies of Samuel and continues through the seventy years of the Babylonian captivity (which Jeremias had foretold[1]) and ends with the rebuilding of the Temple, after the Israelites came home. This period is known as the 'Age of the Prophets,' although, of course, the patriarch Noe, in whose lifetime the whole earth was destroyed by the flood, and others before and after him up to the time of the kings, were Prophets also. At least, they prefigured, in some fashion, many things touching the City of God and the kingdom of heaven, and sometimes actually prophesied. Consequently, it is not too much to speak of these men as Prophets; some of them are explicitly so called in Holy Writ, for example, Abraham and Moses.[2]

Nevertheless, the age of the chief and greatest of the Prophets begins with Samuel. He it was who, at God's bidding, anointed Saul as king and, when Saul had been cast off, David. The remaining kings were to come from David's stock for as long as their succession was ordained.

Now, if I were to dwell upon everything the Prophets foretold of Christ, while the City of God waxed in the birth and waned in the death of its members throughout this era, I would never have done. The reason for this is that even when

---

[1] Jer. 25.11. [2] Gen. 20.7; Deut. 34.10.

the Scriptures truly seem to be annals of one king after another, with the exploits and fortunes of each set down with a chronicler's care, it will be found, provided the Holy Spirit teaches us to read the Scriptures rightly, that they seem even more—assuredly not less—concerned with prophecy than with history. And anyone who has given this problem even a passing thought will realize how many weighty and wearisome tomes it would take to delve into these matters and air them fully. Even in regard to the texts which are unquestionably prophetic of Christ and His kingdom, the City of God, there are so many that a thoroughgoing examination would carry me beyond the modest limits of this work. And so as far as I am able, I shall so govern my pen that, God willing, I may get through this Book, neither leaving out what should be said nor lingering on what is superfluous.

Chapter 2

I have already related[1] how, out of all the promises God made from the beginning, two were made to Abraham. One was that his seed should own the land of Chanaan, for such is the sense of the words: 'Come into the land which I shall show thee, and I will make of thee a great nation.'[2] The other, which is vastly more important than the first, was that, whereas in his fleshly seed he was to sire the Jewish race alone, in his spiritual seed he was to be the father of every people that would follow in the footsteps of his faith. This promise opens with the words: 'In you shall the nations of the earth be blessed.'[3] I also went on to prove, by means of a great many additional texts, that both these pledges were really given.

At the time of which I was speaking, the people of Israel, the carnal seed of Abraham, were not merely dwelling in the promised land, in possession of their foes' cities, but were reigning under their own kings. Already, then, God's promises

---

[1] Bk. 16.16.
[2] Gen. 12.1. Texts cited follow the Confraternity translation except when St. Augustine's original Latin varies considerably from the Latin Vulgate.
[3] Gen. 12.3.

with respect to them had been in large measure fulfilled, not alone the promises that had been made to the ancient fathers, Abraham, Isaac, and Jacob in their day, but others as well which God had given them through Moses, by whose hand He brought them out of the bondage of Egypt and through the desert, and by whose lips He made known all the past history of the race.

Nevertheless, even after the illustrious captain, Josue son of Nun, had conducted them into the promised land, crushed the Gentiles, parceled out the territory among the twelve tribes according to divine command, and then died, God's pledge that Chanaan should reach from a certain river of Egypt to the great Euphrates[4] had not been fulfilled to the letter. Neither, after Josue, was this pledge redeemed in the time of the Judges. Yet it was looked upon not as a matter for further prophecy, but for imminent realization.[5] It was, in fact, realized in David and in his son Solomon. For, when they had put down and made tributary all the peoples round about, Solomon's sway was enlarged to the precise terms of the promise. At this point, the seed of Abraham under its kings was in Chanaan, the earthly land of promise, established in such wise that nothing remained to implement fully God's temporal pledge except that the Hebrews and their descendants should there abide, rooted in unshakeable worldly well-being until the end of time. The condition was that they obey the laws of the Lord their God.

But, since God knew that they would not obey, He made use of temporal chastisements to test the handful of loyal believers He had among them, and to render alert those followers He was to have later on among all those peoples for whose sake He was planning to make good His second promise, in the revelation of His New Testament, in the Incarnation of Christ.

[4] Gen. 15.18.
[5] . . . *nec adhuc prophetabatur futurum, sed expectabatur implendum.*

Chapter 3

The divine revelations made to Abraham, Isaac, and Jacob, and all other signs and prophecies contained in the early Scriptures, are sometimes related to the carnal progeny of Abraham and, at other times, to that spiritual progeny which means all nations that are blessed and called to eternal life in the kingdom of heaven as co-heirs of Christ in the New Testament. This is true, also, of the prophecies belonging to the 'Age of the Kings.' Some of them refer to the terrestrial Jerusalem, the slave-girl, bearing her sons into bondage to serve beside her; others, to the free City of God, the true everlasting Jerusalem above, whose sons are men living by God's law like pilgrims on earth. Yet, there are still others among them which are applicable to both cities at one and the same time, to the slave-girl literally, and figuratively to the free woman.[1]

Thus, the Prophets' sayings are of three classes: one class refers to the earthly, a second to the heavenly Jerusalem, and a third to both simultaneously. It will be best to support this assertion with illustrations. The Prophet Nathan was sent to accuse King David of a grave sin and to foretell what evils were to befall him on this account.[2] Now no one can fail to see that this prophecy refers to the earthly city. There are others like it, sometimes addressed to the people at large for their profit and well-being, and sometimes to an individual who merited a word from God to foreknow some event for the guidance of his temporal life.

In the following prophecy, however, the reference is to the heavenly Jerusalem: 'Behold the days shall come, saith the Lord, and I will make a new covenant with the house of Israel, and with the house of Juda; not according to the covenant which I made with their fathers, in the day that I took them by the hand to bring them out of the land of Egypt; the covenant which they made void, and I had dominion over them, saith the Lord. But this shall be the covenant which I

[1] Cf. Gal. 4.21–31; and above, 15.2, for St. Augustine's discussion of this passage.
[2] 2 Kings 12.

will make with the house of Israel, after those days, saith the Lord, I will give my law in their bowels, and I will write it in their heart; and I will be their God and they shall be my people.'[3] Here, God Himself is Jerusalem's reward. Her highest—her entire—good is to possess Him and to be possessed by Him.

Both cities are meant when Jerusalem is called the City of God and when it is foretold that the house of God is one day to be there—a prophecy that seems to be fulfilled in the magnificent Temple built by King Solomon—for such things both happened historically in the earthly Jerusalem and also forefigured the heavenly Jerusalem.

This kind of prophecy, blending the other two kinds, is very common in the ancient canonical books devoted to history. It has challenged and continues to challenge the interpretative talent of Scripture students. They must search for the allegorical sense to be fulfilled, for example, in the seed of Abraham according to the faith, when they read of something foretold and accomplished in the literal sense with respect to his seed according to the flesh. Some, indeed, have gone so far as to claim that in these books there are no predictions and fulfillments—not even facts which were not predicted—which do not suggest some necessary figurative reference to the City of God and her pilgrim children in this life.

But, if this is so, the sayings of the Prophets are of two, not of three, classes. Moreover, this classification would apply to the whole Old Testament as well. For, if everything foretold there of the earthly Jerusalem or accomplished in her must forthwith be looked upon as a foreshadowing of the heavenly, then there is nothing there pertaining to the former alone. Consequently, only two types of prophecy would be admitted: one having to do with the free City, the other with the free and bond together.

Now, just as I feel that those are greatly mistaken who think that the historical facts in those books have no significance other than that things occurred as described, so I find too venturesome those who maintain that absolutely every-

[3] Jer. 31.31–33.

thing is bound up with allegorical meanings.[4] That is why I called for three classes of prophecies, not for two.

This is my opinion. However, I do not censure those who may have been able to carve out some spiritual interpretation from every historical fact recounted, so long as they take good care first and foremost to adhere to the historical fact.[5] Certainly, passages of such nature that they seem to fit in with neither man's nor God's actions and plans will seem to a believer to be valueless in themselves. He will want to interpret such matters in a spiritual sense, if he can, or at least he will admit that they should be so interpreted by someone else who knows how.

Chapters 4-13

Recounting the history of the Jewish kings, Augustine dwells in particular on the importance of David and Solomon. The promises made to David were fulfilled in Christ.

Chapter 14

As the City of God moved along in the course of history, the first king to rule in that earthly Jerusalem, which foreshadowed the one that was to come, was David. He was a man skilled in the shaping of songs, but one who loved the harmony of music less as a common emotional indulgence than as a religious dedication to His God, who was the true God. And it was to serve Him that David made use of music in order to express a tremendous truth by means of mystical symbols, for what can better suggest the unity in variety of a well-ordered city than the harmony produced by the rational and controlled concord of differing tones?[1]

Nearly all of David's prophecies are to be found in his

---

[4] Bk. 16.2.   [5] Cf. above, 13.21, 14.11.

[1] . . . *qui harmoniam musicam non vulgari voluptate, sed fideli voluntate dilexerit eaque Deo suo, qui verus est Deus, mystica rei magnae figuratione servierit. Diversorum enim sonorum rationalis moderatusque concentus concordi varietate compactam bene ordinatae civitatis insinuat unitatem.*

Book of 150 Psalms. There are some who maintain that out of this number only those were composed by David which bear his name. Still others say that only those prefaced with the note 'Of David' were written by him and that those marked 'For David' were written by others and passed off as his. This opinion, however, is rendered untenable by our Saviour Himself, who says in the Gospel that David in the Spirit calls Christ his Lord.[2] Our Lord was quoting the opening of Psalm 109, which goes like this: 'The Lord said to my Lord: Sit thou at my right hand, until I make thy enemies thy footstool.' Now, this psalm is not inscribed 'Of David' but 'For David,' as are many others.

For this reason I prefer the opinion of those who are persuaded that all 150 Psalms are David's work; but that he prefaced certain ones with the names of other men (who had some symbolic relevance to the matter in hand) and left the remainder uninscribed, as the Lord inspired him in a flexible arrangement, which may be dark to us but is not for that reason devoid of meaning.

No insuperable difficulty for this position is raised by the fact that some psalms bear the names of Prophets who lived long after David's day and even seem to present them as speakers. For the prophetic Spirit could have revealed to King David in the act of prophesying the names of these Prophets-to-be with a view to his foresinging something relevant to them; as was the case when the name of King Josias, more than 300 years before his birth and reign, was revealed to a certain Prophet, who proceeded to foretell even some of the king's exploits.

Chapter 15

At this point in the present Book, my readers may expect me to deal with those prophecies in David's Psalms which concern our Lord Jesus Christ and His Church. It was partly to meet this expectation that I have just dealt with one psalm; but it would be difficult to satisfy the reader fully simply because the material is too abundant—not because there is too

[2] Matt. 22.43,44.

little of it. The fact is that if I am to avoid saying too much, I simply cannot cite all that David has to say. On the other hand, I am afraid that, if I limit myself to one or two texts only, informed readers may think that I am bypassing more important ones. Besides, since the sense of any one verse should be supported by the pattern of the whole psalm or, at least, should not be contradicted by the context, I may appear to be arbitrarily plucking texts out of their context to bolster my own views, like a man who makes a patchwork of verses on a theme quite unlike that of the longer poem from which the verses have been culled. To show the valid use of any excerpt, the entire psalm must be expounded. Now, how much work this entails, my own book,[1] and those of others who have done this, are proof enough. These books, then, I recommend to any reader who may have the inclination and opportunity to read them. Anyone who does so will discover how abundant and magnificent are the prophecies of David, king and prophet, touching Christ the King and the City which He founded, the Church.

Chapter 16

Although there exist on any prophetic theme utterances which are literal, plain-spoken and perfectly clear, there has to be some intermingling of figurative language. It is this latter kind of thing which forces upon teachers the laborious task of discussion and explanation—more particularly for the benefit of those who are rather slow to understand. Nevertheless, there are texts which, on a very first hearing, obviously concern Christ and the Church—even if they contain a residue of less readily intelligible points to be clarified at one's leisure. Here is an example from the Book of Psalms:

'My heart hath uttered a good word; I speak my words to the king; my tongue is the pen of a scrivener that writeth swiftly. Thou art beautiful above the sons of men; grace is poured abroad in thy lips; therefore hath God blessed thee forever. Gird thy sword upon thy thigh, O thou most mighty. With thy comeliness and thy beauty set out, proceed prosper-

---

[1] *Enarrationes in psalmos.*

ously, and reign. Because of truth and meekness and justice; and thy right hand shall conduct thee wonderfully. Thy arrows are sharp; under thee shall people fall, into the hearts of the king's enemies. Thy throne, O God, is for ever and ever; the sceptre of thy kingdom is a sceptre of uprightness. Thou hast loved justice, and hated iniquity; therefore God, thy God, hath anointed thee with the oil of gladness above thy fellows. Myrrh and aloes and cassia perfume thy garments, from the ivory houses; out of which the daughters of kings have delighted thee in thy glory.'[1]

In this passage the reader hears one spoken of as God whose throne is for ever and ever, one anointed by God—as God anoints, of course, with a spiritual chrism visible only to the eyes of faith. Now, is there any reader—however dull-witted —who does not recognize in this person the Christ whom we preach, in whom we believe? Is there any insider so ill-informed in his faith, any outsider so deaf to its universally known character, as not to be aware that Christ's very name is derived from 'chrism,' that is, from His anointing? Anyone, at least, who is already subject to Him whose reign is based on truth, meekness, and justice, will recognize in this description Christ the King. After that, he may, at his leisure, look into the meaning of the rest that is spoken figuratively—how, for instance, He is 'beautiful above the sons of men' (with a spiritual comeliness all the more worthy of love and admiration on that account), what his 'sword' and 'arrows' may be, and much else that is cast in metaphorical language.

Next let him examine in the following text the Church united in spiritual marriage and divine love to her tremendous Spouse:

'The queen stood on thy right hand, in gilded clothing; surrounded with variety. Hearken, O daughter, and see, and incline thy ear, and forget thy people and thy father's house. And the king shall greatly desire thy beauty; for he is the Lord thy God, and him shall they adore. And the daughters of Tyre with gifts, yea, all the rich among the people, shall entreat thy countenance. All the glory of the king's daughter is within in golden borders, clothed round about with varieties.

[1] Ps. 44.2–10.

After her shall virgins be brought to the king; her neighbors shall be brought to thee. They shall be brought with gladness and rejoicing; they shall be brought into the temple of the king. Instead of thy fathers, sons are born to thee; thou shall make them princes over all the earth. They shall remember thy name throughout all generations. Therefore shall people praise thee forever; yea, for ever and ever.'[2]

In my opinion there is no one so lacking in common sense as to imagine that these words are portrait and praise of some insignificant woman—a fit wife, if you please, for Him to whom the words were addressed: 'Thy throne, O God, is for ever and ever; the sceptre of thy kingdom is a sceptre of uprightness. Thou hast loved justice, and hated iniquity; therefore God, thy God, hath anointed thee with the oil of gladness above thy fellows'—Christ, obviously, above all Christian men. These 'fellows' are those who are chosen from all peoples to form, by their unity and harmony that Queen, who is called, in another psalm, 'The city of the great King.'[3] By mystical application she is also called Sion, a word which means 'spying out,' for she spies out the great good of the hereafter and keeps her gaze intently fixed upon it. By the same kind of application, she is called Jerusalem, but I have already spoken abundantly on this point.

Her foe is the Devil's city, Babylon, which means 'confusion.' Yet it is out of this very Babylon that our Queen is created among all nations, by liberation and regeneration, passing over from the worst to the best of kings, from the Devil's dominion to Christ's. This transfer explains the words addressed to her: 'Forget thy people and thy father's house.' To this godless city belong those Israelites who are such according to the flesh alone—not those who are so in faith—for they are among the enemies of this great King and His Queen. For, when Christ came to them and was slain by them, He became instead the King of those whom He never beheld in the flesh. This is the meaning of the words our King speaks in one of the prophetic psalms: 'Thou wilt deliver me from the contradictions of the people; thou wilt make me head of

2 Ps. 44.11–18.
3 Ps. 47.3.

the Gentiles. A people, which I knew not, hath served me; at the hearing of the ear they have obeyed me.'[4] That is, the Gentiles, with whom Christ had no physical contact, believed in Him when He was preached to them, so that quite properly it is said of them, 'At the hearing of the ear they have obeyed me,' for faith comes by hearing. These people together with the authentic Israelites in both flesh and faith make up the City of God which became the mother of Christ Himself, in the flesh, during the time when she existed among the Israelites alone, for the Virgin Mary, in whom He became incarnate, was a citizen of this City.

Of this City another psalm says: 'A mother is Sion, a man shall say, and a man is begotten in her, and the Highest himself hath founded her.'[5] Who is this Highest save God? Accordingly, we must say that Christ as God founded this City in the Patriarchs and Prophets, even before, as a man, He became, through Mary, a citizen.

Long, long ago in prophecy this royal City was told: 'For thy fathers sons are born to thee: thou shalt make them princes over all the earth.'[6] This prediction we see realized before our very eyes, because out of her sons come her rulers and fathers all over the earth, as the nations hasten to join in praising her with a praising that shall go on for ever and ever. These truths are perfectly clear and, therefore, any interpretations of other parts of the psalm, which are somewhat obscure by reason of metaphorical language, must be consistent with what we know to be true.

Chapters 17–22

Further examples are given from the Psalms of foreshadowings of events in Christ's life. The later history of the kings of Juda finds idolatry developing among the Jewish people.

Chapter 23

In the kingdom of Juda, too, as one king succeeded another, there were Prophets. They came, as God saw fit to send them,

[4] Ps. 17.44,45. [5] Ps. 86.5.
[6] Ps. 44.17.

to predict what needed prediction, or to rebuke vice and teach virtue. For there, too, although a great deal less frequently than in Israel, there were kings godless enough to offend Him grievously and to be punished for it along with their sinful subjects—although their punishments were not terribly severe. There were in Juda, beyond question, some devout kings, and Holy Writ praises them amply, whereas we are told that the kings of Israel without exception were all, in larger or smaller degree, wicked.

Thus, each of the kingdoms had its own uplifting consolations and depressing adversities as Divine Providence planned or permitted, such as the afflictions of foreign wars as well as of civil wars between the kingdoms, so that there were unmistakable evidences of the mercy or wrath of God in all these ups and downs.

Finally, however, God's indignation reached such a point that the entire race was conquered by the invading Chaldaeans, overthrown in their own domain, and transported, almost to a man, into Assyrian territory. This happened first to the ten tribes called Israel; later, to Juda as well, after Jerusalem and its magnificent Temple had been destroyed. And this paralyzing captivity[1] lasted for seventy years.

When this time was up, they were released and came back to rebuild the ruined Temple. Many Jews went on living in foreign countries, but the division into two kingdoms under separate kings was a thing of the past. Thenceforward, they all had one leader in Jerusalem, whither Jews from everywhere, as best they could manage, used to come for certain calendar festivals in God's temple. Meanwhile, they never lacked foreign foes and conquerors. Indeed, when Christ came, He found them paying tribute to Rome.

Chapter 24

When the Jews had returned from Babylonia, they had the Prophets Malachias, Aggeus, and Zacharias, whose predictions belong to this period, and also Esdras. From then on, throughout the entire era extending to the Saviour's coming, there

---

[1] . . . *captivum egit otium.*

were no others save the following: just before Christ's birth, that other Zacharias, John's father, and his wife Elizabeth; just after Christ's birth, the old man Simeon and the very aged widow Anna. Then came John himself, the very last of all—which explains our Lord's words: 'For all the prophets and the law have prophesied until John.'[1] Because John and Christ were almost of an age, it would be incorrect to say that John foretold Him as someone to be looked for, yet he was inspired to point Him out when He was still unknown.

But the prophesying of these five people is known to us from the Gospels (wherein the Lord's Virgin Mother herself sings like a prophetess before John). Accordingly, the Jews who rejected the faith do not accept their prophecies, but the countless Jews who have believed in the Gospel do. This is the real splitting-in-two of Israel prefigured by that division which the Prophet Samuel foretold to King Saul as irrevocably determined.

However, even the unbelieving Jews have Malachias, Aggeus, Zacharias, and Esdras in their official canon and they consider these to be the last of the Prophets. Fortunately, these men were among that mere handful in the great throng of Prophets whose writings managed to achieve canonical authority. I realize, therefore, that it will be well for me to quote in this work excerpts from these prophets touching Christ and His Church. But, not wishing to overload this already lengthy Book, I shall, with the Lord's help, do so more easily in the Book to follow.

[1] Matt. 11.13.

BOOK XVIII

The City of Man in Ancient History

Chapter 1

IN CONNECTION with the City of God and the city of the world, I promised to write about their origins, developments and appointed ends as though they were two cities, although, as far as human history goes, the former lives like an alien inside the latter. First, however, I had to refute the arguments of those enemies of the City of God who prefer their own gods to its Founder, Christ, and who hate His followers savagely, to the havoc of their own souls. This I did, with the grace of Christ, in the first ten Books. Only then did I go on to make good the first part of the threefold promise which I have just mentioned. Books XI-XIV dealt with the origins of the two cities; Book XV turned to the simultaneous progress of the two cities and carried the story from Adam to the flood, and the first part of Book XVI continued the story down to the days of Abraham, telling it concurrently, just as in actual history the two currents of development flowed in a single stream.

But in the course of Book XVI there was a change. The second part of this Book dealt with the period from the Patriarch Abraham to the coming of the kings of Israel and Book XVII continued the narrative down to the Incarnation of the Saviour. Here, however, the progress of the City of God is treated in isolation in my narrative, although, in fact, throughout that period, as from the beginning, the two cities continued to progress concurrently and to give their respective colors to human history. My reason for this change was that, although the course of God's City was overshadowed and kept in the dark, by contrast with the other city, I wanted to bring it into the light during the period which begins with God's more outspoken promises and ends with their fulfillment in Christ's birth of the Virgin.

Now, however, I must retrace my steps and describe in some detail the development of the city of the world from the days of Abraham on. In this way, my readers will be able to study the two cities by comparing one with the other.

Chapter 2

The city of man, for all the width of its expansion throughout the world and for all the depth of its differences in this place and that, is a single community. The simple truth is that the bond of a common nature makes all human beings one. Nevertheless, each individual in this community is driven by his passions to pursue his private purposes. Unfortunately, the objects of these purposes are such that no one person (let alone, the world community) can ever be wholly satisfied. The reason for this is that nothing but Absolute Being can satisfy human nature.[1] The result is that the city of man remains in a chronic condition of civil war. Hence, there is always the oppression of those who fail by those who succeed. The vanquished succumb to the victorious, preferring sheer survival and any kind of peaceful settlement to their own continued hegemony—even to liberty itself. In nearly all peoples the voice of nature itself has counseled that, when you have had the bad luck to be beaten, it is better to bow before the conqueror than to risk wholesale annihilation—so much so, in fact, that those who have chosen death rather than slavery have aroused constant admiration in those who do not understand. At any rate, God, in whose mighty providence lie both defeat and victory, has seen to it that wars brought supremacy to some people and subjugation to others.

Among the many earthly empires into which human society (which I call inclusively the city of this world) has been split for the sake of earthly advantage or greed, two have emerged in history far surpassing all the rest: first, the Assyrian, then the Roman, chronologically successive and geographically distinct; the former in the East, the latter in the West; the latter taking up, without interval, where the former left off. In com-

---

[1] . . . *id quod appetitur aut nemini aut non omnibus sufficit, quia non est id ipsum.*

parison with these two, I would call all other kingdoms with their kings mere appendages.[2]

Now, Assyria already had its second king, Ninus, succeeding his father Belus, when Abraham was born in Chaldaea.[3] At that time there also existed the very small kingdom of the Sicyonians.[4] It is this kingdom which the encyclopedic scholar Marcus Varro[5] takes as his earliest point of departure in his *Origins of the Roman People.* From the Sicyonian kings he proceeds to the Athenians, thence to the Latins, finally to the Romans. Actually, however, up to the founding of Rome, it all makes extremely small talk by comparison with Assyrian achievements. Still, the Roman historian Sallust admits that the Athenians were outstanding in Greece—more, however, by reputation than in reality. He has this to say: 'In my opinion, Athenian exploits were quite large and impressive in scope—rather less so, however, than we have been led to believe. The world is convinced that their doings were of first-rate importance because of the brilliant account of them which Athenian historians have given. So it is that the powers of her active men have been judged in the light of the enthusiastic praise her brilliant writers accorded.'[6] Additional great glory came to this city from the literature and philosophy which flourished there.

When it comes to power, however, there was nothing in antiquity to compare with that of Assyria in scope and duration. King Ninus, Belus' son, we are told, conquered all Asia right up to the Libyan frontier—one third of the world in number of subjects, one half of the earth in extent. In the East only India escaped his sway; even so, his widow, Semiramis, attacked these people. So it came about that all the peoples and kings of those lands were brought under Assyria's imperial domination and obediently did as they were told. I have already said that Abraham was born into this empire, in Chaldaea, in Ninus' day.

---

[2] *Regna cetera ceterosque reges velut adpendices istorum dixerim.*

[3] Cf. above, 16.17.

[4] . . . *regnum Sicyoniorum admodum parvum.*

[5] . . . *ille undecumque doctissimus Marcus Varro.* Cf. above, 6.2.

[6] *Bellum Catilinarium* 8.

It happens that Greek history is much more familiar to our people than Assyrian history (because of the Latin historians who have dug out the ancient genealogical roots of the Romans, in passing from the Greeks to the Latins to the Romans, who are Latins). Hence, when necessary, I must introduce the Assyrian kings, in order to bring out how Babylon, the first Rome, so to speak, was related in development to the wayfaring City of God. In general, however, in selecting facts to illustrate the contrast between the earthly and heavenly cities, I shall, in this work, take the bulk of my material from Greek and Roman history. Here, Rome plays the role of a second Babylon.

At Abraham's birth, then, Ninus was second king of Assyria, Europs, second of Sicyon. (Belus had been the first in Assyria, Aegialeus first in Sicyon.) By the time, however, that Abraham left Babylonia on God's promise that he would be the father of a great people and that in his seed all nations were to be blessed, Assyria had its fourth king and Sicyon its fifth. In the former, Ninus' son was ruling, in succession to his mother, Semiramis. History has it that he put her to death because she had shamelessly sought to lie with him in incest. Some writers think that she founded Babylon, and she may very well have built it over. I have already indicated, in Book XVI,[7] the time and circumstances of its founding.

With respect to this king's name, some call him Ninus, too; others, Ninyas by patronymic derivation. Anyway, his contemporary in Sicyon was Telxion, under whose sway times were so pleasant and prosperous that, when he died, his people worshiped him with sacrifices as a god. They also instituted games in his honor—the first instance, history says, of this kind of thing.

Chapters 3–7

A continuation of the survey of events in ancient history before the time of Moses.

[7] Ch. 4, here omitted.

Chapter 8

Moses was born in Egypt during the reigns of Saphrus, fourteenth king of Assyria, Orthopolis, twelfth king of Sicyon, and Criasus, fifth king of Greece. Through Moses, God's people were delivered from that bondage of Egypt which was necessary to arouse in them a desire for God's help. Prometheus, too, some say, lived during the reigns of the kings just mentioned. The word got around that 'he made men out of mud' —because he was considered a most excellent teacher of wisdom. However, we have no evidence who the wise men of his day were. His brother, Atlas, had a reputation as a great astrologer, which accounts for the myth that he carries the sky on his shoulders. There is a mountain named after him, and the height of it may well have given people the idea of Atlas supporting the sky.

Meanwhile, many other fabulous ideas began to be dreamed up in Greece, and from this time up to the reign of Cecrops, king of the Athenians, under whom the city first came to be called Athens—this was the period of the exodus from Egypt under Moses—additional dead people were divinized by the blind, foolish, and superstitious customs of the Greeks. Among others, there were Melantomice, wife of King Criasus, and Phorbas, their son, who became sixth king of Greece after his father, and Jasus, son of the seventh king, Triophas, and Sthenelas, the ninth king. (I find this name spelt as Stheneleus or Sthenelus, in different authors.)

They say, too, that these were the days of Mercury, a grandson of Atlas by his daughter, Maia—a hero even of the popular story-tellers.[1] He was renowned for his skill in many arts which he taught to men. Hence, when he died, men believed he was a god, or, at least, were willing to make him one. Later on came Hercules, still, however, in the era of the Argives. Some authors place him earlier than Mercury, but I think they are mistaken. Be this as it may, responsible historians of antiquity agree that both were human and won divine honors because they had helped mankind to make life more livable.

[1] . . . quod vulgatiores etiam litterae personant.

Minerva, of course, is much earlier than either of these. For it was in the time of Ogygus that she is supposed to have first appeared as a young girl by the shores of Lake Triton—hence her name, Tritonia. Beyond doubt she was the moving spirit behind many fine discoveries, and was all the more readily taken for a goddess because her origin was so obscure. The songs about her having sprung from Jupiter's head are, of course, subject matter for poetry and story-telling, not for history.

Historians do not agree on the dates of Ogygus himself. There was a great flood in his day, greater than the one that came later in Deucalion's time; but not, assuredly, the tremendous flood from which only those in the ark escaped, for neither Greek nor Latin historians knew anything about that. Anyway, in the book I mentioned above, Varro begins with this flood as the point of departure in dealing with Roman history. On the other hand, our Christian chroniclers, Jerome and Eusebius before him, following still older writers, have placed the flood of Ogygus more than 300 years later, during the reign of Phoroneus, second king of the Greeks.

However that may be, Minerva was already adored as a goddess when Cecrops became king of Athens. Some writers claim that the city of Athens was founded under this king; others that it was merely rebuilt.

Chapter 9

The name Athens is certainly derived from *Athēna* which is Greek for Minerva. Varro gives the following explanation of this. It seems that an olive tree suddenly appeared where there was none before, and, in another spot, a gushing stream of water. These phenomena made a mighty impression upon the king, who forthwith dispatched men to Apollo at Delphi to inquire what was to be made of them, and what course of action was to be taken. The oracle replied that the olive tree stood for Minerva, the water for Neptune; further, that it lay in the citizens' power to pick either of the names of the two gods, whose portents these were, as a name for their city. When Cecrops received this answer, he called together all citizens of either sex for a vote. It was a custom there, in those days, to include women in public assemblies. When the throng had been polled, it was found that the men stood for Neptune, the women for Minerva. There was a majority of one woman, and Minerva won. Thereupon, Neptune was so enraged that he sent the ocean boiling in over Athenian land—for demons can use any kind of water to cause a flood. Varro goes on to say that the men of Athens, to placate him, decreed a three-fold punishment for their womenfolk: they were to lose the right of suffrage; they were not to give their own names to their children; they were never to be known as Athenians.

That is how the noblest and most brilliant city Greece ever had, the mother and nurse of liberal studies and of so many great philosophers, got its name! As the demons made sport of this tussle between two of their gods, a male and a female, and of the female's victory by female vote, Athens was driven to penalize the victory of the victorious goddess to placate the vindictive god who was vanquished[1]—quaking more violently, it seems, before Neptune's waves than before Minerva's weapons. Minerva the victor was herself vanquished in the punishment of her women supporters.

Nor did she come to the assistance of her partisans. They were not even permitted to use the title Athenian, to bear the name of the goddess who triumphed by their votes over the male god. And they lost their suffrage and the right to give their names to their own children! How many reflections one is tempted to make! But I must hasten on to other matters.

Chapters 10-21

Augustine attempts to correlate certain events in pagan history with the possibly contemporary incidents of Bible history. Virgil and Varro are his chief sources for ancient secular history.

Chapter 22

To be brief, Rome was founded—a second, and the daughter of the first, Babylon, as it were. It was God's good pleasure,

[1] . . . *a victo laesa ipsam victricis victoriam punire compulsa est.*

by means of this city, to subdue the whole world, to bring it into the single society of a republic under law, and to bestow upon it a widespread and enduring peace. But this was to be accomplished only at the expense of titanic hazards, hair-raising exertions, and much mutual devastation—for by this time the other peoples of the earth had also become stout-hearted and strong, practiced in the use of weapons, and unwilling to yield. It is true that the Assyrian kingdom in a series of wars brought nearly all of Asia under the yoke. But these could not have been wars fraught with such harrowing difficulties, because the nations at that time were still unschooled in self-defense; neither were they as populous and powerful as they later became. When Ninus conquered all of Asia save India, not many more than a thousand years had gone by since the great world-wide flood, from which only eight men escaped in Noe's ark. It was not, you may be sure, with Assyrian speed and ease that Rome came to master thoroughly the Eastern and Western peoples whom we see subject to the Empire today. For, wheresoever she turned in her gradual growth and expansion, she found them rugged and ready to do battle.

At the time Rome was founded, God's people had been in the promised land for 718 years. Of these, twenty-seven were the years of Josue; 329 belonged to the age of the judges; and 362 to the age of the kings. At this point the king in Juda was named Achaz, or, according to others' chronology, Ezechias. It is certain that this latter excellent and most devout king ruled in the time of Romulus. In the other division of the Hebrews, the kingdom called Israel, Osee had begun his reign.

Chapter 23

It was at this time, some authors say, that the Erythrean Sibyl prophesied. Varro, by the way, has pointed out that there were several sibyls—not just one. The Sibyl of Erythrae, at any rate, wrote some things that clearly concern Christ. I first read her sayings in a Latin poetic version marked by poor Latinity and poor metrical structure, but this was the fault of the blundering translator, whoever he was, as I came to

realize later on. For, one day when the distinguished proconsul, Flaccianus, who was a man of great eloquence and learning, was conversing with me about Christ, he brought out a
Greek manuscript containing, he said, the poems of the Sibyl
of Erythrae.[1] In the text he showed me how in a certain passage the initial letters of the verses fell in such sequence you
could read the acrostic, IESOUS XREISTÒS THEOU UIÒS SŌTER,
which is Greek for 'Jesus Christ, Son of God, Saviour.' These
verses, translated into verse, read as follows:

Judgment shall come, and the sweat of the earth be its signal.
Even the monarch eternal shall come from the heavens,
Suddenly come, in His flesh, to the dreaded tribunal.
O faithful and faithless alike shall be seeing their Maker
Uplifted with heavenly friends at the term of the ages.
Souls with their bodies conjoined shall He summon to
　　judgment.
Xanthic with withering brambles the garden untended.
Riches shall many reject and their long-cherished idols.
Enormous the blaze that shall burn the broad seas and the
　　heavens;
Its terrible blasts shall break open the portals of Hades.
Saints in their flesh shall shine free in the light of this wild-
　　fire—
The same that shall roast without ending the flesh of the
　　wicked.
Openly speak shall each man his most secret wrongdoing,
Sounding the depths shall God open their hearts to the day-
　　light.
Then gnashing of teeth shall resound and most horrible
　　weeping.
Even the sun shall not shine and the stars shall fall silent;
Over and done with the moonlight, the sky wrapped in
　　darkness.
Up shall the valleys be leveled, the hilltops be downcast,
Under and over in human affairs shall be ended.
Into the fields the mountains sink down and the billows.

[1] Modern scholars date this 'Sibylline' acrostic toward the end
of the second century of the Christian era. For St. Augustine's own
doubts, cf. below, 18.46.

Over and done with the earth and the whole of its holdings.
Spring-source and river alike shall be boiling with fire.
Swelling, the trumpet shall sound from the height of the
    heavens
Over the criminal damned the sad tale of their wanderings.
Tartarus' pit shall the quake-shaken earth be revealing.
Rivers of brimstone and fire shall fall from the heavens.
Judged before God shall the kings of the world then stand.

However, when the original translator tried to render the
Greek into Latin, he found it impossible to retain perfectly
the sequence of initial letters; for, wherever the Greek letter
for Y occurred, no Latin words beginning with the corresponding letter and at the same time suitable to the verses' meaning
could be found. The refractory verses are numbers five, eight-
een, and nineteen.[2] However, by connecting the initial letters
of all the verses, these three excepted, and then mentally substituting for the initial letters used in the latter the Greek letter
for Y, even the Latin reader could see a transliteration of the
Greek acrostic which read: IESOUS XREISTÒS THEOU UIÒS SŌTER.

The verses are twenty-seven in number, which is the cube
of three. Three times three equals nine; three times nine (raising the square to a cube) equals twenty-seven. If, moreover,
you string along together the initial letters of the five Greek
words in question, you get the Greek word, *Ichthys,* which
means fish. This, by mystical application, is a name for Christ,
because, as a fish can live in the depths of waters, Christ was
able to live in the abyss of our mortality without sin, which is
truly to live.

This Erythrean (or, as some are persuaded, Cumaean) Sibyl's entire poem, of which I have cited but a tiny segment,
contains nothing at all in favor of worshiping false or man-
made gods. Quite to the contrary, it speaks out so openly
against them and their votaries that the prophetess herself, it
seems, must be counted among those who belonged to the City
of God.

Lactantius, too, has woven into one of his books[3] some

---

[2] In Father Honan's English version all of the initial letters of
the Greek acrostic are preserved.
[3] *Institutiones* 4.18.

sibylline prophecies concerning Christ, but he does not indicate their authorship. These passages, which he quoted in different places, I have decided to put down all together in a single connected sequence: 'Afterwards, says she, he shall fall into the unjust hands of unbelievers; they shall strike God with unclean hands and shall spit upon him the poisonous spittle of their impure mouths; but he shall simply give over his holy back to their whips. . . . And silently he shall take their blows so that none may know the source or the meaning of the word he addresses to hell as he is crowned with thorns. . . . For meat they have given him gall, and for drink, vinegar; this is the kind of hospitality they shall show him at table. . . . Thou fool—not to have recognized thy God, displaying himself before the minds of men; instead, you crowned him with thorns and brewed him the cup of bitter-tasting gall. . . . But the veil of the temple shall be rent; and at midday there shall be a night of pitch-blackness lasting for three hours. . . . And, having died, he shall sleep the sleep of death for three days; then he shall come back from hell to the daylight, the first of the arisen, establishing the beginning of resurrection for those whom he has recalled.'

These are the sibylline prophecies which, as I have said, Lactantius used bit by bit to support the progression of his argument. I have strung them along uninterruptedly, taking care to observe his divisions with capital letters—an arrangement which will remain clear if only the copyists hereafter will not neglect to keep the capitals where they belong.

I should say that some writers place the Erythrean Sibyl at the time of the Trojan War rather than in Romulus' day.

Chapter 24

After the 'theological' poets, of whom Orpheus was the most highly esteemed, there came seven other seers to whom was accorded the title, *Sophoi*, which is Greek for Wise Men. One of these, Thales the Milesian, is said to have lived during the reign of Romulus. In this same period the ten tribes known, since the division, as Israel were conquered by the Chaldaeans and led off into captivity. Consequently, there remained in Judea only the two tribes known as Juda with their capital at Jerusalem.

Because the corpse of the dead Romulus, like that of Aeneas, was nowhere to be found, the Romans elevated him also to godhood, as everyone knows perfectly well. This practice had been discontinued, and when it was reverted to later on in the days of the Caesars it was a matter of flattery, not one of faith.[1] At any rate, Cicero[2] gives great credit to Romulus for having won such distinction not in an age when men were primitive, illiterate, and easily taken in, but in one when men were both cultivated and learned, even though the razor-sharp and fine-spun volubility of the philosophers was yet to bud and burst into foaming bloom.[3]

However, granted that more advanced times did cease to divinize any more dead men, they did not leave off worshiping as gods those whom the ancients had so established. What is worse, they enhanced the seductiveness of this empty and impious superstition with graven images—a thing unknown to their forefathers. What is still worse, the unclean demons at work in their hearts (tricking them, too, by means of lying oracles) drove them to portray in filthy plays consecrated to the honor of the false gods the same false gods' mythical crimes, which this more sophisticated age was no longer imaginatively creating.

Numa came to the throne after Romulus. This king's policy was to buttress Rome with quantities of false gods—and the more the better. Yet he himself did not succeed, after his death, in being added to the horde. Apparently, people thought he had so stuffed heaven with divinities that there was no room left for him. While he was ruling in Rome, the godless king Manasses, by whom the Prophet Isaias was put to death, was beginning his reign among the Hebrews. These, they say, were the days of the Sibyl of Samos.

---

[1] . . . *nec postea nisi adulando, non errando, factum est.*

[2] *De re publica* 2.10.18.

[3] . . . *quamvis nondum efferbuerat ac pullaverat philosophorum subtilis et acuta loquacitas.*

Chapter 25

When Sedechias was ruling over the Hebrews and Tarquin Priscus, successor of Ancus Martius, over the Romans, the magnificent Temple which Solomon built in Jerusalem was demolished and the Jewish people were led off captive into Babylonia. These events had been foretold when the Prophets had chided them for their sins and infidelities. Jeremias, specifically, prophesied even the duration of the captivity.[1]

In these days, we are told, Pittacus of Mitylene, another of the Seven Wise Men, lived. Eusebius has written that the other five (besides Thales and Pittacus whom we have mentioned) lived during the Babylonian captivity of God's people; these were Solon of Athens, Chilo of Lacedemon, Periander of Corinth, Cleobalus of Lindus, and Bias of Priene. All seven of them lived later than the period of the 'theological' poets, and were famous for their praiseworthy manner of living and of enunciating their moral precepts. So far as writings are concerned, however, they bequeathed nothing to posterity, save Solon, who is reputed to have given the Athenians some laws, and Thales, who left books on the principles of natural philosophy.

In these days of the Jewish captivity, Anaximander, Anaximenes, and Xenophanes also became famous as natural philosophers. Pythagoras, too, was alive, the man who began to call wise men 'philosophers.'

Chapters 26-36

Continuing the parallelism of the histories of the Jews and the Gentiles, Augustine stresses the many Jewish prophecies of the coming of Christ and the 'calling' of the Gentiles.

Chapter 37

Even in the days when the writings of our Prophets had already attracted close to world-wide attention, there were no pagan thinkers properly called 'philosophers,' in the sense first

[1] Jer. 25.11.

started by Pythagoras of Samos. Now, since Pythagoras won a name and fame for himself only about the time the Babylonian captivity ended, it is obvious that all other philosophers came still later than the Prophets. Socrates the Athenian, for example, master of all the famous philosophers of his age and the outstanding exponent of moral or practical wisdom, is dated later even than Esdras in the Chronicles. Plato was born shortly after Socrates, and was destined to outstrip all of his fellow disciples. Even if we go back beyond Pythagoras to those who were not yet styled 'philosophers,' for example, to the Seven Wise Men or to the Physicists, who followed Thales in the careful scrutiny of nature, to men like Anaximander, Anaximenes, Anaxagoras and others, we shall still find no men of pagan wisdom antedating the first of our Prophets. Thales, who leads this list, became well known during Romulus' reign, at the time when in Israel a torrent of prophecy broke loose in those minor Prophets whose words were destined to flow like rivers over the whole earth.

Consequently, it is only the Greek 'theological' poets— Orpheus, Linus, Musaeus, and the rest—who antedated all of the Hebrew Prophets included in the canon. They did not, however, antedate the first writer in our canon, Moses, the true theologian who truthfully preached the one true God. So far, then, as the Greeks are concerned, they may have reached the highest pitch of perfection in secular literature, but they have no foundation for boasting that, although their wisdom may not be superior to our religion (in which true wisdom lies), it is, at least, older.

On the other hand, I must admit that certain peoples other than the Greeks, the Egyptians, for example, had before Moses' time a certain body of learning which might be called their 'wisdom.' Otherwise, Holy Writ could not have said that Moses was schooled in all the wisdom of the Egyptians.[1] It tells how he was born there, adopted and reared by Pharao's daughter, and put to learning letters.

Even so, if you remember that Abraham himself was a prophet, you will see that Egyptian wisdom, too, is posterior to the wisdom of our Prophets. For, what wisdom could there

[1] Acts 7.22.

have been in Egypt, anyway, before Isis (who was worshiped as a great goddess after death) gave them an alphabet? She was the daughter of Inachus, first king of the Argives, and in this king's day Abraham was already a grandfather.

Chapter 38

I may, in fact, find prophecy far earlier even than Abraham. I might regard—and rightly regard—our patriarch, Noe (who lived even before the great flood), as a prophet; for he was a prophet at least in the sense that the ark which he made, and in which he and his family were saved from the flood, was itself a prophecy of what is happening in the Church today. I might go even beyond Noe to Henoch, who lived as far back as the seventh generation from Adam. Does not the canonical Epistle of St. Jude the Apostle openly declare that Henoch spoke as a prophet?[1]

It is true, indeed, that the alleged writings of these two men have never been accepted as authoritative, either by the Jews or by us Christians, but that is because their extreme antiquity makes us afraid of handing out, as authentic, works that may be forgeries. The fact is that certain irresponsible people who believe anything as their whim dictates do hand about certain writings which are said to have been written by Henoch and Noe. But the canon, which must be kept immaculate, has repudiated these writings; not, of course, because there was any doubt about the holiness of these men themselves—for they were pleasing to God—but simply because it is too difficult to believe that the writings are authentic. Nor should this critical reserve with respect to writings allegedly of such enormous antiquity astonish anyone.

The point of exclusion from the canon may be illustrated from the Book of Kings. This deals with the history of Israel and Juda and contains many historical facts, some of which we have confidently included in the canonical Scriptures, while other facts are not mentioned in full, but are merely alluded to as being narrated in other books written by men who were Prophets and whose names are, in two instances,

[1] Jude 14.

mentioned.[2] The 'other books' are not to be found in the Hebrew canon.

I confess that I know of no satisfactory explanation of this exclusion. However, I will suggest as an hypothesis that authors, to whom the Holy Spirit revealed such matters as should be binding in religious faith, could have written parts of their works in their capacity as careful historians, and other parts in their capacity as divinely inspired prophets, and that the distinction was so clear to the writers themselves that they understood that the former parts should be attributed to themselves while the others should be attributed to God speaking through them. Thus, the human parts would be a matter of fullness of historical knowledge, while the inspired parts would have the full force of religious revelation. It is with this last alone that the canon is concerned.

In regard now to such writings as fall outside the canon, and are passed off under the names of very ancient[3] prophets, these writings have no value even from the point of view of fullness of information, for the simple fact that no one can verify whether they belong to the men whose names they bear. In a word, it is because they might be spurious that they are not to be trusted; and this is pre-eminently the case with works that contain declarations that run counter to the faith as contained in canonical writings, for then we can be absolutely sure that the attribution is spurious.

Chapter 39

We should pay no attention to those who maintain that the Hebrew language, merely as speech, was preserved through Heber (whence the name, Hebrew) and thus came down to Abraham, but that written Hebrew began only with the Mosaic Law. The truth is that Hebrew, both spoken and written, was handed down from one to another of those ancient Patriarchs. Moses, in fact, took care to appoint teachers of reading and writing for God's people before they had any

---

[2] 1 Par. 29.21; 2 Par. 9.29.

[3] Reading *veterum* in place of *verorum* of the Mss.

written record of God's Law.[1] The Septuagint Scripture calls these instructors *grammatoeisagōgoí*, which is Greek for 'bringers-in of letters,' because they brought them, in a sense, into their students' minds, or perhaps introduced their students to them.

Accordingly, no people should foolishly brag about their wisdom antedating that of our Patriarchs and Prophets, whose wisdom was from God. The Egyptians, for example, make a business of boasting about the antiquity of their learning. But it is a false and hollow boast, for, on examination, we discover that even their learning, such indeed as it was, did not antedate that of our Patriarchs. No one is going to be silly enough to say that the Egyptians were deeply versed in studies which are extremely difficult before they had even learned to read and write—that is, before Isis came there and taught them. Besides, what was their extraordinary learning, their vaunted 'wisdom,' except, in the main, astronomy and other cognate studies which furnish more in the way of intellectual calisthenics than any genuine illumination of the mind,[2] such as true wisdom affords.

Speaking of philosophy, it is the essential function of this subject to teach men how to attain happiness. There was nothing of this kind in Egypt until around the time of Mercury or Trismegistus, as he was called, when such studies began to win public attention. This was, admittedly, much earlier than the appearance of the sages and philosophers in Greece. Even so, it was later than Abraham, Isaac, and Jacob. What is more, it was later even than Moses himself. For Moses was a contemporary of Atlas, Prometheus' brother, the eminent astronomer, the maternal grandfather of Mercury the elder of whom Mercury Trismegistus was the grandson.

Chapter 40

Consequently, how utterly unconvincing is the presumptuous prattling of those who maintain that Egyptian astronomi-

[1] Cf. Exod. 18.25, and St. Augustine's *Quaestiones in Heptateucha* 2.69.

[2] . . . *magis ad exercenda ingenia quam ad inluminandas vera sapientia mentes.*

cal science has a history of more than 100,000 years! From what books, pray, did they cull this number, if Queen Isis taught them to write not much more than 2,000 years ago? This point about the origin of Egyptian letters is made by Varro, no negligible authority in matters historical, and it fits in well with what we know from Holy Writ. Besides, since 6,000 years have not yet elapsed from the days of Adam, the first man, should we not ridicule, rather than bother to refute, those who strive to convince us of a temporal duration so different and so utterly contrary to this established truth?

Who can be a more trustworthy chronicler of things past than one who was also a prophet of things future which our eyes behold realized in the things present? The very disagreement of historians among themselves affords us an opportunity to chose for credence those whose contentions are not at variance with the divinely inspired history to which we adhere. Very different is the plight of the ungodly city's citizens scattered over the whole face of the earth! When these people study the books of men so tremendously learned that no one of them, they feel, can be taken lightly as an authority, and find them, nevertheless, entertaining discordant views on matters enormously removed from the memory of living man, they do not know what or whom to believe. We, on the other hand, have the support of divine authority in the history of our religion. Accordingly, whatever in secular histories runs counter to it we do not hesitate to brand as wholly false, while with respect to non-parallel matters we remain indifferent. For, whether they be true or untrue, they make no important contribution to our living righteous and happy lives.

Chapter 41

To discuss historical topics, I left the philosophers alone for a while. Now I come back to them. These men, in all their laborious investigations, seem to have had one supreme and common objective: to discover what manner of living is best suited to laying hold upon happiness. Yet, they have ended up by disagreeing—disciples with masters, and disciples with fellow disciples. Why, except that they sought the answer to their question merely in human terms, depending solely upon human experience and human reasoning? It is true that some of their dissensions may be explained by a less worthy factor: namely, the vainglorious desire to appear wiser and more penetrating than one's colleague, less dependent upon others' opinions, and more of a creative thinker. Nevertheless, we must be ready to allow that some at least, perhaps many, who broke with their teachers or fellow students, did so out of a pure love of the truth, determined to fight for it as they understood it (whether it was actually the truth or not). What does it all go to prove except that human unhappiness cannot get very far along the road to happiness unless divine authority shows the way?

How different is the case of those writers who with good reason have been included in the final canon of Holy Writ. There is no shadow of disagreement among them. That is why such enormous numbers of men, of every conceivable description, have quite rightly found in their writings the voice of God Himself or of God speaking through them—so many, and not just a handful of the formerly disputatious chatterers connected with philosophical societies and schools, men both learned and the unlearned everywhere, farmers in the field, townsmen in the towns. Admittedly, our writers are few in number, but this was quite proper, lest their writings, so precious from a religious viewpoint, seem cheap by their very abundance. On the other hand, they are numerous enough to make their perfect agreement a thing to marvel at. Granted that there is a more copious literary legacy in philosophy, a man still would be hard put to find, in all this abundance, any philosophers in agreement on everything they have taught —a proposition, however, which I cannot take time to prove in this work.

Has any one founder of a philosophical school become so solidly accepted in the demon-adoring city[1] that those with different or diametrically opposed doctrines have been forthwith rejected? Is it not a fact that in Athens the Epicureans and Stoics were equally admired, although the former taught that the gods took no interest in human affairs, while the lat-

---

[1] . . . *in hac daemonicola civitate adprobatus.*

ter taught that the gods constantly governed, guarded, and guided them? These are mutually exclusive opinions. Anaxagoras was condemned for saying that the sun is merely a burning stone and not a god at all. I wonder why, since Epicurus flourished gloriously in the same city and went unmolested, although he claimed that neither the sun nor any of the stars is divine, and that neither Jupiter nor any god at all dwells in the world to hear the prayers and supplications of humankind. Is it not a fact that Aristippus placed the highest good in bodily pleasures, while Antisthenes maintained that only moral virtue can make man happy—both of them in Athens? Were not both of them Socratics of the first rank? Yet they found life's very meaning in such wholly irreconcilable goals. Did not Aristippus teach that a wise man should keep clear of public office and Antisthenes that he should devote himself to it? And both of them went around gathering in followers to promote their ideas.

In Athens in those days the philosophers went milling about with their hangers-on, in broad daylight, here and there, now in the world-renowned Portico, now in the schools, now in little gardens, in every species of public and private place, each one belligerently propounding his own persuasions—some saying that there is only one world, some saying that it began, others, that it had no beginning; some saying it will come to an end, others that it will go on forever; some saying that the world is ruled by divine intelligence, others, that it is driven by fortuitous chance. With respect to the soul, some say it is immortal, others, that it is mortal; of those defending immortality, some say that the soul will turn up again in a beast, others, no such thing; of those defending mortality, some say the soul will die shortly after the body, others, that it will live on after the body; of these, some say that it will survive for a little while, others, for rather a long while, though not forever. With respect to the identity of the highest good, some put it in the body; others, in the mind; still others, in both at the same time; still others drag in extrinsic goods and add them to the body and mind. With respect to the validity of sense experience, some say that the senses are always to be trusted; others, not in every instance; still others, never.

Tell me, has any people, senate, or person with any power or authority in the ungodly city[2] ever bothered to examine these and the other almost innumerable results of philosophical wrangling with a view to approve and accept certain fixed principles and to condemn and reject all contentions to the contrary? Is it not the case, rather, that the ungodly city has, without the smallest degree of critical discrimination, taken all these scrapping ideas from here, there, and everywhere, clutching them in pell-mell confusion to her bosom? Yet, these philosophers were not discussing such relatively indifferent matters as agriculture, architecture, or economics.[3] They were holding forth on the deepest issues of all, the things that have to do with whether mankind is to live in happiness or in utter wretchedness.

Granted that some of the things these philosophers said are true, still, untruth was taught with equal license. No wonder, then, that this earthly city has been given the symbolic name of Babylon, for Babylon means confusion, as I remember having already remarked. Actually, her diabolical king does not care a straw how many contradictory opinions she harbors or how her people squabble over them, so long as he goes on in possession of them and all their errors—a tyranny they deserve by reason of their enormous and manifold ungodliness.

How differently has that other race, that other commonwealth of men, that other City, the people of Israel, to whom was entrusted the word of God, managed matters! No broad-minded, muddle-headed mixing of true prophets with false prophets there! They have recognized and held as the true-speaking authors of Holy Writ only those who are in perfect harmony with one another. These writers are for them their philosophers, that is, their lovers of wisdom, their sages, their theologians, their prophets, their teachers of good living and right believing—all in one. They know that if they think and live according to what these men taught, they are thinking and living according to God—who spoke through the inspired

---

[2] . . . quis umquam populus, quis senatus, quae potestas vel dignitas publica inpiae civitatis.

[3] . . . non de agris et domibus vel quacumque pecuniaria ratione.

writers—and not according to man. They know that when these writers forbid sacrilege, God Himself forbids it. When they say, 'Honor thy father and thy mother; Thou shalt not commit adultery; Thou shalt not kill; Thou shalt not steal,'[4] and the rest, they recognize these for God's commands—not human mouthings, but divine revelations.[5]

Certain philosophers, it is true, did get a glimpse of the truth amid the fog of their own fallacies and did try to build it up to solid conviction and persuasiveness by means of carefully worked-out argumentation—such truths, for example, as God's creation of the world, His providential governance of it, the excellence of virtue, of patriotism, of loyalty in friendship, of good works and all other things pertaining to morality. They saw these things even when they did not know to what final end, or how, they were to be referred. But in the City of God these truths are found in the words of the Prophets—God's words, even though spoken by men. And they were not driven into her people's heads amid the tumult of twisting and turning argumentation, but simply delivered to them.[6] And those who heard them trembled, for they knew that if they despised them they were despising not the wisdom of man, but the word of God.

Chapter 42

Even one of the Ptolomies, kings of Egypt, strove to possess and become acquainted with the Holy Scriptures. Here is the story of how Egypt first came to have this dynasty of kings.

Alexander of Macedon, surnamed the Great, in an extremely brief but absolutely breath-taking show of power,[1] conquered all of Asia—indeed, nearly the whole world—sometimes by using armed aggression, at other times by intimidation. While he was subduing the East, he marched into Judea and took possession. After his death,[2] his higher officers, realizing they

---

[4] Exod. 20.12–15.
[5] . . . *non haec ora humana, sed oracula divina fuderunt.*
[6] . . . *populo commendata sunt, non argumentationum concertationibus inculcata.*

---

[1] . . . *mirificentissiman minimeque diuturnam potentiam.*
[2] 323 B.C.

would not be able to rule, jointly and without conflict, such a gigantic empire, chose to carve it up—or, rather, to cut it to pieces, for their wars were to bring it nothing but destruction and dissolution.

Hereupon, Egypt began to be ruled by Ptolomies, of whom the first, a son of Lagus, brought into Egypt many slave laborers from Judea. His successor, the second Ptolemy, called Philadelphus, emancipated and repatriated all of them. What is more, he sent royal gifts to God's Temple in Jerusalem, begging meanwhile from Eleazar, who was the high priest, copies of the sacred Scriptures which, he had heard, were divinely inspired. The king was, he said, most eager to have a copy for the magnificent library he had built.

When Eleazar had sent him copies in Hebrew, the king then requested that he send him translators. Six men from each of the twelve tribes, seventy-two in all, men deeply versed in both Hebrew and Greek, were appointed. Thus, the translation they made is by prevailing custom called the Septuagint.

Tradition tells the following story.[8] To test their trustworthiness, Ptolemy had them tackle this task, each in solitary confinement. When they had finished, it was discovered that in their versions they had arrived at a wonderful, indeed a stupendous and obviously divinely inspired, unanimity in their choice of words; that they were in agreement in each word (at least so far as meaning and equivalent value are concerned), and in the order of the words they chose. All gave one translation as if there were but one translator, because, in truth, the one Holy Spirit was at work in all. God gave them this marvelous gift so that the authorship of the Scriptures would seem to the Gentiles divine and not human, and so that in time they would believe in and profit by them. We have lived to see this realized.

[8] The story goes back to the so-called Letter of Aristeas, which modern scholars regard as spurious.

Chapter 43

There have, of course, been other translations of the Old Testament from Hebrew into Greek. We have versions by Aquila, Symmachus, Theodotion, and an anonymous translation which is known simply as the 'fifth edition.' Nevertheless, the Church has adopted the Septuagint as if it were the only translation. Indeed, Greek-speaking Christians use it so generally that many of them do not even know that the others exist. From the Septuagint a Latin translation has been made, and this is the one which the Latin churches use. This is still the case despite the fact that in our own day the priest Jerome, a great scholar and master of all three tongues, has made a translation into Latin, not from Greek but directly from the original Hebrew.[1] The Jews admit that his highly learned labor is a faithful and accurate version, and claim, moreover, that the seventy translators made a great many mistakes in their version. Christ's Church, however, thinks it inadvisable to choose the authority of any one man as against the authority of so many men—men hand-picked, too, by the high priest Eleazar for this specific task.[2] For, even supposing that they were not inspired by one divine Spirit, but that, after the manner of scholars, the Seventy merely collated their versions in a purely human way and agreed on a commonly approved text, still, I say, no single translator should be ranked ahead of so many.

The truth is that there shone out from the Seventy so tremendous a miracle of divine intervention that anyone translating the Scriptures from the Hebrew into any other language will, if he is a faithful translator, agree with the Septuagint; if not, we must still believe that there is some deep revealed meaning in the Septuagint. For, the same Spirit who inspired the original Prophets as they wrote was no less present to the Seventy as they translated what the Prophets had written. And this Spirit, with divine authority, could say, through

[1] The so-called Vulgate, which was begun in 390 and finished in 405.

[2] The Catholic Church has long since accepted the Vulgate as official.

the translators, something different from what He had said
through the original Prophets—just as, though these Prophets
had the two meanings in mind, both were inspired by the
Spirit. Besides, the Holy Spirit can say the same thing in two
different ways, so long as the same meaning, in different words,
is clear to anyone who reads with understanding. The Spirit,
too, could omit certain things and add others, to make it clear
that in the translators' work there was no question of their being bound to a purely human, word-for-word, slavish transcription, but only to the divine power which filled and mastered their minds.

Many have felt, of course, that the Greek manuscripts of
the Septuagint need emendations by comparison with the
Hebrew, but they did not presume to leave passages out of
the former merely because they were not to be found in the
latter. They were content to add to the Septuagint passages
lacking there but present in the Hebrew, and they marked
the beginning of such verses with star-shaped signs, called
asterisks, while passages found in the Septuagint but missing
in the Hebrew original were marked with short horizontal
lines such as are used in writing fractions.[3] Many manuscripts
with these critical signs—not only in Greek but in Latin, too—
are in wide circulation. So much for additions and omissions.
With respect to other matters, that is, things expressed differently, whether they yield different meanings not wholly beyond harmonization, or the self-same meaning in synonyms
—such passages cannot be recognized except by comparing
both texts.

At any rate, if in reading the Scriptures we keep an eye, as
we ought, only to what the Spirit of God spoke by the lips of
men, we will conclude, in the case of something in the Hebrew
which is missing in the Septuagint, that the Spirit elected to
say this by the lips of the original Prophets and not by the
lips of their translators. Conversely, in the case of something
present in the Septuagint and missing in the original, we will
conclude that the Spirit chose to say this particular thing by
the lips of the Seventy rather than by the lips of the original
Prophets, thus making it clear that all of them were inspired.

[3] . . . *iacentibus virgulis, sicut scribuntur unciae, signaverunt.*

Not otherwise did the Spirit speak, as He willed, certain things through Isaias, others through Jeremias, still others through this or that Prophet, or the self-same things in divers ways, now through this one, now through that. Whatever is found both in the original Hebrew and in the Septuagint, the one same Spirit chose to say through both; with this difference, however, that the former were inspired while prophesying, the latter were inspired while translating the original prophecy.[4] Just as the one Spirit of peace made the former say things both true and consistent, the same Spirit made the latter, without benefit of mutual consultation, speak all that they spoke as if by one mouth.

Chapters 44-45

The events of Jewish and pagan history in the centuries immediately preceding Christ are rapidly described in these two chapters.

Chapter 46

According to prophecy,[1] Christ was born in Bethlehem of Juda, at the time, as I said, when Herod was king in Judea. At Rome, the republic had given way to the empire, and the Emperor Caesar Augustus had established a world-wide peace.

Christ was born a visible man of a human virgin mother, but He was a hidden God because God was His Father. So the Prophet had foretold: 'Behold the virgin shall be with child, and shall bring forth a son; and they shall call his name Emmanuel, which is, interpreted, God with us.'[2] To prove that He was God, Christ worked many miracles, some of which—as many as seemed necessary to establish His claim—are recorded in the Gospels. Of these miracles the very first was the marvelous manner of His birth; the very last, His ascension into heaven in His body risen from the dead.

---

[4] . . . *sed ita ut illi praecederent prophetando, isti sequerentur prophetice illos interpretando.*

[1] Mich. 5.2.

[2] Isa. 7.14; Matt. 1.23.

Despite all, the Jews who refused to believe that He was destined to die and to rise from the dead slew Him and were ravaged by the Romans worse than before, torn from their fatherland where foreigners were already lording it over them, and scattered over the whole earth—for they are now everywhere. And it is their own Scriptures that bear witness that it is not we who are the inventors of the prophecies touching Christ. That is why many of them, who pondered these prophecies before His passion and more especially after His Resurrection, have come to believe in Him, as was foretold: 'For if thy people, O Israel, shall be as the sand of the sea, a remnant of them shall be converted.'[3] But the rest have been blinded, as was also foretold: 'Let their table become as a snare before them, and a recompense, and a stumbling-block. Let their eyes be darkened that they see not; and their back bend thou down always.'[4] That is why when they refuse to believe in our Scriptures and read their own like blind men, they are fulfilling what their own Prophets foretold.

However, some of them may object that we Christians made up the non-Jewish prophecies concerning Christ which are circulating under the name of the Sibyl—or others under any other names. My answer is that we have no need of any others than the ones in our opponents' books, precisely because these enemies, who are scattered over the whole earth wherever the Church is expanding and who possess and preserve these books, are living witnesses, however reluctant, to the truth of our position. For, in the very psalms which they read there is a prophecy to this effect: 'He is my God. His mercy shall help me. My God has shown this to me in the midst of my enemies. Slay them not lest they forget thy law. Scatter them in thy power.'[5] God has shown the grace of His mercy to His Church 'in the midst of her enemies,' for, as St. Paul says: 'By their offense salvation has come to the Gentiles.'[6]

Although they were conquered and oppressed by the Romans, God did not 'slay' them, that is, He did not destroy them as Jews. For, in that case, they would have forgotten and would have been useless as witnesses to what I am speaking of. Consequently, the first part of the prophecy, 'Slay them

---

[3] Isa. 10.22.   [4] Ps. 68.23,24.
[5] Ps. 58.11,12.   [6] Rom. 11.11.

not lest they forget thy law,' is of small import without the rest, 'Scatter them.' For, if the Jews had remained bottled up in their own land with the evidence of their Scriptures and if they were not to be found everywhere, as the Church is, the Church would not then have them as ubiquitous witnesses of the ancient prophecies concerning Christ.

Chapters 47-50

The Jews were not the only citizens of God in ancient times; Job, for instance, was not a Jew. The prophecies of the reconstruction of the Temple are fulfilled in the growth of the Christian Church, and in the conversion of the Gentiles.

Chapter 51

When the Devil saw the human race abandoning the temples of demons and marching happily forward in the name of the freedom-giving Mediator, he inspired heretics to oppose Christian teaching under cover of the Christian name as though their presence in the City of God could go unchallenged like the presence, in the city of confusion, of philosophers with wholly different and even contradictory opinions!

Heretics are those who entertain in Christ's Church unsound and distorted ideas and stubbornly refuse, even when warned, to return to what is sound and right, to correct their contagious and death-dealing doctrines, but go on defending them. When they leave the Church they are ranked as enemies who try her patience. Even so, their evil-doing profits the loyal Catholic members of Christ's Body, for God makes good use of bad men, while 'for those who love God all things work together unto good.'[1] Actually, all foes of the Church, whether blinded by error or moved by malice, subserve her in some fashion. If they have power to do her physical harm, they develop her power to suffer; if they oppose her intellectually, they bring out her wisdom; since she must love even her enemies, her loving kindness is made manifest; and whether she has to deal with them in the persuasiveness of argument

[1] Rom. 8.28.

or the chastisement of law, they bring into play her power to do good.

So it is that the diabolical prince of the ungodly city is not allowed to harm the pilgrim City of God, even when he stirs up his tools and dupes against her. Beyond all doubt, Divine Providence sees to it that she has both some solace of prosperity that she may not be broken by adversity and some testing of adversity that she may not be weakened by prosperity. Thus, the one balances the other, as one can see from the words of the psalm, 'According to the multitude of sorrows in my heart, so thy consolations have gladdened my soul,'[2] and those of St. Paul: 'Rejoicing in hope, being patient in tribulation.'[3]

St. Paul also says: 'All who want to live piously in Christ Jesus will suffer persecution.'[4] Persecution, therefore, will never be lacking. For, when our enemies from without leave off raging and there ensues a span of tranquility—even of genuine tranquility and great consolation at least to the weak—we are not without enemies within, the many whose scandalous lives wound the hearts of the devout. These people bring discredit upon the Christian and Catholic name—a name so dear to 'all who want to live piously in Christ Jesus'—that they grieve bitterly to see their own brethren love it less than pious people should. There is that other heartache of seeing heretics, too, using the name and sacraments, the Scriptures and the Creed of genuine Christians. They realize how many would-be converts are driven into perplexed hesitancy because of heretical dissension, while the foul-mouthed find in heretics further pretext for cursing the Christian name, since these heretics at least call themselves Christian.

So it is that those who want to live piously in Christ must suffer the spiritual persecution of these and other aberrations in thought and morals, even when they are free from physical violence and vexation. This explains the verse: 'According to the multitude of sorrows in my heart'—there is no mention of the body. On the other hand, they recall the unchangeable, divine promise that no one of them can be lost. As St. Paul says: 'The Lord knows who are his,'[5] and 'For those whom he has foreknown he has also predestined to become conformed to the image of his son.'[6] And the psalm just cited goes on: 'Thy consolations have gladdened my soul.'

Yet, even the mental suffering which the devout undergo because of the lives of bad or pretended Christians is a source of spiritual profit because it flows from their charity, in virtue of which they would not have sinners be lost or go on blocking the salvation of others. Besides, the devout experience immense consolation when conversions flood the souls with a joy as great as the previous anguish on their account was excruciating.

So it falls out that in this world, in evil days like these, the Church walks onward like a wayfarer stricken by the world's hostility, but comforted by the mercy of God. Nor does this state of affairs date only from the days of Christ's and His Apostles' presence on earth. It was never any different from the days when the first just man, Abel, was slain by his ungodly brother. So it shall be until this world is no more.

Chapter 52

No one knows how many persecutions Christ's Church may yet suffer; certainly, there will be a final one, that of Antichrist.

Chapter 53

This much is certain, that, with His second coming, Jesus Himself will quench the fires of that final persecution which will be Antichrist's. For it is written: 'He will slay him with the breath of His mouth, and He will destroy him with the brightness of His coming.'[1]

At this point people usually inquire: When will all this happen? A most unreasonable question, for, if it were good for us to know the answer, the Master, God Himself, would have told His disciples when they asked Him. When they had Him face to face, they did not receive such news in silence, either,

---

[5] 2 Tim. 2.19.   [6] Rom. 8.29.
[1] 2 Thess. 2.8.

but plainly asked Him: 'Lord, wilt thou at this time restore
the kingdom to Israel?' And He replied: 'It is not for you to
know the times or dates which the Father has fixed by his
own authority'[2]—an answer, it should be noted, given to men
who had not sought to know the exact hour, or day, or year,
but only the general time of this fulfillment. Obviously, then,
it is a waste of effort for us to attempt counting the precise
number of years which this world has yet to go, since we
know from the mouth of Truth that it is none of our business.

Not to be put off, however, some men have presumed to
say that the complement of years between our Lord's Ascension and His second coming will be 400, others, 500, others,
as high as 1,000. It would be both a lengthy and pointless
task to show how each one tries to bolster up his opinion.
They fall back on human guesswork, you may be sure, for the
canonical Scriptures afford them nothing clearcut in the way
of supporting evidence.

Suffice it to say that the fingers of all such calculators were
slackened by Him who imposed silence with the words: 'It is
not for you to know the times or dates which the Father has
fixed by his own authority.'

This text, being taken from the New Testament, has, of
course, done nothing to stop the votaries of the false gods from
pretending to define, on the basis of reponses from the demon
gods whom they adore, just how long the Christian religion
was destined to endure. When these people had to face the
fact that many gigantic persecutions, instead of destroying the
faith, had made it grow beyond belief, they trumped up some
Greek verses or other, in the form of an oracle's effusion to a
questing client, to make Christ out blameless in the propagation of this criminally sacrilegious sect. The verses added that
it was Peter who contrived by black magic to have Christ's
name adored, and that this farce would go on for 365 years,
whereupon it would end abruptly.

O these learned men! O these cultivated intelligences! They
refuse to believe in Christ, yet gladly believe such preposterous
things about Christ as that, while He was not the master
magician to his pupil Peter and was guileless while Peter alone

[2] Acts 1.6,7.

was the villain, Peter yet chose to promote the worship of Christ's name rather than of his own, and did this by means of the dark arts he knew, the efforts he made, the perils he underwent and, even, the shedding of his own blood! If Peter made the world love Christ by means of magic, by what innocent means did Christ make Peter love Him to this extent?

Let them answer this question in their own hearts. And let them understand, also, if they can, that heavenly grace alone made the world love Christ, for the sake of everlasting life, the very same grace which made Peter, too, love Christ and, looking to Him for everlasting life, suffer for His name's sake the brief death of the body.

And, by the way, what kind of gods are these that can foretell things, yet cannot prevent their happening? Do they have to collapse completely in the face of one magician and his one act of black magic in killing, as they claim a year-old body, cutting him up and then burying him with abominable ceremonies so as to persuade the god to allow a religion hostile to them to wax big and strong over so long a period, triumph over the horrendous savagery of so many persecutions—and not by resisting, but by suffering them—and, finally, achieve the overthrow of their own statues, temples, rites, and oracles? What kind of god was it—certainly not ours—who was so drawn or driven by Peter's monstrous crime as to grant all this success? For, so the verses say, Peter's magic imposed this on a god, not on any demon. Well, that is the kind of god people have who refuse to have Christ!

Chapter 54

I would produce a great deal more in the way of refutation had not the fatal year, foretold by fraudulent prophecy, and taken on faith by the empty-headed, already elapsed. Several years ago, the religion of Christ, which was established by Himself and His Apostles, had already lasted 365 years. Why, then, seek any further for arguments to scotch that pagan lie? Not to take Christ's birth as the starting point (because in infancy and boyhood He had no disciples), Christian faith and worship certainly became public knowledge when He personally appeared and began to have disciples, after He was baptized by John in the Jordan. This, in fact, is what is referred to in the prophecy concerning Him: 'He shall rule from sea to sea, and from the river to the ends of the earth.'[1]

However, for the sake of this debate, it is best to begin with the Resurrection. He was to suffer, die, and rise from the dead before the content of faith could receive its definitive form. This is what St. Paul had in mind when he said to the Athenians: 'He calls upon all men everywhere to repent; inasmuch as he had fixed a day on which he will judge the world with justice by a man whom he has appointed, in whom he had *defined* faith for all by raising him from the dead.'[2] It was after the Resurrection, too, that the Holy Spirit was to be given in that city from which, as had been ordained, the second Law, the New Testament, was first to be proclaimed. The first Law, the Old Testament, had come out of Mount Sinai by the lips of Moses; but of the Law Christ came to give it was foretold: 'The law shall come forth from Sion, and the word of the Lord from Jerusalem.'[3] This explains why Christ ordered repentance to be preached in His name among all peoples, but beginning in Jerusalem. It was there that the worship of this name arose when men were called upon to believe in Jesus Christ crucified and risen from the dead. It was there that this faith had such an electrifying introduction[4] that several thousands of men turned to Christ with astonishing enthusiasm, sold what they had to give to the poor, embraced voluntary poverty with holy determination and burning love, and steeled themselves, in the midst of enraged and bloodthirsty Jews, to battle unto death for the truth—not with weapons of war, but with the more potent weapon of patient suffering.[5] If this was the result of divine power, rather than of black magic, why should anyone hesitate to believe that the same divine power may have operated in the same way throughout the rest of the world? If, on the other hand, one persists in maintaining that Peter must already have performed his act of sorcery

---

[1] Ps. 71.8.   [2] Acts 17.30,31.
[3] Isa. 2.3.
[4] . . . *tam insignibus initiis incanduit.*
[5] . . . *non armata potentia, sed potentiore patientia.*

for so many men in Jerusalem to have been stirred to worship Christ's name—men who had either caught and crucified Him or had derided Him when He was crucified—then the year of these conversions is the proper starting point, and we must ask when the 365 years were up.

Very well. Now, Christ died in the year when the Gemini were consuls, on the twenty-fifth day of March. He rose from the dead on the third day, as the Apostles could prove from the witness with their own eyes. After forty days He ascended into heaven. Ten days later, on the fiftieth day after His resurrection, he sent down the Holy Spirit. On that day 3,000 men believed when the Apostles preached to them. It was on that day that the Christian religion began, and it was by the efficacy of the Holy Spirit, as we believe and the facts prove, and not by means of Peter's black magic, as impious foolishness has thought or feigned to think. A short time afterwards, 5,000 more men were converted upon the occasion of Peter's working a miracle upon a beggar, lame from birth, who used to be carried to the temple gate to get alms. In the name of Jesus Christ this man leaped to his feet cured. And so, as time went by, the Church grew by one influx after another of believers.

Thus, we can establish the very day on which the first year of Christianity began, namely, the fifteenth of May, the day when the Holy Spirit came down. Starting there and counting the consuls, we find that the 365 years were over on May 15, during the consulate of Honorius and Eutychianus.[6]

Now, in the following year, during the consulate of Manlius Theodorus, when, according to that demonic oracle or human fabrication, there ought to have been no Christianity left, I need not investigate how things were faring in other parts of the world, but I do know what happened in the illustrious city of Carthage in Africa. There, on March 31, Gaudentius and Jovius, officers of the Emperor Honorius, destroyed the temples of the false gods and smashed their statues.

Almost thirty years[7] have gone by since that day and anyone can see how Christianity has grown, especially by the conversion of those who were held back from the faith because

---

[6] A.D. 395.
[7] Thus, St. Augustine was finishing Book XVIII in 425.

they took that prophecy to be true. When the fated number of years had elapsed, however, they realized how senseless and ridiculous it was.

We who are Christians in name and in deed do not believe in Peter, but in Him in whom Peter believed; we have been drawn to Christ by Peter's exhortations, not drugged by his incantations; we have been helped by his services, not hoodwinked by his sorceries.[8] Christ was Peter's teacher in that faith which leads to everlasting life. The same Christ is our teacher, too.

Let me, at long last, end this Book. I have described in such detail as I judged adequate the historical course of the two cities, the heavenly and earthly, intermingled as they have been from the beginning and are to be until the end of time. The earthly one has made for herself, according to her heart's desire, false gods out of any sources at all, even out of human beings, that she might adore them with sacrifices. The heavenly one, on the other hand, living like a wayfarer in this world, makes no false gods for herself. On the contrary, she herself is made by the true God that she may be herself a true sacrifice to Him.

Both of these cities alike make use of temporal goods and both are equally afflicted by temporal ills—but how different they are in faith, how dissimilar in hope, how unlike in love![9] This will go on until they are to be separated in the Last Judgment, when each shall achieve its appointed end—an end which will have no end.

I must undertake now to treat of those ends.

[8] . . . *aedificati sermonibus, non carminibus venenati; nec decepti maleficiis, sed beneficiis eius adiuti.*
[9] . . . *diversa fide, diversa spe, diverso amore.*

PART FIVE

THE ENDS OF THE TWO CITIES

BOOK XIX

Philosophy and Christianity on Man's End

Chapter 1

FROM THIS POINT ON, I see that I must discuss the appointed ends of the two cities of earth and of heaven. But first I must set forth, within the limits which my work allows, the kind of philosophical efforts men have made in their search for happiness amid the sorrows of this mortal life. My purpose is, first, to point out the difference between their hollow aspirations and the holy assurances which God has given us; second, to make clear what is meant by the true beatitude which He will grant. For this latter purpose I shall appeal not only to divine Revelation but to such natural reasoning as will appeal to those who do not share our faith.

In regard to what is supremely good and supremely evil, philosophers have taken many different stands—all striving with the highest earnestness to determine what it is that makes men happy. By definition, our supreme end is that good which is sought for its own sake, and on account of which all other goods are sought. In the same way, the supreme evil is that on account of which other evils are avoided, whereas it is to be avoided on its own account. For the moment, we shall say that the ultimate good is not so much a good to end all goods as, rather, one by which goodness reaches its fullest consummation. In the same way, the ultimate evil is not one in which evil comes to an end, but the one in which evil reaches the very height of harm.[1] It is in this sense that the greatest good and the worst evil are called ends or ultimates.

To determine what these ultimates are and then, in this life, to obtain the supreme good and avoid the supreme evil—such has been the aim and effort of all who have professed a zeal for wisdom in this world of shadows. Of course, for all their aberrations, the nature of man has set limits to men's deviations from the right track, seeing that the ultimate good and evil must be found either in the soul, or in the body, or in both.[2] It was under these three general heads that Marcus Varro, in his work, *On Philosophy*, listed the immense variety of opinions which he examined with such careful and subtle scrutiny; he remarked that, by the application of various differentiating notes, he could easily reach no less than 288 possible species of opinions—not, of course, that there were that many schools in existence.

For the purpose of my exposition, I shall begin with an observation of Varro in the work just mentioned, namely, that there are four ends which men naturally pursue, irrespective of any teacher, formal education, or training in that purposeful art of living which we call virtue, and which is indubitably a matter of learning. These ends are: first, pleasure aroused by the pleasant stirring of our bodily senses; second, calm, in the sense of the absence of all bodily vexation; third, that combination of pleasure and serenity which Epicurus called, in a single word, pleasure; fourth, the primary demands of nature[3] which include, besides pleasure and calm, such needs of our body as wholeness, health, security, and such needs of our soul as man's innate spiritual powers, whether great or small. These four—pleasure, serenity, their combination, and the primary exigencies of nature—are so much a part of us that it is either on their account that we pursue the virtue which education brings us; or else they are sought on account of virtue; or else these four and virtue are sought, each on its own account. Hence, we get twelve schools of thought, since each of the

---

[1] *Finem boni . . . dicimus, non quo consumatur ut non sit, sed quo perficiatur ut plenum sit . . . finem mali non quo esse desinat, quo usque nocendo perducat.*

[2] Cf. above, 8.1.   [3] *Primigenia.*

four ends can be looked at in three ways. A single illustration
will make this whole matter clear.

Take bodily pleasure. This can be either subordinated or
preferred or merely joined to virtue in the soul. Hence, we get
three different schools of thought. Pleasure is subordinate to
virtue when it is a means to the practice of virtue. For example, it is a part of virtue to live in one's native land and
to beget children for the sake of the fatherland—neither of
which is possible without bodily pleasure, since we cannot eat
to live without pleasure nor, without pleasure, take the means
to propagate a family. On the other hand, when pleasure is
preferred to virtue, it is sought for its own sake and virtue is
pursued as a means for the sake of pleasure. This is to say
that virtue makes no effort save to procure or to make secure
some bodily pleasure. Strange life, indeed, where pleasure is
the mistress and virtue is the handmaid! No such handmaid
could, in fact, be called a virtue; yet this shameless and re-
volting theory has found philosophers to back and defend it.

Pleasure is combined with virtue when each is sought for
itself and neither for the other. Thus, just as pleasure is subordinated to, or preferred to, or co-ordinated with, virtue—
making three schools—so calm, a combination of pleasure and
calm, and the primary needs of nature can each be taken as a
criterion to produce three distinct schools. According to the
variety of human opinions, these ends are sometimes subordinated to, sometimes preferred to, and sometimes made co-
ordinate with, virtue; thus, the number of schools becomes
twelve. But this number, in turn, is doubled the moment we
introduce another distinction, that between individual and social life; for, anyone who follows one or other of the twelve
schools mentioned above does so either for himself alone, or
because of some neighbor for whom he ought to wish what
he wishes for himself. Hence, there are twelve schools of those
who hold that each of the opinions is to be held for purely
personal reasons, and a second twelve made up of those who
think they should philosophize in this way or that, not merely
with a view to their own personal living, but because of others
whose good they seek as they seek their own. And these
twenty-four schools become twice as many, namely, forty-

eight, by introducing a distinction from the philosophy of the New Academy;[4] for, each of the twenty-four opinions can be held and defended as certain (as the Stoics defended as certain their opinion that the good which makes a man happy is to be found solely in the virtue of the soul), or each of them can be held as being uncertain (much as the members of the New Academy defended their view merely as a probability). Thus, there are twenty-four schools of those who hold their views as certain because they are true, and another twenty-four made up of those who think they should follow their views because they seem probable, although not certain.

Again, each of these forty-eight schools may be followed either after the manner of the Cynics, or after the manner of other philosophers; and by this distinction the forty-eight becomes ninety-six. Moreover, any of these opinions can be so followed and defended either with a view to the life of contemplative leisure (as in the case of those who would and could devote all their time to the study of the truth), or with a view to an active life (as in the case of those who, though philosophers, are actually engaged in the administration of State affairs or other human enterprises), or, finally with a view to a mixed life, both active and contemplative (as in the case of those who find time to alternate periods of scholarly leisure with periods of necessary business). By such differences the number of the schools can be tripled and brought up to 288.

All this is in Varro's book, but I have summarized what he says as clearly as I could in language of my own. Varro goes on to refute all the other views save the one he thinks to be the view of the Old Academy, as founded by Plato and adhered to up to the time of Polemon, the fourth leader of the school. It seemed to Varro that this school held their views as certain, and thus he distinguishes it from the New Academy (the kind of philosophy that began with Arcesilaus, the successor of Polemon, according to which everything is open to doubt). It seemed to Varro that the school of the Old Academy was free from all doubt and all error. Just how he reached

---

[4] Or, as we would say today, Middle Academy.

these conclusions it would take me too long to show in detail. I cannot, however, forego all discussion of this matter.

What Varro first does is to remove all those distinguishing marks which merely multiply the number of schools but fail to include what is essential, namely, the supreme good. For, he thinks that no school of philosophy is worthy of the name unless it differs from others in what it regards as the ultimate good and the ultimate evil. The reason for this is that no one has any right to philosophize except with a view to happiness. Now, what makes a man happy is the supreme good. Hence, there is no reason for philosophizing apart from the supreme good. From this it follows that no school of philosophy is properly so called unless its search is for the supreme good.

Take the matter of social life. Is it to be entered upon by a philosopher as the supreme good by which he is both rendered happy and also seeks and procures his neighbor's good as he does his own, or should he cultivate it purely out of consideration for his own happiness? When we raise these questions we do not touch the matter of the supreme good itself, but merely ask whether or not our neighbor is to be reckoned as a sharer in this good on our account or on account of the neighbor himself, in the sense that we rejoice in his good as we do in our own.

So, too, with the question of the New Academy and its universal skepticism. When we ask whether all those matters which are the concern of philosophy are to be considered doubtful or whether we should consider them certain as other philosophers do, there is no question here as to what is to be sought as the supreme good, but merely whether or not we should have doubts as to the reality of the supreme good which we think should be pursued. In plain words, the question here is whether the person pursuing the supreme good should so pursue it as to call it a real good, or pursue it in such wise that he is willing to say that it is probably an objective good, although it may not be so—one and the same good, meanwhile, being pursued in both cases.

So, too, there is the distinction drawn from the dress and ways of the Cynics. Here the question raised is not the nature of the supreme good. The question is whether a person pur-

suing the supreme good—whatever he happens to think is the
good that is both true and to be pursued—should pursue it
in the dress and ways of the Cynics.

Finally, there have been philosophers who pursued quite
different ends as being ultimates—some, virtue; others, pleasure—yet observed the idiosyncrasies of life that gave the Cynics
their name. Hence, whatever it was that distinguished the
Cynics from other philosophers, certainly it had nothing to do
with choosing and holding to a good which might make them
happy. For, if manners had anything to do with this matter,
then similarity of manners would compel men to pursue the
same end, and any variety would make this impossible.

Chapter 2

To return to the three types of living noted above, namely,
the life of inactivity (not of mere idleness, of course, but of
contemplation and scholarly search for the truth), the life of
activity in human affairs, and the life of action tempered by
contemplation—if one asks which of these is to be chosen, this
does not raise the issue of the supreme good, but merely asks
which of the three makes it easy or difficult to reach or retain
what is supremely good. For, as soon as a man reaches the
ultimate good, this at once makes him happy. Now, no one
is immediately happy the moment he enjoys the leisure of a
literary life, or the activity of public life, or begins to alternate
one with the other. In point of fact, it is possible for many
men to live in any of these three estates, yet to take the wrong
road to the final good which makes men happy.

It follows that the question of the ultimates in good and
evil, which divide the schools of philosophers, must be distinguished from such other matters as social life, Academic
doubt, the dress and food of the Cynics, the three lives of contemplation, administration, and the mixture of both. There is
no question, in these latter discussions, of any ultimate in
either good or evil. Now, it was by introducing these four
differentiating notes (namely, social life, Academic skepticism,
the Cynics' way of life, and the three types of human living)
that Varro distinguished 288 possible schools of philosophy—

and even more might be added. But the moment he removes all those matters which do not touch the question of the supreme good and, therefore, cannot differentiate schools of philosophy properly so called, Varro is back to the twelve groups whose sole search is for that good which when obtained makes a man happy. He seeks to show that one of these is right and all the others wrong. Merely by removing the question of the threefold kind of life, the number is reduced by two thirds from 288 to ninety-six. Next, by disregarding the question about the Cynics, the ninety-six is cut in two and becomes forty-eight. And once we remove the question about the Skeptics, we have another subtraction of one half, and are left with twenty-four. Let the question of social life be taken away and we are left with the twelve which became twenty-four only by introducing this distinction. As for these twelve, there is no reason why they should not all be reckoned as schools, since the central preoccupation of each is with the question of the ultimate goods and evils—the evils, of course, being the contraries of the goods. However, the number twelve was reached by multiplying by three the four goods, pleasure, repose, their combination, and the primary demands of nature which Varro calls the *primigenia*. The number four was tripled to become twelve schools on the basis of the relations of the goods to virtue: sometimes they are subordinated, as when they are apparently pursued not for themselves but as a means to virtue; sometimes they are put before virtue, on the theory that virtue is not its own end, but is merely a necessary means if the four goods are to be obtained and retained; sometimes they are co-ordinated, in the view that both virtue and the four goods are to be pursued each for its own sake. However, even from the four ends, three of them—namely, pleasure, calm and a combination of pleasure and calm—are removed by Varro, not on the ground that they are bad, but because pleasure and calm are included in the primary satisfactions of nature. And, of course, since the *primigenia* include not merely pleasure and calm but other things, too, there is no need to add a combination of pleasure and calm to make a third thing distinguished from the search of pleasure and calm taken singly.

Thus, Varro is left with the problem of making a careful selection of one of the three schools, since true reason can allow no more than one of differing opinions to be right, whether in the matter of these three or of any others; and this we shall see later. For the moment I shall discuss, as briefly and clearly as I can, how Varro makes his selection of one of the three theories: either the primary needs of nature are to be sought for the sake of virtue; or virtue, for their sake; or nature and virtue, each for its own sake.

Chapter 3

Varro argues as follows in deciding which of the three theories is true and therefore to be embraced. First of all, he thinks that a definition of man must be settled upon, since in philosophy it is the supreme good of man that is in question, not that of a tree or of an animal or of God. In man's nature he finds two elements, body and soul; and he has no doubt whatever that of these two the soul is the better and by far the nobler element. But he discusses the question whether man is the soul alone or the body alone or a combination of body and soul. In the first case, the body would be like the horse to the horseman, where the horseman is not both horse and man but only the man, though he is called a horseman because of a relation to the horse which he rides. In the second case, the body would be to the soul somewhat as the wineglass to the wine. For, although the wineglass is not a glass of wine, that is, not both the glass and the wine in the glass, but only the glass, a wineglass is a glass meant to contain wine. In the third case, man is neither the soul alone nor the body alone, but each of these is a part, and the man is the whole of which they are the parts, much as we say a team is made up of two horses harnessed together, of which both the left-hand one and the right-hand one are parts. We never say that either of them, however closely linked with its mate, is the team, but that the pair is the team.

Of these three views Varro chooses the third, regarding man as neither the soul alone nor the body alone but the combination of body and soul. Consequently, he says that man's supreme good, which constitutes his happiness, is made up out of the goods both of the soul and of the body. And for this reason he considers that the primary demands of nature are to be sought on their own account and that the same is true of virtue—the art of living derived from education—which, of all the soul's goods, is the highest. Once virtue, this art of living, has taken charge of our innate exigencies, which were previously unguided but which existed even when they lacked direction, then virtue seeks all these things with reference to herself, at the same time seeking herself and making use of all while she is making use of herself. In doing so, her purpose is to find delight and joy in all these things, more or less, according to a scale of greater and lesser values. Rejoicing in all without exception, she will forego certain lesser goods, if this is necessary for getting or keeping the greater ones. Meanwhile, there is absolutely no good, whether of soul or body, that virtue prefers to herself. For, virtue makes good use of both herself and of all other goods which can make a man happy. Where virtue is lacking, no number of other goods are really any good to one who has them and, therefore, cannot really be called *his* goods, since they cannot profit one who uses them badly. Thus, the human life which is called happy is one which enjoys both virtue and the other goods of soul and body without which there can be no virtue; life is happier still if it enjoys also any or many of those other goods which are not essential to virtue; life is perfectly happy when it enjoys absolutely all goods of both soul and body, so that nothing is lacking. For, life is not the same thing as virtue, since only a virtuous life, and not any kind of life, is virtue. There can be a kind of life without any virtue, yet there can be no virtue without some kind of life. I could say the same for memory or reason or any other such endowment in a man. These, too, exist before education, nor can there be any education without them; nor, therefore, any virtue, which is a matter of education, without them. Speed in running, physical beauty, matchless strength, and other gifts of this kind are such that they can exist without virtue and virtue without them. Nevertheless, these are goods, too, and, according to the philosophers, virtue loves them for their sake,[1] and uses them and enjoys them as virtue ought.

The happy life is said, further, to be social when the goods of one's friends are loved for what they are[2] as one loves one's own goods, and when one wishes for one's friends what one wishes for oneself. These friends may be in a man's home, as in the case of wife, children, and servants; or may be fellow citizens in the city where one's home is located; or they may be the people of the whole world who make up human society; or they may be elsewhere in the cosmos made up of heaven and earth, like the gods, whom the philosophers claim as friends (or, as Christians would say, more tenderly, like angels[3]).

The philosophers of the Old Academy hold that there can be no doubt about the reality of the supreme good and the ultimate evil. In this, they claim, lies the difference between themselves and the skeptics of the New Academy. So long as any philosopher holds these ultimates to be real, it is for them a matter of no consequence at all if he affects the dress and diet of a Cynic or of anyone else. As for the three kinds of life—contemplative, active, and mixed—they hold for the third.[4]

Such, says Varro, was the position of the Old Academy as held by Antiochus, who taught Cicero and himself—although Cicero, to be sure, makes Antiochus out, on several matters, to be more of a Stoic than an adherent of the Old Academy. However, this is no concern of mine, since I am more intent upon getting at the truth of itself than upon knowing what one philosopher thought about another.[5]

Chapter 4

If I am asked what stand the City of God would take on the issues raised and, first, what this City thinks of the supreme

[1] Reading, with Dombart, *propter se ipsa* rather than, with Hoffmann, *propter se ipsam.*

[2] . . . *propter se ipsa.*

[3] . . . *quos nos familiarius angelos dicimus.*

[4] *Academica priora* 2.43.

[5] . . . *de rebus ipsis iudicare debemus, quam pro magno de hominibus quid quisque senserit scire.*

good and ultimate evil, the answer would be: She holds that eternal life is the supreme good and eternal death the supreme evil, and that we should live rightly in order to obtain the one and avoid the other. Hence the Scriptural expression, 'the just man lives by faith'[1]—by faith, for the fact is that we do not now behold our good and, therefore, must seek it by faith; nor can we of ourselves even live rightly, unless He who gives us faith helps us to believe and pray, for it takes faith to believe that we need His help.

Those who think that the supreme good and evil are to be found in this life are mistaken. It makes no difference whether it is in the body or in the soul or in both—or, specifically, in pleasure or virtue or in both—that they seek the supreme good. They seek in vain whether they look to serenity, to virtue, or to both; whether to pleasure plus serenity, or to virtue, or to all three; or to the satisfaction of our innate exigencies, or to virtue, or to both. It is in vain that men look for beatitude on earth or in human nature.[2] Divine Truth, as expressed in the Prophet's words, makes them look foolish: 'The Lord knows the thoughts of men'[3] or, as the text is quoted by St. Paul: 'The Lord knows the thoughts of the wise that they are vain.'[4]

For, what flow of eloquence is sufficient to set forth the miseries of human life? Cicero did the best he could in his *Consolatio de morte filiae*, but how little was his very best? As for the primary satisfactions of our nature,[5] when or where or how can they be so securely possessed in this life that they are not subject to the ups and downs of fortune? There is no pain of body, driving out pleasure, that may not befall the wise man; no anxiety that may not banish calm. A man's physical integrity is ended by the amputation or crippling of any of his limbs; his beauty is spoiled by deformity, his health by sickness, his vigor by weariness, his agility by torpor and sluggishness. There is not one of these that may not afflict the flesh even of a philosopher. Among our elementary requirements we reckon a graceful and becoming erectness and movement;

---

[1] Gal. 3.11.
[2] . . . *hic beati esse et a se ipsis beati fieri mira vanitate voluerunt.*
[3] Ps. 93.11.   [4] 1 Cor. 3.20.
[5] . . . *prima naturae.*

but what happens to these as soon as some sickness brings on palsy or, still worse, a spinal deformity so severe that a man's hands touch the ground as though he were a four-footed beast? What is then left of any beauty or dignity in a man's posture or gait? Turn, now, to the primary endowments of the soul:[6] senses to perceive and intelligence to understand the truth. How much sensation does a man have left if, for example, he goes deaf and blind? And where does the reason or intelligence go, into what strange sleep, when sickness unsettles the mind? We can hardly hold back our tears when mad men say or do extravagant things—things wholly unlike their customary behavior and normal goodness. To witness such things, even to recall them, makes a decent man weep. Still worse is the case of those possessed by demons. Their intelligence seems driven away, not to say destroyed, when an evil spirit according to its will makes use of their body and soul. And who can be sure that even a philosopher will not be such a victim at some time in his life?

Further, what is to be said of our perception of the truth, at the very best? What kind of truth and how much of it can we reach through our bodily senses? Do we not read in the truth-speaking Book of Wisdom: 'For the corruptible body is a load upon the soul, and the earthly habitation presseth down the mind that museth upon many things'?[7]

And what of the urge and appetite for action—*hormé,* as the Greeks call it—which is reckoned among the primary goods of our nature?[8] Is not this the root, too, of those restless energies of the madmen who fill us with tears and fears when their senses deceive them and their reason refuses to function?

So much for the elementary endowments of nature. Look, now, at virtue herself, which comes later with education and claims for herself the topmost place among human goods. Yet, what is the life of virtue save one unending war with evil inclinations, and not with solicitations of other people alone, but with evil inclinations that arise within ourselves and are our very own.

I speak especially of temperance—*sōphrosynē,* as the Greeks

[6] . . . *animi primigenia.*   [7] Wisd. 9.15.
[8] . . . *primis naturae deputant bonis.*

call it—which must bridle our fleshly lusts if they are not to drag our will to consent to abominations of every sort. The mere fact that, as St. Paul says, 'the flesh is at war with the spirit,' is no small flaw in our nature; and virtue is at war with this evil inclination when, in the same Apostle's words, 'the spirit lusts against the flesh.' These are opposed to each other to such a degree that 'we do not the things that we would.'[9] And when we seek final rest in the supreme good, what do we seek save an end to this conflict between flesh and spirit, freedom from this propensity to evil against which the spirit is at war? Yet, will as we may, such liberty cannot be had in mortal life.

This much, however, we can do with the help of God—not yield by surrender of the spirit and be dragged into sin willingly. Meanwhile, we must not fondly imagine that, so long as we wage this inward war, we may achieve that longed-for beatitude which can be solely the prize of the victor. For there lives no man so perfected in wisdom as not to have some conflict with excessive desires.

Take, next, the virtue called prudence. Is not this virtue constantly on the lookout to distinguish what is good from what is evil, so that there may be no mistake made in seeking the one and avoiding the other? So it bears witness to the fact that we are surrounded by evil and have evil within us. This virtue teaches that it is evil to consent to desires leading to sin and good to resist them. And what prudence preaches temperance puts into practice. Yet, neither prudence nor temperance can rid this life of the evils that are their constant concern.

Finally, there is justice. Its task is to see that to each is given what belongs to each. And this holds for the right order within man himself, so that it is just for the soul to be subordinate to God, and the body to the soul, and thus for body and soul taken together to be subject to God. Is there not abundant evidence that this virtue is unremittingly struggling to effect this internal order—and is far from finished? For, the less a man has God in his thoughts, the less is his soul subject to God; the more the flesh lusts counter to the spirit, the less

[9] Gal. 5.17.

the flesh is subject to the soul. So long, then, as such weakness, such moral sickliness remains within us, how can we dare to say that we are out of danger; and, if not yet out of danger, how can we say that our happiness is complete?

Look, now, at the great virtue called fortitude. Is not its very function—to bear patiently with misfortune—overwhelming evidence that human life is beset with unhappiness, however wise a man may be? It is beyond my comprehension how the Stoics can boldly argue that such ills are not really ills, meanwhile allowing that, if a philosopher should be tried by them beyond his obligation or duty to bear, he may have no choice but to take the easy way out by committing suicide. So stultifying is Stoic pride that, all evidences to the contrary, these men still pretend to find the ultimate good in this life and to hold that they are themselves the source of their own happiness. Their kind of sage—an astonishingly silly sage, indeed—may go deaf, dumb and blind, may be crippled, wracked with pain, visited with every imaginable affliction, driven at last to take his own life, yet have the colossal impertinence to call such an existence the happy life! Happy life, indeed, which employs death's aid to end it! If such a life is happy, then I say, live it![10] Why pretend that evils are not evils, when they not only overcome the virtue of fortitude and force it to yield to evil, but make a man so irrational as to call one and the same life both happy and unlivable? How can anyone be so blind as not to see that if life is happy it should not be shunned? Yet, the moment sickness opens her mouth they say one must choose a way out. If so, why do they not bow their stiff necks and admit life's unhappiness? Now, let me ask: Was it courage or cowardice that made their hero Cato kill himself?[11] Certainly, he would not have done what he did had he not been too cowardly to endure the victory of Caesar. Where, then, was his fortitude? It was a fortitude that yielded, that surrendered, that was so beaten that Cato ran away, deserted, abandoned the happy life. Or, maybe it was no longer the happy life? In that case, it was unhappy. If so,

---

[10] *Si beata est, maneatur in ea!*
[11] Cf. Plutarch, *Cato Minor*, 66–70.

how can anyone deny that the ills that made Cato's life unhappy and unlivable were real evils?

From this it follows that those who admit that such things are evils, so do the Aristotelians and those of the Old Academy whom Varro defends, are nearer the truth than the Stoics, even though Varro also makes the egregious mistake of maintaining that this life is still the happy life in spite of evils so grievous that, for one who suffers them, suicide becomes imperative. 'The pains and afflictions of the body,' Varro admits, 'are evils; and the worse the pains, the greater the evil. To escape them you should end your life.' I ask: Which life? He answers: 'This life which is made grievous by so many evils.' Life, then, is the happy life in the midst of evils which drive a man to escape from life? Is it, perhaps, the happy life precisely because you are allowed to escape its unhappiness by death? Suppose you should be bound by a divine law to remain in its evils and be permitted neither to die nor ever to be free from such misfortunes? Then, at least, you would have to say that such a life would be unhappy. And, surely, if you admit it would be unhappy if unending, you cannot say that it is not unhappy just because there is a quick way out. You cannot maintain that just because unhappiness is short-lived it is really not unhappiness at all; or, what is more preposterous, that because unhappiness is short-lived it deserves to be called happiness.

No, these ills of life must be very real indeed if they can drive even a sage of their type to take his life. For, these philosophers say—and rightly say—that the first and most fundamental command of nature is that a man should cherish his own human life and, by his very nature, shun death; that a man should be his own best friend, wanting and working with all his might and main to keep himself alive and to preserve the union of his body and soul. These ills must be very real indeed if they can subdue the very instinct of nature that struggles in every possible way to put death off; overwhelm it so utterly that death, once shunned, is now desired, sought, and, when all else fails, is self-inflicted. Yes, very real, when they can turn courage into a killer,[12] if, indeed, there be any question of genuine courage, when this virtue, devised to support

[12] . . . quae fortitudinem faciunt homicidam.

and steel a man, is so battered down by misfortune that—having failed to sustain him—it is driven, against its very function, to finish him off. It is true, of course, that a philosopher should face death as well as all other trials, with fortitude, but that means death coming upon him from without.

If then, as these philosophers held, even a wise man must yield to suicide, they ought logically to admit that there are evils—even insufferable evils—that account for this tragic compulsion; and that a life so burdensome, so exposed to fortune's ebb and flow, should not be called happy! Nor would those who talk of 'the happy life' ever have called life happy if they had yielded to the truth and the cogency of reason in their search for the happy life as readily as they yield to unhappiness and the weight of evils when they lose their life by suicide; and if, further, they had given up the idea that they could enjoy the supreme good in this mortal life. They would have realized that man's very virtues, his best and most useful possessions, are the most solid evidences of the miseries of life, precisely because their function is to stand by him in perils and problems and pains.

For, when virtues are genuine virtues—and that is possible only when men believe in God—they make no pretense of protecting their possessors from unhappiness, for that would be a false promise; but they do claim that human life, now compelled to feel the misery of so many grievous ills on earth, can, by the hope of heaven, be made both happy and secure. If we are asked how a life can be happy before we are saved, we have the answer of St. Paul: 'For in hope were we saved. But hope that is seen is not hope. For how can a man hope for what he sees? But if we hope for what we do not see, we wait for it with patience.'[13]

Of course, the Apostle was not speaking of men lacking prudence, fortitude, temperance, and justice, but of men whose virtues were true virtues because the men were living by faith. Thus, as 'we are saved by hope,' so we are made happy by hope. Neither our salvation nor our beatitude is here present, but 'we wait for it' in the future, and we wait 'with patience,' precisely because we are surrounded by evils which

[13] Rom. 8.24,25.

patience must endure until we come to where all good things are sources of inexpressible happiness and where there will be no longer anything to endure. Such is to be our salvation in the hereafter, such our final blessedness. It is because the philosophers will not believe in this beatitude which they cannot see that they go on trying to fabricate here below an utterly fraudulent felicity built on virtue filled with pride and bound to fail them in the end.

Chapter 5

So much for the philosophers' 'happy life.' What we Christians like better is their teaching that the life of virtue should be a social life. For, if the life of the saints had not been social, how could the City of God (which we have been discussing in all these nineteen Books) have a beginning, make progress, and reach its appointed goal? Yet, social living, given the misery of our mortality, has enormous drawbacks—more than can be easily counted, or known for what they really are. Just recall the words of a character in one of the pagan comedies who is applauded for expressing everyone's feeling:

> A wife I wed. What a worry, the shrew!
> The babies were born, and the worries grew.[1]

And remember the troubles of lovers listed by the same Terence:

> Slights and fights and spirits vexed,
> War today and peace the next.[2]

All human relationships are fraught with such misunderstandings. Not even the pure-hearted affection of friends is free from them. All history is a tale of 'slights and fights and spirits vexed,' and we must expect such unpleasantness as an assured thing, whereas peace is a good unguaranteed—dependent upon the unknowable interior dispositions of our friends. Even if we could read their hearts today, anything might happen tomorrow. Take the members of a single family. Who are as fond of one another as, in general, they are or, at least, are expected to be? Yet, who can rely utterly even on family affection? How much unhappiness has sprung from the ambush

---

[1] Terence, *Adelphi* 5.4.13,14.   [2] *Eunuchus* 1.1.14,15.

of domestic disloyalties! And how galling the disillusionment after peace had been so sweet—or seemed to be, though in fact it was nothing but a clever counterfeit. That is why no one can read, without a sigh, those touching words of Cicero: 'No snares are ever so insidious as those lurking as dutiful devotion or labeled as family affection. You can easily escape from an open foe, but when hatred lurks in the bosom of a family it has taken a position and has pounced upon you before it can be spied out or recognized for what it is.'[3]

Even divine Revelation reminds us: 'And a man's enemies will be those of his own household.'[4] It breaks the heart of any good man to hear this, for, even if he be brave enough to bear, or vigilant enough to beware of, the ruses of faithless friends, he must suffer greatly just the same when he discovers how treacherous they are. And it makes no difference whether they were genuine friends who have turned traitors, or traitorous men who had been trading on pretended affection all along.

If, then, the home, every man's haven in the storms of life, affords no solid security, what shall one say of the civic community? The bigger a city is, the fuller it is of legal battles, civil and criminal, and the more frequent are wild and bloody seditions or civil wars. Even when the frays are over, there is never any freedom from fear.

Chapter 6

Even when a city is enjoying the profoundest peace, some men must be sitting in judgment on their fellow men. Even at their best, what misery and grief they cause! No human judge can read the conscience of the man before him. That is why so many innocent witnesses are tortured to find what truth there is in the alleged guilt of other men. It is even worse when the accused man himself is tortured to find out if he be guilty. Here a man still unconvicted must undergo certain suffering for an uncertain crime—not because his guilt is known, but because his innocence is unproved. Thus it often happens that the ignorance of the judge turns into tragedy for the in-

[3] *In Verrem* 2.1.15.　　　　[4] Matt. 10.36.

nocent party. There is something still more insufferable—deplorable beyond all cleansing with our tears.[1] Often enough, when a judge tries to avoid putting a man to death whose innocence is not manifest, he has him put to torture, and so it happens, because of woeful lack of evidence, that he both tortures and kills the blameless man whom he tortured lest he kill him without cause. And if, on Stoic principles, the innocent man chooses to escape from life rather than endure such torture any longer, he will confess to a crime he never committed. And when it is all over, the judge will still be in the dark whether the man he put to death was guilty or not guilty, even though he tortured him to save his innocent life, and then condemned him to death. Thus, to gather evidence, he tortures an innocent man and, lacking evidence, kills him.

Such being the effect of human ignorance even in judicial procedure, will any philosopher-judge dare to take his place on the bench? You may be sure, he will. He would think it very wrong indeed to withdraw from his bounden duty to society. But that innocent men should be tortured as witnesses in trials not their own; that accused men should be so overcome by pain as falsely to plead guilty and then die, as they were tortured, in innocence; that many men should die as a result of or during their torturings, prior to any verdict at all —in all this our philosopher-judge sees nothing wrong. So, too, a judge in his ignorance will condemn to death, as sometimes happens, men who had nothing but the good of society at heart. To prevent crimes from going unpunished, such men go to court; but the witnesses lie and the guilty party holds out inhumanly under the torture and makes no confession; the accusation, in spite of the facts, is not sustained and it is the accuser who is condemned. No, our philosopher-judge does not reckon such abuses as burdens on his conscience because he has no intention of doing harm. Often, he would say, he cannot get at the truth, yet the good of society demands that he hand down decisions. My only point is that, as a man, surely his cannot be the 'happy life' even though his philosophy may save him from a sense of wrongdoing. Granted that his ig-

[1] . . . *intolerabilius magisque plangendum rigandumque, si fieri possit, fontibus lacrimarum.*

norance and his office are to blame for the torture and death of innocent men, is it any consolation to feel free of responsibility unless he is also happy? Surely there is something finer and more humane in seeing and detesting his wretchedness in this necessity and, if he is a Christian, in crying out to God: 'Deliver me from my necessities.'[2]

Chapter 7

After the city comes the world community. This is the third stage in the hierarchy of human associations. First, we have the home; then the city; finally, the globe. And, of course, as with the perils of the ocean, the bigger the community, the fuller it is of misfortunes.

The first misfortune is the lack of communication resulting from language differences. Take two men who meet and find that some common need calls on them to remain together rather than to part company. Neither knows the language of the other. As far as intercommunication goes, these two, both men, are worse off than two dumb animals, even of different kinds. For all its identity in both, their human nature is of no social help, so long as the language barrier makes it impossible for them to tell each other what they are thinking about. That is why a man is more at home with his dog than with a foreigner.

It will be answered that the Roman Empire, in the interests of peaceful collaboration, imposes on nations it has conquered the yoke of both law and language, and thus has an adequate, or even an overflowing, abundance of interpreters. True enough. But at what cost! There is one war after another, havoc everywhere, tremendous slaughterings of men.

All this for peace. Yet, when the wars are waged, there are new calamities brewing. To begin with, there never has been, nor, is there today, any absence of hostile foreign powers to provoke war. What is worse, the very development of the empire accruing from their incorporation has begotten still worse wars within. I refer to the civil wars and social uprisings that involve even more wretched anxieties for human beings, either

2 Ps. 24.17.

shaken by their actual impact, or living in fear of their renewal. Massacres, frequent and sweeping, hardships too dire to endure are but a part of the ravages of war. I am utterly unable to describe them as they are, and as they ought to be described; and even if I should try to begin, where could I end?

I know the objection that a good ruler will wage wars only if they are just. But, surely, if he will only remember that he is a man, he will begin by bewailing the necessity he is under of waging even just wars. A good man would be under compulsion to wage no wars at all, if there were not such things as just wars. A just war, moreover, is justified only by the injustice of an aggressor; and that injustice ought to be a source of grief to any good man, because it is human injustice. It would be deplorable in itself, apart from being a source of conflict.

Any man who will consider sorrowfully evils so great, such horrors and such savagery, will admit his human misery. And if there is any man who can endure such calamities, or even contemplate them without feeling grief, his condition is all the more wretched for that. For it is only the loss of all humane feeling that could make him call such a life 'the happy life.'

Chapter 8

Another of the not uncommon miseries of our human life is to mistake, by a misunderstanding close to madness, enemies for friends and friends for enemies. This apart, even granted the ordinary miseries and mistakes, of which all human relationship is full, there is no greater consolation than the unfeigned loyalty and mutual love of good men who are true friends. Yet, the more friends we have, and the more scattered they are locally, the more widely stretched are our heartfelt fears, lest any of the mountainous miseries of life befall them. We become apprehensive not only about possible afflictions of famine, war, sickness, imprisonment, or such unimaginable sufferings as may be their lot in slavery. What is far harder to swallow is our fear that they may fail us in faithfulness, turn to hate us and work us harm. If and when our fear becomes a fact, and we find it out (and the more friends we have, the more sources of such heartbreak), the fire of pain is whipped to such a blazing in our heart[1] as none can guess who has not felt the smart. Indeed, we would rather hear that our friends are dead.

Yet here is another source of sadness, for the death of those can never leave us free from grief whose friendship during life was a solace and delight. There are some who say men should not grieve. Then, let them try, if they can, to ban all loving interchange of thoughts, cut off and outlaw all friendly feelings, callously break the bonds of all human fellowship, or claim that such human relationships must be emptied of all tenderness. And if this is utterly impossible, it is no less impossible for us not to taste as bitter the death of those whose life for us was such a source of sweetness. It is, in fact, because such grief, in a broken heart, is like a wound or open sore that men feel it a duty to offer us the balm of their condolences. And if the heart is more easily and quickly healed the more virtuous a man is, that does not mean that there was no wound to heal.

There is no escape, then, from that misery of human life which is caused, in varying degrees, by the deaths of very close friends, especially if they have played some important role in public life. Yet it is easier to watch any of our loved ones die, in this sense, than to learn that they have lost their faith, or have fallen into grievous sin, and thus are spiritually dead. It is because of the immensity of this misery filling the earth that the Scripture asks: 'Is not the life of man upon earth a trial?'[2] No wonder the Lord said: 'Woe to the world because of scandals,'[3] and again: 'Because iniquity hath abounded, the charity of many shall grow cold.'[4]

That is why we Christians can feel a real joy when our friends die a holy death. Their death, of course, afflicts our heart, but faith gives us the surer consolation, that they are now freed from those evils of this present life which threaten

---

[1] . . . *quibus cor nostrum flagris uratur.*
[2] Job 7.1, reading *tentatio* in place of the Vulgate *militia.*
[3] Matt. 18.7.
[4] Matt. 24.12.

the best of men with either failure or defilement—and sometimes with both.

Chapter 9

In the philosophy of the Platonists, who hold that the gods are our friends, there is place for a fourth kind of society, which is not merely global but, so to speak, cosmic, in the sense that it embraces even heaven; and in this society our friends are such that there can be no fear whatever of their death or moral degradation causing us any sadness. However, partly because we cannot associate with them as familiarly as we do with men—a further affliction of this present life—and partly because Satan sometimes 'transforms himself into an angel of light,'[1] in order to test those who need testing or to deceive those deserving deception, nothing but the great mercy of God can save a man from mistaking bad demons for good angels, and false friends for true ones, and from suffering the full damages of this diabolical deception, all the more deadly in that it is wily beyond words.

Now, for anyone who needs this great mercy of God, what is this need but another of the great miseries of human life—in this instance, the overwhelming ignorance that makes us such easy victims of the devils' deceit? Certainly, in the unholy city, the philosophers who talked of the gods as their friends had fallen victims to those malignant demons who were unchallenged lords of that city which is doomed to share their eternal suffering. If any proof of this were needed, it is provided by the kind of gods who were worshiped by the sacred or, rather, sacrilegious rites with which they were honored, by the indecent plays in which their sins were re-enacted for the imaginary propitiation of the very gods who have conceived and commanded these filthy celebrations.

Chapter 10

Not even the holy and faithful followers of the one true and supreme God are beyond the reach of demonic trickery

[1] 2 Cor. 11.14.

and temptation in its many forms. Yet our anxiety in this matter is good for us, so long as we inhabit this frail body in this evil world, for it sends us seeking more ardently after that heavenly peace which is to be unshakeable and unending. There, all of our natural endowments—all that the Creator of all natures has given to our nature—will be both good and everlasting, where every wound in the soul is to be healed by wisdom and every weakness of body to be removed by resurrection; where our virtues will be no longer at war with passion or opposition of any kind, but are to have, as the prize of victory, an eternally imperturbable peace. This is what is meant by that consummate beatitude, that limitless perfection, that end that never ends.[1]

On earth we are happy, after a fashion, when we enjoy the peace, little as it is, which a good life brings; but such happiness compared with the beatitude which is our end in eternity is, in point of fact, misery. When we mortal men, living amid the realities of earth, enjoy the utmost peace which life can give us, then it is the part of virtue, if we are living rightly, to make a right use of the goods we are enjoying. When, on the other hand, we do not enjoy this temporal peace, then it is the function of virtue to make a right use of the misfortunes which we are suffering. By genuine Christian virtue we mean here that we refer not only all good things which are being rightly used, and all the right use we are making of blessings and misfortunes, but our very virtue itself to that End in which there will be a peace so good that no peace could be better, a peace so great that a greater would be impossible.

Chapter 11

Thus, we may say of peace what we have said of eternal life—that it is our highest good; more particularly because the holy Psalmist was addressing the City of God (the nature of which I am trying, with so much difficulty, to make clear) when he said: 'Praise the Lord, O Jerusalem; praise thy God, O Sion. Because he hath strengthened the bolts of thy gates,

---

[1] *Ipsa est enim beatitudo finalis, ipse perfectionis finis, qui consumentem non habet finem.*

he hath blessed thy children within thee. He hath placed peace in thy borders.'[1] For, when the bolts of that city's gates will have been strengthened, none will enter in and none will issue forth. Hence, its borders [*fines*] must be taken to mean that peace which I am trying to show is our final good. Note, too, that Jerusalem, the mystical name which symbolizes this City, means, as I have already mentioned, 'the vision of peace.'

However, the word 'peace' is so often applied to conditions here on earth, where life is not eternal, that it is better, I think, to speak of 'eternal life' rather than of 'peace' as the end or supreme good of the City of God. It is in this sense that St. Paul says: 'But now being made free from sin, and become servants of God, you have your fruit unto sanctification, and the end life everlasting.'[2]

It would be simplest for all concerned if we spoke of 'peace in eternal life,' or of 'eternal' or of 'eternal life in peace,' as the end or supreme good of this City. The trouble with the expression 'eternal life' is that those unfamiliar with the Scriptures might take this phrase to apply also to the eternal loss of the wicked, either because, as philosophers, they accept the immortality of the soul, or even because, as Christians, they know by faith that the punishment of the wicked has no end and, therefore, that they could not be punished forever unless their life were eternal.

The trouble with 'peace' is that, even on the level of earthly and temporal values, nothing that we can talk about, long for, or finally get, is so desirable, so welcome, so good as peace. At any rate, I feel sure that if I linger a little longer on this topic of peace I shall tire very few of my readers. After all, peace is the end of this City which is the theme of this work; besides, peace is so universally loved that its very name falls sweetly on the ear.

Chapter 12

Any man who has examined history and human nature will agree with me that there is no such thing as a human heart

---

[1] Ps. 146.12–14. . . . *qui posuit fines tuos pacem.*
[2] Rom. 6.22.

that does not crave for joy and peace. One has only to think of men who are bent on war. What they want is to win, that is to say, their battles are but bridges to glory and to peace. The whole point of victory is to bring opponents to their knees —this done, peace ensues. Peace, then, is the purpose of waging war; and this is true even of men who have a passion for the exercise of military prowess as rulers and commanders.

What, then, men want in war is that it should end in peace. Even while waging a war every man wants peace, whereas no one wants war while he is making peace. And even when men are plotting to disturb the peace, it is merely to fashion a new peace nearer to the heart's desire; it is not because they dislike peace as such. It is not that they love peace less, but that they love their kind of peace more. And even when a secession is successful, its purpose is not achieved unless some sort of peace remains among those who plotted and planned the rebellion. Take even a band of highwaymen. The more violence and impunity they want in disturbing the peace of other men, the more they demand peace among themselves. Take even the case of a robber so powerful that he dispenses with partnership, plans alone, and single-handed robs and kills his victims. Even he maintains some kind of peace, however shadowy, with those he cannot kill and whom he wants to keep in the dark with respect to his crimes. Certainly in his own home he wants to be at peace with his wife and children and any other members of his household. Of course, he is delighted when his every nod is obeyed; if it is not obeyed, he rages, and scolds, and demands peace in his own home and, if need be, gets it by sheer brutality. He knows that the price of peace in domestic society is to have everyone subject in the home to some head—in this instance, to himself.

Suppose, now, a man of this type were offered the allegiance of a larger society, say of a city or of a nation, with the pledge that he would be obeyed as he looks to be obeyed under his own roof. In this case, he would no longer hide himself away in a darksome robber's den; he would show himself off as a high and mighty king—the same man, however, with all of his old greed and criminality. Thus it is that all men want peace in their own society, and all want it in their own way. When they go to war what they want is to make, if they can, their enemies their own, and then to impose on them the victor's will and call it peace.

Now let us imagine a man like the one that poetry and mythology tell us about, a being so wild and anti-social that it was better to call him half-human than fully a man. He was called Cacus, which is Greek for 'bad.' His kingdom was the solitude of a dreadful cave and it was his extraordinary wickedness that gave him his name. He had no wife to exchange soft words with him; no tiny children to play with; no bigger ones to keep in order; no friend whose company he could enjoy, not even his father, Vulcan—than whom he was at least this much luckier that he had never begotten a monster like himself! There was no one to whom he would give anything, but whenever and from whomsoever he could he would take whatever he wanted and whenever he wanted it.

Nevertheless, all alone as he was in a cave that was always 'warm with the blood of some recent victim,'[1] his sole longing was for peace in which no force would do him harm and no fear disturb his rest. Even with his own body he wanted to be at peace, and he was at ease only when peace was there. Even when he was bidding his members to obey him and was seizing, killing, and devouring his victims, his purpose was peace—the speediest possible peace with his mortal nature, driven by its needs to rebellion, and with his hunger, in sedition, clamoring for the breakup of the union of body and soul. Brutal and wild as he was and brutal and wild as were his ways, what he wanted was to have his life and limbs in peace. So much so that, had he been as willing to be at peace with his neighbors as he was active in procuring peace within himself and in his cave, no one would have called him wicked, nor a monster, nor even sub-human; or, at least, despite the shape of his body and the smoke and fire that issued from his mouth and kept all neighbors at a distance, people would have said that what looked like injustice, greed, and savagery were merely means to self-preservation. The truth is, of course, that there never existed any such being or, at least, none just like

[1] *Aeneid* 8.195.

the foil the poets' fancy invented to glorify Hercules at the expense of Cacus. As is the case with most poetic inventions, we need not believe that any such creature, human or sub-human, ever lived.

I turn now to real wild beasts (from which category the animal part of the so-called half-beast,[2] Cacus, was borrowed). They, too, keep their own particular genus in a kind of peace. Their males and females meet and mate, foster and feed their young, even though many of them by nature are more solitary than gregarious, like lions, foxes, eagles, and owls —as contrasted with deer, pigeons, starlings, and bees. Even a tigress purrs over her cubs and curbs all her fierceness when she fondles them. Even a falcon which seems so lonely when hovering above its prey mates and builds a nest, helps to hatch the eggs and feed the young, and makes every effort to maintain with the mother falcon a peaceful domestic society.

It is even more so with man. By the very laws of his nature, he seems, so to speak, forced into fellowship and, as far as in him lies, into peace with every man. At any rate, even when wicked men go to war they want peace for their own society and would like, if possible, to make all men members of that society, so that everyone and everything might be at the service of one head. Of course, the only means such a conqueror knows is to have all men so fear or love him that they will accept the peace which he imposes. For, so does pride perversely copy God.[3] Sinful man hates the equality of all men under God and, as though he were God, loves to impose his sovereignty on his fellow men. He hates the peace of God which is just and prefers his own peace which is unjust. However, he is powerless not to love peace of some sort. For, no man's sin is so unnatural as to wipe out all traces whatsoever of human nature. Anyone, then, who is rational enough to prefer right to wrong and order to disorder can see that the kind of peace that is based on injustice, as compared with that which is based on justice, does not deserve the name of peace.

Of course, even disorder, in whole or in part, must come to some kind of terms either with the situation in which it

[2] *Aeneid* 8.267: *semiferus.*

[3] *Sic enim superbia perverse imitatur Deum.*

finds itself or with the elements out of which it takes its being —otherwise it would have no being at all.

Take a man hanging upside down. Certainly his members are in disorder and the posture of the body as a whole is unnatural. The parts which nature demands should be above and below have become topsy-turvy. Such a position disturbs the peace of the body and is therefore painful. Nevertheless, the soul remains at peace with the body and continues to work for its welfare. Otherwise, the man would not live to feel the agony. And even if the soul is driven from the body by excess of pain, nevertheless, so long as the limbs hold together, some kind of peace among these parts remains. Otherwise, there would be no corpse to go on dangling there. Further, the fact that by gravity the corpse, made out of earth, tends to fall to the ground and pulls at the noose that holds it up proves that there is some order in which it seeks peace, and that its weight is, as it were, crying out for a place where it can rest. Lifeless and insensible though the body now is, it does not renounce that appropriate peace in the order of nature which it either has or seeks to have.

So, too, when a corpse is treated to embalming, to prevent dissolution and decay, there is a kind of peace which holds the parts together while the whole is committed to the earth, its proper resting place, and, therefore, a place with which the body is at peace. If, on the other hand, embalming is omitted and nature is allowed to take its course, the corpse remains a battleground of warring exhalations (that attack our senses with the stench we smell) only until such time as they finally fall in with the elements of this world and, slowly, bit by bit, become indistinguishable in a common peace.

Even afterward, however, the law and ordering of the Creator who is supreme in the whole cosmos and the regulator of its peace are still in control. Even when tiny bacteria spring from the corpse of a larger animal, it is by the same law of the Creator that all these minute bodies serve in peace the organic wholes of which they are parts. Even when the flesh of dead animals is eaten by other animals, there is no change in the universal laws which are meant for the common good of every kind of life, the common good that is effected by bringing like into peace with like. It makes no difference what disintegrating forces are at work, or what new combinations are made, or even what changes or transformations are effected.

Chapter 13

The peace, then, of the body lies in the ordered equilibrium of all its parts; the peace of the irrational soul, in the balanced adjustment of its appetites; the peace of the reasoning soul, in the harmonious correspondence of conduct and conviction; the peace of body and soul taken together, in the well-ordered life and health of the living whole. Peace between a mortal man and his Maker consists in ordered obedience, guided by faith, under God's eternal law; peace between man and man consists in regulated fellowship. The peace of a home lies in the ordered harmony of authority and obedience between the members of a family living together. The peace of the political community is an ordered harmony of authority and obedience between citizens. The peace of the heavenly City lies in a perfectly ordered and harmonious communion of those who find their joy in God and in one another in God. Peace, in its final sense, is the calm that comes of order.[1] Order is an arrangement of like and unlike things whereby each of them is disposed in its proper place.

This being so, those who are unhappy, in so far as they are unhappy, are not in peace, since they lack the calm of that Order which is beyond every storm; nevertheless, even in their misery they cannot escape from order, since their very misery is related to responsibility and to justice. They do not share with the blessed in their tranquility, but this very separation is the result of the law of order. Moreover, even the miserable can be momentarily free from anxiety and can reach some measure of adjustment to their surroundings and, hence, some tranquility of order and, therefore, some slender peace. However, the reason why they remain unhappy is that, although they *may* be momentarily free from worry and from pain, they are not in a condition where they *must* be free both from worry

---

[1] . . . *pax omnium rerum tranquillitas ordinis.*

and pain.[2] Their condition of misery is worse when such peace as they have is not in harmony with that law which governs the order of nature. Their peace can also be disturbed by pain and in proportion to their pain; yet, some peace will remain, so long as the pain is not too acute and their organism as a whole does not disintegrate.

Notice that there can be life without pain, but no pain without some kind of life. In the same way, there can be peace without any kind of war, but no war that does not suppose some kind of peace. This does not mean that war as war involves peace; but war, in so far as those who wage it or have it waged upon them are beings with organic natures, involves peace—for the simple reason that to be organic means to be ordered and, therefore, to be, in some sense, at peace.

Similarly, there can be a nature without any defect and, even, a nature in which there can be no kind of evil whatever, but there can be no nature completely devoid of good.[3] Even the nature of the Devil, in so far as it is a nature, is not evil; it was perversity—not being true to itself—that made it bad.[4] The Devil did not 'stand in the truth'[5] and, therefore, did not escape the judgment of truth. He did not stand fast in the tranquility of order—nor did he, for all that, elude the power of the Ordainer. The goodness which God gave to his nature does not withdraw him from the justice of God by which that nature is subject to punishment. Yet, even in that punishment, God does not hound the good which He created, but only the evil which the Devil committed. So it is that God does not take back the whole of His original gift. He takes a part and leaves a part; He leaves a nature that can regret what God has taken back. Indeed, the very pain inflicted is evidence of both the good that is lost and the good that is left. For, if there were no good left, there would be no one to lament the good that has been lost.

A man who sins is just that much worse if he rejoices in

[2] . . . etsi in aliqua securitate non dolent, non tamen ibi sunt, ubi securi esse ac dolere debeant.

[3] Cf. above, 11.22; 12.3.

[4] . . . perversitas eam malam fecit.

[5] John 8.44. Note St. Augustine's play on the words in veritate (in truth) and perversitas (not being true to itself).

the loss of holiness; but one who suffers pain, and does not benefit by it, laments, at least, the loss of his health. Holiness and health are both good things and, because the loss of any good is more a cause for grief than for gladness (unless there be some higher compensation—the soul's holiness, to be sure, is preferable to the body's health), it is more in accordance with nature that a sinner grieve over his punishment than that he rejoice over his offense. Consequently, just as a man's happiness in abandoning the good of wrongdoing betrays his bad will, so his sorrowing for the good he has lost when in pain bears witness to the good of his nature. For, anyone who grieves over the loss of peace to his nature does so out of some remnant of that peace wherewith his nature loves itself. This is what happens—deservedly, too—in eternal punishment. In the midst of their agonies the evil and the godless weep for the loss of their nature's goods, knowing, meanwhile, that God whose great generosity they contemned was perfectly just when He took these goods away.

God, the wise Creator and just Ordainer of all natures, has made the mortal race of man the loveliest of all lovely things on earth. He has given to men good gifts suited to their existence here below. Among these is temporal peace, according to the poor limits of mortal life, in health, security, and human fellowship; and other gifts, too, needed to preserve this peace or regain it, once lost—for instance, the blessings that lie all around us, so perfectly adapted to our senses: daylight, speech, air to breathe, water to drink, everything that goes to feed, clothe, cure, and beautify the body. These good gifts are granted, however, with the perfectly just understanding that whoever uses the goods which are meant for the mortal peace of mortal men, as these goods should be used, will receive more abundant and better goods—nothing less than immortal peace and all that goes with it, namely, the glory and honor of enjoying God and one's neighbor in God everlastingly; but that whoever misuses his gifts on earth will both lose what he has and never receive the better gifts of heaven.

Chapter 14

In the earthly city, then, temporal goods are to be used with a view to the enjoyment of earthly peace, whereas, in the heavenly City, they are used with a view to the enjoyment of eternal peace. Hence, if we were merely unthinking brutes, we would pursue nothing beyond the orderly interrelationship of our bodily part and the appeasing of our appetites, nothing, that is, beyond the comfort of the flesh and plenty of pleasures, so that the peace of body might contribute to peace of the soul. For, if order in the body be lacking, the peace of an irrational soul is checked, since it cannot attain the satisfaction of its appetites. Both of these forms of peace meanwhile subserve that other form of peace which the body and soul enjoy between them, the peace of life and health in good order.

For, just as brutes show that they love the peace or comfort of their bodies by shunning pain, and the peace of their souls by pursuing pleasure to satisfy their appetites, so, too, by running from death, they make clear enough how much they love the peace which keeps body and soul together.

Because, however, man has a rational soul, he makes everything he shares with brutes subserve the peace of his rational soul, so that he first measures things with his mind before he acts, in order to achieve that harmonious correspondence of conduct and conviction which I called the peace of the rational soul. His purpose in desiring not to be vexed with pain, nor disturbed with desire, nor disintegrated by death is that he may learn something profitable and so order his habits and way of life. However, if the infirmity of his human mind is not to bring him in his pursuit of knowledge to some deadly error, he needs divine authority to give secure guidance, and divine help so that he may be unhampered in following the guidance given.

And because, so long as man lives in his mortal body and is a pilgrim far from the Lord, he walks, not by vision, but by faith. Consequently, he refers all peace of body or soul, or their combination, to that higher peace which unites a mortal man with the immortal God and which I defined as 'ordered obedience guided by faith, under God's eternal law.'

Meanwhile, God teaches him two chief commandments, the love of God and the love of neighbor. In these precepts man finds three beings to love, namely, God, himself, and his fellow man, and knows that he is not wrong in loving himself so long as he loves God. As a result, he must help his neighbor (whom he is obliged to love as himself) to love God. Thus, he must help his wife, children, servants, and all others whom he can influence. He must wish, moreover, to be similarly helped by his fellow man, in case he himself needs such assistance. Out of all this love he will arrive at peace, as much as in him lies, with every man—at that human peace which is regulated fellowship. Right order here means, first, that he harm no one, and, second, that he help whomever he can. His fundamental duty is to look out for his own home, for both by natural and human law he has easier and readier access to their requirements.

St. Paul says: 'But if any does not take care of his own, and especially of his household, he has denied the faith and is worse than an unbeliever.'[1] From this care arises that peace of the home which lies in the harmonious interplay of authority and obedience among those who live there. For, those who have the care of the others give the orders—a man to his wife, parents to their children, masters to their servants. And those who are cared for must obey—wives their husbands, children their parents, servants their masters. In the home of a religious man, however, of a man living by faith and as yet a wayfarer from the heavenly City, those who command serve those whom they appear to rule—because, of course, they do not command out of lust to domineer, but out of a sense of duty—not out of pride like princes but out of solicitude like parents.[2]

Chapter 15

This family arrangement is what nature prescribes, and what God intended in creating man: 'let them have dominion over the fish of the sea, the birds of the air, the cattle, over all the wild animals and every creature that crawls on the

---

[1] 1 Tim. 5.8.
[2] . . . *nec principandi superbia, sed providendi misericordia.*

earth.'[1] God wanted rational man, made to His image, to have no dominion except over irrational nature. He meant no man, therefore, to have dominion over man, but only man over beast. So it fell out that those who were holy in primitive times became shepherds over sheep rather than monarchs over men, because God wishes in this way to teach us that the normal hierarchy of creatures is different from that which punishment for sin has made imperative. For, when subjection came, it was merely a condition deservedly imposed on sinful man. So, in Scripture, there is no mention of the word 'servant' until holy Noe used it in connection with the curse on his son's wrongdoing.[2] It is a designation that is not natural, but one that was deserved because of sin.

The Latin word for 'slave' is *servus* and it is said that this word is derived from the fact that those who, by right of conquest, could have been killed were sometimes kept and guarded, *servabantur*, by their captors and so became slaves and were called *servi*. Now, such a condition of servitude could only have arisen as a result of sin, since whenever a just war is waged the opposing side must be in the wrong, and every victory, even when won by wicked men, is a divine judgment to humble the conquered and to reform or punish their sin. To this truth Daniel, the great man of God, bore witness. When he was languishing in the Babylonian captivity he confessed to God his sins and those of his people and avowed, with pious repentance, that these sins were the cause of the captivity.[3] It is clear, then, that sin is the primary cause of servitude, in the sense of a social status in which one man is compelled to be subjected to another man. Nor does this befall a man, save by the decree of God, who is never unjust and who knows how to impose appropriate punishments on different sinners.

Our heavenly Master says: 'everyone who commits sin is a slave of sin.'[4] So it happens that holy people are sometimes enslaved to wicked masters who are, in turn, themselves slaves. For, 'by whatever a man is overcome, of this also he is a slave.'[5] Surely it is better to be the slave of a man than the slave of

1 Gen. 1.26.
2 Gen. 9.25, 'a servant of servants shall he be.'
3 Dan. 9.5.   4 John 8.34.
5 2 Pet. 2.19.

passion as when, to take but one example, the lust for lordship raises such havoc in the hearts of men. Such, then, as men now are, is the order of peace. Some are in subjection to others, and, while humility helps those who serve, pride harms those in power. But, as men once were, when their nature was as God created it, no man was a slave either to man or to sin. However, slavery is now penal in character and planned by that law which commands the preservation of the natural order and forbids its disturbance. If no crime had ever been perpetrated against this law, there would be no crime to repress with the penalty of enslavement.

It is with this in mind that St. Paul goes so far as to admonish slaves to obey their masters and to serve them so sincerely and with such good will[6] that, if there is no chance of manumission, they may make their slavery a kind of freedom by serving with love and loyalty, free from fear and feigning,[7] until injustice becomes a thing of the past and every human sovereignty and power is done away with, so that God may be all in all.[8]

Chapter 16

Our holy Fathers in the faith, to be sure, had slaves, but in the regulation of domestic peace it was only in matters of temporal importance that they distinguished the position of their children from the status of their servants. So far as concerns the worship of God—from whom all must hope for eternal blessings—they had like loving care for all the household without exception. This was what nature demanded, and it was from this kind of behavior that there grew the designation 'father of the family,' which is so widely accepted that even wicked and domineering men love to be so called.

Those who are true fathers are as solicitous for everyone in their households as for their own children to worship and to be worthy of God. They hope and yearn for all to arrive in that heavenly home where there will be no further need of

---

[6] Eph. 6.5,7.

[7] . . . *non timore subdolo, sed fideli dilectione serviendo.*

[8] 1 Cor. 15.24,28.

giving orders to other human beings, because there will be no longer any duty to help those who are happy in immortal life. In the meantime, fathers ought to look upon their duty to command as harder than the duty of slaves to obey.

Meanwhile, in case anyone in the home behaves contrary to its peace, he is disciplined by words or whipping[1] or other kind of punishment lawful and licit in human society, and for his own good, to readjust him to the peace he has abandoned. For, there is no more benevolence and helpfulness in bringing about the loss of a greater good than there is innocence and compassion in allowing a culprit to go from bad to worse. It is the duty of a blameless person not just to do no wrong, but to keep others from wrongdoing and to punish it when done, so that the one punished may be improved by the experience and others be warned by the example.

Now, since every home should be a beginning or fragmentary constituent of a civil community, and every beginning related to some specific end, and every part to the whole of which it is a part, it ought to follow that domestic peace has a relation to political peace. In other words, the ordered harmony of authority and obedience between those who live together has a relation to the ordered harmony of authority and obedience between those who live in a city. This explains why a father must apply certain regulations of civil law to the governance of his home, so as to make it accord with the peace of the whole community.

Chapter 17

While the homes of unbelieving men are intent upon acquiring temporal peace out of the possessions and comforts of this temporal life, the families which live according to faith look ahead to the good things of heaven promised as imperishable, and use material and temporal goods in the spirit of pilgrims, not as snares or obstructions to block their way to God, but simply as helps to ease and never to increase the burdens of this corruptible body which weighs down the soul. Both types of homes and their masters have this in common, that

---

[1] . . . *verbo seu verbere.*

they must use things essential to this mortal life. But the respective purposes to which they put them are characteristic and very different.

So, too, the earthly city which does not live by faith seeks only an earthly peace, and limits the goal of its peace, of its harmony of authority and obedience among its citizens, to the voluntary and collective attainment of objectives necessary to mortal existence. The heavenly City, meanwhile—or, rather, that part that is on pilgrimage in mortal life and lives by faith —must use this earthly peace until such time as our mortality which needs such peace has passed away. As a consequence, so long as her life in the earthly city is that of a captive and an alien (although she has the promise of ultimate delivery and the gift of the Spirit as a pledge), she has no hesitation about keeping in step with the civil law which governs matters pertaining to our existence here below. For, as mortal life is the same for all, there ought to be common cause between the two cities in what concerns our purely human living.[1]

Now comes the difficulty. The city of this world, to begin with, has had certain 'wise men' of its own mold, whom true religion must reject, because either out of their own daydreaming or out of demonic deception these wise men came to believe that a multiplicity of divinities was allied with human life, with different duties, in some strange arrangement, and different assignments: this one over the body, that one over the mind; in the body itself, one over the head, another over the neck, still others, one for each bodily part; in the mind, one over the intelligence, another over learning, another over temper, another over desire; in the realities, related to life, that lie about us, one over flocks and one over wheat, one over wine, one over oil, and another over forests, one over currency, another over navigation, and still another over warfare and victory, one over marriage, a different one over fecundity and childbirth, so on and so on.

The heavenly City, on the contrary, knows and, by religious faith, believes that it must adore one God alone and serve Him with that complete dedication which the Greeks call *latreía*

---

[1] . . . *ut, quoniam communis est ipsa mortalitas, servetur in rebus ad eam pertinentibus inter civitatem utramque concordia.*

and which belongs to Him alone. As a result, she has been unable to share with the earthly city a common religious legislation, and has had no choice but to dissent on this score and so to become a nuisance to those who think otherwise. Hence, she has had to feel the weight of their anger, hatred, and violence, save in those instances when, by sheer numbers and God's help, which never fails, she has been able to scare off her opponents.

So long, then, as the heavenly City is wayfaring on earth, she invites citizens from all nations and all tongues, and unites them into a single pilgrim band. She takes no issue with that diversity of customs, laws, and traditions whereby human peace is sought and maintained. Instead of nullifying or tearing down, she preserves and appropriates whatever in the diversities of divers races is aimed at one and the same objective of human peace, provided only that they do not stand in the way of the faith and worship of the one supreme and true God.

Thus, the heavenly City, so long as it is wayfaring on earth, not only makes use of earthly peace but fosters and actively pursues along with other human beings a common platform in regard to all that concerns our purely human life and does not interfere with faith and worship.[2] Of course, though, the City of God subordinates this earthly peace to that of heaven. For this is not merely true peace, but, strictly speaking, for any rational creature, the only real peace, since it is, as I said, 'the perfectly ordered and harmonious communion of those who find their joy in God and in one another in God.'

When this peace is reached, man will be no longer haunted by death, but plainly and perpetually endowed with life,[3] nor will his body, which now wastes away and weighs down the soul, be any longer animal, but spiritual, in need of nothing, and completely under the control of our will.

This peace the pilgrim City already possesses by faith and it lives holily and according to this faith so long as, to attain its

---

[2] . . . et de rebus ad mortalem hominum naturam pertinentibus humanarum voluntatum compositionem, quantum salva pietate ac religione conceditur, tuetur adque adpetit.

[3] . . . non erit vita mortalis, sed plane certeque vitalis.

heavenly completion, it refers every good act done for God or for his fellow man. I say 'fellow man' because, of course, any community life must emphasize social relationships.

Chapter 18

Turning now to that distinctive characteristic which Varro ascribes to the followers of the New Academy, namely, universal skepticism, the City of God shuns it as a form of insanity. Its knowledge of truth, gleaned by intelligence and reasoning, is indeed slender because of the corruptible body weighing down the soul. As St. Paul says, 'We know in part.'[1] Still, this knowledge is certain. Believers, moreover, trust the report of their bodily senses which subserve the intelligence. If they are at times deceived, they are at least better off than those who maintain that the senses can never be trusted.

The City of God believes the Old and New Testaments accepted as canonical. Out of these she formulates that faith according to which the just man lives. And in the light of this faith we walk forward without fear of stumbling so long as 'we are exiled from the Lord.'[2] This perfectly certain faith apart, other things which have not been sensibly or intellectually experienced nor clearly revealed in canonical Scripture, nor vouched for by witnesses whom it is reasonable to believe —these we can doubt and nobody in justice can take us to task for this.

Chapter 19

The City of God does not care in the least what kind of dress or social manners a man of faith affects, so long as these involve no offense against the divine law. For it is faith and not fashions that brings us to God. Hence, when philosophers become Christians, the Church does not force them to give up their distinctive attire or mode of life which are no obstacle to religion, but only their erroneous teachings. She is entirely indifferent to that special mark which, in Varro's reckoning,

[1] 1 Cor. 13.9.
[2] 2 Cor. 5.6.

distinguishes the Cynics, so long as it connotes nothing shameful or unbalanced.

Or take the three modes of life: the contemplative, the active, the contemplative-active. A man can live the life of faith in any of these three and get to heaven. What is not indifferent is that he love truth and do what charity demands. No man must be so committed to contemplation as, in his contemplation, to give no thought to his neighbor's needs, nor so absorbed in action as to dispense with the contemplation of God.

The attraction of leisure ought not to be empty-headed inactivity, but in the quest or discovery of truth, both for his own progress and for the purpose of sharing ungrudgingly with others. Nor should the man of action love worldly position or power (for all is vanity under the sun), but only what can be properly and usefully accomplished by means of such position and power, in the sense which I have already explained[1] of contributing to the eternal salvation of those committed to one's care. Thus, as St. Paul wrote: 'If anyone is eager for the office of bishop, he desires a good work.'[2] He wanted to make clear that the office of bishop, *episcopatus*, implies work rather than dignity. The word is derived from *episkopos*, which is Greek for 'superintendent.' Thus, a bishop is supposed to superintend those over whom he is set in the sense that he is to 'oversee' or 'look out for' those under him. The word, *skopein*, like the Latin *intendere*, means to look; and so *episkopein*, like *superintendere*, means 'to oversee' or 'to look out for those who are under one.' Thus, no man can be a good bishop if he loves his title but not his task.[3]

In the same way, no man is forbidden to pursue knowledge of the truth, for that is the purpose of legitimate leisure. But it is the ambition for the position of dignity which is necessary for government that is unbecoming, although, of course, the dignity itself and its use are not wrong in themselves. Thus, it is the love of study that seeks a holy leisure; and only the compulsion of charity that shoulders necessary activity. If no such burden is placed on one's shoulders, time should be passed in study and contemplation. But, once the burden is

---

[1] Cf. above, 19.6. [2] 1 Tim. 3.1.
[3] . . . *qui praeesse dilexerit, non prodesse.*

on the back, it should be carried, since charity so demands.
Even so, however, no one should give up entirely his delight
in learning, for the sweetness he once knew may be lost and
the burden he bears overwhelm him.

Chapter 20

Meanwhile, and always, the supreme good of the City of
God is everlasting and perfect peace and not merely a continuing peace which individually mortal men enter upon and
leave by birth and death, but one in which individuals im-
mortally abide, no longer subject to any species of adversity.
Nor will anyone deny that such a life must be most happy,
or that this life, however blessed spiritually, physically, or
economically, is, by comparison, most miserable.

It is true, however, that a man who makes his life here below a means to that end which he ardently loves and confidently hopes for can even now be reasonably called happy
—though more in hope than in present happiness. Such present felicity apart from this hope is, to tell the truth, an illusory
happiness and, in fact, a great wretchedness, since it makes no
use of the true goods of the soul. No wisdom is true wisdom
unless all that it decides with prudence, does with fortitude,
disciplines with temperance, and distributes with justice is directed to that goal in which God is to be all in all in secure
everlastingness and flawless peace.

Chapter 21

I have arrived at the point where I must keep my promise[1]
to prove, as briefly and clearly as I can that, if we accept the
definitions of Scipio, cited by Cicero in his book *On the Republic,* there never existed any such thing as a Roman
Republic.

Scipio gives a short definition of a commonwealth as the
weal of the people. Now, if this is a true definition, there never
was any Roman Republic, because there never was in Rome
any true 'weal of the people.' Scipio defines the people as 'a

[1] Cf. above, 1.21.

multitude bound together by a mutual recognition of rights and a mutual co-operation for the common good.' As the discussion progresses, he explains what he means by 'mutual recognition of rights,' going on to show that a republic cannot be managed without justice, for, where there is not true justice, there is no recognition of rights.

For, what is rightly done is justly done; what is done unjustly cannot be done by right. We are not to reckon as right such human laws as are iniquitous, since even unjust lawgivers themselves call a right [*ius*] only what derives from the fountainhead of justice [*iustitia,*] and brand as false the wrong-headed opinion of those who keep saying that a right [*ius*] is whatever is advantageous [*utile*] to the one in power.

It follows that, wherever true justice is lacking, there cannot be a multitude of men bound together by a mutual recognition of rights; consequently, neither can there be a 'people' in the sense of Scipio's definition. Further, if there is no 'people,' there is no weal of the 'people,' or commonwealth, but only the weal of a nondescript mob undeserving of the designation 'the people.' To resume the argument: If a commonwealth is the weal of the people, and if there is no people save one bound together by mutual recognition of rights, and if there are no rights where there is no justice, it follows beyond question that where there is no justice, there is no commonwealth.

Let us see. Justice is the virtue which accords to each and every man what is his due. What, then, shall we say of a man's 'justice' when he takes himself away from the true God and hands himself over to dirty demons? Is this a giving to each what is his due? If a man who takes away a farm from its purchaser and delivers it to another man who has no claim upon it is unjust, how can a man who removes himself from the overlordship of the God who made him and goes into the service of wicked spirits be just?

To be sure, in *On the Republic* there is a hard-fought and powerful debate in favor of justice as against injustice. First, the side of injustice was taken. At that point it was claimed that only by injustice could the republic stand firm and be efficiently managed. And this was put down as the most telling proof: that it is unjust that some men should have to serve others as masters; that, nevertheless, the capital of the Empire to which the commonwealth belongs must practice such injustice or surrender her provinces. Then the side of justice made the following rebuttal: that such procedure is, in fact, just because such submission is advantageous to the men in question, that it is for their good, when such sovereignty is properly managed, that is, when the lawless marauding of criminals is repressed and order established. For, the conquered peoples thereafter are better off than they were in liberty.

Next, to bolster this reasoning, a new argument was brought forward in the form of an admirable example taken, so they said, from nature herself: 'Why, otherwise, does God have mastery over man, the mind over the body, reason over lust and the other wrongful movements of the soul?'

Surely, now, this example teaches plainly enough for anyone that it is for the good of some to be in an inferior position, and that it is good for all without exception to be subject to God. The soul that is submissive to God justly lords it over the body; in the soul itself, reason bowing down before its Lord and God justly lords it over lust and every other evil tendency.

Because this is so, what fragment of justice can there be in a man who is not subject to God, if, indeed, it is a fact that such a one cannot rightfully exercise dominion—soul over body, human reason over sinful propensities? And if there is no justice in a man of this kind, then there is certainly no justice, either, in an assembly made up of such men. As a result, there is lacking that mutual recognition of rights which makes a mere mob into a 'people,' a people whose common weal is a commonwealth.

What shall I say of the common good whose common pursuit knits men together into a 'people,' as our definition teaches? Careful scrutiny will show that there is no such good for those who live irreligiously, as all do who serve not God but demons and, particularly, those filthy spirits that are so defiant of God that they look to receive sacrifices as if they were gods. Anyway, what I have said with regard to mutual recognition of rights I consider sufficient to show that, on the basis of the definition itself, a people devoid of justice is not such a people as can constitute a commonwealth.

I am supposing that no one will raise the objection that the Roman Republic served good and holy gods, and not unclean spirits. Surely, I do not have to repeat the same old arguments which I have so often and so more than sufficiently stated. No one but a thickhead or an irrepressible wrangler can have read all the earlier Books of this work and still doubt that the Romans worshiped evil and dirty demons. In any case, what does it matter to what kind of demons they offered sacrifices? In the law of the true God it is written: 'He that sacrificeth to gods shall be put to death, save only to the Lord.'[2] The dreadful sanction of this command makes it clear that God wanted no sacrifices offered to such gods, good or bad.

Chapter 22

But a man may object: Who is this God of yours, and how do we know that the Romans were obliged to adore Him with sacrifices to the exclusion of other gods? One must be blind indeed to be asking at this late date who our God is! He is the God whose Prophets foretold things we see realized under our very eyes. He is the God who gave the reply to Abraham: 'In thy seed shall all the nations of the earth be blessed.'[1] And this promise has been made good in Christ, born in the flesh of Abraham's seed—a fulfillment which those who have remained opposed to Christ's name know so well, though they like it so little. He is the God whose Spirit spoke through Prophets whose predictions are now realized in our visibly world-wide Church and which I quoted in previous Books. He is the God whom Varro, the most learned of Romans, thought was Jupiter, however little he grasped the import of his words. It is at least worth mentioning that a man of his learning was unable to think of our God as despicable or non-existent. In fact, Varro identified Him with his own conception of the supreme deity.

Finally, our God is the one whom Porphyry, most learned

2 Exod. 22.20.
_____
1 Gen. 22.18.

of philosophers and bitter enemy of Christianity, admits to be
a great God, and this on the strength of pagan oracles.

Chapter 23

In his work, *Ek logíon philosophías,* Porphyry brings together in orderly form some so-called 'divine' utterances on
theological topics. I quote his words as translated from the
Greek: 'Apollo gave this admonition in metre to a client seeking to learn which god he should placate with a view to wean-
ing his wife away from Christianity.' There follow the words
which Apollo is supposed to have uttered: 'It would be easier
for you to write lasting words in water, or to fly in the air
like a bird on weightless wings, than to get back any sense
into the head of your corrupted and impious wife. Let her have
her way with her empty illusions, and sing her sad, fond songs
over her dead god who was condemned by upright judges and,
in his lonely years, met the ugliest death, linked with iron.'

Following these verses of Apollo, here translated into prose,
Porphyry comments: 'In this oracle Apollo has shown how incurable are the Christians, for it is the Jews, not they, who
have regard for God.' See how he smears Christ[1] and puts
the Jews ahead of the Christians by saying that they have
more regard for God! He takes Apollo's words about Christ
being killed by upright judges to mean that their verdict was
just and that He got what He deserved. It is not my responsibility to decide whether it was Apollo's lying prophet that
uttered the words about Christ, which Porphyry swallowed, or
whether, possibly, Porphyry made up the whole thing out of
whole cloth. Later on we shall have to see how inconsistent
Porphyry is or, at least, what a job he has getting his oracles
to speak their pieces in unison. What he does say here is that
the Jews, as being upholders of God, judged Christ justly when
they decreed to torture him in the most ignominious of all
deaths. In this case, Porphyry should have lent an ear to what
the God of the Jews, to whom he bears witness, has to say:
'He that sacrificeth to gods shall be put to death, save only
to the Lord.'[2]

---

[1] . . . *decolorans Christum.*   [2] Exod. 22.20.

But let us come now to his more candid avowals, and hear how great he makes the God of the Jews out to be. Once again we have a question addressed to Apollo—this time as to the superiority of speech, or reason, or law. 'He replied,' says Porphyry, 'in verse.' Then he gives these verses, including the following—which are enough for my purposes: 'In God the father and king, older than all things, before whom the heavens, the earth, the ocean, and the sightless reaches of hell tremble, before whom the gods themselves quake with fear. For them the law is the Father whom the devout Hebrews hold in profound regard.' Using this oracle, Porphyry makes his god Apollo say that the God of the Hebrews is mighty enough to make the gods themselves quake with fear before Him. Well, in view of the fact that this God is none other than the one who said, 'He that sacrificeth to gods shall be put to death, save only to the Lord,' I am amazed that Porphyry himself did not quake with fear, too, and tremble lest he, in the act of sacrificing to his gods, be done away with.

Truth to tell, though, our philosopher has some good things to say of Christ. Either he is forgetful of the obloquy of which I have just been speaking, or else it is his gods who cursed Christ in their sleep and then, waking up, realized that He really was good and set out to praise Him becomingly! For he says as something extraordinary and beyond belief: 'What I am about to say is assuredly going to appear as remarkable to some. My gods have pronounced Christ a most religious person, now rendered immortal, and they have spoken very well of him. They say, however, that the Christians themselves are a besmirched and corrupted crew, all tied up in errors. And they have many similar hard things to say of them.'

At this point he cites some divine oracles cursing the Christians. Then, 'Hecate, answering some people who asked her if Christ is God, replied: "You know already that the soul is deathless and journeyeth on after the body. One, however, that is cut off from wisdom wandereth ever. The soul of Christ is the spirit of a man of very great piety. But those who adore it do so in ignorance of the truth."'

Having quoted this so-called oracle, Porphyry weaves this commentary: 'Note that she says he was a most religious man

whose spirit, like that of other devout men, has been endowed
with immortality after death, and that Christians worship him
out of ignorance. In answer to the query, "Why, then, was he
condemned to die," the goddess replied, "The body, to be sure,
is always up against exhausting torture, but the souls of the
devout are enthroned in heaven. The soul you speak of, however, was fated to bring other souls, whom the fates did not
will to receive the gods' gifts nor to come to the knowledge
of Jupiter the Immortal, into the toils of error. These souls are
hateful to the gods because, as they were fated not to know
God nor to receive the gods' gifts, he fatefully involved them
in error. He himself, however, was a devout man and has gone
up into heaven as do all good men. Accordingly, you will on
no account speak ill of him, and you will pity the pathetic
madness of these people, inasmuch as they stand unawares in
headlong peril." '

I ask: Who is so dull-witted as not to perceive that these
oracles were either made up by this clever and implacable
enemy of the Christians or were actually uttered by impure
demons. In either case, the purpose was the same, namely,
by praising Christ to win a confident hearing in their slanderous abuse of His followers, and thus, if possible, to block that
road to eternal salvation upon which one who becomes a
Christian enters. The demons realize that it falls in well with
their astute resourcefulness in doing harm, if they gain credit
by praising Christ, and consequent credit in calumniating
Christians. In this way they can make a man who swallows
both tales the kind of Christ-eulogizer who is loath to be a
Christian, with the result that the Christ whom he extols is
rendered incapable of setting him free from the domination
of the demons. This is all the more true when you reflect that
their praise of Christ is so shaped that anyone accepting Christ
on their testimony would not be a genuine Christian anyway,
but a Photinian heretic who accepts Christ as a man while
rejecting Him as God, and thus can neither be saved by Him
nor avoid, or escape from, the snares of these lying devils.

For our part, we pay no attention either to Apollo slander-
ing Christ or to Hecate praising Him. The former would have
us believe that Christ was a criminal, executed by right-

thinking judges; the latter, that he was a sincerely pious man —but merely a man. Both have a single aim, to dissuade men from becoming Christians and thus keep them in the power of the demons.

I have a suggestion. Let Porphyry or, better still, all who swallow these 'oracles' against the Christians first undertake, if they can, to effect agreement between Apollo and Hecate on the subject of Christ, so that they damn Him in unison or praise Him in unison! Even if they could, we would still shun these demons as ruseful devils whether they praise or blame. Seeing, however, that their damning god and praising goddess disagree concerning Christ, no sensible man will believe them when they curse the Christians.

Now let us examine Porphyry's (or Hecate's) approval of Christ. Assuredly, when he (or she) contends that it was Christ Himself who was the fateful source of His followers' error, he (or she) is supposed to reveal the cause of Christian error. But, before I quote Porphyry's words, I have a question: If Christ caused the Christians to be caught in inevitable error, did He do this deliberately or indeliberately? If deliberately, how can He be just? If indeliberately, how can He be blessed? However, let us hear the causes of this error. 'There exist in certain localities,' says Porphyry, 'certain very small terrestrial spirits who are underlings of the evil demons. The Hebrew sages—of whom Jesus was one according to Apollo's oracle, just cited—taught believers to shun these lesser spirits and dastardly demons and reverence the heavenly spirits, above all, God the Father. I have shown that this is what the gods command when they admonish us to fix our minds on God and adore Him in every place. For all this, ignorant people of irreligious bent who are not fated to receive the gifts of the gods nor to have any conception of Jupiter the Immortal, have paid no heed to the gods and godlike teachers and have dispensed with all the gods, and have revered the banned demons who they should have hated. Pretending to worship God, they do not do what worship calls for. Not that God, the Father of all, needs anything, but it is to our good to worship Him by justice, chastity, and the other virtues, making our whole life a prayer built on seeking him and walking in his footsteps.

Seeking purifies, and following divinizes, our affections, by making Him their object.'

This is, indeed, splendid praise of God the Father and a fine statement of the kind of life a man is commanded to live in His honor; and of such praise and such precepts the Jews' prophetic books are full, wherever holy living is mentioned.

When it comes to the Christians, though, Porphyry is as mistaken or as malicious as the demons, his 'gods,' could desire. As if it were difficult for a man to recall the shameful and unseemly business which used to be staged in theater and temple in honor of these gods, and then contrast the kind of thing read, preached, and listened to in our churches, and the kind of sacrifice we offer to the true God, and thus grasp on which side lies the tearing down and on which side the building up of the good life! Who but a diabolical spirit ever told Porphyry (or inspired him to tell) such a hollow and palpable lie as that Christians do more to reverence than revile the demons whose cult the Jews forbade?

The God of the Hebrew Prophets forbade sacrifices even to those holy angels and heavenly powers whom we in this pilgrimage of mortal life reverence and love as our blessed fellow countrymen. In the Law He gave to the Hebrew people, He thundered these threatening words: 'He that sacrificeth to gods shall be put to death.' Moreover, no one could think that this banning of sacrifice affects only those evil and earthly spirits whom Porphyry dubs 'unimportant' or 'lesser' and who are called even in Scripture 'the gods of the Gentiles,' as is perfectly clear in the Septuagint version of Psalm 95: 'For all the gods of the Gentiles are devils.'[3] It was lest anyone might entertain the idea that sacrifice, forbidden to demons, could be offered to all or even some of the heavenly spirits that God added at once: 'save only to the Lord.' This means 'to the Lord and to nobody else.' I add this paraphrase to prevent anyone thinking that the Latin words, *Domino soli*, mean that to the 'Sun God' sacrifice may be offered. It is the simplest thing in the world to see from the Greek version that such is not the meaning.

This God of the Hebrews, whose greatness even Varro at-

[3] Ps. 95.5.

tests, gave a Law to his chosen people, a law written in Hebrew, not an obscure and little-known law, but one that has long been common knowledge among all people. And it is this Law that contains the words: 'He that sacrificeth to gods shall be put to death, save only to the Lord.' What point is there in seeking for further proof in His Law and Prophets concerning this matter? Indeed, there is no need to 'seek' for evidences which are neither rare nor recondite; nor even to collect all those texts that are so many and so manifest, and to quote them here. They make it clearer than daylight that the supreme true God wishes sacrifice to be paid exclusively to Himself. Now, I offer but one statement. It is brief, majestic, terrifying, and true. It was spoken by that very God whom the most distinguished pagan scholars extol so splendidly. Hear it, fear it, heed it, lest death befall you if you disobey. He said: 'He that sacrificeth to gods shall be put to death, save only to the Lord,' and that, not because God needs anything, but simply because it is good for us to belong to God alone. For the Hebrews' Scripture sings: 'I have said to the Lord, thou art my God, for thou hast no need of my goods.'[4]

We ourselves, who form His City, are His best and most worthy sacrifice. It is this Mystery which we celebrate in our oblations, so familiar to the faithful, as I have explained already.[5] And it was through the Hebrew Prophets themselves that the divine revelations were given that the symbolic sacrifices of the Jews would one day cease, and that thereafter all races would offer one sacrifice from sunrise to sunset, just as we see for ourselves this very day. But I have already quoted enough of such texts throughout this work.

To sum up. Where justice is wanting, in the sense that the civil community does not take its orders from the one supreme God, and follow them out with the help of His grace; where sacrifice is offered to any save Him alone; where, consequently, the civil community is not such that everyone obeys God in this respect; where the soul does not control the body, and reason our evil urges, as proper order and faith require; where neither the individuals nor the whole community, 'the people,'

---

[4] Ps. 15.2, as quoted by Eusebius.
[5] Cf. above, 10.6.

live by that faith of the just which works through that charity which loves God as He should be loved and one's neighbor as oneself—where this kind of justice is lacking, I maintain, there does not exist 'a multitude bound together by a mutual recognition of rights and a mutual co-operation for the common good.' This being so, there is no proper 'people'—if Scipio's definition is correct—nor a commonwealth. For, where there is no 'people,' there is no 'people's' weal.

Chapter 24

It is possible to define a 'people' not as Cicero does but as 'a multitude of reasonable beings voluntarily associated in the pursuit of common interests.'[1] In that case, one need only consider what these interests are in order to determine of what kind any particular people may be. Still, whatever these interests are, so long as we have a multitude of rational beings —and not of irresponsible cattle—who are voluntarily associated in the pursuit of common interests, we can reasonably call them a 'people,' and they will be a better or worse people according as the interests which have brought them together are better or worse interests.

This definition certainly makes the Roman people a 'people' and their weal a 'commonwealth' or 'republic.' However, we know from history what kind of interests this people had, both in primitive times and more recently, and also what kind of morals brought on the rupture and corruption of their voluntary association (which is the health, so to speak, of any community), first, by sanguinary seditions, and, later, by social and civil war. On this subject, I had a good deal to say earlier in this work.[2] However, I would still call the Romans a 'people' and their affairs a 'commonwealth,' so long as they remain a multitude of reasonable beings voluntarily associated in the pursuit of common interests.

Of course, what I have said of the Romans and their Republic applies not less to the Athenians and other Greek com-

[1] *Populus est coetus multitudinis rationalis rerum quas diligit concordi communione sociatus.*
[2] Bks. 2.18; 3.23–29.

munities, to the Egyptians, to the early Assyrians of Babylonia, and, in general, to any other pagan people whose government exercised real political control, however much or little. The fact is that any civil community made up of pagans who are disobedient to God's command that He alone receive sacrifices and who, therefore, are devoid of the rational and religious control of soul over body and of reason over sinful appetite must be lacking in true justice.

Chapter 25

There may seem to be some control of soul over body and of reason over passion, even when soul and reason do not serve God as He demands. Actually, however, there is no such thing. For, what species of control can there be of the body and its bad tendencies if the mistress mind is ignorant of the true God, insubmissive to His authority, and, as a result, a plaything to the corrupting influences of thoroughly evil demons? No, the virtues on which the mind preens itself as giving control over the body and its urges, and which aim at any other purpose or possession than God, are in point of fact vices rather than virtues.[1]

Although some people claim that virtues are authentic and worthy of the name so long as their end is in themselves and they are not means to something else, even they are spoiled by the puff of pride and must, consequently, be reckoned as vices rather than virtues.

Just as our flesh does not live by its own power but by a power above it, so what gives to a man the life of blessedness derives not from himself, but from a power above him. And this applies not just to man but to every heavenly Power and Domination.

Chapter 26

As the life of the body is the soul, so the 'blessed life' of a man is God. As the sacred writings of the Hebrews have it: 'Happy is that people whose God is the Lord.'[1] Wretched, then, must be any people that is divorced from this God.

[1] Cf. above, 5.20.
[1] Ps. 143.15.

Yet, even such a people cherishes a peace of its own which is not to be scorned although in the end it is not to be had because this peace, before the end, was abused. Meanwhile, it is to our advantage that there be such peace in this life. For, as long as the two cities are mingled together, we can make use of the peace of Babylon. Faith can assure our exodus from Babylon, but our pilgrim status, for the time being, makes us neighbors.

All of this was in St. Paul's mind when he advised the Church to pray for this world's kings and high authorities—in order that 'we may lead a quiet and peaceful life in all piety and worthy behavior.'[2] Jeremias, too, predicting the Babylonian captivity to the Old Testament Jews, gave them orders from God to go submissively and serve their God by such sufferings, and meanwhile to pray for Babylon. 'For in the peace thereof,' he said, 'shall be your peace'[3]—referring, of course, to the peace of this world which the good and bad share in common.

Chapter 27

The City of God, however, has a peace of its own, namely, peace with God in this world by faith and in the world to come by vision. Still, any peace we have on earth, whether the peace we share with Babylon or our own peace through faith, is more like a solace for unhappiness than the joy of beatitude. Even our virtue in this life, genuine as it is because it is referred to the true goal of every good, lies more in the pardoning of sins than in any perfection of virtues. Witness the prayer of God's whole City, wandering on earth and calling out to Him through all her members: 'Forgive us our debts as we also forgive our debtors.'[1]

This prayer is effective, not on the lips of those whose faith without works is dead,[2] but only on the lips of men whose faith works through charity.[3] This prayer is necessary for the just because their reason, though submissive to God, has only

2 1 Tim. 2.2.   3 Jer. 29.7.

1 Matt. 6.12.   2 Cf. James 2.17.

3 Cf. Gal. 5.6.

imperfect mastery over their evil inclinations so long as they live in this world and in a corruptible body that 'is a load upon the soul.'[4] Reason may give commands, but can exercise no control without a struggle. And, in this time of weakness, something will inevitably creep in to make the best of soldiers —whether in victory or still in battle with such foes—offend by some small slip of the tongue, some passing thought, if not by habitual actions. This explains why we can know no perfect peace so long as there are evil inclinations to master. Those which put up a fight are put down only in perilous conflict; those that are already overcome cannot be kept so if one relaxes, but only at the cost of vigilant control. These are the battles which Scripture sums up in the single phrase: 'The life of man upon earth is a warfare.'[5]

Who, then, save a proud man, will presume that he can live without needing to ask God: 'Forgive us our debts'? Not a great man, you may be sure, but one blown up with the wind of self-reliance—one whom God in His justice resists while He grants His grace to the humble. Hence, it is written: 'God resists the proud, but gives grace to the humble.'[6]

This, then, in this world, is the life of virtue. When God commands, man obeys; when the soul commands, the body obeys; when reason rules, our passions, even when they fight back, must be conquered or resisted; man must beg God's grace to win merit and the remission of his sins and must thank God for the blessings he receives.

But, in that final peace which is the end and purpose of all virtue here on earth, our nature, made whole by immortality and incorruption, will have no vices and experience no rebellion from within or without. There will be no need for reason to govern non-existent evil inclinations. God will hold sway over man, the soul over the body; and the happiness in eternal life and law will make obedience sweet and easy. And in each and all of us this condition will be everlasting, and we shall know it to be so. That is why the peace of such blessedness or the blessedness of such peace is to be our supreme good.

On the other hand, the doom in store for those who are not

---

[4] Wisd. 9.15.   [5] Job 7.1.
[6] James 4.6; 1 Peter 5.5.

Chapter 28

of the City of God is an unending wretchedness that is called 'the second death,' because neither the soul, cut off from the life of God, nor the body, pounded by perpetual pain, can there be said to live at all. And what will make that second death so hard to bear is that there will be no death to end it.

Now, since unhappiness is the reverse of happiness, death of life, and war of peace, one may reasonably ask: If peace is praised and proclaimed as the highest good, what kind of warfare are we to think of as the highest evil? If this inquirer will reflect, he will realize that what is hurtful and destructive in warfare is mutual clash and conflict, and, hence, that no one can imagine a war more unbearably bitter than one in which the will and passions are at such odds that neither can ever win the victory, and in which violent pain and the body's very nature will so clash that neither will ever yield. When this conflict occurs on earth, either pain wins and death puts an end to all feeling, or nature wins and health removes the pain. But, in hell, pain permanently afflicts and nature continues to feel it, for neither ever comes to term, since the punishment must never end.

However, it is through the last judgment that good men achieve that highest good (which all should seek) and evil men that highest evil (which all should shun), and so, as God helps me, I shall discuss that judgment in the Book that comes next.

BOOK XX

Separation of the Two Cities in the Last Judgment

Chapter 1

IN THIS BOOK, I plan, with God's help, to discuss His day of final judgment and to defend its reality against those who deliberately disbelieve in it. My first duty will be to lay a solid foundation of revealed data. Of those who reject these revelations, some do so on the ground that they deny outright the divine inspiration of Scriptural texts, and others because they try to twist the texts to a different meaning. In both cases, the reasonings are human, specious and false. For there is no human being, I think, who will withhold assent, if only he will take these texts at their face value and realize that the holy men who wrote them were inspired by the true and supreme God. Not everyone, of course, will admit this openly—some because they are too ashamed or afraid to make open profession, and others because they are so psychotic in their bullheadedness that they will strain and strive to defend, at all costs, what they know or believe to be false even when reason or faith tells them it is true.

By the last day or time of divine judgment I mean what the whole Church of the true God means when she believes and openly proclaims that Christ will come from heaven to judge the living and the dead. Just how many days this judgment will take we do not know, since even the most casual reader of Scripture knows that the word 'day' is often used for 'time.' And one speaks of 'last' or 'final' in connection with this particular 'day' of divine judgment because, in fact, God is at all times exercising judgment and, therefore, at the present time just as He has been doing from the creation of mankind. For example, He exercised judgment when He expelled our first parents from Eden and drove the perpetrators of the great sin far from the tree of life. And God exercised judgment when He refused to spare the angels who sinned and, especially, their leader who was the cause, by choice, of his own fall and, by envy and hatred, the cause of the fall of man. Nor is it without God's high and just judgment that the life of the demons in the air and of men on earth is so miserable, so full of ignorance and anguish. And even had there been no sin to punish, there would have been a place for God's good and righteous judgment in rewarding with eternal felicity all of His rational creatures who cling in constancy to Him as Lord.

God judges men and angels not only as groups that deserve wretchedness as the wages of the original sin, but also as individuals who have freely chosen to do what each has done. When the demons beseech God not to torture them, He may quite justly be more sparing to one and more severe with another according to individual wickedness. So, too, human beings—whether manifestly or hiddenly, whether in this life or later—pay a divinely assessed penalty, each for his or her own personal wrongdoing. And it is right to speak of penalty and reward even though no positively good action can be done without divine help, and although there can be no sin of man or angel without a divine permission which is at the same time a perfectly just judgment. For, as St. Paul says in one place: 'Is there injustice with God? By no means!'[1] Again he says: 'How incomprehensible are his judgments and how unsearchable his ways!'[2]

In this Book, however, as God permits, I shall not discuss God's first judgment nor those other judgments which are past nor those that go on today, but only that last judgment when Christ will come from heaven to judge the living and the dead. This will be a day of judgment in the precise sense that there will be no place for any uncomprehending complaint that this sinner has been blessed or that that good man has been punished. On that day, we shall see plainly the true fullness of felicity of all the saints and only of the saints, as we shall see the supreme and deserved misery of the wicked and of the wicked alone.

Chapter 2

While time lasts, however, we are schooled to bear misfortune calmly, for good and bad men without distinction have

[1] Rom. 9.14.   [2] Rom. 11.33.

to bear it; and we set no great store by prosperity, since bad and good men alike may come to enjoy it. So it is that, even in these temporal vicissitudes where God's justice is not apparent, divine Revelation must save us from confusion.

We cannot know, for example, what secret decree of God's justice makes this good man poor and that bad man rich; why this man, whose immoral life should cause him, in our estimation, to be torn with grief, is, in point of fact, quite happy; why that man, whose praiseworthy life should bring him joy, is, in fact, sad of soul; why this innocent party leaves the courtroom not just unavenged but actually condemned, unfairly treated by a corrupt judge or overwhelmed by lying testimony, while his guilty opponent not merely gets off unpunished but goes gloating over his vindication. Here we have an irreligious man in excellent health, there a holy man wasting away to a shadow with disease. Here are some young men, robbers by profession, in superb physical fettle; there, some mere babies, unable to harm anyone even in speech, afflicted with various kinds of implacable disease. A very much needed man is swept off by untimely death; a man who, we think, should not even have been born survives him and lives a long life. One man loaded with crimes is lifted to honors, while another whose life is beyond reproach lives under a cloud of suspicion. And so of innumerable other examples.

It would be intelligible if there were only some consistency in the seeming senselessness of these arrangements. But in this world, where man, as the inspired psalm says, 'is like to vanity; his days pass away like a shadow,'[1] it is not only bad men who enjoy the passing boons of this earth, and it is not only good men who suffer misfortunes. If it were always the case that those who are not going to attain the eternal blessings of beatitude should have the temporal ones, whether in the form of solaces from God's mercy or even as illusory goods to deceive them, and if those not destined to suffer eternally were consistently to have temporal misfortunes, whether in the form of chastisement corresponding to their sins, or in the form of spiritual testings for the attainment of virtue, this consistency might be traced to a just or merciful judgment of God. But it

[1] Ps. 143.4.

is sometimes not so obvious as all this, for not only are the good sometimes unfortunate and the wicked fortunate—a seeming injustice—but, as often as not, bad luck befalls bad men and good luck good men. The whole arrangement makes God's judgments all the more inscrutable and His ways unsearchable.

Accordingly, even though we cannot understand what kind of divine judgment can positively or even permissively will such inequalities—since God is omnipotent, all-wise, all-just, and in no way weak, rash, or unfair—it is still good for our souls to learn to attach no importance to the good or ill fortune which we see visited without distinction upon the good and the bad. We learn, too, to seek the good things that are meant for the good, and to avoid at all costs the evil things that are fit for the bad.

When, however, we come to that judgment of God the proper name of which is 'judgment day' or 'the day of the Lord,' we shall see that all His judgments are perfectly just: those reserved for that occasion, all those that He had made from the beginning, and those, too, He is to make between now and then. Then, too, it will be shown plainly how just is that divine decree which makes practically all of God's judgments lie beyond the present understanding of men's minds, even though devout men may know by faith that God's hidden judgments are most surely just.

Chapters 3-29

This is a long study of Scripture texts having reference to the Last Judgment. Augustine here takes the Millennium as probably meaning the whole Christian era, however long it may be. Texts and prophecies concerning the resurrection of the dead and persecution under Antichrist are very fully discussed.

Chapter 30

There are many other passages, of the divinely inspired Scripture which deal with the last judgment, but it would take too long to assemble them all. Suffice it to say that evidence enough has been adduced to prove that the judgment has been foretold in both Testaments. The fact that it is Christ who is to come from heaven as the Judge is made less explicit in the Old Testament than in the New. The difficulty is that in the Old Testament, when the 'Lord God' says He is to come or when it is stated that the 'Lord God' will come, it is not obvious that Christ is meant.

Now, of course, it is true that the Father, Son, and Holy Spirit is each Lord and God; yet that is no reason why one should not attempt to show that, in the relevant texts, it is Christ that is meant. The first proof is this. In the prophetical books, Jesus Christ speaks under the name of the 'Lord God' in many passages where there can be no doubt at all that it is Christ who is meant. Hence, when there is a reference to the last judgment, indicating that the 'Lord God' is to come, it is at least possible to argue that Christ is meant, even though this is not made explicit. Take, for example, the passage in Isaias where God says, through the Prophet: 'Hearken to me, O Jacob, and thou Israel when I call. I am he, I am the first, and I am the last. My hand also hath founded the earth and my right hand hath measured the heavens: I shall call them and they shall stand together, and all will assemble and all will hear. Who hath declared these things? Loving thee I will do thy will in regard to Babylon, and so take away the seed of the Chaldeans. I, even I have spoken and called him. I have brought him and I have made his way prosperous. Come ye near unto me and hear this. I have not spoken in secret from the beginning. When these things were done I was there and now the Lord God hath sent me and his spirit.'[1] Now, it is Jesus Christ who is speaking here as the 'Lord God'; yet this would not have been obvious if He had not added the final words: 'And now the Lord God hath sent me and his spirit.' These words were spoken by Christ in His 'form' as a 'servant.' He used a verb in the past tense to indicate a future event, much as was done in that other text of the same Prophet: 'He was led as a sheep to the slaughter.'[2] Instead of saying: 'He

[1] Isa. 48.12–16.
[2] Cf. Isa. 53.7; the Vulgate reads: 'He shall be led . . .'

shall be led,' he uses a verb in the past tense to indicate a future event, as is frequently the case in the prophecies.

Another example to prove the same point may be found in a passage of Zacharias where the 'Almighty' sends the 'Almighty.' This can only mean that God the Father sends God the Son. The text runs: 'Thus saith the Lord Almighty. After the glory he hath sent me to the nations that have robbed you; for he that toucheth you, toucheth the apple of my eye. For behold I lift up my head upon them, and they shall be a prey to those who served them; and you shall know that the Lord Almighty sent me.'[3] In this case, the Lord Almighty says that He is sent by the Lord Almighty. How can anyone doubt that it is Christ who is speaking and, in fact, speaking to the lost sheep of the house of Israel. Remember what is said in the Gospel: 'I was not sent except to the lost sheep of the house of Israel.'[4] The comparison of these lost sheep to the pupil of God's eye is explained by the perfection of God's love. And, of course, it was to this flock of sheep that the Apostles belonged. 'After the glory' of His Resurrection—a glory alluded to in the words: 'Jesus had not yet been glorified'[5]—it was in the person of these Apostles that Jesus was sent to the Gentiles; and this was to be the fulfillment of what the Psalmist had prophesied: 'Thou wilt deliver me from the contradictions of the people; thou wilt make me head of the Gentiles.'[6] The result was that the Gentiles, who had 'robbed' the Israelites in the days of their slavery, were themselves robbed, in their turn, but in a different way, when they became 'prey' to the Israelites. This is the point of the promises which Jesus made, first, to a group of the Apostles: 'I will make you fishers of men,'[7] and then to one of them: 'Henceforth, thou shalt catch men.'[8] Thus the Gentiles were to become 'prey' in the good sense that they were to be goods plundered from the 'strong man,' when he was bound by One still stronger.[9]

Here is still another illustration taken from the same Prophet: 'And it shall come to pass in that day that I shall seek to destroy all the nations that come against Jerusalem.

---

[3] Zach. 2.8,9.
[5] John 7.39.
[7] Matt. 4.19.
[9] Matt. 12.29.

[4] Matt. 15.24.
[6] Ps. 17.44.
[8] Luke 5.10.

And I will pour out upon the house of David, and upon the inhabitants of Jerusalem the spirit of grace and of mercy; and they shall look upon me, as one whom they have insulted and they shall mourn for him as one mourneth for a beloved son and they shall grieve over him as the manner is to grieve for the death of the only begotten.'[10] Now, no one will question that it belongs to God 'to destroy all the nations' that are hostile to the holy city of Jerusalem and that 'come against' her in the sense of being opposed to her (or, as other versions have it, 'come down upon her') in order to conquer her. And it equally belongs to God to 'pour out upon the house of David and upon the inhabitants' of that city 'the spirit of grace and mercy.' This, I repeat, belongs to God, in whose name the Prophet is speaking; yet the God who performs these great and divine actions is clearly revealed as Christ in the words that follow: 'And they shall look upon me as one they have insulted, and they shall mourn for him as one mourneth for a beloved son and they shall grieve over him as the manner is to grieve for the death of the only begotten.'

Certainly, in the day of judgment, the Jews, including those who are to receive the spirit of grace and mercy, will grieve for the insults heaped upon Christ in His passion. They will repent when they see Him coming in His majesty, and when they recognize Him as the One whom, in the person of their fathers, they mocked in the days of His lowliness. And those very fathers, who were directly responsible for the great outrage, will see Him when they rise from the dead in a resurrection that will be, not for the sake of purification, but of punishment. It is not, therefore, to such 'fathers' that the words of the text, 'the inhabitants of Jerusalem,' refer but, rather, to those of their descendants who are destined to believe in the days of the preaching of Elias. And, of course, even these converts will still grieve, though they were no more responsible for the actions of their fathers than the present-day Jews who are sometimes called 'Christ-killers.' Of course, when the Jews who are to become believers through the 'spirit of grace and mercy,' and who are not to be punished along with their impious ancestors, grieve as though they were responsible for

[10] Zach. 12.9,10.

the deeds of their fathers, their grief will be one inspired, not
so much by a sense of guilt, but rather by a sense of gratitude.

It is worth noticing that, where the Septuagint text reads,
'And they shall look upon me as one whom they have insulted,' the Vulgate[11] has: 'whom they have pierced.' This
makes the allusion to Christ crucified clearer than ever. However, the word which the seventy translators preferred to use
has a wider reference to the whole passion, since Christ was
'insulted' in His arrest and imprisonment, in the trial and the
ignominy of the robe they put upon Him, in the crown of
thorns and the blows from the reed, in the mock bending of
knees and in the carrying of the cross, and, finally, He was
insulted when He was hanging on the cross. If only we com-
bine the two readings, 'insulted' and 'pierced,' we get a much
fuller picture of our Lord's passion than by taking either the
Septuagint or the Vulgate reading by itself.

The conclusion, then, is that, when we read in the prophetical books that 'God' is to come to pronounce the last judgment, we do not need any indication more specific than the
mention of the judgment to realize that it is Christ who is
meant. The Father, of course, will judge, but He will do so
by means of the coming of the Son of Man. Although the Father will manifest Himself by His presence, He will not 'judge
any man, but all judgment he has given to the Son.'[12] The Son,
on the other hand, will manifest Himself as a man who is to
judge, because it was as a man that He was judged.

This is confirmed by a passage in the Prophet Isaias, where
God uses the names of Jacob and Israel to indicate Christ,
who assumed His body from their descendants. The passage
reads: 'Jacob my son, I will uphold him; Israel my elect, my
soul has assumed him. I have given my spirit upon him, and
he shall bring forth judgment to the Gentiles. He shall not
cry out nor cease, neither shall his voice be heard outside.
The bruised reed he shall not break and the smoking flax he
shall not quench. He shall bring forth judgment unto truth.
He shall shine and shall not be broken until he set judgment

---

[11] *Sane ubi dixerunt septuaginta interpretes . . . sic interpreta-
tum est ex Hebraeo.*
[12] John 5.22.

on earth; and in his name shall the Gentiles hope.'[13] It is true, indeed, that the Vulgate text has 'my servant' in place of 'Jacob' and 'Israel,' but the Septuagint translators preferred to make the meaning more explicit, namely, that the prophecy concerns the 'Highest' in so far as He became the 'lowliest,' in the 'form of a servant.' Hence they placed the name of that man from whose stock the 'form of a servant' was assumed. It was to Him that the Holy Spirit was 'given' and this was made manifest, as the Gospel tells us, under the form of a dove.[14] It was He who brought forth 'judgment to the Gentiles,' in the sense that He predicted to them a judgment of which they had no knowledge. In His meekness He did not 'cry out,' nor did He 'cease' from preaching the truth. His voice was not, nor is not, 'heard outside,' because those who are 'outside,' who are cut off from His Body, do not listen to Him. He did not 'break' nor 'quench' those very Jews who persecuted Him, although they were like a 'bruised reed' because of their lost innocence, and like 'smoking flax' because of the Light they lost. Rather, He spared them, in the sense that He came to be judged by them before He came to be their Judge. Of course, He 'brought forth judgment in truth' when He foretold the time of their punishment to those who should persist in sin. His face 'shone' on the mount and His fame 'shone' throughout the whole world. He was not 'broken,' either in Himself or in His Church, because He has not yielded to the efforts of persecutors who have sought to crush His Church out of existence.

The time has not yet come, nor will it ever come when His enemies can say: 'When shall he die and his name perish?'

In the answer given, 'not until he set judgment on earth,'[15] we have revealed the hidden truth we have been seeking. The 'judgment' mentioned here is that last judgment which Christ is to 'set on earth' when He comes from heaven. And it is in Christ that we see already fulfilled what is mentioned at the end of the prophecy: 'And in his name shall the Gentiles hope.' This, surely, is a fulfillment which no one can deny and, therefore, to disbelieve the rest of the prophecy is little short of

13 Isa. 42.1–4.   14 Matt. 3.16.
15 Ps. 40.6.

impudence. For, who could have hoped to see what even those who refused to believe in Christ cannot help but see before their very eyes? There is the fulfillment, utterly undeniable, and all they can do is to 'gnash their teeth and waste away.'[16] It was certainly hard for anyone to hope that the Gentiles would hope in the name of Christ when He was being arrested, bound, scourged, mocked, and crucified, and when even His disciples lost the hope they once had. Yet, the hope that hardly anyone but a single thief dying on a cross could entertain is now shared by peoples everywhere on earth, who sign themselves with that very Cross on which He died, in the hope that they may escape eternal death. How, then, can anyone deny or even doubt that it is Jesus Christ who will be in charge of the last judgment, just as Holy Writ has preannounced? Or, if there is anyone who can doubt, he must be moved by such unbelievable hatred that he cannot trust those holy Scriptures which have demonstrated their truth to all the world.

In connection with the last judgment, therefore, we who believe can be sure of the following truths: Elias the Thesbite will return; the Jews will believe; Antichrist will persecute the Church; Christ will be the Judge; the dead will rise; the good will be separated from the wicked; the world will suffer from fire, but will be renewed. Of course, what we believe is the simple fact that all these things are to be; but how and in what sequence the events are to occur we must leave to future experience, which alone can teach these truths so much better than human intelligence can at present understand. My own view is that they will occur in the order I have just mentioned.

There now remain two Books still to be written, if I am to keep, with God's help, the promise I made when I began this work. One of these Books will deal with the pains in store for sinners and the other with the bliss of the saints. In these two Books, my main purpose will be to refute, with God's grace, those seemingly skillful arguments by which those who are wise with the wisdom of men try, unhappily, to weaken the force of God's menaces and promises, and to ridicule as false those Scriptural texts that are the very food of our saving faith. Men, however, who are wise with the wisdom of God

16 Cf. Ps. 111.10.

hold that the irrefutable omnipotence of God is an unanswerable argument in favor of all of these predictions which seem too incredible to human intelligence but which are contained in holy writings whose veracity has now been established in countless ways. Men whose wisdom is according to God hold for certain, first, that God in the Scriptures could not possibly lie, and, second, that He has the power to do things that seem impossible to the unbeliever.

BOOK XXI

End and Punishment of the Earthly City

Chapter 1

THE TWO CITIES, of God and of the Devil, are to reach their appointed ends when the sentences of destiny and doom are passed by our Lord Jesus Christ, the Judge of the living and the dead. In the present Book, therefore, I must try, with the help of God, to discuss in some detail the kind of punishment which the Devil and those who belong to the city of the Devil are to endure. My reason for treating eternal pains before dealing with beatitude is that it seems harder to believe that the bodies of the damned are to remain in endless torment than to believe that the bodies of the saints are to continue without pain in everlasting felicity. Once I have proved the possibility of eternal pain, this will greatly help to show how relatively easy it is to believe in the utterly unperturbed immortality of the bodies of the saints.

This order which I have chosen to follow is not out of harmony with Scriptural use. It is true, of course, that in some cases the blessedness of the just is placed first, as in the text: 'And they who have done good shall come forth unto resurrection of life; but they who have done evil unto resurrection of judgment.'[1] At other times, however, it comes second, as in the text: 'The Son of Man will send forth his angels, and they will gather out of his kingdom all scandals and those who work iniquity, and cast them into the furnace of fire, where there will be the weeping and the gnashing of teeth. Then the just will shine forth like the sun in the kingdom of their Father,'[2] and in the text: 'And these will go into everlasting punishment, but the just into everlasting life.'[3] And anyone who examines the Prophets will find texts which I need not here mention, some following the one order and some the other. I hope, at

[1] John 5.29.
[2] Matt. 13.41–43.
[3] Matt. 25.46.

any rate, that I have sufficiently explained my own choice in this matter of sequence.

Chapter 2

It is not easy to find a proof that will convince unbelievers of the possibility of human bodies remaining not merely active, alive, and uncorrupted after death, but also of continuing forever in the torments of fire. Such unbelievers are deaf to any appeal to the power of the Almighty, and demand a demonstration in terms of positive facts. When facts are reported, they deny the value of the evidence; when the evidence is produced, they declare it inconclusive. In regard to facts, it is said that certain animals live in fire, although they are mortal and, therefore, corruptible; that in certain hot springs, too hot for any hand to bear, there is found a species of worm that not merely endures the heat but cannot live without it. But even when the unbelievers see such things with their eyes (or accept reliable witnesses), they object, first, that the animals in question do not live forever and, second, that such animals feel no pain from the heat but, in fact, thrive in it. Strange unbelievers, who find it easier to believe that animals can thrive in fire than survive the pain! Surely, if it is incredible that an animal can feel a fire and go on living, it is still more incredible that it should live in a fire and not feel it. No one who can believe the second marvel has a right to doubt the first.

Chapter 3

Criticizing the Platonic denial of the resurrection of the body, Augustine explains how the soul may feel pain from the fires of hell.

Chapter 4

If we may trust the reports of workers in the field of natural phenomena, the salamander lives in fire. Again, certain well-known volcanoes in Sicily have been continuously active from the earliest times down to our own day, yet, in spite of the fire, the mountains remain intact. Such facts should prove that not everything that burns is consumed; and, as we saw, the soul proves that not everything that is susceptible of pain is susceptible of death. What further evidence, then, do we need to prove that human bodies suffering the penalty of eternal pains, first, remain united with their souls in the fire; second, burn without being consumed; and, third, suffer pain without meeting death?

The truth is that God, who has endowed things with such a marvelous variety of marvelous qualities that their multitude no longer astonishes us, can give to the substance of flesh the qualities requisite for existence in the world to come. After all, it was God the Creator of all things who gave to the flesh of the peacock that quality which keeps it from decaying even when dead. I could hardly believe this to be possible when I was first told of this peculiarity. Once, however, when I was in Carthage and peacock was served at table, I took a fair slice of the breast and had it put on one side. After as many days as it takes for any other cooked meat to become high, I had it brought out and set before me. There was no offensive odor whatever. I then had the same piece of meat kept for more than a month. I still found no change in it. Then, after a whole year, the only difference was that it was somewhat dried and shriveled.

Again, was it not God who gave to straw a power so strange that it keeps snow cold enough not to melt and raw fruits warm enough to ripen? Or who can explain the marvels of fire? Bright as it is in itself, it blackens everything it burns; for all its lovely color, it discolors almost everything it licks with its flames. For example, it turns the blazing glow of burning coal into the black ugliness of cinders. Yet it is bound by no fixed and fast rule; stones, on the contrary, under intense heat become incandescent. And, curiously enough, although the flames are reddish, the stones turn white—which is a color more appropriate to the fire. There is a contrary effect on the wood which is burned in order to heat the stones, although wood and stone are not, by nature, contraries, as white and black are contraries. Yet, in fire, stones become white and wood becomes black. The same bright fire that makes stones brighter makes logs darker, yet neither the fire nor the stone would be bright except for the logs!

Or consider the marvelous qualities of charcoal. It is so brittle that it breaks at the lightest tap and is crushed by the slightest pressure, yet it is so strong that it is neither damaged by dampness nor decays with old age. This is so much the case that, when boundary markers are set up, people put pieces of charcoal below them to serve as a permanent proof in years to come, so that anyone who denies the position of the boundary can be convinced by the presence of the charcoal. Yet the paradox is that while wood, from which the charcoal is made, would have long since rotted in wet ground, what kept the charcoal intact so long was that most destructive of all things—fire!

Or take a look at the miracle of lime. First, it shares in that marvel of stone which I just mentioned, namely, that it becomes white in fire while so many other things turn black. More than that, lime becomes, in a mysterious way, so impregnated with fire that a lump of lime which feels cold to the touch keeps latent within it the slumbering embers of a fire which no sense can perceive but which experiment can show to have been there all the time. That is why we speak of quick, or living, lime as though this unsuspected heat were a principle life, like the invisible soul of a visible body. But there is a further paradox. The fire latent in lime is a fire that flares up when it is put out! For, to bring the latent heat to life, the lime is dampened by, or dipped into, water, with the result that what was cold before now becomes hot, and by means of something we normally use to make hot things cold. But then, hardly has the hidden fire come to life when, like the departing soul of the dying lime, it takes its leave, and the lime lies cold as in death. In fact, no amount of water can now bring the lime back to life, so that what we once called quick or living we now call slaked or dead!

Surely, you would think that no further marvel could be added to this. But listen to this! If, instead of water, you use oil—the very food of fire—no amount of dampening or dipping brings out the heat! Now, if anyone were told or read in a book of a marvel like this happening to some stone in far-off India—and so very difficult to verify—he would either say that the story was a lie or, at least, he would be immensely surprised. And so it is with marvels no less astonishing that happen in daily experience; they no longer surprise us, merely because we are used to them. Even when the wonders of India reach us at last from that remotest corner of the globe, we give up being astonished.

This is the case with diamonds. Plenty of people now have them, and they can be seen in the shops of every goldsmith and jewelry designer. Yet, a diamond is so marvelously hard that neither iron nor fire can crack it. Only goat's blood, so they say, is potent enough for that. Now, the marvel of this hardness amazes only those who are unfamiliar with diamonds, not those who own them or know about them. Many who have never seen a demonstration of this hardness will simply not believe it, or, if they believe, their astonishment is merely the wonder of ignorance. When experience comes, this wonder becomes astonishment in the presence of the unusual, but when the experience is repeated, familiarity soon saps the stirrings of excitement.

Or take the lodestone. Everyone now knows of its marvelous magnetic power of attracting iron, but when I first saw one I was immensely amazed. First of all, it drew an iron ring to itself; then it kept it suspended. Next, I saw a second ring attracted by the first, and hang onto it as though the stone had communicated its power of attraction to the ring; and so with a third ring, and a fourth. Finally, there was a chain of rings hanging in the air, not held together like links, but holding onto each other by sheer attraction. Surely, the power of the stone by itself is marvelous enough, but what shall we say of the marvel of a power communicated to so many rings and holding them together by invisible bonds?

A still more astonishing fact was told me by my brother bishop, Severus of Mileve. Once when he was dining with Bathanarius, formerly Count of the Province of Africa, he saw the count take out a magnet and hold it under a silver plate on which he had placed a piece of iron. Then as the count moved the magnet in his hand, the iron filing began to move.

The silver plate remained unaffected, but, however quickly the magnet was moved, this way and that, the iron on the plate moved correspondingly. One of these marvels I have seen for myself; and the other I have been told by a man whom I trust as I would my own eyes. Now for something I read in a book. It is said that, when a diamond is placed near a lodestone, the stone no longer attracts the piece of iron or, if the iron was already holding onto the stone, the iron drops off as soon as the diamond is brought near.

These lodestones come from far-off India, but, now that we have become used to them, we have ceased to be astonished. And, of course, those who export them and find it so easy to get them must be even less astonished and, no doubt, think as little of them as we do of lime. For, even when lime is made hot by water that ought to cool it and remains cool in spite of being dipped in oil that ought to heat it, the wonder is now so familiar that no one is astonished.

Chapters 5–6

Additional descriptions of the marvels of nature and of human art are here used to argue that even greater wonders may be worked by God's power.

Chapter 7

All this being so, why should God be unable to raise bodies from the dead and allow the bodies of the damned to suffer in eternal fire, seeing that He made a universe filled with uncounted miracles in the heavens and on earth, in the air and in the ocean—a universe, therefore, which is a greater and nobler miracle than any of the miracles of which it is full?

Our adversaries are inconsistent. They believe that there is a God who made the universe, and that He created Intelligences that are used by Him to run the universe. They not merely do not deny but insist that there are powers that can work miracles—either natural, magical, or demoniacal. Yet, when we cite examples of marvelous powers in things which are neither human, nor spirits endowed with reason, as was the case in some of the examples I cited, our opponents have but one answer: 'The force here is purely natural; this is the way their natures work; each nature has its own peculiar powers.' Thus, the only reason why the salt of Agrigentum flows in fire and crackles in water is because it is its nature to do so. You would think, rather, that it is against its nature, since it is natural for water, and not for fire, to melt salt; natural for fire, and not for water, to heat salt. But to this the answer given is: 'Ah, but it is the natural peculiarity of this particular salt to act in a way contrary to other salt.' So, too, with the well of the Garamantes, which is too cold by day and too hot by night and, therefore, always unpleasant to touch. And so with that other well which is cold and fire-extinguishing like other wells, but marvelously unlike them when it lights an extinguished torch. The same explanation goes for the inextinguishable asbestos, which has no fire of its own, but when set on fire never stops burning. And so on. I need not repeat the other marvels. They all involved a peculiarity that seems contrary to nature, but in every case the explanation offered is: 'This is their nature.'

Certainly, that explanation is brief enough and, for all I know, sufficient. Why, then, do these skeptics object to our explanation, 'This is the will of Almighty God.' After all, God is the Creator of all natures, and when something seems impossible and incredible and people ask us to explain it, surely, our answer is better than theirs. The whole point of being Almighty is that God has the power to do whatever He wills to do, and He has shown this power in creating so many things that would certainly seem impossible were they not before our very eyes or, at least, testified by reliable witnesses. Some of the examples I have given are known by everybody; others are less well known. As for the marvels recorded in writings but unconfirmed by eye-witnesses, no one can be blamed for disbelief if the writers were men who could easily be wrong and if they wrote without divine inspiration.

And, therefore, I would not want anyone to be rash enough to believe all the wonders I have mentioned. I am not myself completely convinced, except where I have had personal experience and where verification is easy for anyone: as in the case of lime becoming hot in water and remaining cool in oil; or of magnets attracting iron by some kind of imperceptible suction, while straw remains unmoved; or of peacock's flesh remaining fresh while Plato's was putrescent;[1] or of straw being cool enough to keep snow from melting and warm enough to hasten the ripening of fruit; or of a bright fire making stones white with incandescence while making other things turn black. You get a similar anomaly when dark marks are left by clear oil or when black lines are engraved by white silver. So, too, with the contradictions connected with charcoal. It is ugly, brittle, and lasting, although it is made from wood that is lovely, hard, and subject to rapid decay. Most of these phenomena are universally or, at least, widely known; and so of others too many to mention here.

Some of the examples I know only from my reading and not from experience, and I have been unable to find reliable witnesses to confirm the stories. This is the case with the well which both puts out tapers and lights them when extinguished, and with the apples of Sodom that look so ripe but break into smoke. However, although I have never met anyone who has seen the well in Epirus, I have met people who know of just such a well near Grenoble in France. As for the apples of Sodom, the written accounts are credible enough; besides, so many people say they have seen them that I am unable to doubt them. As for the rest of the marvels I remain undecided. My only point in mentioning them is that they are taken from pagan writers and reveal how many pagans are willing to believe—without being able to explain—any number of marvels recorded in their own writings, while refusing to believe us, merely because we are unable to explain something that Almighty God is to do and something which transcends not only their experience but their very understanding. Where marvels of this kind are involved, what better or more cogent explanation can anyone give than to say that it is Omnipotence who has the power and that Omnipotence will use His power to do something which He prophesied in a book in which so many other of His prophesies can be found which have, in fact, been already fulfilled. We must remember that the God

---

[1] . . . *non putescente pavonis cum putuerit et Platonis.*

who is to do the things which seem impossible is the God who foretold that He will do them, and that this is the same God who made the promise, so clearly fulfilled already, that incredible things would be accepted as credible by incredulous peoples.

Chapter 8

Another argument, using details taken from Varro, shows that God may work wonders exceeding the powers of nature.

Chapter 9

One thing that will happen, and most certainly happen, is what God, through His Prophet, said concerning the punishment of hell being eternal: 'Their worm shall not die, and their fire shall not be quenched.'[1] And it was to emphasize this further that, when the Lord Jesus was counseling us to cut off members that scandalize us (meaning that we should cut off people whom we love as we love our right hand), He said: 'It is better for thee to enter into life maimed, than, having two hands, to go into hell, into the unquenchable fire, where their worm dies not, and the fire is not quenched.' So for the foot: 'It is better for thee to enter into life everlasting lame, than, having two feet, to be cast into the hell of unquenchable fire, where their worm dies not, and the fire is not quenched.' And for the eye, too: 'It is better for thee to enter into the kingdom of God with one eye than, having two eyes, to be cast into hell fire, where their worm dies not, and the fire is not quenched.'[2] He did not hesitate to quote the same text three times. Surely, that repetition and that emphatic warning, coming from divine lips, are enough to make any man tremble.

There are some who think that both the 'fire' and the 'worm' here mentioned are meant as pains of the soul rather than of the body. Their argument is that, since those who repent too late and, therefore, in vain (because cut off from the kingdom of God) burn with anguish of soul, the 'fire' can

[1] Isa. 66.24.   [2] Mark 9.42–47.

be taken very well to symbolize this burning anguish. They quote the words of the Apostle: 'Who is made to stumble, and I am not inflamed?'[3] They hold that the 'worm' also must be taken to mean the soul, as can be seen, they think, in the text: 'As a moth doth by a garment, and a worm by the wood, so the sadness of a man consumeth the heart.'[4]

However, those who have no doubt that in hell there will be sufferings for both soul and body hold that the body will be burned in fire while the soul will be gnawed, as it were, by the 'worm' of grief. This is certainly a probable enough view, since it is absurd to think that either pain of body or anguish of soul will be lacking there. For myself, however, it seems preferable to say that both 'fire' and the 'worm' apply to the body, and that the reason for making no mention in Scripture of the anguish of the soul is that it is implied, though not made explicit. When the body is in such pain, the soul must be tortured by fruitless repentance. Take, for example, this text of the Old Testament: 'The vengeance on the flesh of the ungodly is fire and worms.'[5] It would have sufficed to say: 'The vengeance on the ungodly.' What, then, could have been the reason for saying 'on the flesh of the ungodly,' except that both 'fire' and the 'worm' are to serve as punishment for the body? However, it may be argued that 'vengeance on the flesh' was meant to imply that the vengeance is to fall on man, in so far as he has lived according to the flesh. In support of this interpretation, there are the words of St. Paul: 'For if you live according to the flesh you will die,'[6] words implying that it is because a man lives according to the flesh that he will suffer the 'second death.' Thus, each of us is free to make his own choice, either attributing 'fire' (taken literally) to the body, and the 'worm' (in a figurative sense) to the soul, or attributing both 'fire' and the 'worm,' in their literal meanings, to the body.

Suffice it to say that argument enough was given above to prove, first, that living creatures can continue in fire without being consumed and in pain without suffering death; second, that this is in virtue of a miracle of the omnipotent Creator;

[3] 2 Cor. 11.29.   [4] Prov. 25.20.
[5] Eccli. 7.19.   [6] Rom. 8.13.

and, third, that anyone who denies the possibility of this miracle is simply unaware of the Source of all that is wonderful in all natures whatsoever. This Source is God. It is He who made all the natural marvels, great and small, which I have mentioned and incomparably more which I did not mention, and it is He who embraced all these miracles within a single universe which is itself the greatest of all these natural miracles. And so, I repeat, each one is free to choose whichever of the two interpretations he finds more satisfactory, namely, that the 'worm,' too, in its literal sense, applies to the body or that the 'worm' is to be taken in a figurative sense to apply to the soul. Which of the two views is true the future reality will soon enough reveal, for then the knowledge of the saints will be in need of no experience of these sufferings but only of that full and perfect wisdom which will suffice to teach them all such truth; for, now 'we know in part,' waiting for the time 'when that which is perfect has come.'[7] The one thing which we may by no means believe is that bodies in hell will be such that they will be unaffected by any pains inflicted by fire.

Chapters 10–22

Augustine reviews the objections of both pagans and some Christians to the view that hell's fire is everlasting.

Chapter 23

A first question to be asked and answered is: Why has the Church been so intolerant with those who defend the view that, however greatly and however long the Devil is to be punished, he can be promised ultimately that all will be purged or pardoned? Certainly, it is not because so many of the Church's saints and Biblical scholars have begrudged the Devil and his angels a final cleansing and the beatitude of the kingdom of heaven. Nor is it because of any lack of feeling for so many and such high angels that must suffer such great and enduring pain. This is not a matter of feeling, but of fact. The fact is that there is no way of waiving or weakening the

[7] 1 Cor. 13.9,10.

words which the Lord has told us that He will pronounce in the last judgment: 'Depart from me, accursed ones, into the everlasting fire which was prepared for the devil and his angels.'[1] In this way He showed plainly that it is an eternal fire in which the Devil and his angels are to burn. Then we have the words of the Apocalypse: 'And the devil who deceived them was cast into the pool of fire and brimstone, where also are the beast and the false prophet; and they will be tormented day and night for ever and ever.'[2] In the one text we have 'everlasting,' in the other, 'for ever and ever.' These are words which have a single meaning in the divine Scripture, namely, of unending duration.

Thus, it is Scripture, infallible Scripture, which declares that God has not spared them. This is the only reason why it is held as a fixed and unchanging religious truth that the Devil and his angels are never to return to the life and holiness of the saints; nor could any more valid or cogent reason be discovered. It is from Scripture that we know that God's sentence implies that He 'dragged them down by infernal ropes to Tartarus, and delivered them to be tortured and kept in custody for judgment.'[3] They will be received into 'everlasting' fire, there to be tortured 'for ever and ever.'

And since this is true of the Devil, how can men—whether all or some—be promised an escape, after some indefinitely long period, from this eternity of pain, without at once weakening our faith in the unending torment of the devils. For it is to men that the words will be said: 'Depart from me, accursed ones, into the everlasting fire which was prepared for the devil and his angels.' Now, if some of these men or all of them are not always to remain in everlasting fire, what ground have we for believing that the Devil and his angels are always to remain there? God's sentence will be pronounced on the wicked, both angels and men. Can we suppose that it will hold for angels but not for men? Yes; but, only if men's imaginings have more weight than God's words! Since this is quite impossible, all those who desire to escape eternal punishment should desist from arguing against God and should rather bow in obedience, while yet there is time, to the command of God. Besides, what kind of imagining is this, to take eternal punishment to mean long-continued punishment and, at the same time, to believe that eternal life is endless, seeing that Christ spoke of both as eternal in the same place and in one and the same sentence: 'And these will go into everlasting punishment, but the just into everlasting life.'[4] If both are 'everlasting,' then either both must be taken as long-lasting but not endless or else both must be taken to be unendingly perpetual. For the everlastingness of the punishment and the everlastingness of the life are related as equal to equal. It is highly absurd to say in one and the same sense: 'Life everlasting will be endless, but everlasting punishment will come to an end.' Therefore, since the eternal life of the saints is to be endless, there can be no doubt that eternal punishment for those who are to endure it will have no end.

Chapters 24–27

Detailed answers are given to the various objections against belief in everlasting fires in hell. It is stressed that God's mercy will not disrupt divine justice.

[4] Matt. 25.46.

BOOK XXII

The Eternal Bliss of the City of God

Chapter 1

As I MENTIONED in the preceding Book, the present one is to be the last of the whole work, and is to deal with the eternal blessedness of the City of God. The word 'eternal' as here used means more than any period, however long, of centuries upon centuries which, ultimately, must have an end. It means 'everlasting' in the sense of the text which runs: 'Of His kingdom there shall be no end.'[1] It does not mean the kind of apparent perpetuity produced by successive generations which come and go by births and deaths. Such a perpetuity is merely perennial like the color of an evergreen that seems to continue forever because the new leaves, sprouting while the old ones wither and fall, maintain an unchanging density of foliage. On the contrary, in the eternal City of God, each and all of the citizens are personally immortal with an immortality which the holy angels never lost and which even human beings can come to share. This is to be achieved by the supreme omnipotence of the Creator, the Founder of the City. It is a realization which God, who cannot but keep His word, has promised, and He has given abundant pledges of its fulfillment in the promises which He has already kept and in the uncovenanted blessings which He has already bestowed.

For, it was this same God who, in the beginning, created the universe and filled it with all those things that the eye can see and all those realities which the mind can know. Of all such creations the highest were the spirits to whom He gave the gift of intelligence and the power to behold God and to be filled with His beatitude. These He has linked by a common bond of love in a single society which we call the holy and heavenly City. In this community, God is the life by which the spirits live. He is the food on which their blessedness is

[1] Luke 1.33.

fed. God gave these spirits the gift of freedom, but it was a power of choice so rooted in their nature, as intelligence is, that, once they used their power to fall away from God, the Source of all their joy, misery was bound to follow. Although God foresaw that some of these free angels would try to lift themselves up to a level where they might find their happiness in themselves alone and so abandon God, their only good, God did not take away their freedom. He judged it better and more in accord with His power to bring some greater good even out of evil than to permit no evil whatsoever.

Now, what makes such evil possible is the fact that no created nature can be immutable. Every such nature is made, indeed, by God, the supreme and immutable Good who made all things good, but, by choosing to sin, such a nature brings evil upon itself. This very sinning, however, bears witness to the fact that the nature in itself, as it comes from the hand of God, is good. For, unless the nature in itself were a really great good—though, of course, not good in the measure that the Creator is good—then the falling away from God into the creature's own darkness could not be a misfortune for the nature. Sin is to a nature what blindness is to an eye. The blindness is an evil or defect which is a witness to the fact that the eye was created to see the light and, hence, the very lack of sight is the proof that the eye was meant, more than any other member of the body, to be the one particularly capable of seeing the light. Were it not for this capacity, there would be no reason to think of blindness as a misfortune. So is it with that nature that basked in God as an eye does in light. The very sin which deprived this nature of happiness in God and left it miserable is the best proof of how good that nature was, as it came from the hand of God.

In the case of the deliberate falling away of some of the angels, God most justly imposed the punishment of an everlasting unhappiness. The other angels remained in union with God, their supreme Good, and to these God gave, as a kind of reward for their remaining, the certain assurance that this remaining would be without end.

As for human nature, God made it likewise unfallen, but free to fall away. Man was an animal made out of earth, but not unfit for heaven, if only he would remain close to his Creator. But, as with the angels, if human nature should choose to fall away from God, misery proportionate to the offense was bound to follow. Here, too, God foresaw the fall, the disregard of His law, the desertion from Good, yet He left man's free choice unchecked because He also foresaw to what good He would turn man's evil. And, in fact, out of this mortal race of men, justly doomed by their own deserts, God gathers, by His grace, so numerous a people that out of them He fills the places and restores the ranks emptied by the fallen angels. Thus is it that the beloved City, which is above, is not deprived of the full complement of its citizens and, in fact, may even rejoice in a fuller complement than it had before the angels' fall.

Chapters 2-4

The immutable will of God is described. God's promises of everlasting happiness for the saints are recalled. Pagan arguments against the resurrection of the body are again answered.

Chapter 5

Even if we should grant that the resurrection of the body was once beyond belief, the fact is that the whole world now believes that the earthly body of Christ has been taken up to heaven. Learned and unlearned alike no longer doubt the resurrection of His flesh and His ascension into heaven, while there is but a handful of those who continue to be puzzled. Now, what all these believers believed was either credible or it was not. If it was credible, then the incredulous should ask themselves whether they are not rather ridiculous. If it was not credible and yet was believed, then we have something really incredible, namely that something incredible should be so universally believed. We have then two incredibles: one, the resurrection of any body in eternal life; the other, the world's belief in this incredibility. But notice. The same God predicted both before the event. Now, one of these incredibilities has become a fact before our very eyes, namely, the incredibility of the world believing something incredible. Why, then, should we doubt that the other will be fulfilled, namely, that the incredible truth which the world believed will come to pass as surely as the others agree incredibility has already come to pass, namely, the incredibility of the world believing as incredible a thing—particularly since the same Scriptures which led the world to believe predicted both the impossibilities, both the one we see realized and the other we know by faith?

What is really hard to believe, for anyone who stops to think, is the way the world came to believe. The fishermen whom Christ sent with the nets of faith into the sea of the world were men unschooled in the liberal arts and utterly untrained as far as education goes, men with no skill in the use of language, armed with no weapons of debate, plumed with no rhetorical power. Yet, the catch this handful of fishermen took was enormous and marvelous. They hauled in fish of every sort, not excluding those rare specimens, the philosophers themselves. We may add, then, if you please, this third incredibility to the other two; in fact, it must be added whether one likes it or not, simply because there are three incredibilities which actually occurred. It is incredible that Christ should have risen in His flesh and, with His flesh, have ascended into heaven; it is incredible that the world should have believed a thing so incredible; it is incredible that men so rude and lowly, so few and unaccomplished, should have convinced the world, including men of learning, of something so incredible and have convinced men so conclusively.

Of course, our friends, the skeptics, still shy at the first of these three incredibilities; but the second is a fact before their very eyes, which they are compelled to believe; and if they refuse to believe the third of the incredibilities, they have no explanation of a manifest fact.

It is no less a fact that the Resurrection of Christ and His Ascension into heaven, with the flesh in which He rose, is now preached to the whole world and is believed. If it cannot be believed, then why in the world does the whole world believe it? Of course, the world could believe without a miracle if a multitude of senators, imperial courtiers, and famous scholars had declared that they had seen the Ascension and then took pains to publicize the fact,[1] but the truth is that the world has believed a handful of unknown and unlearned nobodies who said and wrote that they had seen the miracle.

What the little coterie of skeptics must explain is why they still hold out so blatantly against a whole world of believers who have an explanation of their faith. The world has believed this insignificant group of lowly, unimportant, and uneducated men precisely because the divine character of what happened is more marvelously apparent in the insignificance of such witnesses. What gave power to the preachers who persuaded the world was not the eloquence of the words they uttered, but the miracles in the deeds they did.

Those who had not themselves seen Christ rising from the dead and ascending into heaven with His flesh believed the men who said they had seen the miracle, not merely because these men said so, but also because these men themselves worked miracles. For example, many people were astonished to hear these men, who knew but two languages (and, in some cases, only one) suddenly break forth into so many tongues that everybody in the audience understood. They saw a man who had been lame from earliest infancy now, after forty years, stand upright at a word uttered by these witnesses who spoke in the name of Christ. Pieces of cloth that touched their bodies were found to heal the sick. Uncounted people suffering from various diseases set themselves in line in the streets where the Apostles were to pass and where their shadows would fall upon the sick, and many of these people were at once restored to health. Besides many other marvels wrought in the name of Christ, there were even cases of dead men restored to life.

Now, those who read such marvels either believe them or they do not. If they believe them, then we can add ever so many more incredibilities to the three already mentioned. To gain faith in the one miracle of the Resurrection and Ascension of the flesh into heaven, we literally heap up a mass of testimonies to a multitude of incredibilities. Yet, in spite of all

---

[1] I omit the spurious insertion, *sed istos adhuc credere nolle perdurum est.*

this, we fail to bend to our belief the horrendous hardness of the skeptics' hearts. If, on the other hand, skeptics will not believe that these miracles were wrought through the Apostles precisely for the purpose of making it easier to believe their preaching of the Resurrection and Ascension of Christ, we are still left with the one stupendous miracle, which is all we need: the miracle of the whole world believing, without benefit of miracles, the miracle of the Resurrection.

Chapters 6–7

The contrast between the pagans' motives for believing in the divinity of Romulus and the Christian testimony to the divinity of Christ is here fully developed.

Chapter 8

It is sometimes objected that the miracles, which Christians claim to have occurred, no longer happen. One answer might be that they are no longer needed as they once were to help an unbelieving world to believe. As things now are, any lone believer looking for a miracle to help him to believe, in the midst of a world in which practically everyone already believes, is surely himself a marvel of no mean magnitude. However, the malice of the objection is in the insinuation that not even the earlier miracles ought to be believed. It is an insinuation that leaves our friends with two facts unexplained: How do they explain that the Ascension of Christ into heaven has come to be everywhere proclaimed with so firm a faith; and how do they explain that our world, which is so advanced in culture and so critical in mentality, has come, without benefit of miracles, to believe so miraculously in realities so incredible? Perhaps they will say: 'Well, the tales were not wholly incredible and so people came to believe them.' In that case, our friends have still to explain why they themselves have remained incredulous.

Perhaps it is better to meet such irresponsible skepticism in a summary dilemma which would run as follows: Either the world has founded its faith in an unseen and incredible occurrence on the fact that no less incredible occurrences not merely took place but were seen to take place; or else the original occurrence was so palpably credible that it needed no additional miracles to convince men's minds of its truth. In either case, our friends are left with no justification of their own wilful skepticism. It is simply undeniable that, as a fact, there have been any number of miracles attesting the one, sublime, and saving miracle of Christ's Ascension into heaven with the flesh in which He arose from the dead. The books which record these miracles are absolutely trustworthy and, what is more, they record not merely the attesting miracles but the ultimate object of our faith which the miracles were meant to confirm. The miracles were made known to help men's faith and, of course, they are now still better known on account of the faith which the world has embraced. The miracles are read to our people in our churches to nourish their faith, although the people would not be in the churches to hear them read unless the miracles were already believed.

The truth is that even today miracles are being wrought in the name of Christ, sometimes through His sacraments and sometimes through the intercession of the relics of His saints. Only, such miracles do not strike the imagination with the same flashing brilliance as the earlier miracles, and so they do not get the same flashing publicity as the others did. The fact that the canon of our Scriptures is definitively closed brings it about that the original miracles are everywhere repeated and are fixed in people's memory, whereas contemporary miracles which happen here or there seldom become known even to the whole of the local population in and around the place where they occur. Especially is this the case in the more populous cities, where relatively few learn the facts while most of the people remain uninformed. And when the news does spread from mouth to mouth, even in the case of Christians reporting to Christians, it is too unauthoritative to be received without some difficulty or doubt.

This, however, was not the case with a miracle that took place in Milan while I was there. A great many people managed to hear of a blind man whose sight was restored because the city is big and, besides, the Emperor was there at the time and an immense multitude of people was gathered to venerate the relics of the martyrs, Protasius and Gervasius, and so witnessed what took place. The relics had been hidden, and no one knew where they were until the hiding place was revealed in a dream to Bishop Ambrose, who thereupon went and found them. It was on that occasion that the long-enduring darkness dropped from the blind man's eyes and he saw the light of day.

On the other hand, only a handful of people have ever heard of a cure that occurred in Carthage when I was there and which I witnessed with my own eyes. It happened to Innocent, a former advocate in the office of deputy prefect, at the time when my fellow bishop, Alypius, and I (neither of us yet ordained, but both already dedicated to God) had just returned from Italy. Innocent, along with his whole household, was a remarkably devout Catholic and he welcomed us into his home. He was just then undergoing medical care in connection with a complicated case of multiple rectal fistula.[1] The doctors had already incised and were now following up with applied medications. The cutting had caused very acute pains and these continued day after day, the trouble being that one of the sinuses that should have been opened was so recessed that it had escaped the scrutiny of the surgeons. Long after all the other sinuses were healed, this single one remained, and all efforts to relieve the patient's pain were unavailing.

Naturally, he became afraid that a second operation would be called for, particularly since his family doctor, who had not been allowed even to watch the original operation, had told Innocent that this would be the case. On that occasion, Innocent had become so annoyed that he dismissed the doctor from his service. His anxiety, however, continued. One day, in fact, he turned to his surgeons and burst out: 'Do you mean to cut me again? Don't tell me that the man you refused to admit to the operation was right after all!' The surgeons, however, merely scoffed at the family doctor's naïveté and tried

---

[1] For several technical medical expressions the translators are indebted to John Madigan, M.D., of Houlton, Maine.

to calm their patient and, in their best bedside manner, made soothing promises.

But, as day after day dragged on, nothing came of all their medications. The surgeons kept saying that there was no need to operate and that all would respond to treatment. However, they called in for consultation Ammonius, a very old and famous practitioner, who has since died. He examined the patient's rectum and, on the basis of the other surgeons' technique and aftercare, gave the same prognosis as they. Innocent, for the moment, was so assured by the weight of this authority that he began to talk as though he were already cured. He even indulged in cheerful banter at the expense of the poor family doctor who had predicted that more cutting was to come.

Well, to make a long story short, so many days passed to no purpose that the worn-out and humbled surgeons confessed, at last, that nothing short of the scalpel would effect a cure. Poor Innocent turned pale with fear and nearly fainted. As soon as he was sufficiently calm to talk, he told them to get out and never come back again. Worn out with weeping and with no other recourse, he thought that the best thing he could do would be to call in an extremely skillful surgeon from Alexandria, and have him do what he was too angry to let the other surgeons do. This world-famous specialist came, and examined with his trained eye the excellent work the others had done, as was clear from the healthy residual scar tissue. Whereupon, the specialist behaved like a man of principle and persuaded Innocent to allow the surgeons to have the satisfaction of terminating a case on which they had obviously worked so well and so long. He admitted that no cure was possible without a second operation, but protested that it would be utterly against his professional ethics to deprive others of the satisfaction of completing an operation in which so little remained to be done and, especially, to deprive men whose skillful work and careful handling of the patient he so much admired. So the surgeons returned to the good graces of Innocent, and it was agreed that they should incise the remaining sinus in the presence of the Alexandrian specialist. The operation was set for the next day, all the doctors admitting that it was the only way to heal the trouble.

Once they were gone, the whole household set up a wail of grief for their master that was worse than a funeral, and we had the hardest time keeping them calm. Among Innocent's habitual visitors who happened to be there that day were that holy man of blessed memory, Saturninus, then Bishop of Uzalum, and Gulosus, a holy priest, and some deacons of the church at Carthage, one of whom was my highly esteemed friend and now colleague in the episcopate, Aurelius. He is the sole survivor of that group of guests, and I have often compared notes with him regarding this remarkable mercy of God and have found that his memory of the events corresponds with my own. Their visit, as usual, was in the evening, and Innocent begged them, with tearfulness in his voice, to please come the next day to what, he was sure, would be not merely his agony but his death. The very thought of the previous pains filled him with fear, and he was certain that he would die under the hands of the surgeons. Everyone tried to comfort him, and to exhort him to put his trust in God, and face His will unflinchingly.

Then we all began to pray. The rest of us prayed, as we usually do, on our knees and prostrate on the floor, but Innocent literally threw himself flat as though he had been violently struck by some powerful blow, and then burst into prayer so vehemently, so feelingly, so pathetically and wept with such indescribable groaning and sobbing that he shook in every fiber of his being and all but choked. How any of the others could pray, with all this pitiable petitioning to distract them, I do not know. As for myself, no formula of prayer was possible. All I could do was let my heart repeat this short refrain: 'Lord, if Thou dost not hear such prayers, what prayers of any saints can move Thee?' It seemed to me that, with one more sigh, the poor man would have prayed himself to death.

At last, we all arose and, when the bishop had given us his blessing, left. There was one final request that all would be present in the morning and, on our part, one last exhortation for the sufferer to have fortitude.

The dreaded day had hardly dawned when all these men of God were at the door to keep their promises. The doctors entered. The needed preparations were immediately under way. As each piece of frightening metal flashed, we gasped and held our breath. Then, while the patient's body was being properly disposed for the hand of the operating surgeon, Innocent's closest friends stood by, whispering words of comfort to cheer his drooping spirit. The bandages were removed. The site was exposed. The surgeon took a look. With the scalpel in one hand, he palpated for the offending sinus. He searched once more with his eye. He probed again with his fingers. He exhausted every means of medical examination. But there was nothing to be found except perfectly healthy tissue!

Imagine the burst of joy and the flood of grateful tears, the praise and thanks to the God of mercy and of power, that broke from everyone there present. It was a scene too much for any pen to tell. I can only leave it to the meditation of my readers.

Chapter 8, continued

Twelve more pages describe similar miracles witnessed by, or directly reported to, Augustine. All these incidents testify to the credibility of Christian teaching.

Chapter 9

Now, the faith to which all these miracles bear witness is the faith that holds that Christ rose bodily from the dead and ascended with His flesh into heaven, because, of course, the martyrs were witnesses. That, in fact, is what the word 'martyr' means. The martyrs were witnesses to this faith. It was because they bore witness to this faith that they found the world hostile and cruel. Yet, they overcame the world, not by defending themselves, but by preferring to die for Christ. Those whose intercession has the power from the Lord to work these miracles were killed on account of His name and died for faith in Him. First came the miracle of their fortitude in dying for this faith, and then came, as a consequence, the power revealed in these miracles.

This question, then, calls for an answer: If the resurrection of the flesh into eternal life did not occur in the case of Christ and is not to occur hereafter in our case, in accordance with the promises made by Christ and those in the Old Testament which likewise foretold the coming of Christ, then how explain these great wonders wrought by dead martyrs? For, they were put to death precisely for that faith which proclaims this resurrection. It makes no difference whether we say that it is God Himself who works these miracles in the marvelous way that the Eternal operates in the temporal order, or whether we say that God works these miracles through His servants. And, in regard to what He does through His servants, it is all one whether He does these things through the spirits of martyrs, as though they were still living in their bodies, or whether He uses angels and effects His purposes by His orders, which are given invisibly, inaudibly, immutably. In that case, miracles which we think are done by martyrs are the result, rather, of their prayers and intercession, and not of their actions. Or God may have varying means to His different ends and these means may be altogether incomprehensible to the minds of men. But the main point is that all miracles are witnesses to that faith which proclaims the supreme miracle of the resurrection of the flesh into life everlasting.

Chapters 10–21

After another long outline of philosophical and pagan objections to belief in the resurrection of the dead, answers are given to all these difficulties. Augustine's opinion is that all men and women will have mature and normal bodies after the resurrection. Differences between male and female will probably be retained. Those who are too thin or too fat in this life may take comfort: they will look better in a future life. Yet Augustine is not quite clear as to the nature of a spiritualized body.

Chapter 22

This life of ours—if a life so full of such great ills can properly be called a life—bears witness to the fact that, from its very start, the race of mortal men has been a race condemned. Think, first, of that dreadful abyss of ignorance from which all error flows and so engulfs the sons of Adam in a darksome pool that no one can escape without the toll of toils and tears and fears. Then, take our very love for all those things that prove so vain and poisonous and breed so many heartaches, troubles, griefs, and fears; such insane joys in discord, strife, and war; such wrath and plots of enemies, deceivers, sycophants; such fraud and theft and robbery; such perfidy and pride, envy and ambition, homicide and murder, cruelty and savagery, lawlessness and lust; all the shameless passions of the impure—fornication and adultery, incest and unnatural sins, rape and countless other uncleannesses too nasty to be mentioned; the sins against religion—sacrilege and heresy, blasphemy and perjury; the iniquities against our neighbors —calumnies and cheating, lies and false witness, violence to persons and property; the injustices of the courts and the innumerable other miseries and maladies that fill the world, yet escape attention.

It is true that it is wicked men who do such things, but the source of all such sins is that radical canker in the mind and will that is innate in every son of Adam.[1] For, our infancy proves with what ignorance of the truth man enters upon life, and adolescence makes clear to all the world how full we are of folly and concupiscence. In fact, if anyone were left to live as he pleased and to do what he desired, he would go through practically the whole gamut of lawlessnesses and lust—those which I have just listed and, perhaps, others that I refrained from mentioning.

Yet, for all this blight of ignorance and folly, fallen man has not been left without some ministries of Providence, nor has God, in His anger, shut up His mercies.[2] There are still

[1] . . . *ab illa tamen erroris et perversi amoris radice venientia, cum qua omnis filius Adam nascitur.*
[2] Cf. Ps. 76.10.

within the reach of man himself, if only he will pay the price of toil and trouble, the twin resources of law and education. With the one, he can make war on human passion; with the other, he can keep the light of learning lit even in the darkness of our native ignorance.[3] This is the meaning of those many appeals to fear in disciplining the waywardness of growing children. That is why we have tutors and schoolmasters with their ferules and straps and canes, and why, in the training of a child we love, we use the authority of Holy Writ to 'beat his sides . . . lest he grow stubborn'[4]—else he may become too wild ever to be tamed. The point of all such human punishment is to help dispel our ignorance and to bridle our untamed desires—the double birthmark with which we come into this world.

As evidence of this inheritance we have only to recall how difficult it is to remember, how easy to forget; how hard to learn and how easy to be ignorant; how difficult to make an effort and how easy to be lazy. We need go no further to realize to what depths our damaged nature tends to gravitate and what aid it needs to be rescued from its inclinations. We are weighed down in soul and body by sloth and indolence, and disinclined to make an effort because, in fact, this price of effort, even for our good, is a part of the penalty we must pay for sin.

Such, then, are the penalties which must be paid even in childhood and merely for the purpose of learning what our elders want—and this is seldom really useful! But who can describe or even imagine all the later ills that befall mankind? When we are not victims of the lawlessness and lust of wicked men, we have to suffer the miseries that no one in our present condition can escape. Who can be free from fear or grief in a world of mourning and bereavement, of losses and legal penalties, of liars and deceivers, of the false imputations, violences and other wickednesses of our neighbors? Think of the tragedies of being robbed or reduced to slavery, of bonds and

---

[3] . . . *in ipsis sensibus generis humani prohibitio et eruditio contra istas, cum quibus nascimur, tenebras vigilant et contra hos impetus obponuntur.*

[4] Eccli. 30.12.

prison walls, of banishment and torture, of limbs cut off and eyes torn out, of bodies made to minister to an oppressor's lusts, and of all other no less dreadful possibilities.

And think of the dread we have of the countless accidents of nature, of the extremes of heat and cold, of winds and rains and floods, of thunder, lightning and winter storms, of earthquakes, landslides and openings in the earth; of stumbling, shying, biting horses; of poisoned fruits and waters, of pestilential air and animals diseased; of the harmful and often fatal bites of wild animals. Take, for example, the rabies resulting from the bite of a mad dog. Here we have the gentlest and most friendly of all animals making his own master more afraid of a dog than of lions or of dragons, because when a man has been infected by this poison he becomes so raging mad that he frightens his whole family far more than the wildest animals ever could.

Or think of the perils of voyagers at sea and of travelers on land. Even a man taking a walk is liable to the most unsuspected accidents. Here is a man in perfect health returning from downtown to his home; he slips and breaks his leg; the wound festers and he dies. Or take a man sitting down. You would think that no one could be safer, yet Heli, the priest, slipped from a chair and was killed.[5] Or take farmers and all who depend on them. There is the weather to be feared, the soil, the blights that ruin crops. At least, you might think, the fears would vanish when the crops are gathered and are in the barns. Yet I have known cases where a sudden flood has not only driven the men from the fields but has swept the grain from the barns.

Then there are the demons in a thousand forms that fill mankind with dread. Not even innocence is safe from their incursions. No innocence is greater than that of newly baptized children, yet, to give us a lesson in holy diffidence, even they are sometimes attacked by demons. God, who permits this tragedy, could not teach us more emphatically how much the misery of this life is to be moaned and how greatly the blessedness of eternity is to be desired.

Turn, now, to the maladies that afflict our bodies. Not even

[5] 1 Kings 4.18.

medical libraries have catalogued all the diseases; in most cases, it takes pain to drive out pain, so that medical care and cures can be as cruel as the complaints themselves.[6] Then there is hunger and thirst. Desperate men have been driven to drink human urine, sometimes their own, and to eat human flesh, and sometimes to kill others in order to eat them—and not always their enemies. There have been mothers driven to desperation by hunger and to the unbelievable monstrosity of devouring their own children.

Even sleep, which we think of as perfect rest, is made restless by dreadful dreams and nightmares so filled with unspeakable phantoms that seem so real that our whole being is filled with fear. And even when we are awake, we are often tortured even more cruelly by delirium induced by some toxic or diseased condition. Worse still are those weird phantasms evoked by malignant demons in the imaginations of perfectly healthy men; even when such men are not seduced by these imaginations to serve the Devil's purposes, the delusions are painfully humiliating.

From this all but hell of unhappiness here on earth, nothing can save us but the grace of Jesus Christ, who is our Saviour, Lord and God. In fact, the very meaning of the name, Jesus, is Saviour, and when we say 'save' we mean, especially, that He saves us from passing from the misery of this mortal life to a still more miserable condition, which is not so much a life as death. It is true that, even in this life on earth, through the intercession of the saints we have many holy comforts and great remedies. Nevertheless, such favors are not always given to those who ask—lest such favors be mistaken for the real purpose of religion, which is felicity in that other life in which all our ills will be no more. What grace is meant to do is to help good people, not to escape their sufferings, but to bear them with a stout heart, with a fortitude that finds its strength in faith.

To gain such fortitude we need, as even the wisdom of this world assures us, that true philosophy which, as Cicero says,[7] is given by the gods to very few and is a gift greater

---

[6] . . . *etiam ipsa adiumenta et medicamenta tormenta sunt.*
[7] *De finibus* 5.21.

than any which the gods have given men, or even have the power to give. Here, surely, in this insistence on a true as opposed to any kind of philosophy, we have an admission by our main opponent, the pagan world, of the reality of super-natural grace. And what is more, if it is only to a few that there is given from on high this sole source of solace in the miseries of this life, the pagans should conclude that our human race, taken as a whole, has been condemned to pay mortal misery as a penalty for sin. And if, as they confess, there is no greater gift from God than this, then they should admit that it can be given by no less a divinity than the One than whom, as even the polytheists admit, there is no greater.

Chapter 23

Continued vigilance and struggle are needed to overcome human frailty.

Chapter 24

From all this misery, in which we admire the justice by which God punishes mankind, we must now turn to consider the multitude and munificence of the blessings which God's goodness bestows on the creatures who are ruled by His providence.

First, think of the blessing of fecundity which was bestowed upon man before he fell. God said: 'Be fruitful and multiply and fill the earth.'[1] That blessing did not cease because man sinned, for God willed it to remain in the race even after the race was condemned. Not even the canker of sin, which has involved mankind in the blight of death, was able to take from human seed the miracle of life, nor have human bodies lost that still more mysterious power, woven into their very texture, whereby the seed itself is produced. Thus, in the torrential stream of human history, two currents meet and mix: the current of evil which flows from Adam and that of good which comes from God. The original good includes two quite

[1] Gen. 1.28.

different things: the procreation of the body and the inbreathing of a soul.

As for the elements of evil, namely, sin which resulted from
man's audacity and the penalty imposed by God's judgment,
I have already said all that the theme of this work requires.
My present purpose is to speak, rather, of the endowments of
human nature which, by God's bounty, have been bestowed
and continue to be bestowed upon us, even though we have
been wounded by sin and condemned to pay its penalties.
For, the penalties imposed do not mean the total deprivation
of all that God has given. For, had that been the case, there
would have been no human nature left at all. Nor did God
renounce the governance of our nature even though He permitted us, in punishment, to fall under the tyranny of the
Devil. The truth is that the Devil himself is still under God's
power, since it is God (the Supreme Being that brings into
being whatever in any way exists) who permits that the nature of the Devil should even subsist.

Thus it was from a fountain, so to speak, of divine goodness
that there flowed into a nature, fallen by reason of sin and
condemned to punishment, the two blessings I have mentioned. The first of these, the power of procreation, was
granted by God in a blessing He pronounced during those
seven days of creative work, on the last of which He rested.
The second of the blessings, the inbreathing of the soul, is a
part of that work whereby God 'works even until now.'[2] For,
if God withdrew, even from inanimate things, His creative
power, they could not continue to be what they became by
creation, let alone complete that series of movements which
were meant to measure the span of their existence. As for man,
when God created him, He gave him, in addition to being
and movement, the power of propagating other men, who,
in turn, were born with this same power. (It was, however,
a power which no individual was obliged to exercise. Actually,
in certain cases, God Himself withdrew this gift of potency
and fertility. However, to mankind in general, God continued
the blessing of fecundity which He pronounced on Adam and
Eve.)

[2] John 5.17.

Of course, it does not follow that this power of propagation, which was left intact even after sin, is identical with what it would have been had man not sinned. For, man who was once 'in honor' sinned, and after that 'he is compared to senseless beasts'[3] and has become like them in the matter of procreation, even though that light of reason which makes man an image of God has not been extinguished altogether. It was only because God added to the animal power of procreation this conformation to God's image that man's offspring retain the form and essence of our specifically human nature. For, of course, God could have chosen to fill the earth with human beings without the exercise of the mating process, since He could have created all men out of nothing, just as He created the first. And, even as things now are, unless God's creative power concurred, no mating of man and maid would result in generation.

There is a parallel between natural generation and supernatural regeneration. Speaking of the way in which a man is fashioned into supernatural life,[4] St. Paul says: 'Neither he who plants is anything, nor he who waters, but God who gives the growth.'[5] So, too, in regard to natural generation, it may be said: Neither the wife nor the husband's part is anything, but it is God who fashions the form of the offspring; nor is the mother who bears and brings the child to birth anything, but it is God who gives the growth. For, it is by that creative process by which God 'works even until now'[6] that human seed unfolds its multiple potentialities, evolving from the invisible latencies of the womb into the visible beauty of forms that we behold. And, by a marvelous mating, He brings a spiritual nature into union with one that is material and makes the soul and body active and passive principles, respectively, of a single human whole. This operation of God, so marvelous and mysterious, He performs not only in the case of man, who is a rational animal and the highest and noblest of all animals on earth, but also in the case of the tiniest insects. And no one can reflect on this marvel without a sense

---

[3] Ps. 48.13.
[4] . . . *de institutione spiritali, qua homo ad pietatem iustitiamque formatur.*
[5] 1 Cor. 3.7.   [6] John 5.17.

of astonishment and some expression of admiration for the Creator.

In regard to the principle of human life, God infused into it a capacity for reasoning and intellection. In infancy, this mental capacity seems, as it were, asleep and practically non-existent, but in the course of years it awakens into a life that involves learning and education, skill in grasping the truth and loving the good. This capacity flowers into that wisdom and virtue which enable the soul to battle with the arms of prudence, fortitude, temperance, and justice against error, waywardness, and other inborn weaknesses, and to conquer them with a purpose that is no other than that of reaching the supreme and immutable Good. Even when this Good is not attained, there still remains, rooted in all rational nature, a divinely given capacity for goods so high that this marvel of God's omnipotence is beyond any tongue to express or any mind to comprehend.

And, quite apart from those supernatural arts of living in virtue and of reaching immortal beatitude which nothing but the grace of God which is in Christ can communicate to the sons of promise and heirs of the kingdom, there have been discovered and perfected, by the natural genius of man, innumerable arts and skills which minister not only to the necessities of life but also to human enjoyment. And even in those arts where the purposes may seem superfluous, perilous and pernicious, there is exercised an acuteness of intelligence of so high an order that it reveals how richly endowed our human nature is. For, it has the power of inventing, learning and applying all such arts.

Just think of the progress and perfection which human skill has reached in the astonishing achievements of cloth making, architecture, agriculture and navigation. Or think of the originality and range of what has been done by experts in ceramics, by sculptors and by painters; of the dramas and theatrical spectacles so stupendous that those who have not seen them simply refuse to believe the accounts of those who have. Think even of the contrivances and traps which have been devised for the capturing, killing, or training of wild animals; or, again, of the number of drugs and appliances that medical science has discovered in its zeal for the preservation and restoration of men's health; or, again, of the poisons, weapons, and equipment used in wars, devised by military art for defense against enemy attack; or even of the endless variety of condiments and sauces which culinary art has discovered to minister to the pleasures of the palate.

It was human ingenuity, too, that devised the multitude of signs we use to express and communicate our thoughts—and, especially, speech and writing. The arts of rhetoric and poetry have brought delight to men's spirits by their ornaments of style and varieties of verse; musicians have solaced human ears by their instruments and songs; both theoretical and applied mathematics have made great progress; astronomy has been most ingenious in tracing the movements, and in distinguishing the magnitudes, of the stars. In general, the completeness of scientific knowledge is beyond all words and becomes all the more astonishing when one pursues any single aspect of this immense corpus of information. Last, but not least, is the brilliance of talent displayed by both pagan philosophers and Christian heretics in the defense of error and falsehood. (In saying this, of course, I am thinking only of the nature of the human mind as a glory of this mortal life, not of faith and the way of truth that leads to eternal life.)

Now, the Creator of this noble human nature is the true and supreme God whose providence rules all that He has created, whose power is unlimited, and whose justice is infinite; and, therefore, man could never have fallen into the miseries that he now suffers and is destined to suffer in eternity—excepting only the elect—unless the first man, the father of all the rest, had committed an enormous iniquity.

Turn now from man's mind to his body. It is true that it is no better than the body of a beast as far as dying is concerned and, in life, it is even weaker than that of many of the animals. Nevertheless, the human body is a revelation of the goodness of God and of the providence of the body's Creator. It is a body obviously meant to minister to a rational soul, as you can see from the arrangement of the human organs of sense and of man's other members. This is obvious, too, in man's specific appearance, form, and stature. The bodies of irrational animals are bent toward the ground, whereas man was made to walk erect with his eyes on heaven, as though to remind him to keep his thoughts on things above. And if we need further evidence to show to what kind of a mind the body was meant to minister, we have only to think of the marvelous mobility of the tongue and hands, so perfectly suited for speaking and writing, for the arts, and for the countless other activities of men.

What is more, quite apart from these practical purposes, there is in a man's body such a rhythm, poise, symmetry, and beauty that it is hard to decide whether it was the uses or the beauty of the body that the Creator had most in mind. It is clear that every organ whose function we know adds to the body's beauty, and this beauty would be still more obvious if only we knew the precise proportions by which the parts were fashioned and interrelated. I do not mean merely the surface parts which, no doubt, could be accurately measured by anyone with proper skill. I mean the parts hidden below our skin, the intricate complex of veins and nerves, the inmost elements of the human viscera and vital parts, whose rhythmic relationships have not yet been revealed. Surgeons, of course, have done something in their relatively crude anatomical study of corpses (and in the course of their hardly less inhuman operations on living bodies) to explore the last recesses of the organs they have had to handle in order to learn the best technique in dealing with this or that disorder. But what I have in mind is the rhythm of relationships, the *harmonia*, as the Greeks would say, whereby the whole body, inside and out, can be looked upon as a kind of organ with a music all its own. The beauty of this music no one has yet discovered, because no one has dared look for it. Nevertheless, if this total organic design could only be discerned, even in the seemingly ugly elements of the human viscera, there would be revealed to the soul so ravishing a beauty that no visible shapeliness of form that delights the eye—the mere minister of our mind—could be compared with it.

Of course, some parts of the human body appear to have no other purpose than to add to beauty, as the mamillae on a man's chest or the beard on his face. Certainly, if the beard were meant for protection rather than for beauty, it would have served a better purpose for the weaker sex, whose face remains uncovered. If, then, we argue from the facts, first, that, as everyone admits, not a single visible organ of the body serving a definite function is lacking in beauty, and, second, that there are some parts which have beauty and no apparent function, it follows, I think, that in the creation of the human body God put form before function. After all, function will pass and the time will come when we shall delight solely in the unlibidinous contemplation of one another's beauty, knowing that our joy will be giving glory to the Creator, of whom the Psalmist says: 'Thou hast put on praise and beauty.'[7]

And now, to pass from man to the rest of creation, what beauty for contemplation and what bounties for use God has scattered like largesse for man amid the weariness and miseries of his fallen and penalized lot! What words can describe the myriad beauties of land and sea and sky? Just think of the illimitable abundance and the marvelous loveliness of light, or of the beauty of the sun and moon and stars, of shadowy glades in the woods and of the colors and perfume of flowers, of the songs and plumage of so many varieties of birds, of the innumerable animals of every species that amaze us most when they are smallest in size. For example, the activity of ants and bees seems more stupendous than the sheer immensity of whales. Or take a look at the grandiose spectacle of the open sea, clothing and reclothing itself in dresses of changing shades of green and purple and blue. And what a delight when the ocean breaks into storm and can be enjoyed—at least from the shore where there is no fear of the fury of the waves!

Or think of God's bounty in the never-ending stores of foods that banish hunger; in the variety of flavors which a generous nature provides without calling on the skill of cooks to stimulate our sluggish appetite; in the medicinal value of so many foods, whether we are sick or healthy. We have to thank God, too, for the alternations of day and night, for the solace of soothing breezes, and for the plants and animals that provide the linen and wool for the making of our clothing. No one

7 Ps. 103.1.

person could catalogue all of God's bounties. Each of the blessings which I have, as it were, piled up in a heap, contains a multitude of lesser blessings wrapped up within it, and if I were to unfold each of these packages and deal with the blessings in detail I should never end.

And, remember, all these favors taken together are but the fragmentary solace allowed us in a life condemned to misery. What, then, must be the consolations of the blessed, seeing that men on earth enjoy so much of so many and of such marvelous blessings? What good will God not give to those predestined to eternal life, if He gives so much to those who are doomed to death? What joys in the life of beatitude will God not shower on those for whom, in that life of misery, He allowed His only-begotten Son to suffer so many sorrows, even unto death? It was this that St. Paul had in mind when he wrote: 'He who has not spared even His own Son but delivered Him for us all, how can He fail to grant us also all things with Him.'[8] Just imagine how perfectly at peace and how strong will be the human spirit when there will be no passion to play the tyrant or the conqueror, no temptation even to test the spirit's strength. And think of the mind's universal knowledge in that condition where we shall drink, in all felicity and ease, of God's own wisdom at the very source. Think how great, how beautiful, how certain, how unerring, how easily acquired this knowledge then will be. And what a body, too, we shall have, a body utterly subject to our spirit and one so kept alive by spirit that there will be no need of any other food. For, it will be a spiritual body, no longer merely animal, one composed, indeed, of flesh but free from every corruption of the flesh.

Chapter 25

It is true that, in regard to the rewards which the soul is to enjoy in the blessedness which is to follow the present life, the best of the pagan philosophers agree with us. What they object to, however, in our faith is the resurrection of the body; on this point, they are emphatic in their denial. However, the

[8] Rom. 8.32.

fact is that the majority of men have moved away from the small minority of skeptics and have turned to Christ who, by His own Resurrection, realized in fact what seems absurd in theory. This majority of men, whose hearts are now filled with faith, includes the learned and unlearned alike, philosophers along with simple folk. And it is to be noted that God had revealed in prophecy not only the faith which the world has believed but also the fact that the world would believe as it now believes; certainly, it was not by means of any sorceries of Peter[1] that God was compelled to reveal what, to the joy of all believers, He had predicted so long before the event. For, this is the God before whom, as I have said and rejoice to repeat, Porphyry admits, on the basis of pagan oracles, that all lesser divinities tremble.[2] This is the God whom Porphyry himself hails as the Supreme God, the Father and King.

As for the meaning of the divine predictions, certainly no one should rely on the interpretations of those who have remained skeptical while the rest of the world has believed what God predicted it would believe. It is surely far better to believe like the world, whose believing was predicted, than as a handful of gabblers believe who have refused to follow the world in believing what it was predicted the world would believe. The pagans justify their position by saying that it would dishonor the God they esteem so highly if they believed that the Scriptures set forth predictions which have not been fulfilled. But, surely, it is just as grave an injury to God—if not graver—to offer an interpretation which runs counter to the faith of the whole world that believes as God predicted it would believe, and praised it for believing, and prepared it to believe.

Let us ask the pagans this question: Should we withhold faith in the resurrection and eternal life of the body, on the ground that such a thing is impossible to God; or should we refuse to believe on the ground that such a thing is wicked and unworthy of God? Impossible? Need I say more than I have in regard to that Omnipotence which has demonstrably accomplished so many things that seem unbelievable? If the pagans are really in search of something impossible even to

---

[1] Cf. above, 18.53,54.   [2] Cf. above, 19.22,23.

Omnipotence, I shall give them a hint: Not even God can tell a lie. But, by simply refusing to believe that God has told a lie, we are driven to believe that He has done what He had the power to do. Just let the pagans refuse to believe that God can lie and they will come to believe that He will accomplish what He has promised to accomplish; and so they will come to believe as the rest of the world believes—the world whose believing God predicted, praised, promised, and has now demonstrably brought to pass. The resurrection, therefore, is possible.

Wicked? How can the pagans prove that the resurrection of the body involves some kind of evil? It involves no corruption. Therefore, it involves no evil for the body. I have already discussed the hierarchy of the elements;[3] and I have said all that needs to be said of other hypothetical difficulties.[4] In Book XIII, I have, I think, sufficiently proved the agility of the glorified body from the relative agility enjoyed during good health even in this present life,[5] for this agility is, of course, incomparably less than that enjoyed in immortal life. Anyone who has not read these earlier parts of the present work (or who wishes to recall them to memory) can read them for himself.

Chapters 26–28

Plato and Porphyry did not think that human bodies could be resurrected. Yet these Platonists held many views reconcilable with Christianity. Even Varro approached in his thinking the notion of the resurrection.

Chapter 29

And now, with such help as the Lord will grant us, let us try to see what is to be the activity of the saints in those spiritual and immortal bodies in which their flesh is to be alive, not merely with a carnal but with a spiritual life. I speak of activity, although, perhaps, I should rather say calm

[3] Bk. 22.11, here omitted.　　　[4] Bk. 22.12–20, here omitted.
[5] Cf. above, 13.18.

or repose. To tell the truth, I have no real notion of what eternal life will be like, for the simple reason that I know of no sensible experience to which it can be related. Nor can I say that I have any mental conception of such an activity, for, at that height, what is intelligence or what can it do? In heaven, as St. Paul assures us, 'the peace of God . . . surpasses all understanding.'[1] Certainly, it surpasses ours. Maybe it surpasses that of the angels as well. Of course, it does not surpass God's 'understanding.' This much is sure. If the redeemed are to live in the peace of God, they are to live in a peace 'which surpasses all understanding.' As to ours, there is no doubt at all, and, when St. Paul says 'all understanding' he seems to imply no exception for the angels. We ought, therefore, to take the text to mean that neither men nor angels can understand, as God does, that peace of God by which God Himself is at peace. Thus, 'all understanding' means all except God's.

Nevertheless, since we are to be sharers of His peace, in the measure of our capacity, we are to receive, within ourselves and in our relations to one another and to God, a supreme degree of peace—whatever that supreme degree for us may be. So, too, in the measure of their capacity, do the holy angels understand that peace. Men on earth, whatever the perfection of understanding they may reach, understand far less than the angels. For we must remember that not even St. Paul, for all his greatness, could say more than this: 'We know in part and we prophesy in part; until that which is perfect has come. . . . We see now through a mirror in an obscure manner, but then face to face.'[2]

Face to face—this is how the holy angels, who are called *our* angels, already see. They are our angels in the sense that, once we have been delivered from the power of darkness, have received the pledge of the spirit, and have been translated to the kingdom of Christ, we shall have begun to belong to the angels, with whom we are to be fellow citizens in that holy and supremely satisfying Communion which is that City of God about which I have been writing all these pages. The angels, who are God's angels, are our angels in the

[1] Phil. 4.7.   [2] 1 Cor. 13.9,12.

way that the Christ of God is our Christ. They are God's, because they never deserted God. They are ours, because they have begun to accept us as their fellow citizens.

Now, the Lord Jesus said: 'See that you do not despise one of these little ones; for, I tell you, their angels in heaven always behold the face of my Father in heaven.'[3] In the way, then, that they see, we, also, shall one day see. But we do not see in that way yet. That is why St. Paul said what I have just quoted: 'We see now through a mirror in an obscure manner, but then face to face.' This implies that there is in store for us a reward for our faith, that Vision which St. John had in mind when he said: 'When he appears, we shall be like him, for we shall see him just as he is.'[4] For, of course, 'face' is to be understood not as the kind of face we now have as part of our body, but as a manifestation of what God is.

And so it is that, when anyone asks me what the activity of the saints in their spiritual bodies will be, I do not tell him what I now see; I tell him what I believe. I follow the rule suggested by the psalm: 'I have believed, therefore have I spoken.'[5] What I answer is: The saints will see God with their bodily senses, but whether they will see Him by their sense in the same way we now see the sun and moon and stars, the land and sea and all that they contain—that is a difficult problem.[6] It is difficult to admit that bodies in heaven will be such that the saints cannot open and close their eyes at will; on the other hand, it is still harder to admit that, if one closes his eyes in heaven, he will cease to see God. After all, the prophet Eliseus, when he was nowhere near his wicked servant, Giezi, secretly (as he thought) saw him receiving the gifts which Naaman the Syrian gave him, after Eliseus had healed Naaman of his leprosy.[7] Why, then, should not the saints, in their spiritual bodies, be much more able to see all things, not merely with their eyes closed, but even when they are far away from what they see.

This is the kind of perfection of sight which St. Paul refers

[3] Matt. 18.10. [4] 1 John 3.2.
[5] Ps. 115.10.
[6] Cf. St. Augustine's *Retractationes* 67.
[7] 4 Kings 5.26.

to in the words: 'For we know in part and we prophesy in part; but when that which is perfect has come, that which is imperfect will be done away with.'[8] The Apostle goes on to indicate, as best he can, by a comparison, the gap between the future life and the present life even of men of outstanding holiness: 'When I was a child, I spoke as a child, I felt as a child, I thought as a child. Now that I have become a man, I have put away the things of a child. We see now through a mirror in an obscure manner, but then face to face. Now I know in part, but then I shall know even as I have been known.'[9]

Although, therefore, even in this life, Eliseus could see his servant, who was nowhere near, receiving gifts, such a vision even in the case of man who could work miracles was, in comparison with the Vision in the other life, what a child is to a mature man. Can we not argue, therefore, that, 'when that which is perfect has come,' and when there will be no burden of a corruptible body weighing down the soul but, rather, an incorruptible body that will prove to be no impediment, the saints will have no more need of their bodily eyes, when they want to see, than Eliseus had need of his eyes to see what his servant was doing, even though the servant was a long way off. Notice the words of the Prophet to Giezi. In the Septuagint version, they run: 'Did not my heart go with you when the man turned from his chariot to meet thee and thou didst take his money?' And, in the translation made directly from the Hebrew text by the priest, Jerome, the words are: 'Was not my heart present, when the man turned back from his chariot to meet thee?'[10] Thus, it was with his 'heart' that the Prophet says he saw; and, of course, no one can doubt that he was miraculously helped in this by God.

Now just think, when God will be 'all in all,'[11] how much greater will be this gift of vision in the hearts of all! The eyes of the body will still retain their function and will be found where they now are, and the spirit, through its spiritual body, will make use of the eyes. After all, even Eliseus used his

[8] 1 Cor. 13.9,10. [9] 1 Cor. 13.11,12.
[10] 4 Kings 5.26. [11] 1 Cor. 15.28.

eyes to see things near him, even though he had no need of them to see a man who was not present. And he could have seen things present by his spirit, even with his eyes closed, just as well as he saw things that were not present when he was a long way off. Hence, we should not dream of saying that the saints in heaven will be unable to see God with their eyes closed, since they will see Him at all times with their spirit.

The question still remains whether they will see God with their eyes open and by means of these bodily eyes. For, of course, if spiritual eyes in a spiritual body can see in a no better way than that in which our present eyes can see, then it will certainly be impossible for even spiritual eyes to behold God. If that immaterial Nature, which is circumscribed by no place but is everywhere wholly present, is to be visible to the eyes of a spiritual body, then these eyes will most certainly have to have a power altogether unlike the power of any eyes on earth. It is true that we say that God is in heaven and on earth, and He Himself, through a Prophet, says: 'I fill heaven and earth.'[12] But this does not mean that, in heaven, we shall say that God has one part there and another part on earth. For, He is wholly in heaven and He is wholly on earth; and He is in both simultaneously, not merely successively— which is utterly impossible in the case of any material substance.

When we speak of eyes in heaven having a more powerful vision, we do not mean the kind of sharper sight which snakes and eagles are said to have. For, however keen such animal vision may be, it is limited to material objects. What is meant is that in heaven eyes can see realities that are immaterial. It is the kind of vision that may have been given to holy Job even while he was in his mortal body, when he said to God: 'With the hearing of the ear, I have heard thee, but now my eye seeth thee. Therefore, I reprehend myself, and do penance in dust and ashes.'[13] I say, 'may have been,' because there is no reason why we should not take the 'eye' in this text to mean 'the eye of the heart of the mind,' in the sense that St. Paul meant in his expression, 'the eyes of your mind being

[12] Jer. 23.24.   [13] Job 42.5,6.

enlightened.'[14] It was the Divine Master who said: 'Blessed are the pure of heart, for they shall see God.'[15] Hence, no Christian reading these words in a spirit of faith has any doubt that, when God is to be seen, it will be by the eyes of the heart. But, of course, the problem I am now dealing with is whether, in heaven, God will also be seen by the eyes of the body.

Take the text: 'And all mankind shall see the salvation of God.'[16] There is no difficulty at all in taking this to mean: 'And all mankind shall see the Christ of God.' After all, Christ was seen in the body and will be seen in the body when He is to come to judge the living and the dead. Scripture has many texts showing that He is the 'salvation of God,' particularly in the words of the venerable old man, Simeon, who took the Child in his arms and said: 'Now thou dost dismiss thy servant, O Lord, according to thy word, in peace; because my eyes have seen thy Salvation.'[17] And then there is the declaration of holy Job, as his words appear in the translation direct from the Hebrew: 'And in my flesh I shall see my God.'[18] This is an undoubted prophecy of the resurrection of the flesh. Had Job said: 'by means of my flesh,' we might have taken him to be referring to Christ, rather than to 'God,' since Christ in the flesh will be seen by the senses. But as the words stand, they can be taken to mean: 'I shall be in my flesh when I shall see God.'

At the same time, not even St. Paul's expression, 'face to face,'[19] compels us to believe that we shall see God by means of our physical face, in which we have material eyes, since we shall have an uninterrupted vision of God in our spirit. For, unless there were some spiritual face of the interior man, St. Paul would not have written the words: 'But we all, with face unveiled, reflecting as in a mirror the glory of the Lord, are being transformed into his very image, from glory to glory, as through the Spirit of the Lord.'[20] So, too, in the psalm, I take the words, 'Come ye to him and be enlightened; and your faces shall not be confounded,'[21] to refer to this inner

14 Eph. 1.18.   15 Matt. 5.8.
16 Luke 3.6.   17 Luke 2.29,30.
18 Job 19.26.   19 1 Cor. 13.12.
20 2 Cor. 3.18.   21 Ps. 33.6.

face. The truth is that we shall draw near to God by faith, which is a power to see which is not in our body, but in our mind. However, since no one knows what ways of approaching God the spiritual body will have, for the simple reason that no one has any experience of a spiritual body, we have to remember, in the absence of any completely unambiguous text to rescue us from all doubt, that we are in the condition described in the Book of Wisdom: 'The thoughts of mortal men are fearful, and our counsels uncertain.'[22]

As far as the reasoning of philosophy reaches, intelligible realities are so correlated to the vision of the mind, as sensible or material things are to the senses of the body, that the intelligibles cannot be perceived by the senses nor material things by the immediate intuition of the soul. Now, if philosophy were our most certain source of knowledge, we could be sure that not even a spiritual body could have eyes capable of seeing God. But, of course, such logic becomes laughable in the light of reality and of divine Revelation.[23] Only a traitor to the truth[24] would dare to argue that God has no knowledge of material things, on the ground that God has no body and, hence, no bodily eyes to see such things. Moreover, the revelation concerning Eliseus which I mentioned above is a clear indication that material objects can be perceived by the spirit, independently of the body. Certainly, what Giezi did in taking material gifts was a material action, yet the Prophet saw these material movements, not by the senses of his body, but by the eyes of his spirit. And, if it is a fact that bodies can be perceived by the soul, there is no reason why some special faculty of a spiritual body should be unable to see a spiritual reality by means of the senses; and, of course, God is such a spiritual reality.

Moreover, each of us has a perception of his own life, that is, of the principle by which we are alive in our bodies and which gives our members their growth and movement; and this perception is by means of an interior sense, not by means of our eyes. It is different with our perception of other people's

---

[22] Wisd. 9.14.

[23] *Sed istam ratiocinationem et vera ratio et prophetica inridet auctoritas.*

[24] . . . *aversus a vero.*

lives. These are invisible and we see them only by seeing their bodies. In fact, the reason why we distinguish living from non-living bodies is that we see bodies along with their lives, even though we cannot see the living bodies as such, except through the bodies. However, where there is a life, by itself and apart from a body, this we do not see with the eyes of our body.

What, therefore, is possible and highly probable is that we shall be able to see the material bodies of the new heaven and the new earth in such a way that, by means of our own bodies and of all the others which we shall see wherever our eyes are turned, we shall see God, and we shall see Him with the utmost clarity as being everywhere present and as regulating the whole universe, including material things. We shall see Him in a way different from the way in which His 'invisible attributes' are now seen, 'being understood by the things that are made,'[25] for 'we see now through a mirror in an obscure manner' and only 'in part,'[26] and we must rely more on the eyes of faith, whereby we believe, than on the eyes of the body, whereby we see the beauty of the material universe.

Recall again the living men among whom we now live, at the moment when they are performing vital actions. As soon as we turn our eyes on them, we not merely believe that they are living, we see that they are living. Even though we have no power to see the 'living' apart from the 'living bodies,' nevertheless, we see with the eyes of our bodies, and in no kind of 'obscure manner,' the 'life' in the living bodies. In some such way, in heaven, wherever we shall turn the eyes of our spiritual bodies, we shall see the immaterial God, ruling all things, and we shall see Him by means of our bodies.

Thus, we have two hypotheses. Either God will be seen by these eyes of ours, because they will possess, among other high endowments, something resembling the powers of a mind to enable them to perceive what is by nature immaterial—an hypothesis for which there is no support in experience or in Revelation and which is difficult, if not impossible, to establish; or else—what is easier to comprehend—God will be made known to and be perceived by us, in many ways. He will be

[25] Rom. 1.20.   [26] 1 Cor. 13.12.

seen in the spirit (whereby each of us will see Him within ourselves and in one another); He will be seen in Himself; He will be seen in the new heaven and the new earth and in every creature then existing; and, by means of our bodies, He will be seen in every material object toward which the eyes of our spiritual bodies happen to direct their gaze. Even our very thoughts will then be made known to one another.[27] For, then will be fulfilled what St. Paul said: 'Pass no judgment before the time, until the Lord comes, who will both bring to light the things hidden in darkness and make manifest the counsels of hearts; and then everyone will have his praise from God.'[28]

Chapter 30

Who can measure the happiness of heaven, where no evil at all can touch us, no good will be out of reach; where life is to be one long laud extolling God, who will be all in all; where there will be no weariness to call for rest, no need to call for toil, no place for any energy but praise. Of this I am assured whenever I read or hear the sacred song: 'Blessed are they that dwell in thy house, O Lord: they shall praise thee for ever and ever.'[1] Every fiber and organ of our imperishable body will play its part in the praising of God. On earth these varied organs have each a special function, but, in heaven, function will be swallowed up in felicity, in the perfect certainty of an untroubled everlastingness of joy. Even those muted notes in the diapason of the human organ, which I mentioned earlier, will swell into a great hymn of praise to the supreme Artist who has fashioned us, within and without, in every fiber, and who, by this and every other element of a magnificent and marvelous Order, will ravish our minds with spiritual beauty.[2]

These movements of our bodies will be of such unimagi-

---

[27] Cf. *Retractationes* 25,48. [28] 1 Cor. 4.5.

[1] Ps. 83.5.

[2] *Omnes quippe ille . . . qui nunc latent harmoniae corporalis numeri non latebunt . . . rationales mentes in tanti artificis laudem rationabilis pulchritudinis delectatione succendent.*

nable beauty that I dare not say more than this: There will be such poise, such grace, such beauty as become a place where nothing unbecoming can be found. Wherever the spirit wills, there, in a flash, will the body be. Nor will the spirit ever will anything unbecoming either to itself or to the body.

In heaven, all glory will be true glory, since no one could ever err in praising too little or too much. True honor will never be denied where due, never be given where undeserved, and, since none but the worthy are permitted there, no one will unworthily ambition glory. Perfect peace will reign, since nothing in ourselves or in any others could disturb this peace. The promised reward of virtue will be the best and the greatest of all possible prizes—the very Giver of virtue Himself, for that is what the Prophet meant: 'I will be your God and you shall be my people.'[3] God will be the source of every satisfaction, more than any heart can rightly crave, more than life and health, food and wealth, glory and honor, peace and every good—so that God, as St. Paul said, 'may be all in all.'[4] He will be the consummation of all our desiring—the object of our unending vision, of our unlessening love, of our unwearying praise. And in this gift of vision, this response of love, this paean of praise, all alike will share, as all will share in everlasting life.

But, now, who can imagine, let alone describe, the ranks upon ranks of rewarded saints, to be graded, undoubtedly, according to their variously merited honor and glory. Yet, there will be no envy of the lower for the higher, as there is no envy of angel for archangel—for this is one of the great blessednesses of this blessed City. The less rewarded will be linked in perfect peace with the more highly favored, but lower could not more long for higher than a finger, in the ordered integration of a body, could want to be an eye. The less endowed will have the high endowment of longing for nothing loftier than their lower gifts.

The souls in bliss will still possess the freedom of will, though sin will have no power to tempt them. They will be more free than ever—so free, in fact, from all delight in sinning as to find, in not sinning, an unfailing source of joy. By

3 Lev. 26.12.   4 1 Cor. 15.28.

the freedom which was given to the first man, who was constituted in rectitude, he could choose either to sin or not to sin; in eternity, freedom is that more potent freedom which makes all sin impossible. Such freedom, of course, is a gift of God, beyond the power of nature to achieve. For, it is one thing to be God, another to be a sharer in the divine nature. God, by His nature, cannot sin, but a mere sharer in His nature must receive from God such immunity from sin. It was proper that, in the process of divine endowment, the first step should be a freedom not to sin, and the last a freedom even from the power to sin. The first gift made merit possible; the second is a part of man's reward. Our nature, when it was free to sin, did sin. It took a greater grace to lead us to that larger liberty which frees us from the very power to sin. Just as the immortality that Adam lost by his sin was, at first, a mere possibility of avoiding death, but, in heaven, becomes the impossibility of death, so free will was, at first, a mere possibility of avoiding sin, but, in heaven, becomes an utter inability to sin.[5]

Our will will be as ineradicably rooted in rectitude and love as in beatitude. It is true that, with Adam's sin, we lost our right to grace and glory, but, with our right, we did not lose our longing to be happy. And, as for freedom, can we think that God Himself, who certainly cannot sin, is therefore without freedom? The conclusion is that, in the everlasting City, there will remain in each and all of us an inalienable freedom of the will, emancipating us from every evil and filling us with every good, rejoicing in the inexhaustible beatitude of everlasting happiness, unclouded by the memory of any sin or of sanction suffered, yet with no forgetfulness of our redemption nor any loss of gratitude for our Redeemer.

The memory of our previous miseries will be a matter of purely mental contemplation, with no renewal of any feelings connected with these experiences—much as learned doctors know by science many of those bodily maladies which, by suffering, they have no sensible experience. All ills, in fact, can

---

[5] . . . *prima immortalitas fuit . . . posse non mori, novissima erit non posse mori: ita primum liberum arbitrium posse non peccare, novissimum non posse peccare.*

be forgotten in the double way in which we learn them, namely, notionally and experientially. It is one thing to be a philosopher, learning by ethical analysis the nature of each and every vice, and another to be a scoundrel, learning his lessons from a dissolute life. So, too, the student who becomes a doctor forgets in a way different from that of a patient who has suffered disease. The one forgets by giving up his practice; the patient, by being freed from pains. Now, it is into this second kind of oblivion that the previous miseries of the saints will fall, for not a trace of any sensible experience of suffering will remain.

However, in virtue of the vigor of their minds, they will have not merely a notional remembrance of their own past but also a knowledge of the unending torments of the damned. For, if they had no kind of memory of past miseries, how could the Psalmist have said: 'The mercies of the Lord they will sing for ever'?[6] And, surely, in all that City, nothing will be lovelier than this song in praise of the grace of Christ by whose Blood all there were saved.

Heaven, too, will be the fulfillment of that Sabbath rest foretold in the command: 'Be still and see that I am God.'[7] This, indeed, will be that ultimate Sabbath that has no evening and which the Lord foreshadowed in the account of His creation: 'And God rested on the seventh day from all his work which he had done. And he blessed the seventh day and sanctified it: because in it he had rested from all his work which God created and made.'[8] And we ourselves will be a 'seventh day' when we shall be filled with His blessing and remade by His sanctification. In the stillness of that rest we shall see that He is the God whose divinity we ambitioned for ourselves when we listened to the seducer's words, 'You shall be as Gods,'[9] and so fell away from Him, the true God who would have given us a divinity by participation that could never be gained by desertion. For, where did the doing without God end but in the undoing of man through the anger of God?

Only when we are remade by God and perfected by a greater grace shall we have the eternal stillness of that rest

6 Cf. Ps. 88.2.   7 Ps. 45.11.
8 Gen. 2.2,3.   9 Gen. 3.5.

in which we shall see that He is God. Then only shall we be
filled with Him when He will be all in all. For, although our
good works are, in reality, His, they will be put to our account as payment for this Sabbath peace, so long as we do not
claim them as our own; but, if we do, they will be reckoned
as servile and out of place on the Sabbath, as the text reminds
us: 'The seventh day . . . is the rest of the Lord. . . . Thou
shalt not do any work therein.'[10] In this connection, too, God
has reminded us, through the Prophet Ezechiel: 'I gave them
my sabbaths, to be a sign between me and them, that they
might know that I am the Lord that sanctifies them.'[11] It is
this truth that we shall realize perfectly when we shall be perfectly at rest and shall perfectly see that it is He who is God.

There is a clear indication of this final Sabbath if we take
the seven ages of world history as being 'days' and calculate
in accordance with the data furnished by the Scriptures. The
first age or day is that from Adam to the flood; the second,
from the flood to Abraham. (These two 'days' were not identical in length of time, but in each there were ten generations.)
Then follow the three ages, each consisting of fourteen generations, as recorded in the Gospel of St. Matthew: the first, from
Abraham to David; the second, from David to the transmigra-
tion to Babylon; the third, from then to Christ's nativity in the
flesh. Thus, we have five ages. The sixth is the one in which
we now are. It is an age not to be measured by any precise
number of generations, since we are told: 'It is not for you to
know the times or dates which the Father has fixed by his
own authority.'[12] After this 'day,' God will rest on the 'seventh
day,' in the sense that God will make us, who are to be this
seventh day, rest in Him.

There is no need here to speak in detail of each of these
seven 'days.' Suffice it to say that this 'seventh day' will be
our Sabbath and that it will end in no evening, but only in
the Lord's day—that eighth and eternal day which dawned
when Christ's resurrection heralded an eternal rest both for
the spirit and for the body. On that day we shall rest and
see, see and love, love and praise—for this is to be the end

[10] Deut. 5.14.   [11] Ezech. 20.12.
[12] Acts 1.7.

without the end of all our living, that Kingdom without end, the real goal of our present life.

I am done. With God's help, I have kept my promise. This, I think, is all that I promised to do when I began this huge work. From all who think that I have said either too little or too much, I beg pardon; and those who are satisfied I ask, not to thank me, but to join me in rejoicing and in thanking God. Amen.

INDEX

OTHER IMAGE BOOKS

OTHER IMAGE BOOKS

OTHER IMAGE BOOKS

A 88-3

OTHER IMAGE BOOKS

A 88-4

OTHER IMAGE BOOKS

A 88-5

OTHER IMAGE BOOKS